V&R unipress

UNIVERSITÄT OSNABRÜCK

UNIWERSYTET ŚLĄSKI
W KATOWICACH

MIX
Papier aus verantwortungsvollen Quellen
FSC® C083411

Bibliografische Information der Deutschen Nationalbibliothek
Die Deutsche Nationalbibliothek verzeichnet diese Publikation in der Deutschen Nationalbibliografie; detaillierte bibliografische Daten sind im Internet über https://dnb.de abrufbar.

Veröffentlichungen des Universitätsverlags Osnabrück erscheinen bei V&R unipress.

Diese Publikation wurde von der Schlesischen Universität in Katowice finanziell unterstützt.
This publication was financially supported by University of Silesia in Katowice, Poland.

Druck und Bindung: CPI books GmbH, Birkstraße 10, D-25917 Leck
Printed in the EU.

Vandenhoeck & Ruprecht Verlage | www.vandenhoeck-ruprecht-verlage.com

ISSN 2198-7041
ISBN 978-3-8471-1044-6

Contents

List of Shortcuts 11

Preface 13

I. Introduction 15
1. The scope, structure and method of the book 15
2. The main areas of focus of the book 21

II. The bridge between the law of obligations and animal ethics 25
1. Man and animal – a philosophical and ethical background 25
2. Animal "personhood" 28
2.1. Animal ethics – modern approaches for reforming animal law 28
2.2. Animals as subjects or objects of law? 30
2.3. The actual position of animals versus their legal status 35
2.4. Ownership of an animal in the Polish and German Civil Codes 36
2.5. Animals' legal position with reference to the subject of this book 40
3. Where are we now in protecting animals? 43
3.1. Animal law in the EU 43
3.2. Is there a need to protect animals in a European perspective?. 47
3.3. Is there a need to protect animals in a global perspective? . . 52
3.4. Correlation between local traditions, culture and animal protection 56
3.5. The problem of strays as an example of how local traditions and culture determine levels of animal protection – comparative remarks 60

III. Contracts aimed at the transfer of property 65
1. General characteristic of contracts aimed at the transfer of property with reference to contracts with an animal as their object 65
2. Performance of contracts aimed at the transfer of property with reference to contracts having an animal as the object 72
2.1. General remarks 72
2.2. Consumer sale and related legal problems concerning B2B, B2C and C2C relations 74
2.3. Conclusion of contracts aimed at the transfer of property with reference to contracts having an animal as the object . . 80
2.3.1. Estimation of the price 80
2.3.2. Exchange of horses with a partial payment 82
2.3.3. Extortion in the sale of an animal 84
2.4. Applicability of specific types of sale contracts to animals . . 89
2.4.1. Animals as specific objects of sale on approval 89
2.4.2. Animals as specific objects of sale while reserving the right to repurchase 92
2.4.3. Animals as specific objects of sale with a pre-emptive right 95
2.5. Contracts aimed at the transfer of property with reference to animals other than a sale contract 95
2.5.1. Donation 95
2.5.2. Barter 99
2.5.3. Contracts of delivery of pre-contracted agricultural produce (*umowa kontraktacji*) 101
3. Results of the improper performance of contracts aimed at the transfer of property with reference to contracts having an animal as the object 102
3.1. Legal foundations of the seller's liability in connection with the sale of animals 102
3.2. The warranty regime with reference to animals as specific objects of obligations 105
3.2.1. Definition of a defect with reference to animals as specific objects of obligations 105
3.2.2. General overview of the buyer's warranty rights with reference to contracts aimed at the transfer of property of an animal 114
3.2.3. The applicability of seller's right to cure animals 118
3.2.4. Applicability of warranty rights to the continuous medical treatments of animals 123

3.2.5. Reduction in price and termination of contract with reference to contracts aimed at the transfer of property of an animal 125
3.2.6. Monetary damages and excessive costs with reference to exercising a warranty right in the case of animals as specific object of obligations 127
3.2.7. Animals as used goods? 131
3.2.8. Peculiarities of the sale of horses – the importance of pre-contractual information, medical examination and x-ray images as the basis for the horse's seller's liability 132
3.3. Applicability of the institution of guarantee as to the quality of the good to animals 140
3.4. Results of the improper performance of contracts aimed at the transfer of property of an animal other than the sale contract 141
3.4.1. Donation 141
3.4.2. Barter 143
3.4.3. Delivery of pre-contracted agricultural produce 144

IV. Service contracts 145
1. General characteristics of service contracts with reference to contracts having an animal as their object 145
1.1. General remarks 145
1.2. General characteristics of specific types of service contracts with an animal as their object 152
1.2.1. Commission contracts having an animal as their object 153
1.2.2. Agency contracts having an animal as their object . . . 157
1.2.3. Teaching/training contracts having an animal as their object 159
1.2.4. Safe-keeping contracts having an animal as its object . 167
1.2.5. Other service contracts having an animal as their object 170
2. Performance of service contracts with reference to contracts having an animal as their object 173
2.1. Commission contracts having an animal as their object . . . 173
2.2. Agency contracts having an animal as their object 180
2.3. Teaching/training contracts having an animal as their object . 191
2.4. Safe-keeping contracts having an animal as their object . . . 196
2.5. Other service contracts having an animal as their object . . . 201

3. Results of the improper performance of service contracts with reference to contracts having an animal as its object 206
3.1. Commission contracts having an animal as its object 206
3.2. Agency contracts having an animal as their object 211
3.3. Teaching/training contracts having an animal as their object . 219
3.4. Safe-keeping contracts having an animal as its object 225
3.5. Other service contracts having an animal as their object . . . 228

V. Contracts for the use of someone else's things 231
1. General characteristics of contracts for the use of someone else's things having an animal as their object 231
1.1. General remarks 231
1.2. Differentiation between lease contracts and tenancy contracts in reference to contracts having animals as their object 236
2. Performance of contracts for the use of someone else's things having an animal as their object 240
2.1. Performance of lease contracts and tenancy contracts in reference to contracts having animals as their subject 240
2.2. Performance of undefined/atypical contracts having the use of animals as their subject 246
2.3. Performance of loan for use contracts in reference to contracts having animals as their object 252
3. Results of the improper performance of contracts aimed at the transfer of property of things with reference to contracts having an animal as their object 255
3.1. Results of the improper performance of contracts in reference to lease and tenancy contracts having animals as their object 255
3.2. Results of the improper performance of contracts in reference to loan for use contracts having animals as their subject 259

VI. Final remarks 267
1. Conclusions in reference to the legal status of animals 267
2. Remarks *de lege ferenda* concerning animals in the Polish legal system (to the extent of private law) 269

References 277

Online resources 295

Legal acts and public documents 299

Court rulings 305
Polish court rulings 305
German court rulings 306
Rulings of the European Court of Justice 307

European Parliament petitions 309

List of Shortcuts

ACP	Archiv für die civilistische Praxis
AG	Amtsgericht
APAA	Greek charity Animal Protection Aegina Agistri
Article	Article
B2B	Business to Business Relation
B2C	Business to Consumer Relation
BGB	Bürgerliches Gesetzbuch
BGH	Bundesgerichtshof (German Federal Supreme Court of Justice)
BYIL	British Yearbook of International Law
C2C	Consumer to Consumer Relation
CISG	United Nations Convention on Contracts for the International Sale of Goods
CITES	Convention on International Trade in Endangered Species of Wild Fauna and Flora
DCFR	Draft Common Frame of Reference
Dir.	Directive
EC	European Council
ECHR	European Court of Human Rights
ECJ	European Court of Justice
ECPHRFR	The European Convention for the Protection of Human Rights and Fundamental Freedoms
ed.	Editor
eds.	Editors
etc.	et cetera
EU	European Union
GAWF	Greek Animal Welfare Fund
HGB	Handelsgesetzbuch
i. e.	id est
INP PAN	Instytut Nauk prawnych Polskiej Akademii Nauk
IUCN	The World Conservation Union
JuS	Juristische Schulung Zeitschrift
KC	Kodeks cywilny
KPP	Kwartalnik Prawa Prywatnego

LG	Landesgericht
MoP	Monitor Prawniczy
NGO	Non-government organization
NJW	Neue Juristische Wochenschrift
NJW-RR	Neue Juristysche Wochenschrift Rechtssprechung-Report Zivilrecht
No.	Number
OLG	Oberlandesgericht
OJ C	The Official Journal of the European Union, information and notices
OJ L	The Official Journal of the European Union, legislation
OSNCP	Orzecznictwo Sądu Najwyższego – Izba Cywilna/Pracy
OSP	Orzecznictwo Sądów Polskich
p.	page
PAP	Polska Agnecja Prasowa
PAWS	Paros Animal Welfare Society
PETI	Committee on Petitions, European Parliament
PiP	Państwo i Prawo
pos.	Position
pp.	pages
PWN	Wydawnictwo Naukowe PWN
PZJ	Polski Związek Jeździecki
RöLF	Rönthenleitfaden (x-ray images guide)
Rome I Regulation	Regulation (EC) No. 593/2008 of the European Parliament and of the Council of 17 June 2008 on the law applicable to contractual obligations
Rutgers L. Rev	Rutgers Law Rev
S.C.	Studia Cywilistyczne
SN	Sąd Najwyższy (Polish Supreme Court)
System…	System Prawa Prywatnego
TFEU	The Treaty on the Functioning of the European Union
trans.	translated
UN	United Nations
US	United States of America
Vet. Radiol, Ultrasound	Veterinary Radiology & Ultrasound Journal
Vol.	Volume
ZeUP	Zeitschrift für Europäisches Privatrecht
ZGS	Zeitschrift für das gesamte Schuldrecht
ZNUJ	Zeszyty Naukowe Uniwersytetu Jagiellońskiego

Preface

This book is based on a Doctoral Dissertation (Co-tutelle) written in the Faculty of Civil Law and Private International Law of the University of Silesia under the mentorship of prof. dr hab. Ewa Rott-Pietrzyk (UŚ) and in the European Legal Studies Institute of the University of Osnabrück under the mentorship of prof. dr hab. Fryderyk Zoll (UJ and Universität Osnabrück) in 2018.

I would like to send special thanks to my mentors – prof. dr hab. Ewa Rott-Pietrzyk (UŚ) and prof. dr hab. Fryderyk Zoll (UJ and Universität Osnabrück), as well as to the faculty members of the University of Silesia, who have always offered me support and advice. I would also like to express my infinite gratitude to my parents and my husband, who have always believed that this book will finally emerge, and to my sons, without whom I would probably not have enough motivation to make it happen.

I. Introduction

"The day may come, when the rest of the animal creation may acquire those rights which never could have been withholden from them but by the hand of tyranny."
J. Bentham[1]

1. The scope, structure and method of the book

This book looks at the conclusion, performance and results of the non-performance of contracts with animals as their object. The work concerns private law provisions addressed to animals (which can be found by reference in all the civil codes referred to in this book) and not administrative provisions, which are already referred to in numerous publications covered by the field of animal law (in the meaning of the part of law referring to animal rights).[2] As to the scope of animals covered herein, it had to be established according to their usage in the private law. The animals falling within the scope of this book are all animals that constitute objects of contractual obligations. Therefore, the study refers rather to animals owned by private individuals. Thus, animals destined for slaughter[3] or for producing farm products usually do not constitute further objects of

1 J. Bentham, *An Introduction To The Principles Of Morals And Legislation*, pp. 235–236, Clarendon Press Oxford 1907 (1823); J. Bentham, *Wprowadzenie do Zasad Moralności i Prawodawstwa* (Bogdan Nawroczyński trans.), Warszawa 1958, pp. 418–420.

2 With reference to the melting difference between private and public law, see: J. Nowacki, *Prawo publiczne – prawo prywatne*, Katowice 1992; W. Popiołek, *Znaczenie przepisów "prawa publicznego" różnych systemów prawnych dla stosunków umownych handlu zagranicznego*, Problemy Prawne Handlu Zagranicznego 1988, Issue 12, pp. 56–78; J. Łętowski, *W sprawie granicy między prawem publicznym a prywatnym* [in:] B. Kordasiewicz, E. Łętowska (eds.), *Prace z prawa cywilnego. Wydane dla uczczenia pracy naukowej Profesora Józefa Piątowskiego*, Wrocław/Warszawa/Kraków/Łódź 1985, pp. 353–362; R. Szczepaniak, *W zamkniętym kręgu podziału na prawo publiczne i prywatne, czyli o możliwości dochodzenia odsetek od zasądzonych kosztów procesu*, Studia Prawa Prywatnego 2015, Issue 3, pp. 49–59. See also: ECJ, ruling from 28.7.2016, C-191/15.

3 See more with reference to animals kept for slaughter in: M. Lubelska-Sazanów, *Prawne regulacje dotyczące transportu zwierząt na terenie Unii Europejskiej* [in:] B. Błońska, W. Gogłoza, W. Klaus, D. Woźniakowska-Fajst (eds.), *Sprawiedliwość dla zwierząt*, Warszawa 2017; M. Rudy, A. Rudy, P. Mazur, *Ubój rytualny w prawie administracyjnym*, Warszawa 2013. Compare also: T. Pietrzykowski, *Recenzja książki M. Rudego, A. Rudego, P. Mazura, Ubój rytualny w prawie administracyjnym, Warszawa 2013,* Prokuratura i Prawo 2014, Issue 3, pp. 162–167.

contractual obligations (at least from the moment when they reach the slaughterhouses or animal production farms).[4] However, before that, they are treated as regular objects of potential obligations falling within the scope of this book. Hence, animals that undergo beauty- and health-checks, are sold or offered for lease are privately owned animals and – as such – form the subject of this book. Additionally, the book refers to animals as specific objects of contractual obligations. Therefore the problematic issue of the owner's/keeper's liability *ex delicto* arising as a result of damage caused by an animal is not the subject of these considerations. The problem of the liability of an owner/keeper is very broad and covers, also in the Polish-German context, several differences of its regulation. This problem by itself could constitute the subject of a separate book. Thus, despite a rich vein of German jurisprudence[5] in this matter, the issue of liability *ex delicto* arising as a result of damage caused by an animal – as a delict, not a contractual obligation – is not the subject of this book, referring strictly to contract law.

Due to private contractual obligations forming a focus point of the book, it was necessary to address also the bond that arises between an animal and its owner. This bond begins morality considerations towards animals and is the main reason for bringing animal ethics into a private law book. Thus, the only aspect that justifies the presentation of a legal philosophy, animal ethics and its impact on a legal culture expressed in private law provisions is the specific object of obligations – animals, as addressed in this book referring to civil law.

The first two chapters constitute background for subsequent civil law considerations concerning the fact that the object of a contractual obligation is an animal, and the impact this has on the conclusion, performance and consequences of non-performance or improper performance of the contract. Chapter I contains introductory remarks referring to the scope, structure and method used in this book, while Chapter II combines the needs to address animal interests in contract law with Polish contract law itself. Chapters III, IV

4 Due to this limitation of the scope of this book, the problem of animal slaughter is not subject of this book. However, at this point it is necessary to mention a famous discussion referring to ritual slaughter of animals, see: E. Tuora-Schwierskott, *Rytualny ubój zwierząt w świetle wolności sumienia i wyznania oraz zasady proporcjonalności w ustawodawstwie i orzecznictwie Niemiec, Szwajcarii i USA*, Państwo i Prawo 2016, Issue 4, pp. 64–73; A. Młynarska-Sobaczewska, *Rytualne ofiary a moralność publiczna. Analiza argumentacji Trybunału Konstytucyjnego (K 52/13) i Sądu Najwyższego USA (508 U.S.520.1993)*, Państwo i Prawo 2017, Issue 4, pp. 34–47.

5 See, e.g.: OLG Hamm, ruling from 22.4.2015 – 14 U 19/14; OLG Koblenz, ruling from 7.1.2016 – 1 U 422/15; BGH, decision from 13.1.2015 – VI ZR 204/14; BGH, ruling from 30.4.2013 – VI ZR 13/12; LG Duisburg, ruling from 27.04.2016 – 8 O 286/14; OLG Koblenz, ruling from 18.1.2017 – 5 U 1021/16; OLG Jena, ruling from 8.6.2016 – 7 U 573/15; BGH, ruling from 14.2.2017 – VI ZR 434/15; OLG Nürnberg, ruling from 29.3.2017 – 4 U 1162/13. See also: S. Hensen, *Die Haftung des Nutztierhalters*, NJW-Spezial 2017, p. 265.

and V refer respectively to contracts transferring the ownership of an animal, service contracts and contracts on the deliberate use of somebody else's animal. Each of these chapters is divided into: a subchapter concerning introductory remarks and subchapters concerning the conclusion, performance and results of non-performance or improper performance of these contracts. However, Chapter IV – referring to service contracts – has a slightly different structure, being divided into subchapters each referring to a different service contract (commission contracts, agency contracts, teaching/training contracts, safe-keeping contracts and other service contracts with an animal as the object of the contractual obligation), and with each of these subchapters being itself divided into subchapters concerning the conclusion, performance and results of non-performance or improper performance of these contracts. Chapter VI, closing the considerations undertaken in this book, summarizes the conclusions made during the research and – most importantly – contains some *de lege ferenda* remarks with reference to possible changes in the Polish Civil Code.

The impact of animals being objects of contractual obligations – especially in reference to the conclusion, performance and consequences of improper performance of a contract, as well as non-performance, has not been addressed comprehensively this way in the Polish legal doctrine and is rarely addressed in Polish jurisprudential records. However, the situation is different in the neighboring country – Germany. Therefore, this country is used as a referential legal system in this book, due to the common roots and broad similarities in the Polish[6] and German[7] Civil Codes, but also due to the fact that Germany is globally renowned for its high-quality standards in the areas of breeding, selling, training and competition of horses, as well as of the highest number of horses in Europe (after Great Britain).[8] At this point, it is worth explaining that the majority of the factual situations described in this book refer to horses, because of their potentially high economic value which affects their frequent presence as

6 The Polish Civil Code in the version promulgated on 23.4.1964, last version: J L No. 16, item 93, as amended.

7 The German Civil Code in the version promulgated on 2.1.2002, J L of 8.1.2002, part I, No. 2, item 2787, as amended.

8 I.e. 1,000,000 of 5,750,000 horses kept in the whole of Europe, according to a study made by C. Liljenstolpe, see: C. Liljenstolpe, *Horses in Europe*, Swedish University of Agricultural Sciences 2009, available at: http://www.wbfsh.org/files/EU%20Equus%202009.pdf (last visited: 3.3.2018). According to more recent research, Romania is the country with the highest number of horses (though Romania is rather not identified with horse sports and the horse industry as such) and the following three countries (including Germany) show small differences in the number of horses kept there, see: https://www.statista.com/statistics/414913/eu-european-union-number-of-horses-by-country/ (last visited: 22.6.2018). Nevertheless, there is also different research showing different numbers (though Germany is still in the top 6 of these countries), compare: https://www.theguardian.com/news/datablog/2015/jun/12/how-many-horses-european-union-eu-equine-census-population (last visited: 22.6.2018).

objects of contractual obligations. Thus, the annual total expenses in the German horse sector are approximated to be EUR 2.6 billion, with total sales within the sector reaching nearly EUR 5 billion[9] (the entire turnover of the equestrian industry is estimated to range between five and six billion Euro per year),[10] proof that the horse market is vital for the national economy, which – as a result – means more judicial reasonings and a larger number of doctrinal considerations in this topic. Although there are about the same numbers of cats and dogs in Poland and Germany,[11] this does not have such a significant impact on the economy as the horse market, and so leads to fewer judicial reasonings referring to the sale of these animals. Germany, answering the needs of the horse market – namely investors, breeders, horse dealers and other people employed in the horse industry[12] – has sufficient jurisprudence and doctrine to serve as a role model for applying the legal provisions concerning things to animals in Poland. Therefore, I have taken into account the similarities in the Polish and German legal systems and used the method applied in the project *"The Bilateral German-Polish Harmonization of Private Law in the Integration of the European Union. Addition or Opposition?"*[13] The subject of this project, undertaken by two universities that I attended as a PhD student, was to examine Polish and German law from a case-law perspective. The German cases and the main findings of the German courts were subsequently analyzed from the perspective of the Polish black letter law, as well as from the perspective of the Polish law in action, mainly by analyzing the civil law provisions used in the practice of Polish courts. The method used in the publication produced within this project – *"Limits of Harmonization and Convergence, Dissimilarities and Similarities of Polish and*

9 C. Liljenstolpe, *Horses in Europe,* Swedish University of Agricultural Sciences 2009, available at: http://www.wbfsh.org/files/EU%20Equus%202009.pdf (last visited: 3.3.2018).

10 *Idem.*

11 IBF International Consulting, VetEffecT, Wageningen University & Research Centre (WUR), Istituto Zooprofilattico Sperimentale dell'Abruzzo e del Molise "G. Caporale" (IZSAM), *Study on the welfare of dogs and cats involved in commercial practices* (Specific Contract SANCO 2013/12364 – project financed by the European Commission), available at: https://ec.europa.eu/food/sites/food/files/animals/docs/aw_eu-strategy_study_dogs-cats-commercial-practices_en.pdf (last visited: 3.3.2018).

12 With reference to the scale and importance of horse market in Germany, see: C. Liljenstolpe, *Horses in Europe,* Swedish University of Agricultural Sciences 2009, available at: http://www.wbfsh.org/files/EU%20Equus%202009.pdf (last visited: 3.3.2018).

13 *"Die bilaterale deutsch-polnische Privatrechtsharmonisierung im Prozess der Integration der Europäischen Union. Ergänzung oder Opposition?"/"Bilateralna niemiecko-polska harmonizacja prawa prywatnego w procesie integracji prawa Unii Europejskiej. Uzupełnienie czy opozycja?"* This monograph is part of a Project financed by the German-Polish Fund for Science (Deutsch-Polnische Wissenschaftsstiftung), Agreement number: 2014–16 from 15.4.2014.

German Contract Law"[14] – forced me, as one of the authors analyzing the cases of a foreign court, but with a similar legal tradition, to reconsider Polish law. That inspired me to establish the scope of this book.

The tension between the similarity and proximity of the Polish and German legal systems creates a fascinating field for experimentation with the process of the harmonization and unification of law.[15] This, together with the German experience in the sale of horses (and the extraordinary high number of other civil law contracts connected with such a large number of horses kept in Germany) made the choice of the German legal system as referential to the Polish legal system obvious, while the main legal system of this book remains Polish. References to the German legal system occur systematically in this book, since the Polish legal solutions are compared with those offered by the German legal system. Some interesting judicial reasonings of the German courts have been presented applying the method used in the project "*The Bilateral German-Polish Harmonization of Private Law in the Integration of the European Union. Addition or Opposition?*" Thus, first there is a presentation of the facts of each case considered by the German court, followed by its reasoning. Secondly, the same facts of the case have been transposed to the Polish realities, and then considered with reference to the provisions of Polish law. Therefore, this book purposefully refers mostly to German judicial rulings, which are described herein comprehensively in order to show whether it is possible to pattern Polish law constructions on German law solutions referring to animals.

The method mostly used in the book is dogmatic[16], with the use of empirical materials,[17] like the practice of courts of lower instance, legal contracts and

---

14 M. Jagielska, E. Macierzyńska-Franaszczyk, E. Rott-Pietrzyk, F. Zoll, G. Żmij (eds.), *Limits of Harmonisation and Convergence. Dissimilarities in Similarities of Polish and German Contract Law*, Warszawa 2018.

15 Thus, the similarities, as well as the differences may be very deep-lying, e. g. it was disputable under Polish law whether non-performance and lack of conformity (*rękojmia*) create separate regimes (e. g. M. Podrecka, *Rękojmia za wady prawne rzeczy sprzedanej*, Warszawa 2011, pp. 27–32), while under German law, the lack of conformity (*Mangel*) is a special category of the *Pflichtverletzung* (H. Westermann [in:] Münchener Kommentar zum BGB, München 2016, § 434, side-number. 1; F. Faust [in:] H. Bamberger, H. Roth, W. Hau, R. Poseck (eds.), *Beck'sche Online Kommentare, BeckOK, BGB*, 45. Ed., München 2017, BGB § 437, side-number 1, *BeckOnline (last visited: 12. 3. 2018*; I. Saenger [in:] R. Schulze, H. Dörner, I. Ebert, T. Hoeren, R. Kemper, I. Saenger, K. Schreiber, H. Schulte-Nölke, A. Staudinger (eds.), *Bürgerliches Gesetzbuch. Handkommentar*, Baden-Baden 2016, *Bürgerliches Gesetzbuch. Handkommentar*, Baden-Baden 2016, § 437, side-number 1). See, comprehensively: F. Zoll, *Rękojmia. Odpowiedzialność sprzedawcy*, pp. 1–7; 101–103.

16 With reference to methods of research, see also: Z. Ziembiński, *Metodologiczne zagadnienia prawoznawstwa*, Warszawa 1974, p. 80. For a comprehensive summary about dogmatic method, see: T. Pietrzykowski, *Naturalizm i granice nauk prawnych. Esej z metodologii prawoznawstwa*, Warszawa 2017, pp. 46–68.

forms (used in the market practice of the problems mentioned in the book), the mass media (press articles) and – in particular – materials from foreign law of a different nature. Thus, the book was written with support from the comparative method.[18] Nevertheless, this is also not a typical comparative work, since the German legal system has been used only as a reference (with the Polish legal system being the main subject of the legal analysis in this book) in order to obtain a broader scope of possibilities with reference to the changes proposed to Polish law. Therefore the dogmatic method and the method of adjusting the various legal solutions acknowledged by some representatives of the doctrine (i.e. animal ethics philosophers),[19] to the actual law in practice (i.e. jurisprudence of the German courts), has been strengthened by elements of legal comparison.[20] The German legal solutions serve here as a reference and as source of consideration as to whether such solutions could be applicable in the Polish legal system as well. In the end, I see this book as a dogmatic work, strengthened by a functional analysis of legal solutions acknowledged by the law in action in another legal system (legal comparison).[21] Therefore, my primary goal was to find the most appropriate legal solutions to the problems considered in this book after analyzing the positivist, as well as empirical materials of both the Polish and German legal systems.[22] In the end, the book may also serve in the future as a practical instruction on how to deal with various factual situations concerning animals, and result in reference to contractual obligations that have not yet been addressed (in this scope) by the Polish jurisprudence and doctrine.

17 With reference to legal science, legal positivism and empiricism, see: C. Sandgren, *On Empirical Legal Science,* Scandinavian studies in law 2000, Issue 40, pp. 445–482; T. S. Ulen, *A Nobel Prize in Legal Science: Theory, Empirical Work, and the Scientific Method in the Study of Law,* Illinois Law Review 2002, Issue 4, pp. 875–920.

18 With reference to the comparative method, see: J. Husa, *Methodology of Comparative Law Today: From Paradoxes to Flexibility?,* Revue Internationale de Droit Comparé 2006, Vol. 58, No. 4, pp. 1095–1117.

19 See: T. Pietrzykowski, *Naturalizm i granice nauk prawnych…,* pp. 46–68.

20 With reference to methodologies used for the legal doctrine, see: M. Van Hoecke (ed.), *Methodology of Legal Research. What Kind od Method for What Kind of Discipline?* Oxford/Portland 2011, Chapter I, especially pp. 11–17.

21 With reference to the trends towards empiricism and legal theory in the legal science, see: T. S. Ulen, *A Nobel Prize in Legal Science: Theory, Empirical Work, and the Scientific Method in the Study of Law,* Illinois Law Review 2002, Issue 4, pp. 875–920.

22 With reference to definitions of legal positivism and empirical legal science, see: C. Sandgren, *On Empirical Legal Science,* Scandinavian studies in law 2000, Issue 40, pp. 445–482.

2. The main areas of focus of the book

The main areas of focus of the book concern the role that animals play in civil law contracts (in particular concerning obligation law). Since this role cannot be simply limited to the technical issues connected with the process of contracting and using an animal, the book also covers, to a more limited extent, topics from the borders of legal philosophy and ethics. Thus, what is typical for contracts involving animals and what turns out to be most important in the main chapters (i. e. Chapters III–V) of this book, is the emotional bond between an animal and its owner. The observance of the practice and the problems arising from the improper performance of contracts shows that it is this bond that makes animal as an object of a contract so special. Therefore, the idea that animals used by people should not be treated like inanimate possessions, but should be protected from actions that might cause suffering, is very old and already widespread in human society.[23] Animals should not be treated merely as property, and this is also dealt with in legal provisions in all European countries.[24] However, what is

23 So: D. Broom, *Sentience and Animal Welfare*, Wallingford, 2014, p. 200. Compare: European Parliament, *Animal Welfare in the European Union*, a study for the PETI- Committee, available at: http://www.europarl.europa.eu/RegData/etudes/STUD/2017/583114/IPOL_STU(2017)583114_EN.pdf (last visited: 5.9.2017).

24 The need to change the way animals are treated by the law has been expressed in numerous petitions addressed by EU citizens in the years 2013–2014 alone, listed in the reference list of the European Parliament, *Animal Welfare in the European Union*, a study for the PETI-Committee, available at: http://www.europarl.europa.eu/RegData/etudes/STUD/2017/583114/IPOL_STU(2017)583114_EN.pdf (last visited: 5.9.2017), i. e.: Petition to the European Parliament 0103/2013 by Joron Dominique (French), on banning the use of animals in circuses in the EU; Petition to the European Parliament 0214/2013 by Ronald Schirmer and Annekatrin Pötschulat (German) on fur farming in Germany; Petition to the European Parliament 0337/2013 by Lorenzo Croce (Italian) on the online sale of pets; Petition to the European Parliament 0471/2013 by Gian Marco Prampolini (Italian), bearing 27 signatures, on animal testing and vivisection for cosmetic research purposes; Petition to the European Parliament 0691/2013 by Julia Knorr Alonso (Spanish), on animal welfare in Spain and the European Union; Petition to the European Parliament 1024/2013 by Aurore Bardeau (French) seeking provisions to regulate animal euthanasia; Petition to the European Parliament 1158/2013 by T.Ch. (Belgian), on Animal rights; Petition to the European Parliament 1248/2013 by Pedro Pozas Terrados (Spanish) representing Projecto Gran Simio; Petition to the European Parliament 1553/2013 by Diana Patricia Giraldo Tejada (Spanish) on the protection of animal rights in Spain; Petition to the European Parliament 1619/2013 by C.J. (German), on a ban on hunting all songbirds and penalties for countries failing to comply; Petition to the European Parliament 1690/2013 by Sylvia Van Atta (unknown), on behalf of Many Tears Animal Rescue, on animal rights; Petition to the European Parliament 2218/2013 by C.J. (German) on banning the import of leather, leather goods and fur from China; Petition to the European Parliament 2377/2013 by G.J. (German) on the use of ear tags for the identification of livestock; Petition to the European Parliament 2391/2013 by C.J. (Dutch), on a ban on birdcages containing zinc; Petition to the European Parliament 0251/2014 by Pia Berrend (Luxembourgish) on the mistreatment of stray dogs in Romania; Petition to the

interesting is that the main reason for animal protection in civil law contracts is the connection between the animal and its owner.[25] Hence, is the law protecting the interests of the animal, or the interests of its owner?

If an animal has an owner who does not care for its well-being, other humans have very limited means of counteracting the owner's actions against the animal. In this case, there are only animal rights that can protect the individual animal, and these rights are only public law provisions. Therefore, although treating animals as sentient beings is guaranteed not only in local civil law provisions, but also in the Treaty of Lisbon,[26] the real fate of a privately owned animal

European Parliament 0561/2014 by Sven Niederstrasser (German) on the abolition of the compulsory use of ear tags on free-range calves; Petition to the European Parliament 0721/2014 by Joanna Swabe (British), on behalf of Human Society International, and two signatories, on the Routine docking of pigs' tails; Petition to the European Parliament 0723/2014 by M-J F. (Portuguese / Canadian) on Food safety and Free trade agreements; Petition to the European Parliament 1071/2014 by Linda Mäki-Sulkava (Finnish) on breeding of unhealthy traits in animals (dogs); Petition to the European Parliament 1141/2014 by Fredrick Federley (Swedish), on the cutting of pigs' tails; Petition to the European Parliament 1307/2014 by A. K. (German) bearing 582 signatures, on a ban on the use of ear tags for the identification of cattle; Petition to the European Parliament 1546/2014 by R. P. S. (Spanish) against the immobilisation of horses with pliers; Petition to the European Parliament 1560/2014 by Corinna Haussmann (German) on the use of helium in place of CO2 for stunning animals for slaughter; Petition to the European Parliament 2301/2014 by Moona Hellsten (Finnish), on the cruel treatment of animals in a zoo (Zoo du Mont) in Toulon, France; Petition to the European Parliament 0094/2015 by Pia Berrend, on the terminology used for stray domestic animals in the proposal for a Regulation of the European Parliament and of the Council on Animal Health (COM/2013/0260); Petition to the European Parliament 0545/2015 by Dieter Soβna (German) on the transport of animals for slaughter; Petition 0820/2015 by Annick Pillard (French) on prohibition of the glue traps to catch rodents in the EU; Petition to the European Parliament 1320/2015 by Susanne Prahm (German) supported by eight co-signatories, on the ill-treatment of cats and dogs in China; Petition to the European Parliament 1336/2015 by Patrick Katzer (German) on a ban on scientific experiments on primates; Petition to the European Parliament 1379/2015 by Gisela Urban and Gabriele Menzel (German) on behalf of several animal welfare organisations, supported by 4.680 co-signatories, on the protection of humans and animals against toxins and pesticides; Petition to the European Parliament 1417/2015 by M.V. (Italian) on animal cruelty in China; Petition to the European Parliament 2015 on the Welfare of Dairy Cows by 18 animal protection societies; Petition to the European Parliament 0224/2016 by P.A. (Italian) on cruelty to dogs in China. Thus, in recent years, knowledge of animal functioning, particularly their behaviour and physiology, has increased rapidly and has been the subject of much media attention. This is a major reason for increased concern about the welfare of animals. So: European Parliament, *Animal Welfare in the European Union*, a study for the PETI- Committee, p. 36, available at: http://www.europarl.europa.eu/RegData/etudes/STUD/2017/583114/IPOL_STU(2017)583114_EN.pdf (last visited: 5.9.2017).

25 At least in the current legal situation. See, arguments for animal personhood in: S. M. Wise, *Rattling the cage. Towards Legal Rights for Animals*, Cambridge, Mass.: Perseus Books, 2000.

26 However, it is still not included in all European Regulations (i.e. Regulation (EU) No. 576/2013 of the European Parliament and the Council of 12 June 2013 on the non-commercial movement of pet animals and repealing Regulation (EC) No 998/2003, OJ 178, 28.6.2013, pp. 1–26).

depends on its owner's attitude. The administrative rules, which could protect it from maltreatment, are difficult to execute, as mistreatment by a private owner is hard to prove.[27] Nevertheless, private and public law are intertwined.[28] Hence, public law provisions may also impact the content of a contractual obligation.[29] This is also the case of contractual obligations with an animal as its object under Polish law, where, for example, the content of the Polish Animal Protection Act from 21.8.1997,[30] referring to the competence of the Polish public authorities, may affect either the content of the right of an animal owner or, to some extent, the content of the contractual obligation. Thus, according to Articles 1.1, 5 and 6 of the Polish Animal Protection Act, an animal owner has to treat his or her animal with respect, so it is forbidden to cause harm to this animal, to beat it, to overload it, to scare it, etc.[31] This example shows[32] how the borders between public and private law are melting in reference to legal provisions concerning animals.[33] Would it not be easier if animals had their own civil rights? Although I

27 With reference to the melting difference between private and public law, see: J. Nowacki, *Prawo publiczne – prawo prywatne*, Katowice 1992; W. Popiołek, *Znaczenie przepisów "prawa publicznego" różnych systemów prawnych dla stosunków umownych handlu zagranicznego*, Problemy Prawne Handlu Zagranicznego 1988, Issue 12, pp. 56–78; J. Łętowski, *W sprawie granicy międzyprawem publicznym a prywatnym* [in:] B. Kordasiewicz, E. Łętowska (eds.), *Prace z prawa cywilnego. Wydane dla uczczenia prany naukowej Profesora Józefa Piątowskiego*, pp. 353–362; R. Szczepaniak, *W zamkniętym kręgu podziału na prawo publiczne i prywatne, czyli o możliwości dochodzenia odsetek od zasądzonych kosztów procesu*, Studia Prawa Prywatnego 2015, Issue 3, pp. 49–59.

28 The same refers to other European countries national legislations, since animals are still treated as objects of law and the only provisions that could grant them protection are public law provisions (since they do not have legal personaleity). In Germany, although the obligation to treat animals with care can be found in the German Civil Code, the legal act that comprehensively covers these matters is the German Animal Protection Act from 24.7.1972 in the version of 18.4.2006 (German J.L. I of 2006, p. 1206, item 1313), latest amendment of 17.12.2018 (German J.L. I of 2018, p. 2586).

29 So: W. Popiołek, *Znaczenie przepisów "prawa publicznego" różnych systemów prawnych dla stosunków umownych handlu zagranicznego*, Problemy Prawne Handlu Zagranicznego 1988, Issue 12, pp. 56–78.

30 Polish Animal Protection Act from 21.8.1997 (J.L. of 2013, item 856), see especially Arts: 1, 5, 6, etc.

31 See: content of Article 6 of the Polish Animal Protection Act from 21.8.1997.

32 See also, exemplary: Article 56 of the Polish Act on the animal's health protection and prevention of contagious diseases of animals, J.L. of 2004, No. 69, position 625 (*Ustawa o ochronie zdrowia zwierząt oraz zwalczaniu chorób zakaźnych zwierząt*) referring to the duty to vaccinate animals; Council Regulation (EC) No 1/2005 of 22 December 2004 on the protection of animals during transport and related operations and amending Directives 64/432/EEC and 93/119/EC and Regulation (EC) No. 1255/97 referring to the duties of persons transporting living animals.

33 J. Zwolińska, *Sześć zasad prawa ochrony zwierząt* [in:] T. Gardocka, A. Gruszczyńska, *Status zwierzęcia, zagadnienia filozoficzne i prawne*, Toruń 2013, pp. 351–364.

am not the first to formulate this question,[34] I am leaving the answer open and trying to find an answer in the further part of this book.

The book aims to show whether such a legal solution would be possible at all, and whether it would bring any positive effects to contract law. However, my goal was also to show how often an animal is the object of a civil contract between private parties, and to prove that Poland does not yet have sufficient legislation, jurisprudence or literature covering these matters. At the same time, I have looked for solutions for these problems in the German law system, defined what could be changed in Polish law, and checked whether this change could be patterned on respective provisions of the German Civil Code.

At the beginning of this book, I want to make an assessment that the fact that an animal constitutes the object of a contractual obligation has a direct and significant impact on the conclusion, performance and results of the non-performance/improper performance of that contract. Without any deep analysis, it seems obvious that an animal – being the object of a contractual obligation – creates a different bond of duties to the parties to the contract. The scope of these duties, with reference to all stages – conclusion, performance and results of non-performance, as well as improper performance of the contract – has been the subject of research performed for the purpose of this book. Nevertheless, these legal problems are inseparably connected with the place that animals take in the legal systems of modern European countries, the ethics, legal culture and philosophical background justifying the current situation.

In conclusion, the main area of focus of the book was answering the following questions:

1. What impact does the fact that an animal constitutes the object of a contractual obligation have on the conclusion, performance and results of the non-performance/improper performance of the contract?
2. Is it necessary – in order to sufficiently protect animals in the civil law – to grant them the status of legal persons, or would it be sufficient to define them as a separate group of objects of law, and to address more provisions of the civil code to animals, differentiating their treatment from the treatment of things?
3. What legal position does Polish contract law grant to animals and – after comparison with the German legal systems – what changes to the law would be advisable? Which of the attitudes presented above would be advisable to introduce in the Polish Civil Code in the future?

34 See (especially, though among many others): P. Singer, *Wyzwolenie Zwierząt* [Animal Liberation] (Anna Alichniewicz, Anna Szczęsna trans.), Warszawa 2004; S. M. Wise, *Rattling the cage. Towards Legal Rights for Animals.*

II. The bridge between the law of obligations and animal ethics

1. Man and animal – a philosophical and ethical background

Anywhere there have been human beings, there have always been animals as well - and not only dogs,[35] but also other pets. Some of these animals have even gained the status of "holy" animals, like cows in India[36] or cats in ancient Egypt.[37] In a country with widespread agriculture like Poland, keeping animals was very often a necessity. Therefore, before agricultural technology, transport and logistics became as advanced as they are nowadays, almost every household needed their own chickens and cows (not mentioning the use of horses and cattle for agricultural purposes, though that was rather the case where the family ran a larger business). Even though animals in former times were used mostly as tools needed to perform work that people had to do in order to provide food and money, animals then appeared to be more respected than they are nowadays. Acquiring a farm animal was a challenge that could only be made by undertaking a long trip to a marketplace, where cows and pigs were offered, or to a different farm where they were bred. Such a trip could sometimes take more than a day, as the family had to walk the animal back home again. The same applied to other farm animals, though smaller animals could be transported more easily. Thus, small animals could have been transported on vehicles that were available on farms (a cage with chickens could even be attached to a bicycle), and horses could be ridden back home. Nevertheless, acquiring an animal was always connected with a lot of effort and money and it was a very time-consuming process. Therefore, animal owners have always taken good care of their animals. They knew that it is not that easy to replace them, and that their psychical and health condition is important, as the state of medicine and technology available

35 A. Banaszak-Kulka, *Kilka uwag o psach służbowych* [in:] B. Banaszak (ed.), *Przegląd Prawa i Administracji*, Vol. LXII, Wrocław 2004, pp. 127–128.

36 T. Gadacz, B. Milerski, *Religia: Encyklopedia PWN*, Vol. 6, Warszawa 2002, p. 145.

37 So also: M. Lubelska-Sazanów, *Odpowiedzialność z tytułu rękojmi za wady fizyczne przy sprzedaży zwierząt*, Transformacje Prawa Prywatnego 2015, No. 4, pp. 21–22.

was not sufficient to allow animal owners to improve an animal's health as quickly and easily as happens nowadays. So, although – at least at first glance – modern technology has given many advances and incentives to humans, it has potentially caused much more harm to animals.[38] Therefore, it is worth considering what the actual standards of due care are with reference to obligations having an animal as their subject. Thus, it is not only obligational relationships at hand, but also obligations of an absolute character arising from ownership rights over an animal. The standards of taking care of an animal by its owner usually serve as a benchmark for others who possess an animal, basing this right on a different obligational relationship.

The position of an animal as a human's companion has long been the subject of philosophical analysis. One of the reasons was the disproportion that humans felt with reference to the diverse treatment of animals – some of them were killed and eaten afterwards and some of them were treated as pets. Already in the XVII century, J. Locke expressed feelings of disgust (which he probably could not name correctly) when he observed children mistreating animals. That is why he came on the idea that mistreating animals is bad to the wrongdoer himself, as it has a destructive impact on their psyche.[39] Additionally, there always came an inaccuracy into a person's mind when thinking why some animals, such as dogs, were treated rather as a human's friends from the very beginning, and some rather as food or working tools. Another example is horses, which have been the subject of paintings and books and have always been considered to be majestic and beautiful. In Polish art and literature, this trend could be observed especially in the XIX century, when the most recognizable classical pieces of art concerning horses were created.[40]

The XVIII century saw a change. The English philosopher Jeremy Bentham gave the foundations for the idea of animal equality. He was the founder of the reforming utilitarian school of moral philosophy, and incorporated the essential

---

38 With reference to the expansion of animal production due to modern technology, which has led to changes in the morphology of animals and keeping them in cages with little room to perform their natural behaviour, see: M. Verrinder, N. McGrath, C. Philips, *Science, Animal Ethics and Law* [in:] D. Cao, S. White (eds.), *Animal Law and Welfare – International Perspectives*, pp. 63–65.

39 W. Tatarkiewicz, *Historia filozofii*, Vol. 2, Warszawa 1988, pp. 97–104; T. Pietrzykowski, *Spór o prawa zwierząt*, Katowice 2007, pp. 17–28.

40 See: e.g. horses in the paintings of Juliusz, Karol, Jerzy and Wojciech Kossak, Józef Chełmoński, Jan Metejko and other Polish painters of the XIX and XX century. Compare the list of selected Polish paintings including horses from the XIX and XX century by "Artyzm" Art Gallery, *Konie w malarastwie polskim,* available at: http://artyzm.com/theme.php?id=8 (last visited: 20.3.2018). See also: the XIX century "trilogy" of Henryk Sienkiewicz: H. Sienkiewicz, *Ogniem i mieczem, Warszawa 1884;* H. Sienkiewicz, *Potop,* Warszawa 1886; H. Sienkiewicz, *Pan Wołodyjowski*, Warszawa 1888.

basis of moral equality into his system of ethics by means of the principle: "Everybody to count for one, nobody for more than *one.*"[41]

However, even before Bentham, there were philosophers who have taken into account that wrongdoing to animals is something morally wrong.[42] Thus, already the ancient Greek vegetarian philosopher Pythagoras was called the first animal advocate.[43] Nevertheless, his philosophy had no opportunity to spread because of the influence of the later philosophy of Aristotle, who saw animals as creatures lower in hierarchy than humans, without a soul and made solely to serve humankind.[44] The same happened with the philosophy of Francis of Assisi, who proclaimed love and respect to animals, but his philosophy was not even adopted by the medieval Catholic Church. A real interest in the impact that wrongdoing to animals had on the human nature was observed many years later, in the XVII/XVIII centuries. Thus, although J. Locke (already mentioned above) and Emmanuel Kant did not acknowledge animal rights, they did represent the idea that it is morally wrong to mistreat animals.[45] Thus, although the XVII and XVIII century were very generous to animals – in philosophy as well as in art and consideration of an animal creature – it was still Jeremy Bentham, who made a change.

J. Bentham wrote: "*The day may come when the rest of the animal creation may acquire those rights which never could have been withholden from them but by the hand of tyranny. The French have already discovered that the blackness of the skin is no reason why a human being should be abandoned without redress to the caprice of a tormentor. It may come one day to be recognized that the number*

41 Jeremy Bentham's dictum has been misquoted in several sources – the closest variant to be found in his works is "Every individual in the country tells for one; no individual for more than one," which occurs in: John S. Mill, Rationale Of Judicial Evidence, Specially Applied To English Practice From The Manuscripts Of Jeremy Bentham 475, IV (book 8, chapter 29), (Hunt & Clarke 1827). Cited after: Katarzyna De Lazari-Radek & Peter Singer, *The Point Of View Of The Universe: Sidgwick And Contemporary Ethics* 349 (2014).

42 See also: T. Kaleta, *Człowiek a zwierzę*, Wiedza i Życie 1996, issue 2, 2 http://archiwum.wiz.pl/1996/96023100.asp (last visited: 20.6.2018); M. Kwapiszewska-Antas, *Człowiek wobec zwierząt na przestrzeni dziejów*, Słupskie Studia filozoficzne 2007, Issue 6, http://www.ssf.apsl.edu.pl/baza/wydawn/ssf06/kwapiszewska.pdf (last visited: 20.6.2018); O. Kłosiewicz, Zwierzęta Zaratustry. Symbolika świata zwierzęcego w pismach Friedricha Nietzschego, Uniwersytet Warszawski, Warszawa 2011. pp. 92, 112, 118.

43 So: A. Taylor, *Animals and Ethics: An Overview of the Philosophical Debate,* Toronto 2003, pp. 34–35.

44 See: W. Tatarkiewicz, *Historia filozofii*, Vol. 1, Warszawa 1988, pp. 53–61.

45 See: J. Locke, *Some Thoughts Concerning Education,* London 1963, pp. 130–134; E. Kant, *The Metaphysics of Morals*, Cambridge 1996. Compare also: C. Sunstein, M. Nussbaum (eds.), *Animal Rights: Current Debates and New Directions*, New York 2004, pp. 21 et seq.

of legs, the villosity of the skin, or the termination of the os sacrum are reasons equally insufficient for abandoning a sensitive being to the same fate.. (…)."[46]

With these words, Bentham began to change the way people see animals, and where their place is in the legal structure. This change is a long, still ongoing process. The same principle used by Bentham formed the foundation for the principle of equality espoused by Peter Singer, one of the most recognizable and important animal rights philosophers of our times. He has used Bentham's statements to explain why animals deserve equal protection to human beings.[47] According to Singer's principle of equality, the interests of the being must be applied to all beings, black or white, masculine or feminine, human or nonhuman. He claims that equality between animals and humans should be understood as something natural, and it is just a matter of time before societies accept this – just as it was in the case against racism, and in the case against sexism.[48]

The problem of animal welfare is still a broadly discussed problem. Although various legal systems provide higher standards of animal rights protection every year, it is still difficult to define precisely where the border of wrongdoing to animals lies. This difficulty is especially easy to observe in the field of contract law, where mistreating animals is not a basic premise. Namely, these are no public law provisions with the goal of protecting animals, but a field of law with an absolutely different background and goals, concentrated on private individuals and their needs. However, in order to meet the needs of these individuals, it is necessary to find a proper place for animals in this legal structure. Where do the needs of contracting parties end, and where does the mistreatment of animals begin? How will the process of change, begun by Jeremy Bentham, come to a conclusion?

2. Animal "personhood"

2.1. Animal ethics – modern approaches for reforming animal law

Since the philosophers like Bentham, Aristotle, Locke and Kant were rather concerned with the philosophy of morals, research into animal ethics may be treated as a side effect of their work. And although the works of the first animal

46 J. Bentham, *An Introduction To The Principles Of Morals And Legislation*, pp. 235–236; J. Bentham, *Wprowadzenie Do Zasad Moralności I Prawodawstwa*, pp. 418–20.

47 P. Singer, *Wyzwolenie Zwierząt* [Animal Liberation], p. 17.

48 So also: M. Lubelska-Sazanów, *The Wild Differences in Law when Trading in Wild Animals: a US and EU Perspective*, American Journal of Trade and Policy 2018, [S.l.], Vol. 4, No. 3, pp. 87–96, available at: https://journals.abc.us.org/index.php/ajtp/article/view/1040 (last visited: 1.3.2018).

ethics philosophers were published already in the second part of the XX century,[49] a field of research where this issue was broadly discussed was veterinary ethics. The first veterinary ethics text comes from 1995 and was written by J. Tannenbaum.[50] He argued that, while there is ethical truth, ethics is intensely personal, i. e. each of us must decide for ourselves what we think is right.[51] His philosophy did not change the fate of animals due to his individual attitude towards each person's morals justifying a different treatment of animals. However, the book that may be considered a milestone in animal ethics is a textbook from 2008 under the title "*The Ethics of Animal Use.*"[52] Its authors – P. Sandøe and S. Christiansen – presented five conceptual tools applied to a range of animal ethics issues. The first of them was the **contractarian view** (one shows consideration for other rational self-interested persons who have entered into an agreement, whereas both parties should gain from the contract; since animals cannot enter into a contract with people, they can do what they like with animals); the **utilitarian view** (the interests of every living being affected by a decision deserve equal consideration, interests being the capacity for suffering and/or enjoyment); the **animal rights view** (it is unacceptable to treat a sentient being merely as a means to achieve a goal); **relational view** (animals differ from a moral point of view in the relationships they have with human beings, therefore pet dogs and other companion animals have a special status as individuals), the **respect for nature view** (the protection of the species is more important than the individual).[53] These views have a much broader scope than the purpose of this book and, although it is not possible to present them comprehensively, it was necessary to point them out in order to keep the book coherent.

Nowadays, there are three modern approaches for reforming animal law[54] that are important for the issues at the core of this book. These are: classical welfarism, new welfarism and abolitionism. At a practical level, classical welfarism and new welfarism seek to refine the status quo welfarist approach to legislation to further reduce any unnecessary suffering that animals currently experience.[55]

49 See: especially, P. Singer, *Animal Liberation*, New York 1975.

50 J. Tannenbaum, *Veterinary ethics: Animal welfare, client relations, competition and collegiality*, St Louis 1995.

51 J. Verrinder, N. McGrath, and C. Phillips, *Science, Animal Ethics and the Law* [in:] D. Cao, S. White (eds.), *Animal Law and Welfare – International Perspectives*, Switzerland 2016, pp. 63–86.

52 P. Sandøe, S. Christiansen, *The Ethics of Animal Use*, Copenhagen 2008.

53 P. Sandøe, S. Christiansen, *The Ethics of Animal Use*; cited after: J. Verrinder , N. McGrath, C. Phillips, *Science, Animal Ethics and the Law* [in:] D. Cao, S. White (eds.), *Animal Law and Welfare – International Perspectives*, p. 67.

54 According to G. Fraser, see: G. Fraser, *Legal personhood for animals in New Zealand*, New Zealand 2016, also available at: http://www.otago.ac.nz/law/otago638163.pdf (last visited: 13.3.2018), pp. 4–6.

55 So: G. Fraser, *Legal personhood for animals in New Zealand*, pp. 4–6.

However, there is one very important difference between these two approaches. Namely, classical welfarists believe that animals are inferior to humans, whereas new welfarists believe in the equality of animals and humans. The consequence of these approaches is the fact that classical welfarists agree with animals being classified as property, whereas new welfarists do not.[56] Nevertheless, the most ambitious legislative reform is the aim of the third group, i. e. the representatives of abolitionism. This ideology seeks to remove not only the use of animals, but also their property status and give them the rights they deserve, i. e. the right not to be property.[57] After the revolutionary P. Singer, who is equated with this ideology, there were many other authors following his point of view. The most interesting position, in my opinion, is a book by Saskia Stucki, whose very bold views[58] are presented in the subchapter below.

2.2. Animals as subjects or objects of law?

Ethical considerations of the subchapters above lead to the conclusion that the modern legal philosophy, based on the experience of centuries, acknowledges the need to protect animals and to provide them with some art of substantial rights. **However, the rights that are conferred to animals are passive by nature.** These rights are expressed by prohibiting the mistreatment of animals by humans in the administrative laws of various EU countries' legal systems.[59]

Almost every EU country contains a provision of law stating that "animals are not things",[60] though the answer to the question as to whether animals are things

56 Compare: G. Francione, *Rain without Thunder – The ideology of the Animal Rights movement,* Philadelphia 1996, pp. 8; 35.

57 G. Francione, *Animal Rights and Animal welfare,* Rutgers L. Rev 48/1996, p. 398.

58 Especially as the author is a PhD Senior research fellow at the Max Planck Institute for Comparative Public Law and International Law, and her works go far beyond legal philosophy, combining considerations in the field of public and private law, also in the international context. See: S. Stucki, *Grundrechte für Tiere: eine Kritik des geltenden Tierschutzrechts und rechtstheoretische Grundlegung von Tierrechten im Rahmen einer Neupositionierung des Tieres als Rechtssubjekt,* Baden-Baden 2016.

59 See: Polish Animal Protection Act from 21. 8. 1997; German Animal Protection Act from 24. 7. 1972 and German executive acts referring to animals: Animal Protection – German Executive Act referring to dogs (*Tierschutz-Hundeverordnung*) from 2. 5. 2001 (J.L. I p. 838), last amendment of 12. 12. 2013 (J.L. I p. 4145) and the German Executive Act for protection of farm animals and different products derived from animals in the household (*Verordnung zum Schutz landwirtschaftlicher Nutztiere und anderer zur Erzeugung tierischer Produkte gehaltener Tiere bei ihrer Haltung*) of 25. 10. 2001 in the version of 22. 8. 2006 (J.L. I of 2006, p. 2043), last amendment of 5. 2. 2014 (J. L. I of 2014, p. 94).

60 With reference to Polish and German Civil Code, see: § 90a BGB; Article 1 of the Polish Animal Protection Act from 21. 8. 1997 (J.L. 2013, item 856). This issue has been elaborated in

(objects of property) or not is not yet the solution to the whole legal problem of their position in civil law.[61] Thus, animals are not legal persons,[62] but they are also not *pure* things.[63] Although even soulless companies have legal personality, animals do not – even though there are rules made for the benefit of animals, these rules do not confer any rights on the animals.[64] In addition, animals may be objects of legal contracts and the provisions concerning property things should be used to animals only accordingly, taking into account their living nature.[65]

S. Stucki writes about why animals are not considered legal persons in the modern legal culture, presenting a very comprehensive analysis of the correlation between the terms "legal person" and "natural person" in the law.[66] She proves that the exclusion of animals from the group of legal persons can only be justified by limiting the term "natural person" to mankind, whereas legal philosophers and lawmakers represent the opinion that speciesism is not a reason for excluding animals from creatures able to be qualified to the group of natural persons. Stucki shows the incoherence and lack of logic in the argumentation

the Subchapter II.2.2. ("The bridge between law of obligations and animal ethics" – "Animal personhood" – "Animals as subject or objects of law?").

61 This refers to the civil law of all European countries, however this book addresses solely Polish law – comparing its solutions with other national civil code solutions, especially with the German legal system. See also: J. A. R. L. Gonzales, *Direitos dos animais?,* available at: https://lis-ulusiada.academia.edu/joségonzález (last visited: 18.3.2018).

62 There are considerations, whether legal personality should be granted to animals, which are undertaken in research papers, movies and press articles. See e.g.: J. C. Ju, *When is an animal a legal person?,* Pacific Standard Magazine 28.4.2015, available at: https://psmag.com/environment/is-a-chimpanzee-a-person; C. Hegedus, D. A. Pennbaker, *Unlocking the cage, (the film)* available athttps://www.unlockingthecagethefilm.com; A. Herbert, *If corporations can have legal personality, why not animals?,* Law Society of New South Wales, available at: http://www.lawsociety.com.au/cs/groups/public/documents/internetyounglawyers/023594.pdf; S. Stucki, *The Personhood Beyond the Human: On The "Animal Person" as Legal Persons,* Institute for Ethics and Emerging Technologies 31.12.2013, available at: https://ieet.org/index.php/IEET2/more/personhood201401; G. Shyaam, *The legal status of animals: The world rethinks its position,* Alternative Law Journal 2015, available at: http://www.altlj.org/feature-articles/980-the-legal-status-of-animals-the-world-rethinks-its-position (all websites: last visited 20.3.2018).

63 See e.g.: German Civil Code, § 90a; Swiss Civil Code, art 641a; Austrian Civil Code, art 285; Article 1 of the Polish Animal Protection Act from 21.8.1997 (J.L. 2013, item 856).

64 So: Malanczuk, *Akehurst's Modern Introduction to International Law,* Routledge 1997, p. 91. Compare: S. Stucki, *Grundrechte für Tiere,* p. 185.

65 See: K. Sowery, *Sentient beings and tradable products: the curious constitutional status of animals under Union law,* Common Market Law Review 2018, Issue 55, pp. 55–100.

66 See also, some brief considerations of these matters in the Polish doctrine: J. Białocerkiewicz, *Status prawny zwierząt. Prawa zwierząt czy prawna ochrona zwierząt,* pp. 61–67; 177–190; A. Breczko, M. Andruszkiewicz, *Przejawy reifikacji moralnej i prawnej zwierząt w XXI wieku* [in:] E. W. Pływaczewski, J. Bryka (eds.), *Meandry prawa – teoria i praktyka. Księga jubileuszowa prof. zw. dra. hab. Mieczysława Goettela,* Szczytno 2017, pp. 63–81.

represented in the legal dogma and claims that granting rights to the mentally challenged who are not able to undertake legal actions independently, whereas denying them to animals is inconsequent.[67]

In her book, *"Grundrechte für Tiere: eine Kritik des geltenden Tierschutzrechts und rechtstheoretische Grundlegung von Tierrechten im Rahmen einer Neupositionierung des Tieres als Rechtssubjekt"*,[68] S. Stucki presented three main propositions of possible legal solutions changing the legal position of animals for the better.

According to her first proposition, there is no need to create any new legal category for animals. Thus, if animals were to be qualified as a category between legal persons and things, nothing would significantly change since they already form a third category that lies between legal persons and things (even though this category is not directly addressed by the existing legal systems). Still, this third category of animals should be named and formally qualified in the group of legal persons, in addition to natural persons and legal entities, in order to achieve the aim of enhancing the legal position of animals and granting more legal protection to animals.[69] In my opinion, this solution could be adopted in the national legal systems of European countries most easily. Hence, the only change that would have to be made could amount to one sentence in the national civil codes of EU Member States and – whereas this change will not mean a lot to people not interested in this issue – it would be a milestone for legal ethicists and foundations for a different interpretation of private law as a whole. I believe that people not interested in politics and law would not feel affected by such a small change, though this change would have massive implications throughout the modern world of philosophy.

A second possibility that S. Stucki considers is qualifying animals as one of the already recognized legal subjects, and – since it is obviously more logical than qualifying them as legal entities – to qualify them as natural persons.[70] Nevertheless, I believe that, at least ideologically, that would not be a good solution. Thus, both classical lawyers as well as people without a deep knowledge of law and ethics (which is necessary to understand the logic and, above all, the aim of this legal qualification) would definitely criticize this solution because of

67 See: comprehensive analysis presented by S. Stucki in the whole Chapter D of her book *Grundrechte für Tiere: eine Kritik des geltenden Tierschutzrechts und rechtstheoretische Grundlegung von Tierrechten im Rahmen einer Neupositionierung des Tieres als Rechtssubjekt*, Baden-Baden 2016, pp. 173–333.

68 Independent English translation: Fundamental animal rights: critics of the applicable animal protection laws and legally theoretical foundation of animal rights in the context of repositioning of the animal as a subject of law.

69 S. Stucki, *Grundrechte für Tiere*, pp. 302–303.

70 *Idem*, pp. 303–304.

ideological prejudice. In my opinion, the aim of changing the legal qualification of animals is not to make a revolution and to try to legalese something deeply controversial, but rather to formalize a situation for which acknowledgment was just a matter of time.

There is also a third solution proposed by S. Stucki, namely creating new terminology and qualifying animals as a third category of "animal persons". Although I do not really admire this idea, it is the favored option of Saskia Stucki herself.[71] My view is that, in the modern world where national legislators are overwhelmed with legislation following the legal harmonization in the EU and the need to constantly implement legal changes as a result of changes in modern society, and where the problem of animal rights has been neglected for such a long time due to the lack of time and the magnitude of other legal problems, the legal solution to this issue should not cause more legal complications than is necessary.

I see solely the first of the options proposed by S. Stucki as possible to be taken into account by the European Member States' legislators. This is because there would not be many changes needed – solely by adding several provisions addressing animals in the civil law of national countries. Nevertheless, (although it is worth consideration and is perhaps advisable), I do not think it necessary to add the group of animals into the group of legal persons. Maybe it would be sufficient to define animals as a separate group of objects of law in the European civil codes (just as the German Civil Code does in § 90a BGB)[72] and to address more civil code provisions to animals, differentiating their treatment from the treatment of things? Maybe there is no need to change anything at all and it is solely the interpretation of laws that should change?

At the beginning of this book, I make the assumption that there does not need to be a revolution in order to achieve a better legal position for animals, but there must be a middle way to achieve this goal. Thus, the legal group of animals should be named properly (i. e. not as "goods") in order to start undertaking legal procedures having on purpose their better treatment by humans. Therefore, in the following subchapters of this book, I compare the Polish legal solutions and the law in action with the situation in Germany. In the closing chapter of this book, I set out my conclusions concerning whether I was wrong to make this assumption or not.

However, S. Stucki is not the only voice pushing these issues. Another legal work that I consider as interesting is the dissertation of G. Fraser, who also thinks that animals should be recognized as legal persons. This author proposed that, under the mixed exclusionary/governance regime, the relationship between

71 *Idem*, pp. 304–305.
72 See: following subchapters of this book, where this issue is broadened.

humans and animals should be redefined to be one of human guardian and animal ward. Such an attitude would respect the equal moral standing of animals and humans, while also permitting greater interaction between them. Thus, current family laws already show that the law is capable of adopting solutions consisting in recognizing animals as legal persons.[73] Strengthening the relationship between humans (as animals' guardians) and animals as their wards requires the European Member States' legislators to change the way of thinking and take a look from a different perspective. However, this could be achieved also by adding singular provisions to the national civil codes of EU countries, and by the approach of the jurisprudence and doctrine in cases, where it lacks detailed legislation with reference to animals.

Indeed, the idea that animals could be considered as subjects and not objects of law is interesting and has many supporters.[74] Here, it is important to mention that Polish scholars have also looked into the problem of the legal status of animals.[75] J. Białocerkiewicz covers the issue of whether animals should be treated as object or subjects of law, not compromising the first of these options and stressing that treating animals as objects of law does not constitute equality between humans and animals.[76] He sees the problem arising with reference to animal rights in establishing a correct catalogue of rights that can be granted to animals, taking into account that there are no obstacles to differ the rights granted to certain groups of animals.[77] E. Łętowska has also briefly addressed the problem of the legal status of animals in Polish law, while – sadly – confirming that its provisions are far from the idea of legal dereification of animals.[78]

Nevertheless, it is worth taking a moment to consider whether or not this would be a rational option in order to also meet the needs of a growing group of

73 G. Fraser, *Legal personhood for animals in New Zealand,* pp. 41–42.

74 See e.g. Peter Singer, Tom Reagan. See: P. Singer, *Wyzwolenie Zwierząt* [Animal Liberation]; T. Reagan, *The Case for Animal Rights*; S. Stucki, *Grundrechte für Tiere.* Compare: N. Preston, *Understanding Ethics*, Sydney 2014, pp. 180–182.

75 J. Białocerkiewicz, *Status prawny zwierząt. Prawa zwierząt czy prawna ochrona zwierząt,* Toruń 2005; T. Pietrzykowski, *Spór o prawa zwierząt*; W. Pisula, *Psychologia zachowań eksploracyjnych zwierząt,* Gdańsk 2003 (briefly with reference to the legal status of animals on pp. 9–16).

76 So: *Idem,* pp. 61–67. The author reports remarks that there are stereotypes according to which words referring to human's emotions and behaviour should not be used with reference to animals: *Idem,* p. 65.

77 *Idem,* p. 67. The author proves that some of the rights that could be granted to a certain group of animals do not conform to other groups of animals since they do not need such rights. Therefore, it is solely problematic to set a catalogue of "personal" rigths granted to animals if it would have a universal character (the word "personal" is carefully put between quotation marks, since *de lege lata* it is not possible to refer to animals other than as to objects of law).

78 E. Łętowska, *Dwa aspekty praw zwierząt, dereifikacja i personifikacja* [in:] A. Szpunar (ed.), *Studia z Prawa Prywatnego. Księga pamiątkowa ku czci prof. dr B. Lewaszkiewicz-Petrykowskiej*, Warszawa 1997, pp. 71–92.

animal rights supporters. It is undoubtedly impossible to consider animals as equal to humans under civil law,[79] but granting them rights equal to those granted to children when they are born could be a solution. S. Stucki and P. Singer both claim that the group of people who have been granted substantial civil rights is a circle that has been growing throughout the centuries.[80] Thus, in 1792 the idea of granting rights to animals was used as means to deride the idea of granting substantial civil rights to women.[81] Afterwards, the circle of people qualified as legal persons was expanded to black people. Therefore, according to philosophers, expanding this circle of individuals enjoying substantial rights to also cover animals is the next step in the evolution of legal culture and just a matter of time.[82] The realistic consideration of these options, which came to mind after a thorough consideration of civil law solutions in Poland and Germany, is presented as final remarks in this book.

2.3. The actual position of animals versus their legal status

Animals in the modern world are living in boundaries set by humans. They are not allowed to live freely except in locations where the humans allow them to, and generally their population and every movement is controlled. There are game and nature reserves, but as soon as an animal takes one step too far and – just by being in proximity to humans – appears to harbor a potential danger to people, it is captured, drugged or killed. On what basis do people feel that they stand above animals? Animals are different to us, their ability to think creatively and logically is maybe limited in comparison to humans, but their instincts are stronger, they are often quicker, more limber, stronger and also more empathic or compassionate than many humans.[83] Therefore, it seems overwhelmingly logical that humans – as the ones who have taken power over this planet – should care about animals, but not only that. They should not be treated as species of

79 Compare: the contractarian view in philosophy, see: M. Verrinder, N. McGrath, C. Philips, *Science, Animal Ethics and Law* [in:] D. Cao, S. White (eds.), *Animal Law and Welfare – International Perspectives*, pp. 73–75; N. Preston, *Understanding Ethics*, pp. 43–44.

80 See: P. Singer, *Wyzwolenie Zwierząt*; T. Reagan, *The Case for Animal Rights;* S. Stucki, *Grundrechte für Tiere.*

81 P. Singer, *Wyzwolenie Zwierząt*, p. 16.

82 J. Bentham, *Wprowadzenie do Zasad Moralności i Prawodawstwa* (Bogdan Nawroczyński trans.), Warszawa, 1958, pp. 418–420; S. Stucki, *Grundrechte für Tiere*, pp. 173–333; P. Singer, *Wyzwolenie Zwierząt*, pp. 16–25.

83 Similarly, D. Morris, *Nasza umowa ze zwierzętami,* Warszawa 1995, p.16; N. Łukaszewicz, *Prawa zwierząt w kontekście społeczeństwa obywatelskiego i przeobrażeń cywilizacyjnych – praca magisterska na kierunku Stosunki międzynarodowe, Specjalność nauki polityczne na Wydziale Studiów Międzynarodowych i Politologicznych Uniwersytetu Łódzkiego,* Łódź 2010, p. 21.

"lower" importance. The correlation between humans and animals should bring profits to both sides; humans could learn a lot from animals[84] since they have lost of their instincts – especially nowadays, in the century of internet and modern technology. At this point, it is worth taking a look at how advanced some modern legal systems are with reference to granting legal status to institutions other than humans. A prime example of this happened, for example, in New Zealand, which granted the same legal rights that are granted to human beings to a river.[85] This took place in 2017 following a 140-year old struggle by a local Māori tribe – the Whanganui – on the North Island, which was fighting for the recognition of their river as an ancestor. The legal situation achieved by this legal recognition of a river means that if someone "harms" it, the law sees no differentiation between harming the tribe or harming the river, because they are one and the same.[86] Ethnic tribes live in harmony with nature, recognizing and cultivating their instincts, therefore it was important to them to achieve the status of legal personhood for the river. I believe that this precedence should give national legislators of EU Member States some idea that animals should at least constitute a separate object of obligations.[87]

2.4. Ownership of an animal in the Polish and German Civil Codes

Legal relations of having an animal as object of a contractual obligation are inextricably connected with the issue of ownership of an animal. Thus, since animals are not independent objects of law (like legal persons for example), an animal being an object of a contractual obligation is always owned by someone. Additionally, the fact that animals are not things, but are treated as such, is important especially with reference to property rights.[88]

84 Compare: a controversial novel book that has already gained huge popularity and been claimed as a modern classic, written by a Dutch primatologist and ethnologist, currently connected with most prominent American universities, F. De Waal, *Are We Smart Enough to Know How Smart Animals Are?*, New York 2016.

85 See press articles, referring to this issue, e. g.: E. A. Roy, The Guardian 16. 3. 2017, available at: https://www.theguardian.com/world/2017/mar/16/new-zealand-river-granted-same-legal-rights-as-human-being; A. Michalak, Rzeczpospolita 16. 3. 2017, available at: http://www.rp.pl/Spoleczenstwo/170319159-Nowa-Zelandia-Rzeka-Whanganui-zostala-uznana-za-osobe-prawna.html; (all – last visited: 28. 9. 2017).

86 See: E. A. Roy, The Guardian 16. 3. 2017, available at: https://www.theguardian.com/world/2017/mar/16/new-zealand-river-granted-same-legal-rights-as-human-being (last visited: 28. 9. 2017).

87 See also: D. Fraser, *Understanding Animal Welfare – the Science in its Cultural Context*, Ames 2008.

88 See: W. Radecki, *Ustawy: o ochronie zwierząt, o doświadczeniach na zwierzętach – z komentarzem*, Warszawa 2007, p. 39.

At the beginning of these considerations it is important to state that the regulation of ownership (as well as numerous regulations of the law of obligations, especially those referring to contract law, which – as already mentioned – is inseparably connected with the issue of ownership) in the Polish Civil Code (*Kodeks cywilny*,[89] abbreviation: KC) and in the German Civil Code (*Bürgerliches Gesetzbuch*,[90] abbreviation: BGB) is regulated on common foundations.[91] Thus, both of these legal systems are based on the modern pandect system,[92] resulting in similarities in the methodology of legal interpretation in Polish and German civil law. Therefore, the methodology of legal interpretation and the methodology of using legal provisions in one country justify their usage in the other country, and Polish legislators derive a great number of legal solutions from the experience of their German neighbors.[93] This means, firstly, inspiration with reference to legal regulations and secondly, in cases where the Polish system shows a similar solution as the German legal system, in the methodology of legal interpretation and methodology of using legal provisions in the German legal system.

The ownership right in both the Polish and German civil law systems (both arising on the foundation of Roman law) is always defined with three types of

89 Polish Civil Code in the version promulgated on 23.4.1964, last version: J L No. 16, item 93, as amended.

90 German Civil Code in the version promulgated on 2.1.2002, J L of 8.1.2002, part I, No. 2, item 2787, as amended.

91 Compare: M. Siems, *Comparative Law*, Cambridge 2014, pp. 74–82; 85–89, referring to similarities and dissimilarities in different legal systems.

92 S. Frankowski (ed.), *Introduction to Polish Law*, Warszawa 2005, p. 38.

93 See for example: the removal of provisions according to the sale of animals as a manner of implementation of Directive 1999/44/EC of the European Parliament and of the Council of 25 May 1999 on certain aspects of the sale of consumer things and associated guarantees, OJ 171, 7.7.1999, p. 12–16 in both countries, whereas Germany scratched out special provisions applicable to animals already in 2002 and Poland copied that legal solution in 2014, although it has been criticised by some representatives of the German doctrine; e.g. J. Adolphsen, *Tierkauf* [in:] B. Dauner-Lieb, W. Langen, *BGB Schuldrecht. Nomos Kommentar*, pp. 1970–1971; P. Rosbach, *Pferderecht*, München 2011, p. V–Vorwort. See also general remarks concerning the reform of the law of obligations with reference to animals: J. Adolphsen, J. Adolphsen, *Die Schuldrechtsreform und der Wegfall des Viehgewährleistungsrechts*, Agrarrecht 2001, No 7, pp. 203–208. Already before the reform of old and obsolete provisions on the sale of an animal, there were different ideas according to the form of the law after the reform, see: M. Sommer, *Der Pferdekauf*, Münster/Westfalen 2000, pp. 109–118. This solution is quite new in the Polish legal system, but has also already been criticised, see: W. Katner [in:] D. Karczewska, M. Namysłowska, T. Skoczny, *Ustawa o prawach konsumenta*, Warszawa 2015, p. 272. With reference to the regulation of the warranty regime from the comparative perspective and influence of various legal systems on the Polish law of obligations, see also: E. Łętowska/ K. Osajda [in:] E. Łętowska (ed.), *System Prawa Prywatnego, Vol. V, Prawo zobowiązań – część ogólna*, Warszawa 2013, pp. 86–100; M. Podrecka, *Rękojmia za wady prawne rzeczy sprzedanej*, pp. 27–32.

owner's rights.[94] Thus, the owner is entitled to possess the owned good (*ius possidendi*), to use it (*ius utendi, ius fruendi, ius abutendi*) and to dispose of it (*ius disponendi*). The right to use a good encompasses the right to use it in accordance with its purpose (*ius utendi*), to collect profits and different revenues from the good (*ius fruendi*), as well as to consume it (*ius abutendi*). The right to dispose of a good (*ius disponendi*) encompasses the right to divest oneself of the good, the right to encumber the ownership right of a good, and the right to pass this right to somebody else.

Whether an animal can be owned, or is it solely a right similar to ownership with reference to animals, is disputable under Polish law. According to some representatives of the Polish doctrine, with reference to animals one can only use the term of a right similar to ownership,[95] whereas other representatives explicitly refer to animals as objects of property.[96] This issue has also been the subject of considerations by the Polish Court of Appeals in Cracow in a case[97] concerning the validity of a contract between the local government (*gmina*) and a private company, which – according to the contract – was supposed to take over the local government's ownership of ownerless animals and the duties connected therewith. Taking care over stray animals consisted, for example, in catching them, giving them shelter and giving them appropriate care. The claimant – an association whose statutory aim concerns animal welfare – alleged that passing the duties to take care over ownerless animals from a public entity to a private one has the aim of passing over liability for these animals' fate. Although the Court denied the claimant's allegations, it made many interesting statements. Firstly, it confirmed that, according to Article 1 of the Polish Act on the Protection of Animals,[98] an animal – as a living being, capable of suffering – is not a

---

94 With reference to the Polish Civil Code, see: E. Skowrońska-Bocian, M. Warciński [in:] K. Pietrzykowski (ed.), *Kodeks cywilny. Komentarz*, Warszawa 2015, p. 494; M. Orlicki, in: M. Gutowski (ed.), *Kodeks cywilny, Vol I, Komentarz do Artykułów 1-449*^{11}, Warszawa 2016, pp. 766–771; W. Szydło [in:] E. Gniewek, P. Machnikowski (eds.), *Kodeks cywilny. Komentarz*, Warszawa 2017, pp. 322–337. With reference to the German Civil Code, see: J. Fritzsche [in:] H. Bamberger, H. Roth, W. Hau, R. Poseck (eds.), *Beck'sche Online Kommentare, BeckOK, BGB*, 45. Ed., München 2017, BGB § 903 side numbers 17–19.

95 G. Matusik [in:] K. Osajda (ed.), *Kodeks cywilny.* Komentarz. *Tom II.* Własność I inne prawa rzeczowe, Ustawa o księgach wieczystych i hipotece (Artykuły 2–22, 65–111^{1}), Ustawa o zastawie rejestrowym I rejestrze zastawów,, Warszawa 2017, p. 7.

96 See: M. Orlicki [in:] M. Gutowski (ed.), *Kodeks cywilny, Vol I, Komentarz do Artykułów 1-449*^{11}, Warszawa 2016, p. 766. See also: SA Krakow, ruling from 17.6.2014, I ACa 528/14, Legalis (featured below), in which it was pointed out that the owner abandoning a dog loses his property, and the one who takes such dog under his or her protection will become its owner; this solution is a proper use of provisions referring to regular things to animals, which is why an animal abandoned, caught and put into a shelter can be sold.

97 SA Krakow, ruling from 17.6.2014, I ACa 528/14, Legalis.

98 Polish Act on the Protection of Animals from 21.8.1997 (J.L. 2014, item 856).

thing. Man owes it respect, protection and care. However, according to Article 2 of this Act, the provisions concerning things apply respectively to animals. Therefore, the Court underlined that it is a respective applicability, directly related to the attitude of humanism towards animals. The Court stated that such an interpretation of the Polish Act on the Protection of Animals makes the ownership of an animal a right similar to the ownership of things. Thus, the ownership of an animal – since it is not a thing – is not the ownership right in the meaning of Article 140 KC. According to the Court, the provisions of the Polish Civil Code referring to ownership in the meaning of Article 140 KC have only respective applicability. The respective applicability of provisions means that these provisions can be applied directly, with modifications or does not have to be applied at all – depending on the content of a certain contract.[99] On the contrary, the German doctrine seems not to have any problems with using the term "ownership" with reference to animals[100] (with the acknowledgment of the fact that animals are sentient beings and have a different legal character).[101]

The Court also stated that the applicability of the provisions of the Polish Civil Code to animals does not mean a lack of humanism towards animals, basing its considerations on the example of Articles 180 and 181 KC, referring to divesting oneself of an animal. Thus – according to the Court – it is accurate that the owner divesting himself of an animal loses ownership of it, while one who takes care of an animal at this time gains ownership of it. According to the Court, it is an example of a respective applicability of the provisions of the Polish Civil Code referring to things to animals.

However, according to Supreme Administrative Court in Warsaw,[102] this does rule not apply with reference to animals that are lost or have run away. Thus, in such a situation the owner does not lose his ownership of the animal, since in this case the provision regulated in Article 183 § 2 KC referring to found goods applies.

---

99 Compare: SN, ruling from 28.10.1999 – II CKN 530/98, with an approving gloss of Ewa Rott-Pietrzyk concerning the applicability of Article 761 § 1 KC to a contract of one-time agency: E. Rott-Pietrzyk, *Glosa do wyroku Sądu Najwyższego z dnia 28 października 1999 r.*, II CKN 530/98, OSP 2000, No, 7/8, pp. 393–394; P. Machnikowski [in:] E. Gniewek, P. Machnikowski (ed.), *Kodeks cywilny. Komentarz*, pp. 1411–1413. See also: Subchapter IV.1.1. ("General characteristic of service contracts with reference to contracts having an animal as their object" – "General remarks").

100 Compare e.g.: J. Fritzsche [in:] H. Bamberger, H. Roth, W. Hau, R. Poseck (eds.), *Beck'sche Online Kommentare, BeckOK, BGB*, BGB § 903 side numbers 17–19; H. Westermann, *Zu den Gewährleistungsansprüche des Käufers*, ZGS 2005, pp. 342–348.

101 See: German Animal Protection Act from 24.7.1972 in the version of 18.4.2006 (German J.L. I of 2006, p. 1206, item 1313), latest amendment of 17.12.2018 (German J.L. I of 2018, p. 2586).

102 See: Naczelny Sąd Administracyjny w Warszawie, ruling from 03.11.2011 – II OSK 1628/11.

Whereas the application of the provisions of the Polish Civil Code to animals used commonly in Polish courts presented above is factual and undisputable, I do not agree that it does not lack humanism towards animals. Thus, since man owes protection and care to animals, the right similar to ownership, applicable to animals (and referred herein, below, as ownership of an animal in order to avoid ambiguities in this book) should not allow for simply discarding an animal. The German Civil Code states in (3) of § 960 BGB that a tamed animal becomes ownerless if it gives up the habit of returning to the place determined for it. However, according to § 903 BGB, whereas the owner may divest oneself of the good, the owner of an animal must, when exercising his powers, take into account the special provisions for the protection of animals. The German legal solution of the problem of divesting oneself of an animal seems to have a much more humanistic approach to this issue. I believe that the introduction of a provision similar to the one regulated in § 903 BGB to the Polish Civil Code, especially by adding it to the definition of ownership (just as it is in the German Civil Code), would impact the application of legal provisions to animals. Thus, German law foresees the possibility that an animal might not return to the owner itself, and this way becomes ownerless, but – taking into account the owner's responsibilities referred to in § 903 BGB – it seems impossible to accept the idea of discarding an animal under German law.

Nevertheless, *de lege lata* provisions of the Polish Civil Code referring to things should be applicable respectively to animals, which means that an animal should be used with due consideration to its sentient being (e.g. a horse cannot be overstretched by prolonged working hours or overly-heavy riders or load) and – in my opinion – the owner should not be allowed to divest oneself of this duty of care (the owner should retain ownership and serve as the animal's guardian, ensuring appropriate care even if no longer wanted by the owner). In the following chapters of this book, I propose alternative legal methods of dealing with the problem of passing on the ownership of an animal.

2.5. Animals' legal position with reference to the subject of this book

Animals should be protected, but rather in the meaning of gaining enough respect from humans.[103] If they were respected by humans and humans would acknowledge the possibility of living alongside these different species (not in the way that humans are building their world without respecting nature and limiting

103 Which I believe could be achieved by adding respective private law provisions to the EU Member States' national laws, in particular civil codes, in order to show their significance (or other legal acts). This issue is expanded on in subsequent chapters of this book.

the living space of animals to the minimum possible, which can no longer be interrupted due to minimum standards of animal care that used to be observed), then animal protection would automatically become a part of the system. This acknowledgment of an animal's place in a world ruled by humans should also serve as one of the elements defining the standards of due care with reference to the ownership of an animal, but also in relationships between animals and humans that arise from obligations. Thus, an appropriate respect for animals should not take into account permission to divest oneself of an animal, leaving it without the minimum standards of due care owed – in my opinion – to an owned animal.

The position of animals under the law has to change. This can be done in two ways. Either by leaving the animal protection provisions as they are now, but by improving the manner of ensuring they are respected, and by adding additional civil law provisions referring to animals, or by simply granting animals the limited status of a legal person. Although the second option would solve many problems with reference to the mistreatment of animals and is claimed by philosophers as an unavoidable solution given the cultural evolution of humankind, it faces too many adversities at the moment. Thus, in the solution proposed by P. Singer,[104] S. Stucki[105] and T. Reagan,[106] it would be humans who would have to undertake legal actions in the name of the animals being under their custody (the box in a stable would be rented for an animal and in its name; custody over a pet would be passed between their caretakers rather than buying an animal, etc.). Although such measures could help grant more protection to animals, it would be difficult to adjust this legal model of treating animals to practice. Animals – by living among humans – are an integral part of our culture, used for sports and farming. Building the conclusions of these introductory problems on my personal observations, many of those animals are treated well since their owners are thankful to them for the work they are giving them by serving humans. Racing horses often have a much better life and more loving owners who take more care for their health than any other wild animal.[107] Therefore, it would be difficult to qualify contracts connected with using animals in sports, shows or agriculture as contracts against the wellbeing of these animals, as they do not serve directly their own good. Granting animals the status of a legal person would have to be connected – in my opinion – with abandoning their exploitation for man's entertainment, work or sport. Already the con-

104 P. Singer, *Wyzwolenie Zwierząt* [Animal Liberation].

105 S. Stucki, *Grundrechte für Tiere*, pp. 302–305.

106 Reagan T., *The Case for Animal Rights*, Berkeley/Los Angeles 2004 (first published in 1983).

107 At this point, it is worth mentioning that, although I believe that freedom is the highest value – also for animals – it has definitely changed its meaning and worth in the modern world ruled by humankind.

sequences of granting more protection to wildlife by CITES has revealed that more protection and a prohibition on the use animals in a certain way may have a contrary effect, namely – in case of CITES – such a situation has led to a drop in population of some animal species.[108]

I am a supporter of balanced approaches and believe that humans would still be able to use animals for the same purposes as they do now, as long as the animals are respected and taken care of. Not allowing people to attend obedience training with dogs would rather lead to in decrease in the number of dogs taken from dog shelters, and prohibiting the use of horses in sport could lead to overcrowding in stables, with horses who are lacking the exercise they physically need and are not nursed everyday (as sport horses usually are due to their daily training). Maybe it would be a better solution to convene institutions that would randomly inspect the conditions in which animals are kept, and to implement an obligatory register of all animals owned by humans so that their wellbeing can be monitored more easily. Thus, the means of public law to react to the mistreatment of animals, and penalties for the wrongdoers should be improved and increased.[109]

108 Thus, according to R. Martin, the only species that seem to profit from CITES are those where in fact CITES failed on its protection and different factors (for example, the status of the Nile crocodile [*Crocodylus niloticus*] improved not as a result of applying CITES, but only when CITES shifted from a policy of restricting trade to one of promoting the sustainable use of crocodiles; the same situation happened in the case of the black rhino [*Diceros bicornis*], whose population increased when the trade ban failed. See: R. Martin, *When CITES works and When it Does Not* [in:] J. Hutton, B. Dickson (eds.), *Endangered species threatened convention: the past, present and future of Cites, the Convention on International Trade in endangered species of wild fauna and flora*, pp. 30–34. To read more on the topic of wildlife protection and the effectiveness of CITES, see: M. Lubelska-Sazanów, *The Wild Differences in Law when Trading in Wild Animals: a US and EU Perspective*, American Journal of Trade and Policy 2018, [S.l.], Vol. 4, No 3, pp. 87–96, available at: https://journals.abc.us.org/index.php/ajtp/article/view/1040 (last visited: 1.3.2018).

109 See: W. Popiołek, *Znaczenie przepisów "prawa publicznego" różnych systemów prawnych dla stosunków umownych handlu zagranicznego*, Problemy Prawne Handlu Zagranicznego 1988, Issue 12, pp. 56–78; J. Łętowski, *W sprawie granicy międzyprawem publicznym a prywatnym* [in:] B. Kordasiewicz, E. Łętowska (eds.), *Prace z prawa cywilnego. Wydane dla uczczenia prany naukowej Profesora Józefa Piątowskiego*, Wrocław/Warszawa/Kraków/Łódź 1985, pp. 353–362, who already in the 1980s pointed to the melting distinction of public and private law provisions. W Popiołek stresses also in his publication that it is not unusual for public law provisions to also impact the context of a contractual obligation.

3. Where are we now in protecting animals?

3.1. Animal law in the EU

The civil codes of most European states – including the Polish Civil Code – do not provide special regulations concerning animals. However, some of the provisions of these national civil codes do refer to obligations that may exceptionally address animals. Such provisions do not constitute any coherent system describing the legal situation of animals in a certain legal system. Taking the Polish Civil Code (as the leading legal system of this book) as an example, Article 182 KC refers to the ownership of bees (which are not covered by the scope of this book), Article 424 refers to the state of higher necessity in general (therefore also to the fact that this danger may also come from an animal), Articles 431 and 432 KC refer to animals with reference to the liability *ex delicto* of its owner, Article 449^1, KC covers the liability for a dangerous product and Article 846 KC refers to the lack of right of retention on animals of the hotel owner.

In the past, European civil codes recognized provisions signaling that animals are different object of obligations and that, depending on its interpretation, could have been considered as serving the well-being of animals. However, these provisions referred only to warranty rights arising as a result of sale contracts and were scratched out from the civil codes of the European countries as a result of the harmonization of civil law in the European Union.[110] Whereas these provisions were repealed from the German Civil Code already in 2002, in Polish civil law the provisions applicable to property things became applicable to animals accordingly, as objects of civil contracts, first in 2014.[111] All EU Member States' laws include provisions stating that "animals are not things",[112] though some legal systems – like Germany, Austria and Switzerland – include this provision inside national civil codes and some – like Poland – include it else-

110 So, taking the Polish Civil Code as an example, it includes *de lege lata* solely singular provisions of a more general character referring briefly to animals, whereas these provisions are not meant to serve the well-being of animals.

111 Before that, according to Article 570 of the Polish Civil Code in the version of 17.12.2013, J.L. of 2014, item 121, liability for defects in an animal was regulated in the Executive Act of the Ministry for Agriculture referring to the seller's liability for substantive defects with reference to certain animal species (*Rozporządzenie Ministra Rolnictwa w sprawie odpowiedzialności sprzedawców za wady główne niektórych gatunków zwierząt)*, J.L. of 7.10. 1996, No 43, item 257.

112 A provision of a similar meaning, but without the same wording, can be observed in almost all of the laws of the European countries, for example: § 494 of the Czech Civil Code [*Zákon č.*] 89/2012 Sb., *občanský zákoník*, as amended, which underlines the special meaning of an animal and provides that other provisions applicable to movables can be applied to animals only if they do not contradict the nature of the animal.

where.[113] Which of all these solutions seems to be the most rational is described in the further parts of this book.[114]

Due to unavoidable changes in the mindset of European society since the Second World War, connected with an enhanced awareness of the need to protect the natural environment, the rights of plant and animal species in the EU have undergone a long evolution.[115] The last significant change in environmental law concerning the primary law of the EU was introduced with the Treaty of Lisbon,[116] which came into force in 2009 and amended the 'Treaty on the Functioning of the European Union' (TFEU).[117] Namely, the EU countries agreed to set out an explicit competence to the European Union including nature conservation,[118] and to introduce the recognition of animals as sentient beings.[119]

---

113 See: § 90a BGB; Article 1 of the Polish Animal Protection Act, § 641a of the Swiss Civil Code [ZGB]; § 285a of the Austrian Civil Code [*Allgemeines Bürgerliches Gesetzbuch*] of 1.5. 1812, J.L. 946/1816, as amended.

114 Compare also: K. Sowery, *Sentient beings and tradable products: the curious constitutional status of animals under Union law*, Common Market Law Review 2018, Issue 55, pp. 55–100.

115 See: the main achievements of the European Union in the field of animal welfare on the website of the European Commission: https://ec.europa.eu/food/animals/welfare/strategy_en; https://ec.europa.eu/food/animals/welfare/main_achievements_en (last visited: 27.2. 2018). See also: Communication from the Commission to the European Parliament, the Council and the European Economic and Social Committee on the European Union Strategy for the Protection and Welfare of Animals 2012–2015, available at: https://ec.europa.eu/food/sites/food/files/animals/docs/aw_eu_strategy_19012012_en.pdf (last visited: 1.3. 2018).

116 Treaty of Lisbon amending the Treaty on European Union and the Treaty establishing the European Community, 13 December 2007, O.J. (C 306) 01.

117 See: Consolidated version of the Treaty on the Functioning of the European Union, O.J. 326, 26.10.2012. Note, however, that already the Protocol on protection and welfare of animals annexed to the Treaty establishing the European Community with the Treaty of Amsterdam from 1997 has changed the position of animals in the EU by stating that, "*In formulating and implementing the Community's agriculture, transport, internal market and research policies, the Community and the Member States shall pay full regard to the welfare requirements of animals, while respecting the legislative or administrative provisions and customs of the Member States relating in particular to religious rites, cultural traditions and regional heritage.*"; see: Treaty of Amsterdam amending the Treaty on European Union, the Treaties establishing the European Communities and certain related acts of 1997, OJ C 340, 10.11. 1997, p. 93. The protocol is available at the website of the European Parliament: http://www.europarl.europa.eu/topics/treaty/pdf/amst-en.pdf (last visited: 4.6.2018).

118 Nevertheless, one should bear in mind that, although environmental law became an EU competence, in most cases it is still crucial for the law binding on each Member State as to how directives are implemented there. See: Articles 191 to 193 TFEU. Compare: Ludwig Kraemer, *EU Environmental Law*, London, 2012, p. 181; J. Białocerkiewicz, *Status prawny zwierząt. Prawa zwierząt czy prawna ochrona zwierząt*, p. 138.

119 According to Article 13 of the TFEU, introduced by the Treaty of Lisbon, "*In formulating and implementing the Union's agriculture, fisheries, transport, internal market, research and technological development and space policies, the Union and the Member States shall, since animals are sentient beings, pay full regard to the welfare requirements of animals,*

Thus, the core of European legislation concerning animal welfare comprises:
- The European Convention on the Protection of Animals kept for Farming purposes, 10 March 1976[120] (together with the Protocol of Amendment to the European Convention for the Protection of Animals kept for Farming Purposes, 6 February 1992[121]);
- The European Convention for the Protection of Animals for Slaughter, 10 May 1979;[122]
- The European Convention for the Protection of Animals during International Transport (Revised), 6 November 2003;[123]
- The European Convention for the Protection of Vertebrate Animals used for Experimental and Other Scientific Purposes, 18 March 1986[124] (together with the Protocol of Amendment to the European Convention for the Protection of Vertebrate Animals used for Experimental and other Scientific Purposes, 22 June 1998[125])
- and The European Convention for the Protection of Pet Animals (13 November 1987).[126]

Together with the Treaty of Lisbon,[127] these treaties constitute the core of European legislation concerning animal welfare, due to its legal character as main legal sources of the EU law.[128]

---

while respecting the legislative or administrative provisions and customs of the Member States relating in particular to religious rites, cultural traditions and regional heritage."

120 European Convention on the Protection of Animals kept for Farming purposes, 10/3/1976, ETS No. 087; Protocol of Amendment to the European Convention for the Protection of Animals kept for Farming Purposes, 6/2/1992, ETS No. 145. See also EU documents connected with implementation of this Convention: Council Directive 98/58/EC of 20 July 1998 concerning the protection of animals kept for farming purposes, OJ 221, 8.8.1998, pp. 23–27; Commission staff working document – Annex to the Communication from the Commission to the European Parliament and the Council on a Community Action Plan on the Protection and Welfare of Animals 2006–2010 and Commission working document on a Community Action Plan on the Protection and Welfare of Animals 2006–2010 – Strategic basis for the proposed actions – Impact assessment {COM(2006) 13 final} {COM(2006) 14 final}, SEC/2006/0065.

121 Protocol of Amendment to the European Convention for the Protection of Animals kept for Farming Purposes, 6/2/1992, ETS No. 145.

122 European Convention for the Protection of Animals for Slaughter, 10/5/1979, ETS No. 102.

123 European Convention for the Protection of Animals during International Transport (Revised), 6/11/2003, ETS No. 193.

124 European Convention for the Protection of Vertebrate Animals used for Experimental and Other Scientific Purposes, 18/3/1986, ETS No 123.

125 Protocol of amendment to the European Convention for the Protection of Vertebrate Animals used for Experimental and other Scientific Purposes, 22/6/1998, ETS No, 170;.

126 European Convention for the Protection of Pet Animals, 13/11/1987, ETS No. 125.

127 The Treaty of Lisbon is not referred to herein as the core European legislations concerning animal welfare, since it constitutes European primary law. Thus, it amends two fundamental

In the context of animal welfare, the most important (especially due to its successful implementation) EU legal act other than the abovementioned main sources of the EU law is Council Directive 98/58/EC on the protection of animals kept for farming purposes,[129] which protects only animals kept for the production of food, wool, leather or fur, or for other farming purposes. The act sets out 'Five Freedoms' that ought to be granted to animals in order to protect them from mistreatment by humans: freedom from hunger and thirst; freedom from discomfort; freedom from pain, injury and disease; freedom to express normal behavior; and freedom from fear and distress.[130] At this point, it is necessary to remind the reader that these five freedoms have a direct impact on the public of EU Member States, and may also influence the content of contractual obligations concluded under the law of these countries. Nevertheless, these provisions impact mostly European and national public laws referring to farm animals, and are especially aimed at the mass transportation of animals for slaughter and its farming,[131] which are not covered with the scope of this book. Although animals kept for slaughter remain out of the scope of the book, due to the fact that they only marginally constitute objects of contractual obligations, and due to the of owner's lack of interest in its well-being (not in the meaning that he is not willing to provide them with sufficient living/transporting conditions, but with the lack of an emotional bond, and because of the initial purpose of the contract), it is

laws of the European Union: the Treaty on European Union and the Treaty establishing the European Community. See, the website of European Parliament: European Parliament, *Sources and Scope of European Union Law,* http://www.europarl.europa.eu/ftu/pdf/en/FTU_1.2.1.pdf (last visited: 26.2.2018).

128 Compare: the EUR-Lex website, http://eur-lex.europa.eu/legal-content/EN/TXT/?uri=LEGISSUM%3Al14534 (last visited: 1.3.2018).

129 Council Directive 98/58/EC on the protection of animals kept for farming purposes, O.J. L 221 , 08/08/1998, pp. 23–27; see also: Report from the Commission to the European Parliament and the Council on the implementation of Council Directive 98/58/EC concerning the protection of animals kept for farming purposes (COM(2016) 558 final), http://eur-lex.europa.eu/legal-content/EN/TXT/?uri=CELEX:52016DC0558 (last visited: 27.2.2018).

130 See: M. Lubelska-Sazanów, *The Wild Differences in Law when Trading in Wild Animals: a US and EU Perspective*, American Journal of Trade and Policy 2018, [S.l.], Vol. 4, No. 3, pp. 87–96, available at: https://journals.abc.us.org/index.php/ajtp/article/view/1040 (last visited: 1.3.2018). For more information see the official website of European Commission in the field of animal welfare. European Commission website, http://ec.europa.eu/food/animals/welfare/index_en.htm. (last visited:. 11.7.2016). See also: S. Corson, L. Anderson, *Europe* [in:] M. C. Appleby, V. Cussen, L. Garces, L. A. Lambert, J. Turner, *Long Distance Transport and Welfare of Farm Animals,* Wollingford/Cambridge 2008, p. 360.

131 See, e.g.: Council Regulation (EC) No 1/2005 of 22 December 2004 on the protection of animals during transport and related operations and amending Directives 64/432/EEC and 93/119/EC and Regulation (EC) No. 1255/97; M. Lubelska-Sazanów, *Prawne regulacje dotyczące transportu zwierząt na terenie Unii Europejskiej* [in:] B. Błońska, W. Gogłoza, W. Klaus, D. Woźniakowska-Fajst (eds.), *Sprawiedliwość dla zwierząt*, Warszawa 2017.

important to keep in mind that these EU provisions impact the content of contractual obligations in such cases.

Apart from the Treaty of Lisbon introducing Articles 13, 191–193 of the TFEU indirectly protecting animals, and apart from the laws referred to above as the core of European legislation concerning animal welfare, the European Union has also implemented several other legal acts directly protecting animals. Those that deserve mentioning include: Council Directive 79/409/EEC of 2 April 1979 on the conservation of wild birds (known as the "Birds Directive"; though no longer in force)[132] and Council Directive 92/43/EEC of 21 May 1992 on the conservation of natural habitats and of wild fauna and flora (known as the "Habitats Directive"),[133] which form the cornerstone of Europe's nature conservation policy and build a *Natura 2000* network of protected areas.[134]

3.2. Is there a need to protect animals in a European perspective?

Although the EU still faces accusations of not doing enough to properly protect animals, etc., making references to wild fishes[135] or timber,[136] the EU law is still

132 Council Directive 79/409/EEC of 2 April 1979 on the conservation of wild birds, OJ L103 of 25.4.1979, pp. 1–18, available at the website of the EUR-Lex: http://eur-lex.europa.eu/legal-content/EN/ALL/?uri=CELEX%3A31979L0409, (last visited: 7.3.2018). See also: Report from the Commission on the Implementation of Directive 79/409/EEC on the Conservation of Wild Birds, Part I Composite Report on Overall Progress Achieved, Update for 1999–2001 is available at: http://eur-lex.europa.eu/legal-content/EN/TXT/PDF/?uri=CELEX:52006DC0164&from=PL (last visited: 18.3.2018).

133 Council Directive 92/43/EEC of 21 May 1992 on the conservation of natural habitats and of wild fauna and flora, OJ 206 of 22.7.1992, pp. 7–50, available at the website of the EUR-Lex: http://eur-lex.europa.eu/legal-content/EN/TXT/?uri=celex%3A31992L0043, (last visited: 7.3.2018).

134 Ludwig Kraemer, *EU Environmental Law*, pp. 187–193. Compare also: M. Lubelska-Sazanów, *The Wild Differences in Law when Trading in Wild Animals: a US and EU Perspective*, American Journal of Trade and Policy 2018, [S.l.], Vol. 4, No. 3, pp. 87–96, available at: https://journals.abc.us.org/index.php/ajtp/article/view/1040 (last visited: 1.3.2018).

135 *See:* Ludwig Kraemer, *EU Environmental Law*, p. 193, in order to learn more about the Council Directive 78/659 of 18 July 1978 on the quality of fresh waters needing protection or improvement in order to support fish life, OJ L222/1 and Directive 79/923 of 12 December 2006 on the quality required of shellfish waters, OJ L281/47, which completely failed in the opinion of the author.

136 In fact, forestry is not part of the Common Agricultural Policy, and trees and forestry products do not normally come under the notion of "agricultural products" – see more: Ludwig Kraemer, *EU Environmental Law*, p. 183 (2012). *See also:* Sara F. Oldfield, *The Evolving Role of CITES in Regulating the International Timber Trade*, 22 Review Of European Comparative & International Environmental Law, 29/2013, pp. 291–300.

making ongoing attempts to improve protection for animals.[137] For example, the European Commission is still working to strengthen EU Member States' compliance with already existing regulations, supporting international cooperation, and studying how to improve the treatment of farmed fish. Nevertheless, EU laws tend to focus on farm animals, which provide the biggest group of animals lacking appropriate care in the EU. The European Commission is aware of the fact that consumers are often not given or do not know how to find credible information about the treatment of the animals from which meat, cheese, milk and egg products are produced.[138] What is more, farmers, veterinarians, local officials and others involved with raising livestock often do not have enough information themselves about the latest developments in animal welfare practices.[139]

Nevertheless, it is not only farm animals that are covered by the EU laws concerning animal welfare. Thanks to the *Natura 2000* programme, many animal habitats in Poland and Germany could be saved. Still, the animal protection laws of the EU are focused on animals living in Europe (i. e. not big game animals like lions or zebras) and so far obviously concern public law rules. However, as EU laws they have a direct impact on the public of EU Member States, and may also influence (indirectly) the content of contractual obligations concluded under the law of these countries (to the extent of the scope of regulation set out in these laws).[140] The laws granted to wild animals by the EU protect the animals living there, e.g. birds or reptiles in their natural habitats.[141] In addition, the effectiveness of EU law depends mostly on its implementation by the EU

137 Compare: I. Veissiera, A. Butterworth, B. Bock, E. Roe, *European approaches to ensure good animal welfare*, Applied Animal Behaviour Science 2008, Issue 4/113, pp. 279–297; J. Tawse, *Consumer attitudes towards farm animals and their welfare: a pig production case study*, Bioscience Horizons: The International Journal of Student Research 2010, Vol.3, Issue 2, pp. 156–165.

138 European Commission, *EU Animal Welfare strategy: 2012–2015*, available at: https://ec.europa.eu/food/sites/food/files/animals/docs/aw_brochure_strategy_en.pdf (last visited: 1.3.2018), p. 2. Compare also: G. A. Maria, *Public perception of farm animal welfare in Spain*, Livestock Science 2006, Vol. 3, Issue 103, pp. 250–256.

139 *Idem.*

140 Nevertheless, W. Popiołek underlines that it is not unusual for public law provisions to also impact the content of a contractual obligation, see: W. Popiołek, *Znaczenie przepisów "prawa publicznego" różnych systemów prawnych dla stosunków umownych handlu zagranicznego*, Problemy Prawne Handlu Zagranicznego 1988, Issue 12, p. 69.

141 There is also a Council Directive 1999/22/EC of 29 March 1999 relating to the keeping of wild animals in zoos that cannot be omitted, see: Council Directive 1999/22/EC of 29 March 1999 relating to the keeping of wild animals in zoos, OJ 94, 9.4.1999, pp. 24–26. With reference to other non-EU legal acts protecting animals within the EU, see the European Commission website: https://ec.europa.eu/food/animals/welfare/other_aspects_en (last visited: 1.2.2018).

Member States,[142] and the EU lacks sufficient powers to demand obedience on this issue.[143]

Summing up, the achievements of the EU in the field of granting basic protection for farm animals kept for commercial purposes cannot be underestimated,[144] but there is still a lot to be done in the legal field of animal protection in EU law.[145] Thus, the protection of animals at EU level is important and necessary in order to achieve equal animal protection in all EU Member States, and the problem of granting more rights to animals is still open. Due to the scope of EU competences in reference to the harmonization of law within EU Member States, the EU legal provisions aimed at the protection of animals have a brief and accidental character (despite being only administrative law provisions).[146] Hence, EU laws do not deal directly with privately owned animals, which are subjects of various private law contracts (creating numerous different obligational – *inter partes* – relationships). However, these EU laws may still impact private law contracts by creating (to some extent) different content of this obligation than in reference to regular goods. The issue of the factual melting distinction between public and private law provisions is very current in this area

142 See the European Commission website, e. g. with reference to animal welfare of animals kept for farming purposes: https://ec.europa.eu/food/animals/welfare/legislative_aspects_en (last visited: 1. 2. 2018). With reference to the harmonisation of law and its impact on the implementation processes in the EU Member States, see: A. Kunkiel-Kryńska, *Metody harmonizacji prawa konsumenckiego w Unii Europejskiej i ich wpływ na procesy implementacyjne w państwach członkowskich,* Warszawa 2013.

143 See: V. A. Cussen, *Enforcement of Transport Regulations: the EU as Case study* [in:] M. C. Appleby, V. Cussen, L. Garces, L. A. Lambert, J. Turner, *Long Distance Transport and Welfare of Farm Animals,* pp. 113–136. Compare: Press articles referring to potential penalties that Poland could be charged for implementing laws that do not conform with EU laws, e. g.: M. Domagalski, *Unia i jej władze nie mają wyraźnego i przetestowanego sposobu na przełożenie zaleceń na sankcje wobec Polski,* Rzeczpospolita 27. 10. 2016, available at: http://www.rp.pl/Spor-o-Trybunal-Konstytucyjny/310279981-Zalecenia-Komisji-Europejskiej-wobec-TK-raczej-bez-sankcji.html (last visited: 1. 2. 2018) (last visited: 7. 3. 2018) and the lack of real sanctions despite the disobedience of one of the Member States. Compare also the article referring to the year-long wrongful implementation of one of the EU Directives: M. Lubelska-Sazanów, *The implementation of consumer directives into Polish law from the perspective of Directive 2011/83/EU of the European Parliament and of the Council of 25 October 2011 on consumer rights,* Právní ROZPRAVY 2016 (Vol. VI), Hradec Králové 2016, pp. 46–54.

144 One of the biggest achievements of the EU legislation made for the welfare of animals kept for farming, not mentioned in the main text, was also the Ban on Conventional Cages for Laying Hens. See: M. C. Appleby, *The European Union Ban on Conventional Cages for Laying Hens: History and Prospects,* Journal of Applied Animal Welfare Science 2003, Vol. 6, Issue 2, pp. 103–121.

145 See: S. White, *Into the Void: International Law and the Protection of Animal Welfare,* Global Policy Journal 2013, Issue 4/4, pp. 391–398.

146 See: Subchapter II.3.2. ("Is there a need to protect animals in a European perspective?"), Article 3,4 and 6 TFEU.

of law. Thus, for example, the vaccination of animals is an important issue for the citizens of the EU and for its authorities. However, if an animal is an object of a contractual obligation of a permanent character (e. g. lease), the question arises, who is responsible for this duty. Additionally, changes in the possession or ownership of a privately owned animal may easily and without any control result in the deterioration of the animal's well-being and – in the case of exceptionally bad living conditions at its new user/owner's premises – even death.

At this point, it is worth considering whether the **EU could – even theoretically – have the power to bring about harmonization in these matters.**[147] The EU's competence to harmonize law is regulated in Articles 3,4 and 6 TFEU. However – when looking at the possibility to harmonize the legal provisions of the EU Member States in a way that they could change the legal status of an animal – only the EU competences that fall within the scope of Article 4 TFEU could potentially be considered. According to Article 4 TFEU, the EU gains competence in the scope of the internal market. However, providing provisions serving the well-being of animals does not aim at enhancing and improving of the internal market – even with reference to animal sales (as provisions protecting animals are unlikely to improve the functioning of the internal market).[148] On the other hand, the EU competence in reference to environment issues,[149] also based on Article 4 TFEU, does not serve the well-being of animals, but rather on achieving a healthy environment for EU citizens. Thus, it seems that EU does not have any powers that would allow it to change the legal status of animals. Consequently, the potential introduction of provisions aimed at better protection for animals being the subject of contractual agreements does not fall within the scope of EU powers to harmonize the law of EU Member States. Therefore, the European Commission communicates solely the need to simplify and develop clear principles for animal welfare,[150] which is (at this stage) the only

147 With reference to harmonisation of law and its impact on the implementation processes in the EU Member States, see: A. Kunkiel-Kryńska, *Metody harmonizacji prawa konsumenckiego w Unii Europejskiej i ich wpływ na procesy implementacyjne w państwach członkowskich*, Warszawa 2013.

148 See also: European Commission, *The European Union explained – Internal Market*, Brussels 2014, available at: https://publications.europa.eu/pl/publication-detail/-/publication/f85c0e8f-4cdf-4859-be26-f9c17e7fbb6f/language-en (last visited: 15.6.2018).

149 See, the Environment Action Programme of the EU: Decision No 1386/2013/EU of the European Parliament and of the Council of 20 November 2013 on a General Union Environment Action Programme to 2020 'Living well, within the limits of our planet', OJ L from 28.12.2013, item 354, pp. 171–200 . See also: European Commission, *The European Union explained – Environment*, Brussels 2014, available at: https://publications.europa.eu/pl/publication-detail/-/publication/3456359b-4cb4-4a6e-9586-6b9846931463/language-en (last visited: 15.6.2018).

150 See: Communication from the Commission to the European Parliament, the Council and the European Economic and Social Committee on the European Union Strategy for the

thing that can be done by the EU institutions except of introduction of administrative provisions (public law provisions) protecting rather humans than animals.[151] However, by introduction of these public law provisions, EU may indirectly influence the content of private law relationships (both, those having a character of an *erga omnes* obligation and those of having a character of an *inter partes* obligation). Therefore, **firstly** these public law provisions may be considered as criterion limiting the freedom of contract of the parties in reference to their freedom to create the content and goal of their contractual obligation (Article 353[1] KC and § 311 BGB to the extent of law as a freedom of contract limitation). **Secondly**, the provisions referring to the owner's duties to treat an animal with respect, arising from public law provisions may exceptionally complement the content of a contractual obligation (Article 56 KC[152]).[153] **Thirdly**, public law provisions may also impact the standards of performing an obligation (Article 354 KC and § 311 BGB). Nevertheless, as we can observe, these issues that are to be solved under Articles: 56, 353[1] and 354 KC remain predominantly under the competence of national legislators of the EU Member States.

Protection and Welfare of Animals 2012–2015, p. 5, available at: https://ec.europa.eu/food/sites/food/files/animals/docs/aw_eu_strategy_19012012_en.pdf (last visited: 1.3.2018).

151 As already mentioned, in my opinion administratory provisions do only provide a partial protection of animals; the legislatory bodies of the EU are the European Parliament and the Council of the European Union, whereas the European Commission has the legislatory initiative in the ordinary legislative procedurę, referring to a regulation, directive or decision, see: Article 289 and 294 TFEU.

152 Article 56 KC does not have its direct equivalent in the German Civil code, however its content under the German law may be derived from § 242 BGB with the support of *Willenserklärungtheorie* (rozszerzająca teoria woli). Since it is a complicated issue, connected with differences in the structure of the Polish and German legal systems, whereas the German legal system serves only as comparison for this book, I solely signalise these differences. Nevertheless, see more: H.-W. Micklitz, K. Purnhagen [in:] J. Säcker (ed.), *Münchener Kommentar zum BGB, Vol. I*, München 2015, Vorbemerkung zur §§ 13–14, side number 38, *BeckOnline* (last visited: 23.6.2018); H. Mansel [in:] R. Stürner (ed.), *Jauernig, Kommentar zum BGB*, München 2015, Vorbemerkungen, side numbers 1–13. See also, an exemplary ruling of the German Supreme Court (which – however – refers to horses, nevertheless With reference to the delictual liability, hence out of the scope of this book): BGB, ruling from 09.6.1992 – VI ZR 49/91 (Düsseldorf).

153 See: W. Popiołek, *Znaczenie przepisów "prawa publicznego" różnych systemów prawnych dla stosunków umownych handlu zagranicznego*, Problemy Prawne Handlu Zagranicznego 1988, Issue 12, pp. 56–78; J. Łętowski, *W sprawie granicy międzyprawem publicznym a prywatnym* [in:] B. Kordasiewicz, E. Łętowska (eds.), *Prace z prawa cywilnego. Wydane dla uczczenia prany naukowej Profesora Józefa Piątowskiego*, Wrocław/Warszawa/Kraków/Łódź 1985, pp. 353–362, who indicates that it is not unusual that public law provisions may also impact the contect of a contractual obligation.

3.3. Is there a need to protect animals in a global perspective?

The protection of animals in a global perspective is just as important as at the EU level, though such legislation always has a varied aim, purpose and roots.[154] As the EU aims at harmonization, and as most EU Member States share the same basic cultural foundations (mostly connected with the religion of the majority of the members of each EU state and the common history of the EU states), it implements laws that are generally consistent with the interests and goals of most of the Member States. Moreover, as the EU is limited to certain climate zones, it implements laws aimed directly at the animals living or passing through Europe. Due to these factors and the possibility to impose more concrete sanctions on EU Member States, it has a broader spectrum of possibilities with reference to animal protection than global legislation has. Nevertheless, animal protection in a global perspective is also needed, although it would have different goals.

The term *international law* in the global perspective is understood to cover public law provisions that are binding countries only if they decide to be a party to a certain treaty,[155] which makes these laws less effective than in the case of EU laws (since EU Member States have already decided to be bound by all directly applicable EU laws upon accessing the EU; in addition, the EU has its own jurisdiction and executive bodies, which may adopt sanctions in the event of infringements of EU law provisions by EU Member States).[156] International treaties are usually limited to the most important issues, and as such have a global connection (e.g. the transportation of animals,[157] cross-continental wildlife trade,[158] etc.). What is more, it usually takes a lot of time for all countries to sign the treaty. And last, but not least – international law lacks the legal institutions to execute provisions of these treaties, as it is mainly concerned self-help and self-defense.[159]

154 See: A. Peters, *Global Animal Law: What it is and why we need it,* Transnational Environmental Law 2016, Issue 1, Vol. 5, pp. 9–23.

155 Compare: the definition of an international treaty, being the main source of *ius cogens* rules of law in International Law, W. Czapliński, A. Wyrozumska, *Prawo międzynarodowe publiczne. Zagadnienia systemowe,* Warszawa 2004, p. 33; K. Widdows, *What is an agreement in International Law?*, BYIL 50 1979, p. 117.

156 Compare: EU Institutions, listed on the EU website: https://europa.eu/european-union/about-eu/institutions-bodies_pl (last visited: 1.9.2017).

157 Council Regulation (EC) No 1/2005 of 22 December 2004 on the protection of animals during transport and related operations and amending Directives 64/432/EEC and 93/119/EC and Regulation (EC) No. 1255/97.

158 Convention on International Trade in Endangered Species of Wild Fauna and Flora of 3 March 1973, *Konwencja o międzynarodowym handlu dzikimi zwierzętami i roślinami gatunków zagrożonych wyginięciem sporządzona w Waszyngtonie dnia 3 marca 1973 r.*, Polish J.L. 1991 No 27, item 112.

159 See: W. Czapliński, A. Wyrozumska, *Prawo międzynarodowe publiczne*, p. 586.

A legal act that deserves mentioning at this point, as the first complex act covering animal rights in the international scope – despite the lack of legal measures to execute its provisions – is the UNESCO Universal Declaration of Animal Rights of 15 October 1978. It is crucial to mention this declaration, since it signaled the problem of an animal's legal position in a global context and significantly impacted the legislation of several national legal systems in reference to animals. According to G. Rejman, it also served as a role model for the Polish Animal Protection Act of 1997.[160] Nevertheless, due to inability to execute its provisions and the voluntarily nature of its accession, its importance lies mainly in serving as a role model.

However, the UNESCO Universal Declaration of Animal Rights of 15 October 1978, as other international treaties aimed at protecting animals, cannot be successfully executed in Europe, unless the EU becomes a party to a treaty itself. This can be observed using the example of EU accession to the European Convention for the Protection of Human Rights and Fundamental Freedoms (ECPHRFR).[161] Through accession, the EU strengthened the protection of human rights by submitting the Union's legal system to independent external control. Since then, any individual was able to bring a complaint about an infringement of ECHR rights by the EU before the European Court of Human Rights, thereby placing the EU in the same situation as the Member States.[162] The accession of the EU to any international convention is also the best means of achieving a coherent system of fundamental rights' protection across Europe. Another example that will be presented is already connected with animal protection (though apart from the ECHR, there are no special courts with jurisdiction specially dedicated for a certain purpose, therefore I decided that ECPHRFR presents the best example of strengthening the applicability of an International Convention in the EU).

Thus, although some may claim that animal welfare is not currently regulated by a single, comprehensive international law instrument,[163] there is one international convention whose application and effectiveness may raise many doubts, but should still be considered as a successful legal act. This is the Convention on International Trade in Endangered Species of Wild Fauna and Flora (CITES),

160 See: G. Rejman, *Ochrona Prawa Zwierząt*, Studia Iuridica 2006, Issue XLVI, p. 255.

161 See: European treaty Series No 5, Convention for the Protection of Human Rights and Fundamental Freedoms as amended by the Protocols No 11 and No 14 and supplemented by Protocols Nos 1, 4, 6, 7, 12 and 13.

162 See: Accession by the European Union to the European Convention on Human Rights. Answers to frequently asked questions, available at the European Court of Human Rights website: http://www.echr.coe.int/Documents/UE_FAQ_ENG.pdf (last visited: 1.9.2017).

163 See: S. White, *Into the Void: International Law and the Protection of Animal Welfare*, Global Policy Journal 2013, Issue 4/4, pp. 391–398.

which was drafted as a result of a resolution adopted in 1963 at a meeting of members of IUCN (The World Conservation Union).[164] The text of the Convention was finally agreed at a meeting of representatives of 80 countries in Washington, D.C. on 3 March 1973, and so CITES entered in force on 1 July 1975.[165] As CITES is legally binding on the parties, each party has to adopt it into national law in order to enforce the treaty. Therefore, it is a basic principle of international law that a State party to an international treaty must ensure that its own domestic law and practice are consistent with the provisions of the treaty.[166] In the EU, CITES is implemented and enforced primarily through the Endangered Species Act and in Europe through two regulations: Council Regulation (EC) No 338/97 of 9 December 1996 on the protection of species of wild fauna and flora[167] by regulating trade therein, including the annexes containing a list of species regulated in trade (the framework regulation) and Commission Regulation (EC) No 865/2006 of 4 May 2006[168] laying down detailed rules concerning the implementation of Council Regulation (EC) No 338/97 on the protection of species of wild fauna and flora[169] by regulating trade therein (the implementing regulation).[170] As Article 288 TFEU makes EU regulations "directly applicable", any further transposition into the national law of each European Member State is not needed. Thus, the EU regulations can be relied upon in a national court as a cause of actions.[171]

Even though CITES seeks to protect wildlife solely by the regulation of international trade, leading commentators often call it the most successful of all

164 See: CITES official website, https://cites.org/eng/disc/what.php (last visited: 6.3.2016).

165 See the list of contracting parties on the CITES website: *https://cites.org/eng/disc/parties/chronolo.php* (last visited: 6.3.2016). Compare: M. Lubelska-Sazanów, *The Wild Differences in Law when Trading in Wild Animals: a US and EU Perspective*, American Journal of Trade and Policy 2018, [S.l.], Vol. 4, No 3, pp. 87–96, available at: https://journals.abc.us.org/index.php/ajtp/article/view/1040 (last visited: 1.3.2018).

166 With reference to the implementation of International Conventions, see: United Nations website (here, on the issue of the implementation the Convention on the Rights of Persons with Disabilities and its Optional Protocol (A/RES/61/106). United Nations, http://www.un.org/disabilities/default.asp?id=235 (last visited: 26.7.2016).

167 Council Regulation (EC) No. 338/97 of 9 December 1996 on the protection of species of wild fauna and flora.

168 Commission Regulation (EC) No. 865/2006 of 4 May 2006 laying down detailed rules concerning the implementation of Council Regulation (EC) No. 338/97 on the protection of species of wild fauna and flora by regulating trade therein, OJ 166, 19.6.2006, pp. 1–69.

169 Council Regulation (EC) No. 338/97 of December 9, 1996 on the protection of species of wild fauna and flora by regulating trade therein, OJ 61, 3.3.1997, pp. 1–69.

170 European Commission, *An Introduction to CITES and its Implementation in the European Union* (2010), http://ec.europa.eu/environment/cites/pdf/trade_regulations/short_ref_guide.pdf; http://ec.europa.eu/environment/cites/legislation_en.htm (last visited: 9.3.2018).

171 *See e.g.:* D. Cahill, N. Connery, T. Kennedy, V. Power, *European Law*, Oxford 2011 (1987).

international treaties concerned with the conservation of wildlife.[172] My observations presented in the article "*The Wild Differences in Law…*"[173] show that the European Union – by implementing CITES as a whole – made its application quite successful. By contrast, the US has been a party to CITES for a longer time, but the control of wildlife is not as effective, which might be caused by the lack of any centralized control or the lack of popular acceptance.[174] Thus, a centralized implementation of a global legal act by the introduction of directives[175] forcing EU Member States to undergo necessary legal changes, which are then similar in all EU Member States, and by leading all of them along the same legal path, is the key to its successful implementation, respect and control.

There is a strong need to protect animals globally. The most pressing confirmation of this need, and justification for it, can be seen from the success of CITES. Whereas animal protection may be achieved by both public and private law means, the examples presented in this subchapter (i.e. ECPHRFR and mainly CITES) concern only public law (as they are international treaties). There are different goals to be achieved at a global level and at an EU level. Whereas the EU aims also at the harmonization of private law among its Member States, this goal may not be achieved in a global perspective (there are many reasons, not least of them being that there are simply irreconcilable differences between *civil law* and *common law* legal systems). Therefore, it would appear that animal protection at a global level can only be introduced by administrative laws, such as international conventions, which unfortunately are rarely executed with a

172 *Idem*, p. 84; S. Lyster, *International Wildlife Law: An Analysis of International Treaties concerned with the Conservation of Wildlife*, Cambridge 1993 (1985), p. 240; S. Carpenter, *The devolution of conservation: why cites must embrace community-based resource management*, 2 Arizona Journal Of Environmental Law & Policy 1, 3–5 (2011). About CITES' effectiveness in general, *see:* R. Martin, *When CITES Works and When it Does Not* [in:] J. Hutton, B. Dickson (eds.), *Endangered Species, Threatened Convention: The Past, Present And Future Of CITES*, 2000.

173 See: M. Lubelska-Sazanów, *The Wild Differences in Law when Trading in Wild Animals: a US and EU Perspective*, American Journal of Trade and Policy 2018, [S.l.], Vol. 4, No. 3, pp. 87–96, available at: https://journals.abc.us.org/index.php/ajtp/article/view/1040 (last visited: 1.3.2018).

174 See: *http://www.humanesociety.org/assets/pdfs/wildlife/exotics/state-laws-dangerous-wild-animals.pdf* in order to observe the lack of consistency in the US state laws concerning the legality of keeping wild animals as pets and: R. Martin, *When CITES works and When it Does Not* [in:] J. Hutton, B. Dickson (eds.), *Endangered species threatened convention*, pp. 31–32. See: M. Lubelska-Sazanów, *The Wild Differences in Law when Trading in Wild Animals: a US and EU Perspective*, American Journal of Trade and Policy 2018, [S.l.], Vol. 4, No. 3, pp. 87–96, available at: https://journals.abc.us.org/index.php/ajtp/article/view/1040 (last visited: 1.3.2018).

175 With reference to the implementation of directives in international private law from the German perspective, see: Y. Schnorbus, Die richtlinienkonforme Rechtsfortbildung im nationalen Privatrecht, Archiv für die civilistische Praxis (ACP) 2001, Issue 6/201, pp. 860–901.

great deal of success. On the other hand, the very nature of internationally connected issues, such as international trade or the international transportation of animals, mean that they will never be successful if adopted piecemeal, so global solutions would be required. Thus, although there is no ideal way to tackle with this issue, and in the global perspective an administrative law solution is not perfect, it is clear that without International Public Law, some issues could simply not be addressed at all. Therefore, individual countries, as well as unions of states (e.g. the European Union) should seek means to implement international conventions into national laws in order to make respecting these issues more successful. A unified implementation (taking the example of the European Union, which – by implementing CITES as a whole – made the application of CITES more successful than anything in the US) of international treaties at the EU level is the key to its effectiveness within the EU. Thus, there is a need to protect animals globally, since animal protection can only be achieved by correlating activities in this field of law at a global level and at an EU level. Still, it should always be kept in mind that European and globally binding law provisions referring to animals are always public law provisions.

3.4. Correlation between local traditions, culture and animal protection

After an EU constitution failed to pass, there were considerations as to whether the harmonization of laws within the EU is possible at all, since it was not possible to find a compromise in reference to the most important part of our legal culture, i.e. the fundamental rights of EU citizens.[176] T. Wilhelmsson denied this possibility, but evaluated the failure to pass the EU constitution as positive, stating that a systematic harmonization of the law would, in his view, destroy rather than strengthen the identity of Europe, resulting in "abolishing the Idea of Europe".[177] He claimed that the harmonization of European contract law should be created on the basis of traditional values, and sees the strength of Europe and the core of its identity in recognizing the plurality of its languages, social structures and cultures. Therefore, although there is no common EU constitution, the EU still aims at harmonization, while also recognizing the plurality

176 Compare: S. Broß, *Grundwerte und Grundrechte in Europa. Systematische und konstruktive Überlegungen* [in:] C. Robertson-von Trotha (ed.), *Kultur und Gerechtigkeit*, Baden-Baden 2007, pp. 155–169.

177 T. Wilhelmsson, *Towards a (Post)modern European Contract Law* [in:] Juridica International 6/2001, pp. 23–29. See also: M. Lubelska-Sazanów, *The "principle of no freedom of contract" – a postmodern version of the freedom of contract principle?* [in:] M. De Maestri, S. Dominelli (eds.), *Party autonomy in European private (and) international law*, Rome 2014, pp. 15–31.

of cultures at the same time.[178] Therefore, there exists a commonly represented view that a European legal culture either already exists or is being created through the Europeanisation of law.[179] However, firstly, it is necessary to define the term "**law**" and its connection to culture. Beginning with the basics, G. Murdock[180] names law alongside property, government, trade and many other elements common to all human cultures. Going further in these considerations, A. Radcliffe-Brown defines law very strictly, namely as "social control through the systematic application of the force of politically-organized society.[181]"[182] However, the next two definitions are more liberal. Thus, according to E. Hoebel, the "law" covers "cases, where the hurt individual takes action to redress the wrong against him, at least if public opinion uphold him and sanctions his actions",[183] and according to L. Poispil, the "law" is any kind of coercion at all.[184] Although the term "law" might be understood as a more or less comprehensive term, in all these interpretations it is to be understood as part of a culture.[185]

Secondly, it is necessary to define the term "**culture**". According to W. Goodenough, "culture [is located] in the minds and hearts of men," and "society's culture consists of whatever it is one has to know or believe in order to operate in a manner acceptable to its members."[186] According to E. Tylor, it is also "that complex whole which includes knowledge, belief, art, morals, law, custom and any other capabilities and habits acquired by man as a member of society."[187]

---

178 See: G. Dannemann, *Comparative Law: Study of Similarities or Differences?* [in:] M. Reimann, R. Zimmermann (eds.), *The Oxford handbook of comparative law*, Oxford 2008, pp. 383–420.

179 See: R. Michaels, *Comparative Law* [in:] J. Basedow, K. J. Hopt, R. Zimmermann (eds.), *Max Planck Encyclopedia of European Private Law*, Oxford 2012; available as a pdf under: https://scholarship.law.duke.edu/cgi/viewcontent.cgi?referer=&httpsredir=1&article=3012&context=faculty_scholarship (last visited: 1.3.2018), p. 4.

180 G. Mudrock, *Social structure*, New York 1949, pp. 4–5. Quoted after: A. Köbben, *The logic of cross-cultural analysis: why exceptions?* [in:] S. Rokkan (ed.), *Comparative Research across Cultures and Nations*, Paris-The Hague 1968, p. 23.

181 A. Radcliffe-Brown, *A note on Functionalist Anthropology*, Man 46/1946, pp. 38–41.

182 Whereas some societies do not have any law under this point of view, compare: A. Köbben, *The logic of cross-cultural analysis: why exceptions?* [in:] S. Rokkan (ed.), *Comparative Research across Cultures and Nations*, p. 23.

183 E. Hoebel, *The law of Primitive Man*, Cambridge, 1954. Quoted after: A. Köbben, *The logic of cross-cultural analysis: why exceptions?* [in:] S. Rokkan (ed.), *Comparative Research across Cultures and Nations*, pp. 23, 50.

184 L. Poispil, *Kapauku Papuans and their law*, New Haven 1958.

185 However, compare philosophical remarks with reference to the issue whether the law itself may be understood as a culture: T. Gutmann, *Recht als Kultur?*, Baden-Baden 2015.

186 Quoted after: C. Geertz, *The interpretation of cultures*, New York 2000, p. 11.

187 E. Tylor, *Primitive Culture: Researches into the Development of Mythology, Philosophy, Religion, Art, and Custom*, New York 1974 [1871].

Thirdly, there is **legal culture** (connected with the most problematic issues of European legal culture presented above) and **legal tradition.** Legal culture often describes merely an extended understanding of law and – according to the classics, i. e. E. Ehrlich or R. Pound – is synonymous with "living law"[188] or "law in action".[189] Sometimes, the term legal culture is used interchangeably with the term "legal family" or "legal tradition",[190] since many comparatists use the concepts of 'legal culture' and 'legal tradition' as synonyms.[191] Nevertheless, according to P. Glenn, the concept of 'legal culture' is a conflicting concept, whereas the concept of 'legal tradition' is epistemologically more tolerant.[192]

The presentation of the various terms describing law, culture, legal culture and legal tradition is important for the aim of this subchapter, though philosophical considerations connected with defining these terms are not the main subject of this book. Therefore, the presented definitions are, in my opinion, most suitable in its context.

After defining what legal culture is, and acknowledging that the law is a part of it, there is little doubt that local traditions and culture determine animal protection. Thus, EU law in the Treaty of Lisbon confirms solely that "*animals are sentient beings*" and basically leaves detailed legislation to the Member States. Moreover, the EU allows Member States to protect animals "*in accordance with their cultural traditions and customs*",[193] which has turned out to be a very unfortunate formulation, the consequences of which are shown in the following

188 Compare: E. Ehrlich, Funda*mental Principles of the Sociology of Law*, New Brunswick/ London 2009 (originally published on 1936 by Harvard University Press).

189 R. Pound, *Law in Books and Law in Action*, American Law Review 1910, Vol. 44, Issue I, pp. 12–36.

190 R. Michaels, *Comparative Law* [in:] J. Basedow, K. J. Hopt, R. Zimmermann (eds.), Max Planck Encyclopedia of European Private Law, Oxford 2012; available as pdf under: https://scholarship.law.duke.edu/cgi/viewcontent.cgi?referer=&httpsredir=1&article=3012&context=faculty_scholarship (last visited: 1.3.2018), p. 1.

191 J. Husa, *Legal Culture vs. Legal Tradition – Different Epistemologies?*, Maastricht European Private Law Institute Working Paper 2012, Issue 18/2012; available at: http://works.bepress.com/jaakko_husa/23/ (last visited: 25.1.2018). With reference to the similarities and differences in different legal cultures, see: M. V. Hoecke (ed.), *Epistemology and Methodology of Comparative Law*, Portland 2004.

192 See: P. Glenn, *Comparative Legal Families and Comparative Legal Traditions* [in:] M. Reimann, R. Zimmermann (eds.), *The Oxford handbook of comparative law*, pp. 421–440. Compare: J. Husa, *Legal Culture vs. Legal Tradition – Different Epistemologies?*, Maastricht European Private Law Institute Working Paper 2012, Issue 18/2012; available at: http://works.bepress.com/jaakko_husa/23/ (last visited: 25.1.2018).

193 According to Article 13 TFEU, the EU and Member States "shall pay full regard to the welfare requirements of animals, while respecting the legislative or administrative provisions and customs of the Member States relating in particular to religious rites, cultural traditions and regional heritage". Compare: Article 13 TFEU.

subchapter.[194] Nevertheless, achieving a uniform understanding of the mentioned notion seems to be difficult. In various legal orders (in the frame of EU) this all depends on the methodology of the interpretation of law and its application, what is strictly connected with legal culture and legal traditions.

One of the most substantial problems acknowledged by the European Parliament is the problem with stray dogs in several Member States.[195] The welfare of these dogs is sometimes very poor, since there is no EU legislation on this matter.[196] In addition, while retail company standards can have a large beneficial effect on farm animal welfare, there are no such standards for companion and working animals. Many Member States have laws about cruelty to animals, but it is anomalous that there is no community-wide legislation on the welfare of pets and working animals (however, as already mentioned, the EU unfortunately does not have direct legislative competence in these matters).[197] I find the source of this problem in the statement that the EU and Member States will respect the law and customs of the Member States relating in particular to religious rites, cultural traditions and regional heritage when referring to animal welfare issues on the other hand.[198] This neutral attitude of the EU, consisting in acceptance of obsolete customs (e.g. the *corrida* in Spain[199] or the Greek allowance and indifference to enormous numbers of stray cats and dogs caused by an outdated and unaware attitude to their sterilization[200]) will never allow the Union to meet its goals of granting animal welfare within EU – as being more important than the protection of animals in Europe as a whole, and a vision of a modern unity of a certain standards of laws.

194 See: Subchapter II.3.5 ("The problem of strays as an example of how local traditions and culture determine levels of animal protection – comparative remarks").

195 Compare the example presented in Subchapter II.3.5 ("The problem of strays as an example of how local traditions and culture determine levels of animal protection – comparative remarks").

196 See: European Parliament, *Animal Welfare in the European Union*, a study for the PETI-Committee, p. 52, available at: http://www.europarl.europa.eu/RegData/etudes/STUD/2017/583114/IPOL_STU(2017)583114_EN.pdf (last visited: 5.9.2017).

197 *Idem.*

198 Compare: Article 13 TFEU.

199 See: G. Dannemann, *Comparative Law: Study of Similarities or Differences?* [in:] M. Reimann, R. Zimmermann (eds.), *The Oxford handbook of comparative law*, pp. 383–420; R. Michaels, *Comparative Law* [in:] J. Basedow, K. J. Hopt, R. Zimmermann (eds.), *Max Planck Encyclopedia of European Private Law*, p. 4. Compare also press articles referring to that issue, e.g.: J. Badcock, *Will Spain ever ban bullfighting?*, BBC News 3.12.2016, available at: http://www.bbc.com/news/world-europe-38063778; P. Richardson, *Why bullfighting is making Spain see red*, The Guardian 6.6.2010, available at: https://www.theguardian.com/world/2010/jun/06/bullfighting-outlawed-catalonia (last visited: 20.3.2018).

200 Compare the example presented in Subchapter II.3.5 ("Some comparative remarks concerning animal care determined by tradition and culture").

3.5. The problem of strays as an example of how local traditions and culture determine levels of animal protection – comparative remarks

Even if one sees the strength of Europe and the core of its identity in recognizing the plurality of its languages, social structures and cultures – just as T. Wilhelmsson[201] suggested – this plurality of cultures often represents such significant differences that it is impossible to impose the same laws throughout the EU. This is especially the case when taking into account that protecting local customs is still more important for the EU than animal welfare. With reference to animal law, Greece is a good example of local customs leading to a serious problem, with the lack of any legislation or administrative actions. Thus, Greece acceded to the EU back in 1975, mainly because of its history and its contribution to European culture, which can also be expressed in the words "the Greek spirit contributed the idea of Freedom, Truth and Beauty" to European culture.[202] This was the case despite the fact that the European Commission, when issuing its opinion on Greece's membership bid, warned that the Greek economy had a weak industrial base that would limit its capacity to "combine homogeneously" with other member states.[203] German Chancellor Helmut Schmidt worried about Greece's problematic public administration, and its inability to collect taxes from its wealthiest citizens.[204] What is important for defining the Greek nation's culture and general attitude to fundamental issues at that time, it is worth mentioning that levels of corruption in Greece back then were below the European average,[205] and the percentage of citizens who have internet access at home were well below the EU average.[206]

This is important in the context of this book, as the difference in culture and awareness of Greeks can also be observed by the way they treat animals – still today. Thus, although the Treaty of Lisbon has granted a certain level of pro-

201 T. Wilhelmsson, *Towards a (Post)modern European Contract Law* [in:] Juridica International 6/2001, pp. 23–29.

202 Compare: the words of K. Karamanlis, the Greek prime minister during the time period of accession to the EU, See: J. Angelos, *Why on earth is Greece in the EU? Reverence for the ancient Greeks led to the modern Greek crisis* [in:] Politico, available at: http://www.politico.eu/article/why-is-greece-in-the-eu-grexit/ (last visited: 5.9.2017). Compare also: J. Rankin, *Greece in Europe: a short history* [in:] The Guardian, available at: https://www.theguardian.com/world/2015/jul/03/greece-in-europe-a-short-history (last visited: 5.9.2017).

203 *Idem.*

204 *Idem.*

205 *Idem.*

206 See: The APC European Internet Rights Project: M. Anestopoulou, A. McKenna, Country Report – Greece, available at: http://europe.rights.apc.org/c_rpt/greece.html (last visited: 5.9.2017).

tection to animals,[207] Greece is well known for its stray cats and dogs living on the streets. This is a serious problem, reported by many animal welfare organizations[208] and connected with practices that reflect older village attitudes towards animals and many Greeks treating the sterilization of cats and dogs as something unnatural.[209] The biggest problem in matters like the one at hand is not only the lack of animal protection laws, but its execution – and even worse – the way the government generally deals with difficult problems, just as it was in the case of stray dogs.[210] Although the effective enforcement of laws on animal welfare is desirable, it is not a substitute for completeness in the coverage of the law (i. e. it should cover also privately owned animals, like dogs).[211] The problem with reference to stray cats and dogs, however, is not only the government, but also the mentality of regular Greek people, who see solutions like an owner abandoning a dog as socially acceptable. Without changing the attitude of a nation, the law cannot be changed. This led to a situation where, during the financial crisis of 2015, there were over a million stray dogs in Athens. There are also human health and wildlife problems resulting from the presence of stray cats and dogs. This subject has been raised in petitions to the European Parliament (e. g. Petitions 0251/2014[212] and 0094/2015[213]) and there is a need for EU

207 Compare: Subchapter II.3.1. ("The bridge between law of obligations and animal ethics" – "Where are we now in protecting animals?" – "Animal law in the EU").

208 See e. g.: European Society of Dog and Animal Welfare – ESDAW: http://www.esdaw.eu/society-and-animal-welfare-greece.html; Paros Animal Welfare Society – PAWS: http://paws.gr; European Society of Dog and Animal Welfare – ESDAW: http://www.esdaw-eu.eu/the-eu-and-animal-welfare.html; Greek Animal Welfare Fund – GAWF: https://www.gawf.org.uk/what-we-do-1 (all links last visited: 5.9.2017).

209 Compare: http://www.aeginagreece.com/aegina/pages/articles/animals/animal_issues_greece.html, https://www.athensguide.com/straydogs/; http://greece.greekreporter.com/2011/07/13/disapproval-over-new-law-regarding-animals/ (all links last visited: 5.9.2017).

210 Compare: Suspicions of poisoning large numbers of stray dogs in Greece before the Olympics in 2004, http://www.esdaw.eu/greece-massacre.html (last visited: 5.9.2017). See also: a press article referring to the consequences of the Greek financial crisis and the fate of dogs: http://www.bbc.com/news/av/world-europe-34432580/a-million-stray-dogs-victims-of-greek-debt-crisis (last visited: 5.9.2017).

211 European Parliament, *Animal Welfare in the European Union*, a study for the PETI-Committee, p. 10, available at: http://www.europarl.europa.eu/RegData/etudes/STUD/2017/583114/IPOL_STU(2017)583114_EN.pdf (last visited: 7.3.2018). Compare: V. A. Cussen, *Enforcement of Transport Regulations: the EU as Case study* [in:] M. C. Appleby, V. Cussen, L. Garces, L. A. Lambert, J. Turner, *Long Distance Transport and Welfare of Farm Animals*, pp. 113–136.

212 Petition No. 0251/2014 by Pia Berrend (Luxembourgish) on the mistreatment of stray dogs in Romania.

213 Petition 0094/2015 by Pia Berrend (Luxembourgish) on the terminology used for stray domestic animals in the proposal for a Regulation of the European Parliament and of the Council on Animal Health (COM/2013/0260).

legislation in this area.[214] Although Spain and Portugal also struggle with financial difficulties, the problem of stray cats or dogs has never existed in these countries on a scale comparable to Greece,[215] which is the best proof of the very close connection between culture and the fate of animals. Indeed the fate of animals is not only dependent on the laws of a country, but also on the people's will to obey this law, and the government's will to execute it. This will and the law are elements of culture and, as can be clearly seen, they have had a dramatic impact on the fate of dogs and cats in certain European countries – despite common EU legislation[216] and goals.[217]

Although the EU does not have the ability to draw up EU legislation to improve the status of animals under civil law, it should still undertake actions to improve the public law provisions allowing for the better treatment of animals, also by bringing about improvements in the situation of stray animals on Europe's streets. For example, J. Wojciechowski takes the view that the EU should acknowledge improvements in the field of animal welfare as its aim, establishing a special fund for this purpose. These funds could, for example, be used to sterilize stray animals or for educational purposes.[218] The author also acknowledges that the problem of stray animals is the first burning problem that should be looked at by the EU in connection with animal welfare. However, when considering the problem of stray dogs in Greece, the sterilization of stray animals could possibly interfere with the EU respecting the customs of the Member States relating to religious rites and cultural traditions. Despite not having competence in civil law legislation, I fully agree that animal welfare should be acknowledged as an EU goal with high priority. In this way, the EU could educate and promote an appropriate attitude towards animals, granting them the legal

214 European Parliament, *Animal Welfare in the European Union*, a study for the PETI-Committee, p. 61, available at: http://www.europarl.europa.eu/RegData/etudes/STUD/2017/583114/IPOL_STU(2017)583114_EN.pdf (last visited: 7.3.2018).

215 The problem of strays in Spain does exist, but is connected with certain regions and a certain social groups (i. e. hunters, whose treatment of animals leaves a lot to be desired in all parts of the world and with reference to all kinds of animals), thus it is not a "national", but rather a regional problem and is not connected with the general attitude of Spanish people to animals, nor with the economic crisis, compare: http://www.telegraph.co.uk/expat/expatlife/8382998/The-starving-dogs-that-give-Spain-a-bad-name.html (last visited: 14.9.2017).

216 I.e. the Treaty of Lisbon and "five freedoms", see: Subchapter II.3.1. ("Animal law in the EU").

217 Compare: European Parliament, *Animal Welfare in the European Union*, a study for the PETI- Committee, available at: http://www.europarl.europa.eu/RegData/etudes/STUD/2017/583114/IPOL_STU(2017)583114_EN.pdf (last visited: 5.9.2017).

218 So: J. Wojciechowski, *Ochrona zwierząt w UE – w dobrym kierunku zbyt małymi krokami* [in:] T. Gardocka, A. Gruszczyńska, *Status zwierzęcia. Zagadnienia filozoficzne i prawne*, Toruń 2012, p. 293.

status they deserve without changing the law. *De lege lata* such undertakings are not performed by the EU due to its obligation to respect rites and traditions allowing particular nations to discard animals, to organize *corridas* or to deny the need to sterilize stray animals.

III. Contracts aimed at the transfer of property[219]

1. General characteristic of contracts aimed at the transfer of property with reference to contracts with an animal as their object

Neither the Polish Civil Code, nor the referential legal system of Germany, provide regulations concerning animals of a systematic nature in the law of obligations. Additionally, the laws applicable to property things are only **respectively** applicable to animals (meaning that **animals are not things**[220]). Therefore, many questions concerning the legal character of these laws arise, among them is the issue of whether animals can even be owned, if it is accepted that they are not things.[221] Thus, contracts transferring ownership having an animal as its object may simply be understood as the transfer of ownership of an animal (just as it is in case of transfer of ownership over things, though with the

219 The title of obligational relationships refers to the aim of the contracts described therein, due to the differences in understanding the legal character of contracts aimed at the transfer of ownership. Although Polish law distinguishes between the obligation and the act transferring the ownership, in the case of sales and other contracts described by the legislator (to the extent of individual goods), a transfer of ownership supervenes *ex lege* (however, the parties may also decide that ownership will be passed at a different time). Thus, whereas Polish law follows the principles of unity (*zasada podwójnego skutku*) and causality (*zasada kauzalności czynności prawnej*) based on Article 155 KC, the German law follows the principles of separation (*Trennungsprinzip*) and abstraction (*Abstraktionsprinzip*). Therefore, as the term "contracts transferring ownership" would refer rather to Polish law, which – unlike under German law – follows the principles of unity and causality (where each transfer of ownership is connected with a corresponding *causa*), I tried to address the differences in the Polish and German legal systems by using the term "contracts aimed at the transfer of ownership". See: E. Rott-Pietrzyk, F. Zoll [in:] M. Jagielska, E. Macierzyńska-Franaszczyk, E. Rott-Pietrzyk, F. Zoll, G. Żmij (eds.), *Limits of Harmonisation and Convergence…*, p. 29; See also: Z. Radwański, *System Prawa Prywatnego, Vol II, Prawo cywilne – część ogólna*, Warszawa 2008, pp. 189–190 and the literature cited therein.

220 See: § 90a BGB and Article 1 of the Polish Animal Protection Act from 21.8.1997 (J.L. 2013, item 856).

221 See: Subchapter II.2.4. ("Ownership of an animal in the Polish and German Civil Codes").

assumption that special conditions concerning the wellbeing of an animal must be met). However, these contracts may also be understood as the transfer of ownership that cannot be qualified as ownership, since animals, as living creatures with their own rights, may not be owned at all. The second attitude has – *de lege lata* – no foundation in Polish law (nor in the referential system of German law). Thus, even though the idea that animals may be simply owned just as regular things seems to be obsolete with reference to modern philosophical theories referring to animal rights, there is no other possibility than to accept it.[222] Thus, although the Polish legal order – just as it is in the German legal order – grants several rights to animals and underlines that they are not things, the terminology used in reference to animals is the same as in case of obligations concerning regular things. Nevertheless, one has to keep in mind the fact that, despite this terminology animals constitute a different object of obligations – a specific one, therefore several different rules described in this book apply. Thus, the ownership of an animal includes not only the owner's right to control the fate of the animal, but also several duties consisting in taking care over this animal and accepting the animal rights that are granted to it. Due to lack of rules directly addressing these issues, the scope of these duties is subject to legal disputes on how to apply the provisions of contract law (concerning things) to animals.

Taking into account these considerations, there are several types of contracts resulting in the transfer of ownership of things described in this chapter that apply respectively to animals (thus, not all contracts transferring ownership of things are applicable to animals, mainly for practical reasons).[223] The considerations as to what are its peculiarities and dissimilarities to contracts transferring ownership of things are described in this chapter with reference to their applicability to animals.

The most significant agreements involving animals in this field of obligation contracts are sales contracts and donation agreements, although barter agreements or contracts with an element of a barter agreement will also apply. As can be seen from a comparison of judicial records in Germany and Poland, the first one has broad and consolidated foundations in matter of jurisprudence according to the sale of animals. In Polish jurisprudence, court rulings on these matters are very difficult to find. The reason for this situation is the fact that the sale of more expensive horses (apart from auctions of Arabian horses)[224] and the

222 *Idem.*

223 For example, although there are no legal obstacles to animals being objects of leasing agreements or annuity contracts, such agreements are not found in legal practice because of the lack of its practicality and the wide range of different agreements with a wider range of applicability in such cases.

224 Nevertheless, the sale of Polish Arabian horses occurs only at public auctions, see: Subchapter IV.1.2.1. ("Commission contracts having an animal as their object").

popularization of equestrian sports are effects of operations undertaken by riders and several equestrian organizations in the last few years. The number of sales of pedigree dogs has also risen in Poland in the last 20 years, reaching better numbers every single year, while in Germany this market was already flourished many years earlier.

Although there are not many Polish court rulings referring to the sale of animals, it is the most commonly concluded contract with reference to animals – in Germany as well as in Poland. The main reason for the popularity in the **sale of animals** in both countries is the nature of industry in these countries, as they are the leading Member States in terms of their agricultural industry in Europe.[225] However, the increasing significance of the sale of animals is also connected with the development of equestrian sports in both countries.

The existence **of animals in barter** agreements is more closely connected with the agricultural industry than sale contracts, as local farmers have always exchanged the things they produced on a larger scale. Although the domination of larger farming companies and landlords has lessened the significance of barter agreements in the agricultural industry, it does not mean that they have lost all their significance. What is more, the growth of the sport horses market has caused an increased need to exchange these animals. In the sporting reality, it is not extraordinary to exchange horses, especially ponies with similar skills or predispositions but different heights, whose substitution can be connected, for example, with the unavoidable growth of junior riders.

Donations concerning animals are undoubtedly popular, though they do not raise as many practical questions as the agreements mentioned above. Thus, donation agreements in both countries are regulated on a similar basis[226] and are used in order to perform a complimentary transfer of an ownership of a good or – respectively – an animal.[227] Since the characteristics of several types of con-

---

225 Compare: European Union Directorate-General for Agriculture and Rural Development, *Agriculture In The European Union – Markets Statistical Information 2014*, last visited: 20.1.2016 from the website: http://ec.europa.eu/agriculture/markets-and-prices/market-statistics/index_en.htm.

226 Nevertheless, it is important to bear in mind that Polish law acknowledges the principle of double effect of contracts transforming ownership of things defined in its identity (Article 155 § 1 KC), which is expressed by the fact that contracts forming a duty to transfer ownership also transfer this ownership at the moment of conclusion (unless the good in which the ownership is being transferred is not identified, see Article 155 § 2 KC). The German Civil Code does not recognise such a principle.

227 Although this is not important to the topic of this book, since it includes references to the German legal system, it is important to bear in mind that there are some differences in the construction of this type of contract in in both legal systems. Thus, Polish law acknowledges the principle of double effect of contracts transforming the ownership of things defined by their identity (Article 155 § 1 KC), which is expressed by the fact that contracts forming a duty to transfer ownership do also transfer this ownership at the moment of conclusion

tracts in this paper will be mentioned only to the extent to which an animal, as an object of the contract, influences the contractual obligation of the parties (its creation, performance and non-performance), there is no need here to make further remarks concerning the general structure of a donation agreement. Animals have always been objects of these types of contracts, though it mainly concerns animals of unregistered bloodline, or animals paired accidently on the countryside or other rural areas, donated later voluntarily to other family members or colleagues. Although under both the Polish and German Civil Codes, the form of a notarial act is an obligatory formal requirement for conclusion of a donation agreement, there is a possibility to validate such contract afterwards, even if the parties did not keep this formal requirement – namely through a factual donation of an animal. Thus, under both legal systems (under the Polish Civil Code as well as under the German Civil Code), a donation agreement concluded without observing the formal requirements set out by national civil codes is invalid.[228] Only the situation where the donation agreement is already performed – even though formal requirements have not been observed – constitutes an exception validating this agreement.[229] In practice, the exception leading to the validation of an invalid donation by its performance is also the most common manner of concluding contracts similar to donation that have animals as their objects. Both Germany and Poland have considerable numbers of such agreements concluded every day, even though the parties are often not aware of concluding a legal relationship and often do not meet all formal requirements. This concerns mainly the donation of crossbred dogs and cats in both countries.[230]

As already mentioned above, it is important that the **ownership of an animal** is connected with several duties consisting in taking care for it.[231] Since animals do not have their own civil rights (despite the fact that there are several rights granted to animals, referred to as "animal rights"[232]), it is the owner who is

(unless the good in which the ownership is being transferred is not identified, see Article 155 § 2 KC). In contrary, the German Civil Code does not recognise this principle.

228 See: the wording of § 518 (2) BGB and the wording of Article 890 KC.

229 *Idem.*

230 Such agreements take place not only between relatives and colleagues, but also a result of newspaper and internet announcements, which are very common nowadays. See such announcements on websites like: www.olx.pl, www.gumtree.pl, www.allegro.pl, www.deinetierwelt.de, www.ebay.de.

231 Compare: the provisions of Polish and German Civil Codes referring to the ownership over things in Article 140 KC and § 903 BGB.

232 Nevertheless, these rights grant the right to react to animal mistreatment only to administrative organs, see: Polish Animal Protection Act from 21.8.1997 (J.L. 2013, item 856). The German legal system also grants specific rights to animals, see: German Animal Protection Act from 24.7.1972 in the version of 18.4.2006 (German J.L. I of 2006, p. 1206, item 1313), latest amendment of 17.12.2018 (German J.L. I of 2018, p. 2586).

responsible for providing decent living conditions for an animal. When transferring ownership, it should be a condition for the previous owner – no matter whether it is a breeder, a foundation, an animal shelter or a private individual transferring occasionally ownership of a single animal – to ensure that the living conditions of this animal will be decent also after the transfer. Still, apart from a situation where the conclusion of a sale contract occurs in the form of a sale with the reservation of the right to repurchase the animal,[233] there are no provisions that would allow a previous owner to regain an animal in the event of its maltreatment by the new owner. I qualify this as a legal gap that should be considered by lawmakers in the future, since it is a natural result of granting more and more animal rights in the meaning of administrative provisions abolishing maltreatment, and an issue worth addressing due to changes in the awareness of society and its sensitivity to the wellbeing of animals. Although there are laws that forbid the maltreatment of animals, these are always only public law provisions, which means that they allow for the public authorities undertaking actions. However, since there is no private law protection of animals, they do not allow the previous owner (or any other private individual) to undertake any actions.[234] Since it might be difficult and, in particular, time-consuming to initiate the process of taking an animal from its owner by the public authority.[235] My proposal is that the civil codes of modern European countries should contain a claim that would enable the previous owner of an animal to dissolve the contract, entailing a duty to return the animal to its previous owner and to pay damages for any reduction in value. In my opinion, animals are specific objects of obligations, and as such they deserve special treatment, and there should at least be basic constructions in place allowing the previous owner to grant the animal previously owned by him a decent life. Therefore, in the existing legal situation, I would suggest that the person transferring ownership of an animal include in the contract a duty of accurate care over an animal (including a specific definition thereof) under the threat of the contract being declared invalid, followed by the need to return the animal and pay damages for any reduction in its market valuation. Due to the freedom of contract principle (compare: Article 353[1] KC and § 311 BGB), this should not constitute any difficulties with reference to **sale**

233 See: Article 593 KC and § 456 BGB.

234 E. g. under Polish law, this is only possible under Article 7 of the Polish Animal Protection Act from 21. 8. 1997, whereas this decision is left to the discretion of an administrative organ.

235 See: Article 7 (1a) of the Polish Animal Protection Act from 21. 8. 1997. However, the biggest problem with reference to the reaction of a public entity in a case of the maltreatment of an animal is the fact that animal foundations are not physically possible to observe every case of maltreatment of an animal. Additionally, there needs to be hard evidence that such a situation took place, which is not always easy to prove.

contracts. However, the situation is more complicated in the case of contracts similar to **barter agreements**, where the dissolution of a contract would lead to an animal being returned to a person who has been shown to maltreat animals. Therefore, in the case of a barter agreement, the only way to achieve a solution that would grant accurate care over an animal would be by granting more rights to animals (e.g. by granting them the status of quasi-legal persons), or by making their previous owners "guardians" over animals (as happens in the case of parental care over minors). Nevertheless, such a far-reaching change in the legal position of an animal is too revolutionary for it to be included in the national civil codes of EU countries at the moment, and it may remain solely in the sphere of hypothetical considerations for the distant future. This makes it rather an issue to be considered by the legal philosophers, and for now should not constitute a rational suggestion of this civil law book.

However, under Polish and German law, the institution of **donation** foresees taking the object of donation back in case of gross ingratitude of a donor.[236] This may lead to problems as to whether the maltreatment of an animal could, under certain circumstances, be qualified as ingratitude against the donor. Although the Polish Civil Code does not foresee directly such a factual situation, an analysis of the jurisprudence seems to point to its admissibility.[237] Despite none of the currently published rulings of the Polish Supreme Court addressing this issue with reference to animals, M. Goettel – concerned as a Polish specialist in the field of animals in civil law – has admitted in his book that the maltreatment of an animal should be qualified as ingratitude against the donor.[238]

When comparing the Polish civil law provisions referring to donation with the German legal system, the provision included in § 530 BGB foresees the possibility of cancelling the donation in the event of ingratitude towards the donor or his or her close family members. Thus, the scope of anyone falling under this regulation is described more broadly, but still does not include animals.

236 See: Article 898 KC and § 530 BGB.

237 See the rulings, where the Polish Supreme court stated directly that it is enough when the act of ingratitude against the donor does not have to be aimed directly at him, e.g.: SN, ruling from 5.1.1999 – III CKN 783/98; SN, ruling from 7.4.1998 – II CKN 688/97 (pointing, however, to the fact that relations between the donor and the person against which the donee showed gross ingratitude has to be very close, and also be seen as such by his surroundings); SN, ruling from 11.3.2003 – V CKN 1829/00 (where the Court admitted that the act of gross ingratitude does not have to be aimed directly at the donor, though it denied the qualification of marital betrayal against the donors' daughter as such). So also: M. Safjan [in:] K. Pietrzykowski (ed.), *Kodeks cywilny. Komentarz*, Warszawa 2015, p. 863. See also the SN ruling from 22.3.2001 – V CKN 1599/00, where the Court confirmed that the act of gross ingratitude may also be expresssed by the passive behaviour of the donee.

238 M. Goettel, *Sytuacja zwierzęcia w prawie cywilnym*, Warszawa 2013, pp, 155–156.

Although some voices in the Polish doctrine[239] admit that maltreatment of an animal should be qualified as ingratitude against the donor, these are still singular opinions rather than a doctrinal viewpoint. Since it is not absolutely clear whether the provisions of Article 898 KC and § 530 BGB could apply also to animals, it is worth considering whether it would be advisable for the legislator to directly confirm that animals also fall within the scope of this regulation. Hence, *de lege lata* – according to the Polish and German black letter law – provisions concerning goods are respectively applicable to animals, and animals do not have legal personality, therefore do not fall within the scope of family members (according to the Polish and German black letter law).

Addressing animals in such a provision of law would definitely strengthen the position of animals under the civil law and directly serve its well-being. Additionally, this solution would not be connected with a revolution in the way the civil law of European countries concerns animals (by granting them legal personality), but would also not leave the interpretation of legal provisions solely to a certain judge, and only in the case of court proceedings at a final stage. The legislators treating animals as something more than a simple object of obligation could make a change; already at the moment when this legal provision is commonly acknowledged. Hence, it is not necessary to qualify an animal as a subject of law in order to create provisions that would allow the donor or the previous owner to retrieve an animal back in the event of its maltreatment. The inclusion of such a specific provision referring directly to ingratitude against animals would definitely make their application to animals easier, and therefore such a solution should be considered by legislators.

Summing up, I consider three possible solutions in the event of gross ingratitude against a donated animal: granting animals the status of quasi-legal persons, providing more legal provisions directly concerning animals (also in the civil law) or avoiding more legislation and leaving the interpretation of legal provisions to the jurisprudence and doctrine. Since granting animals the status of quasi-legal persons is rather too abstract at this moment – it should be taken into consideration which of the other two solutions would be better in order to provide animals with a proper legal position. Whereas on this particular issue I would consider addressing animals directly in the applicable legal provision as being most desirable, my general conclusions in reference to these three options are presented in the final subchapter of this book.

239 *Idem.*

2. Performance of contracts aimed at the transfer of property with reference to contracts having an animal as the object

2.1. General remarks

According to the standards concerning due performance, the debtor performs an obligation according to the content of this obligation, which always has to be established in reference to each specific obligation. The content of this obligation should be interpreted in accordance with Articles 56 and 65 KC.[240] According to Article 56 KC, the debtor has to perform the obligation not only in accordance with the parties' contractual declarations, but also in accordance with the binding laws, the principles of community life (*zasady wspóżycia spłecznego*) and the established custom (*ustalone zwyczaje*). Additionally, Article 65 KC refers to the interpretation of the parties' declaration of intent that – in addition to the abovementioned factors – should also take into account the circumstances in which it was made.[241] Article 354 KC addresses directly the criteria of due performance to contractual obligations. Firstly – according to this regulation – the parties have to perform the obligation in accordance with their contractual declarations. Secondly, they should perform the obligation in accordance with its socioeconomic purpose (*cel społeczno-gospodarczy*) and the principles of community life (*zasady wspóżycia społecznego*). Thirdly, the parties should observe established customs when performing their obligations (if such customs are established in reference to a certain obligation).

The factors constituting the content of the obligation (strictly: the effects of the parties' declarations of intent) are established *expressis verbis* in the Polish Civil Code (Article 56 KC). The German Civil Code includes similar provisions in § 242, addressing the good faith principle and established customs. Hence, although Article 56 KC does not have its direct equivalent in the German Civil Code, its content under German law may be derived from § 242 BGB with the support of *die Willenserklärungtheorie* (*rozszerzająca teoria woli*).[242] As the

240 See: T. Dybowski, A. Pyrzyńska [in:] E. Łętowska (ed.), *System Prawa Prywatnego, Vol. V, Prawo zobowiązań – część ogólna*, p. 194; also in the comparative context: E. Rott-Pietrzyk, *Klauzule generalne a wykonanie zobowiązania (z uwzględnieniem koncepcji systemu klauzul generalnych w projekcie KC)* [in:] E. Gniewek, K. Górska, P. Machnikowski (ed.), *Zaciąganie i wykonywanie zobowiązań*, Warszawa 2010, pp. 333 *et seq.*

241 More with reference to the interpretation of declarations of intent in Polish law, see: A. Jędrzejewska, *Koncepcja oświadczenia woli w prawie cywilnym*, Warszawa 1992; Z. Radwanski, *Wykładnia Wykładnia oświadczeń woli składanych indywidualnym adresatom*, Warszawa 1992; E. Rott-Pietrzyk, *Wykładnia oświadczenia woli (studium prawnoporównawcze)*, Studia Prawa Prywatnego 2007, Nos 3–4, pp. 31 *et seq.*

242 Since it is a complicated issue, connected with differences in the structure of the Polish and German legal systems, whereas the German legal system serves only as comparison for this

Polish Civil Code is strongly based on the German Civil Code, it is obvious that they share the same principles concerning the standards of due contract performance. Nevertheless, consistency with established customs (*die Verkehrssitten*) and good faith (*der Grundsatz von Treu und Glauben*) when performing the obligation is fundamental for the sense of the law of obligation and, in a more or less similar construction, can be found in all European legal orders.[243] In contracts involving animals (bearing in mind the paucity of private law provisions concerning animals), these components of general clauses with various wordings (e.g. good faith,[244] principles of community life[245] and usage[246]) seem to have major importance. Taking into account the fact that the provisions concerning movables are only respectively applicable to animals, the usage (connected with the way animals are used and treated in certain types of contracts, and how this affects the conclusion, performance and results of the non-performance of these contracts) plays a very important role. Hence, it is very important to define the content of the contract and to establish the scope of duties of the contracting parties – also with reference to the consequences of the non-performance or improper performance of the contract. Therefore, the parts of the book concerning the performance of various contracts are based not only on the legal regulations, which can mostly be found in the specific rules dedicated to a certain contract, but they are also closely connected to the practice. The observation of law in action allows for observation of the methodology of interpretation used by the German courts with reference to obligations having an animal as the object of its contractual obligation. In particular, it shows how the general clauses and usage are applied in individual cases of animals being objects of contractual obligations. What is more, taking into account the rule evoked at the beginning of this subsection – the book would not be possible without combining the legal foundations with this practical knowledge concerning animals and their nature as an object of contractual obligation.

---

book, I merely signal these differences. Nevertheless, see more: H.-W. Micklitz, K. Purnhagen [in:] J. Säcker (ed.), *Münchener Kommentar zum BGB, Vol. I*, München 2015, Vorbemerkung zur §§ 13–14, side number 38, *BeckOnline (last visited: 23.6.2018);* H. Mansel [in:] R. Stürner (ed.), *Jauernig, Kommentar zum BGB*, München 2015, Vorbemerkungen, side numbers 1–13. See also, an exemplary ruling of the German Supreme Court (which – however – refers to horses, but with reference to delictual liability, hence out of the scope of this book): BGB, ruling from 09.6.1992 - VI ZR 49/91 (Düsseldorf).

243 See in details: The correlation of the Polish contract law with other European legal systems, D. Kemptner, *Der Einfluss des europäischen Rechts auf das polnische Zivilgesetzbuch*, Baden-Baden 2007, pp. 90–226.

244 Article 56 KC, § 157 BGB *(Zasady współżycia społecznego, Grundsatz von treu und Glauben).*

245 Article 56 KC.

246 Article 56 KC § 157 BGB (*Zwyczaj, Verkehrssitten*).

The performance of contracts transferring ownership of an animal is presented below in some detail, but due to its complex character it is divided into numerous subchapters presenting specific problems arising therefrom. These are: a subchapter presenting the impact of B2B (Business to Business Contracts), B2C (Business to Consumer Contracts) and C2C (Consumer to Consumer Contracts) relations on contracts transferring the ownership of an animal; a subchapter referring to problems connected with concluding contracts aimed at the transfer of ownership of animals; a subchapter referring to the various types of sale contracts; and also a subchapter referring to various types of contracts aimed at the transfer of ownership of animals, divided into smaller subsections and presenting problematic issues related to donation and barter agreements (see: below).

2.2. Consumer sale and related legal problems concerning B2B, B2C and C2C relations

When writing about contracts of sale, it is impossible not to mention the issue of distinguishing between consumer contracts (known as Business to Consumer Contracts – B2C) and non-consumer contracts (Business to Business Contracts – B2B and Consumer to Consumer Contracts – C2C, where the latter occurs much more often in connection with the sale of animals).[247] An observation based on the last decade shows that the EU consumer law strives to full harmonization as the inconsistencies between consumer laws of the Member States of the EU are seen as an obstacle to the international trade of things. The legal differences in various EU Member States cause an investment flow to the countries with the lowest standards of consumer protection. Therefore, there are several consumer directives that have remarkably influenced all European civil codes[248] and that is

247 Nevertheless, horses have been subject of cases ruled with reference to United Nations Convention on Contracts for the International Sale of Goods, Vienna, 11 April 1980, S.Treaty Document Number 98–9 (1984), UN Document Number A/CONF 97/19, 1489 UNTS 3, covering only B2B contracts. The full text of the CISG is available in pdf format at http://www.uncitral.org/uncitral/en/uncitral_texts/sale_goods/1980CISG.html at 22 December 2007. See: U. Magnus, *UN-Kaufrecht – Aktuelles zum CISG aufgespießt,* ZeUP 2017, Issue 1, pp. 14–16.

248 See, in particular: Directive 2011/83/EU of the European Parliament and of the Council of 25 October 2011 on consumer rights and two other very important consumer directives that it amends: Council Directive 93/13/EEC of 5 April 1993 on unfair terms in consumer contracts and Directive 1999/44/EC of the European Parliament and of the Council of 25 May 1999 on certain aspects of the sale of consumer things and associated guarantees, O. J. L 171, 07/07/1999, pp. 12–16. See: Directive 2011/83/EU of the European Parliament and of the Council of 25 October 2011 on consumer rights (OJ L 304, 22.11.2011, pp. 64–88); Council Directive 93/13/EEC of 5 April 1993 on unfair terms in consumer contracts, OJ 95, 21.4.1993, pp. 29–

the reason why the consumer law in both Polish and German legal systems is so similar.

Although there is a clear definition of a consumer and a business, **the qualification of a contract of sale of an animal as a consumer sale** raises many questions. Directive 2011/83/EU of the European Parliament and of the Council of 25 October 2011 on consumer rights has introduced a unified consumer definition to all EU countries. According to Article 2 of this directive, a consumer is "any natural person who, in contracts covered by this Directive, is acting for purposes that are outside his trade, business, craft or profession." This definition corresponds with the definition of a consumer that was recently amended in the Polish and German Civil Codes as a result of the implementation of Directive 2011/83/EU.[249] As to the definition of a business, the directive defines this as a natural or legal person or an organizational entity that, when entering into a legal transaction, acts in exercise of its trade, business or profession.[250] This means that a person can act as a business as long as the legal form of the entity or the actions made in a certain business field signals this.[251] The Polish legal system also recognizes the institution of an entity without legal personality but with legal capacity, and allows them also to act as a business.[252] The German legal order, on the other hand, recognizes: natural persons, legal persons and partnerships with legal personality.[253]

Since the qualification of an animal seller as a business causes doubts in a doctrine, and since the definitions of consumer and entrepreneur are crucial for the qualification of the contract as a consumer contract (which is further connected with several facilitations for the consumer), this chapter will describe the problematic qualification of a consumer contract sale. However, the specific nature of consumer sales, concerning mostly the warranty rights of the buyer, will be presented in section 3, describing the improper performance of contracts transferring the ownership of animals.

Polish law provides several definitions of a business,[254] with each of them applying in the context of a certain legal act containing this particular definition.

34; Directive 1999/44/EC of the European Parliament and of the Council of 25 May 1999 on certain aspects of the sale of consumer things and associated guarantees, OJ 171, 07/07/1999, pp. 12–16.

249 The novelisation of the Polish Civil Code (the Polish Civil Code in the version promulgated on 23.4.1964, last version: J.L. No 16, item 93 as amended) as a result of the implementation of Directive 2011/83/EU of the European Parliament and of the Council of 25 October 2011 on consumer rights occurred on 25.12.2014.

250 Compare: § 12 BGB and Article 43[1] KC.

251 K. Schmidt, *Handelsrecht*, Köln 2014, p. 345.

252 See: Article 33[1] KC.

253 See: § 14 BGB.

254 So e.g.: Article 43[1] KC; Article 4 (1) of the Polish Act on Freedom of Business Activity [*Ustawa o swobodzie Działalności Gospodarczej*] of 2.7.2004, J L of 2004 No. 173 item 1807;

Nevertheless, the qualification of a person selling animals as his or her economic activity under Polish law raises questions as to the applicability of the provisions referring to businesses to animal breeders. Thus, according to Article 3 (1) of the Polish Act on Freedom of Business Activity, its provisions are not applicable to activities connected with keeping and breeding animals. However, this provision should be interpreted in the context of the applicability of provisions of this particular legal act to persons keeping and breeding animals, and should not be understood as its exclusion from the scope of the definition of a business. As a result, anyone keeping and breeding animals is a business as long as the commercial or occupational activity qualifies it as such, and it just means that the provisions of the Polish Act on Freedom of Business Activity do not apply with reference to them.[255] In a decision of the Polish Supreme Court dated in 2015,[256] the Court stated that, in order to define whether a person acts as a business, the qualification from Article 43[1] KC applies. Therefore, the breeder (and seller) of pigs, in the case at hand,[257] was qualified as a business since he met all the conditions under Article 43[1] KC: his activity had an occupational and profit-making purpose and was performed in an organized and continuous way. However, Polish jurisprudence still lacks cases referring to such matters, so that the borders of qualifying a person performing a certain activity as a business or not are not yet set in stone under Polish law.

On the other hand, the referential legal system of Germany does exactly the opposite. The German Civil Code does not define what acting **as a business** means, though the German Federal Supreme Court of Justice (BGH) defines it[258]

Article 2 of the Polish Unfair Competition Act (*Ustawa o zwalczaniu nieuczciwej konkurencji*) of 16.04.1993, J L 47/211 of 1993; Article 4 of the Polish Protection of Competition and Consumers Act [*Ustawa o ochronie konkurencji i konsumentów*] of 16.2.2007, J.L. of 2007, No. 50 item 331.

255 See also: M. Etel, *Pojęcie przedsiębiorcy w prawie polskim i prawie Unii Europejskiej oraz w orzecznictwie sądowym*, Warszawa 2012, pp. 192 et seq.; W. Katner, *Prawo działalności gospodarczej. Komentarz*, Warszawa 2003, pp. 42–45 and important judicial reasonings of the Polish Supreme Court, which already confirm the jurisprudence in the direction of this interpretation of Article 3 of the Polish Act on Freedom of Business Activity: SN, ruling of 3.10.2014, V CSK 630/13; SN, ruling of 26.2.2015, III CZP 108/14. However, some representatives of the doctrine do not agree with this point of view and represent the opinion that animal breeders are not businesses, see: T. Kocowski [in:] A. Borkowski, A. Chełmoński, M. Guziński, K. Kiczka, T, Kocowski, M. Szydło, L. Kieres (eds.), *Administracyjne prawo gospodarcze*, Wrocław 2009, p. 31.; Z. Radwański, *Podmioty prawa cywilnego w świetle zmian kodeksu cywilnego przeprowadzonych ustwą z dnia 14 lutego 2003 r.*, Przegląd Sądowy 2003, Nos 7–8, p. 18.

256 SN, ruling of 26.2.2015, III CZP 108/14.

257 *Idem.*

258 BGH ruling from 29.3.2006 (NJW 2006, 2250).

exactly as the Polish Act on Freedom of Business Activity[259] does, and provides that a business activity needs to be a profit-making activity that is conducted in an organized and continuous fashion. However, a rider or a hobby breeder may act as a business if they sell horses from time to time in order to reduce expenses.[260] Thus, the differentiation between a business and an occasional seller is not obvious and may be very difficult to discern. P. Rosbach, in his book *Pferderecht,* goes into some details when setting out how many horses have to be sold annually, or for what price, in order to qualify the activity as a profit-making activity conducted in an organised and continuous manner.[261] First of all, as already mentioned, he underlines that making an actual profit is not necessary, it is enough to sell animals in order to reduce expenses in one's hobbyist's activity. He focuses on three criteria to establish whether the sale of a horse has been performed by a business or not: the number of horses sold in one year, the price of the sold horses and the general look of the seller's activity. He proposes a detailed calculation that results in the conclusion, that "selling" more than three foals a year should be qualified as a business activity, and the person who undertakes it should be qualified as a business. He then goes on to propose the price factor, taking into account the data from 2010 and calculating one third of the average income of EUR 10,667. This is, therefore, the price of a sold animal that indicates that the sale of a horse was performed as economic activity.[262] P. Rosbach explains that a hobby rider or breeder would not be able to reach this price level without detailed planning of a horse's breed and education (high prices of horses depend usually on their parentage and skills).

I would not advise applying the concept presented by P. Rosbach (see: above), i.e. describing such strict and detailed criteria for qualification as a business, to the Polish system. Equestrian sports are subject to growing interest by the public, and it is common for a horse bought by a junior or amateur rider as a young and promising horse to prove its extraordinary skills while being ridden by this particular rider, and can then be sold afterwards for a higher price. It is common for amateur riders to buy horses for their own purposes and to then take part in competitions and receive several purchase proposals from professional riders or horse brokers. An amateur is very often not in a position to reject such an offer, as his riding activity is only a hobby and he still has to earn money to be able to do it. What is more, it is rarely the case that he undertakes the decision about buying a certain horse on his own; usually this decision is

259 Polish Act on Freedom of Business Activity (*Ustawa o swobodzie Działalności Gospodarczej*) of 02.07.2004, J L 173/1807 of 2004.

260 J. Adolphsen, *Tierkauf* [in:] B. Dauner-Lieb, W. Langen, *BGB Schuldrecht. Nomos Kommentar*, p. 1971.

261 P. Rosbach, *Pferderecht*, p. 57.

262 *Idem*, p. 62.

made with instructions and advice from a professional trainer, who should at least act with the attitude of choosing the best possible horse for their pupil. It can also happen that an amateur rider has two or three horses and has to sell all of them at once because of financial difficulties or – which is often the case – because he starts college or other form of education at a higher level and has to move away, or simply does not have enough time for his hobby anymore. On the other hand, there are several businesses that own their own stables, also undertake actions as trainers and breeders and, although they sell only one or two horses a year, it leads to a profit almost every time. Adjusting the calculations introduced by P. Rosbach to the Polish reality, I would take into account a percentage of income coming from the sale of horses in comparison to the income achieved from the other business activity of the seller. Taking into account my observations, a horse seller should be qualified as a business under Polish law if the sale of horses provides more than 1/3 of the average income in Poland, or more than half of the seller's annual income for more than two consecutive years. Nevertheless, the presented proposals are only speculations, as it is not possible to calculate the distinguishing factors theoretically and generally. It is a role of courts to create its own jurisprudence in this matter and to base their rulings on the individual characteristics of each case. Given that animals constitute specific objects of obligations and – as the German jurisprudence[263] (which has proven to be applicable to the Polish legal system as well) acknowledged – their purchase is dependent on an emotional bond between the animal and its buyer,[264] it is advisable to provide the elasticity that would allow for a proper adaptation of legal norms in each individual case.

A very interesting issue related with consumer contracts, which does not exist in Polish law but is an important issue under German law, is the fact that the German Civil Code provides for an exclusion of warranty for used goods sold at public auctions, which is respectively applicable to animals.[265] Thus, **auction sale** is very popular for the sale of horses, especially in Germany.[266] Selling horses at public auctions occurs usually in one of two most frequently observed forms: it may either be an auction performed by a certain horse stud selling its own horses, or it may be an auction organized by horse breeders associations, where horses that are being offered to the public are owned by different private principals (where, in case of the second type of auctions, a commission agent in-

263 OLG Düsseldorf, ruling from 16.04.2002 – 21 U 140/01.
264 See: OLG Düsseldorf, ruling from 16.04.2002 – 21 U 140/01.
265 See § 474 (1) BGB concerning the sale of used goods on public auctions and § 90a BGB, providing that the rules applicable to the things are to be respectively applied to animals.
266 See: Subchapter III.2.2 ("Consumer sale and related legal problems concerning B2B, B2C and C2C relations").

termediates in the transfer of ownership[267]). Therefore, in order to establish whether an exclusion of warranty occurs in a particular case, it is important to define how to qualify an animal as a used good or not. On the matter itself, the legal importance of the question as to **whether animals are used goods or not**, is important purely for legal issues concerning consumer sale contracts.[268] Namely, under German law, the notions that strengthen the inexperienced buyer's position in relation to his experienced contracting partner (such as the invalidity of contractual provisions excluding the buyer's warranty rights, the reverse burden of proof that a defect existed at time of the conclusion of contract for the first six months after the contract was concluded to the seller,[269] etc.) are applicable to consumer contracts of sale, as long as it does not concern the sale of used goods at public auctions, as long as the buyer concludes the sale contract in person. In Polish law, the warranty regime is unified in accordance to used and new things, so the only difference that occurs with reference to used goods is the possibility to reduce the period of time to claim the buyer's warranty rights to one year (whereas it lasts two years with reference to new things and five years with reference to real estate[270]).

Summing up, under the German law, the qualification of an animal as unused leads to notions strengthening the consumer's position for goods purchased at public auction, which does not apply under Polish law. With reference to Polish law, the issue of whether an animal should be treated in a certain factual situation as a used good or not is important solely in reference to the possibility to shorten the term for acknowledgement of a defect under the warranty regime (Article 568 § 1 KC). Therefore, this problem is presented in the Chapter III.3.2.7. ("Animals as used goods?"), falling within the scope of the part of this Dissertation referring to the results of the improper performance of contracts aimed at the transfer of property with reference to animals.

---

267 See: Chapters IV.1.2.1., IV.2.1., IV.3.1. of this book with reference to general remarks, performance and wrongful-non-performance of commission contracts.

268 The change with reference to warranty rights to used goods in both legal systems is a result of implementing Article 5 of Directive 1999/44/EC of the European Parliament and of the Council of 25 May 1999 on certain aspects of the sale of consumer goods and associated guarantee.

269 Whether the rules set out in § 476 BGB, reversing the burden of proof to the business, are applicable to the sale of animals or not is controversial. The German doctrine recognises both positive (H. Westermann, *Zu den Gewährleistungsansprüche des Käufers*, ZGS 2005, pp. 342–348; P. Wertenbruch, *Tierkauf und Sachmangel*, NJW 2012, No. 29, p. 2069) and critical opinions (J. Adolphsen, *Die Schuldrechtsreform…*, pp. 203–208; See also: LG Verden, ruling from 16.02.2005 – 2 S 394/03; OLG Oldenburg, ruling from 17.06.2004 – 14 U 41/04) concerning the applicability of § 476 BGB to animals.

270 M. Tulibacka [in:] K. Osajda (ed.), *Kodeks cywilny. Komentarz. Tom IIIB*, Warszawa 2017, p. 166; J. Jezioro [in:] E. Gniewek, P. Machnikowski (ed.), *Kodeks cywilny. Komentarz*, pp. 1218–1222.

2.3. Conclusion of contracts aimed at the transfer of property with reference to contracts having an animal as the object[271]

The main obligations of the parties in **contracts** transferring ownership of an animal is the transfer of this law by the seller and – respectively – the collection of the animal and payment of the price by the buyer.[272] Passing the duty to collect an animal to the buyer corresponds with an old principle of the law of obligations with reference to non-monetary services, and happens to be a perfect solution for the sale of animals and other contracts with an animal as the object.[273] Thus, the transportation of larger animals like horses or cows is always connected with a high risk, and there is no reason to place this risk on the seller.[274] As to other duties – although handing an animal and transferring its ownership are not difficult to define, estimating the price and paying it may cause several problems for the contracting parties. The value of an animal changes constantly, especially where it concerns purebred animals sold for animal husbandry, like cats or dogs, or other animals that are used in sport, like horses. A young puppy might have been sold for a higher price than it is later found to be worth, if it does not grow into the dog that its pedigree and breeding would have suggested. This problem is even more problematic where it concerns sport horses, where the price can differ from one competition to another, depending on the results.

2.3.1. Estimation of the price

The estimation of the price of an animal is one of those matters that has to be agreed between the parties when concluding the contract (i. e. it constitutes the *essentialia negotii* of sale contract) and might be extremely problematic. Ani-

271 The problems addressed in this subchapter, referring to the most frequently discussed issues with reference to the conclusion of contracts aimed at the transfer of property with reference to animals (i. e. estimation of the price and extortion) occur in a pre-contractual stage, therefore they do not neceessary fall within the scope of the chapter referring to the performance of the contract, or the chapter referring to its wrongful performance. However, since they are strongly connected with the content of the contract, they have been presented in this subchapter in order to keep a consistent and clear structure of the book, and to avoid adding an additional unit, which will not be presented separately in the following chapters of this book.

272 Compare: Article 535 KC and § 433 BGB.

273 However, passing the duty to collect an animal to the buyer can also be connected with the risk that this will not happen on time. Such a delay by the buyer with reference to a living animal needing food and care, may cause several problems to the seller, and even be dangerous. See: F. Peters, *Der Anspruch auf Abnahme bei Kauf und Werkvertrag* [in:] P. Forstmoser, H. Giger, A. Heini, W. Schluep (ed.), *Festschrift für Max Keller zum 65. Geburtstag*, Zürich 1989, p. 222.

274 With reference to service contracts consisting in transportation of animals, see: IV.1.2.5.

mals are living creatures and, although there is a certain market where a value of a horse can be estimated with reference to the class of the competition he is taking part in, and there is also a certain market of kennels selling puppies of a certain breed, there are various factors that cannot be overlooked.[275] Namely, the emotional bond to a certain puppy and the fact that a rider feels attracted to a certain horse that is meant to be his sport partner in the future is invaluable. Animals have a certain value on the market, but the personal affections of the potential buyer can easily increase this value.[276] The problem of estimating the price of an animal has also been addressed in case 21 U 140/01 ruled by the German court of second instance - OLG Düsseldorf. The case referred to a situation where a horse bought by the claimant as a sport horse of a higher jumping class, classified by a veterinary doctor as healthy at the time of purchase, turned out to have problems with joints and "kissing spines" a few days afterwards.[277] The claimant's daughter found that the horse was on offer and it was bought for her since - although she had already been looking for a new jumping horse for a half a year - she particularly liked this one. However, the claimant claimed that the horse is not eligible to be used in show jumping due to its health condition, and alleged that the horse does not represent the value that he paid for it. The court - in my opinion, accurately - compared the purchase of a living, constantly progressing horse taking part in sport competitions at a certain level to the purchase of a piece of art, where the affection of the buyer is a very important factor, but the future progress of the artist and the price of his paintings depend on many details and is not predictable.[278] Estimating **a horse's price** is always to be made individually and the price of an animal will always depend on the amount of money that one is willing to pay. These subjective issues refer to the looks of a particular animal or its predispositions in sport, and are just as is important as the individual's emotional bond, which usually arises afterwards, between an animal and its owner and these are the most important factors impacting the price of a purchased animal. In the case at hand, the Court ruled that the price of horses sold for jumping competitions above a certain national level is strongly influenced by the sentiments of the rider. Namely, there needs to be a harmony between the horse and its rider. The estimate of price by the buyer can also be influenced by the feeling that the harmony that the rider feels riding a certain horse will allow them, as a couple, to be promoted to a higher class of competitions than the horse is, in reality, able to jump.[279]

275 With reference to the inequality of the parties' contractual performance and the horse's sale: OLG Hamm, ruling from 15.10.2004 - 19 U 75/04.

276 See also: P. Rosbach, *Pferderecht*, p. 75.

277 OLG Düsseldorf, ruling from 16.04.2002 - 21 U 140/01.

278 *Idem.*

279 *Idem.*

Therefore, I agree with the above presented ruling of OLG Düsseldorf, which made a perfect description of the impact that the personal affection of the rider has on the choice of a high-class horse. The conclusions of the German court in the case of OLG Düsseldorf ruling from 16.04.2002 – 21 U 140/01 are so general that they should be considered as independent of any legal order. Therefore – taking into account the similar facts of the case – I would recommend a similar interpretation of the civil law provisions of the Polish Civil Code to the sale of horses in Poland.

2.3.2. Exchange of horses with a partial payment

A very interesting aspect from the practical side of **the sale of horses** is the fact that the price of a horse is often paid by part exchange, i. e. part in cash, with the remainder being paid by taking another horse in exchange. The Polish doctrine and jurisprudence does address such cases, though not in comprehensive way with reference to animals (which, as a specific object of an obligation, deserve to be treated differently). Still, contracts based on the **part exchange of horses,** with a partial payment for a more expensive one, should be qualified as an undefined or mixed contract under both the Polish and German legal systems.[280]

With reference to sale contracts with the exchange of horses, the German doctrine often addresses the problem of *datio in solutum* – though this is the case only if the buyer accepts a different performance in the sale contract after its conclusion.[281] The Polish law foresees the institution of *datio in solutum* as

280 Z. Radwański and W. Katner represent the opinion that contracts not qualifying to any types of contracts defined in the Polish Civil Code should not be considered as "mixed contracts" (regarding this as a rather obsolete point of view), but – simply – as undefined contracts, to which one of the following possibilities apply:
1) there are no provisions referring to any type of contracts defined in the Polish Civil Code that could be applied to this particular contract;
2) provisions referring to a certain type of contract defined in the Polish Civil Code may be applied to this particular contract;
3) provisions referring to a certain type of contract defined in the Polish Civil Code may be applied to this particular contract with certain modifications.
So: Z. Radwański, *Teoria umów*, Warszawa 1977, pp. 241–242; W. Katner [in:] W Katner (ed.), *System Prawa Prywatnego, Vol. IX, Prawo zobowiązań – umowy nienazwane*, pp. 13–14. See more: Subchapter IV.1.2.3. of this book.

281 § *365 BGB;* P. Rosbach, *Pferderecht*, pp. 70 et seq. However, the German doctrine discussed this problem comprehensively, considering whether whether the character of institution *datio in solutum* consists of a contract changing the obligation (*Austauschvertrag*) or changing the performance itself (*Erfüllungsvertrag*). P. Drapała suggested applicability of its classification as *Erfüllungsvertrag* also in the Polish law. So: P. Drapała, *Świadczenie w miejsce wykonania (datio in solutum)*, Państwo i Prawo 2003, No. 12, p. 30. See also: K. Larenz, Lehrbuch des Schuldrechts, t. I, Allgemeiner Teil, München 1987, p. 249; R. Stürner [in:] Jauernig Bürgerliches Gesetzbuch, München 1999, p. 361. Cited after: M. Pyziak-

well[282] (although there are no references in the doctrine to its applicability to the sale or exchange of horses). Therefore, offering a different performance in the sale contract should also be qualified as *datio in solutum* under Polish law, but – as already mentioned – only in the event of accepting a different performance after the conclusion of the contract.[283] In this case, the parties agree to qualify it as such (thus, they are allowed to do so according to the freedom of contract principle).[284] Otherwise, if the agreement to pay part of the price by taking another horse in exchange occurs at the stage of concluding the contract, the contract is simply qualified as a mixed contract. The institution of *datio in solutum* is foreseen in the Polish and German Civil Code in Article 453 KC and § 364 (1) BGB respectively, and provides a warranty for defects to the provisions on the warranty for defects in the case of a sale contract.

Several questions arise in connection with one party terminating (*odstąpienie, das Rücktritt*) the contract by exercising its warranty rights. According to the German doctrine, if the buyer terminates a contract, the seller has to return the partial price that was paid by the buyer, as well as the horse that has been taken as a partial performance.[285] If the horse has already been sold to a third party, the buyer is entitled to receive damages. A different situation occurs where the horse that was treated as a partial performance turns out to be defective. In this case, the seller in entitled to all the rights arising from the warranty,[286] pursuant to Article 560 KC and § 365 BGB. At the same time, the sale contract of the other horse remains untouched (even if the other party terminates the contract with reference to the defective horse).[287] Although the Polish courts and Polish doctrine do not cover the problem of exchanging horses, the

Szafnicka [in:] A. Olejniczak (ed.), *System Prawa Prywatnego, Vol. VI, Prawo zobowiązań – część ogólna*, Warszawa 2014, p. 1466.

282 See: Article 453 KC.

283 The possibility of accepting a different performance and a partial payment acknowledges also (K. Osajda, Article 453 nb7) and qualifies it as an example of *datio in solutum*. See also the Polish Supreme Court – SN, ruling from 15.9.2005 – II CK 68/05.

284 A. Olejniczak [in:] A. Olejniczak (ed.), *System Prawa Prywatnego*, pp. 1079–1080; W. Popiołek [in:] K. Pietrzykowski (ed.), *Kodeks cywilny. Komentarz*, pp. 11–13. See: M. Pyziak-Szafnicka [in:] A. Olejniczak (ed.), *System Prawa Prywatnego, Vol. VI, Prawo zobowiązań – część ogólna*, p. 1466, where the author underlines that the freedom of contract principle does obviously allow for *datio in solutum* with a partial payment. So also: A. Olejniczak [in:] A. Olejniczak (ed.), *System Prawa Prywatnego, Vol. VI, Prawo zobowiązań – część ogólna*, p. 1479; P. Drapała, *Świadczenie w miejsce wykonania (datio in solutum)*, pp. 31–32.

285 P. Rosbach, *Pferderecht*, pp. 70 et seq.

286 However, there are several doubts according to the rights arising from the warranty that may be exercised in such case: A. Olejniczak [in:] A. Olejniczak (ed.), *System Prawa Prywatnego, Vol. VI, Prawo zobowiązań – część ogólna*, p. 1479; P. Drapała, *Świadczenie w miejsce wykonania (datio in solutum)*, pp. 31–32, W. Popiołek [in:] K. Pietrzykowski (ed.), *Kodeks cywilny. Komentarz*, Warszawa 2015, pp. 11–13.

287 P. Rosbach, *Pferderecht*, p. 70.

same applies to Polish law, since the institution of *datio in solutum* is recognized and regulated in a similar way under both the Polish and German legal systems.

At this point, upon first mentioning of the term "termination" in this book, it is worth explaining that under Polish and German law there are two terms that might be confused when translating them into English: *odstąpienie/das Rücktritt* and *wypowiedzenie/die Kündigung.*[288] Whereas the first of these means of finishing the contractual bond between the parties is used in reference to contracts having only a one-time performance of a certain obligation of a debtor, the second one is used with reference to contracts in which the performance of the obligation has a permanent character (regardless of whether the performance occurs by tolerating a certain behavior, or by an active performance of the debtor). Additionally, under Polish law, finishing the contract through *odstąpienie/das Rücktritt* has – according to the majority of the representatives of the doctrine – an effect *ex tunc,*[289] whereas finishing it by the means of *wypowiedzenie/die Kündigung* – is treated as being *ex nunc.*[290] In order to keep the book clear, each time I will use the Polish and German meaning of the word termination with reference to each case of its use in this book.

2.3.3. Extortion in the sale of an animal

A problem that often arises with reference to the estimation of the price of an animal is the qualification of an obligatory relationship as **extortion.** Thus, this institution can be useful and profitable for the buyer, since the rights arising from extortion do not exclude the applicability of warranty rights.[291] Even if the parties have reached an agreement according to the price of the horse at the time

288 See: G. Tracz, *Sposoby jednostronnej rezygnacji z zobowiązań umownych,* Warszawa/Kraków 2007, pp. 74–93.

289 See: F. Zoll in F. Zoll, R. Cierpiał, A. Kraft, M. Thurner, *Ausgewählte Fragen über die dinglichen Auswirkungen des Rücktritts vom Vertrag* [in:] Wokół problematyki cywilno-procesowej, Księga pamiątkowa K. Korzana, Katowice 2001, p. 88; W. Popiołek [in:] K. Pietrzykowski (ed.), *Kodeks cywilny. Komentarz,* pp. 1311–1312; Z. Radwański, *Recenzja pracy autorstwa A. Kleina, Elementy stosunku zobowiązaniowego,* RPEiS 1965, no 1, p. 308; E. Drozd, *Recenzja pracy autorstwa A. Kleina, Elementy stosunku zobowiązaniowego,* PiP 1964, no 7, p. 146; G. Tracz, *Sposoby jednostronnej rezygnacji z zobowiązań umownych,* pp. 34;35; A. Szpunar, *Odstąpienie od umowy o przeniesienie własności nieruchomości,* Rejent 1995, no 6. Otherwise, however, with reference to the previously binding *Kodeks zobowiązań:* A. Klein, *Ustawowe prawo odstąpienia,* Wrocław 1964.

290 With reference to the distinction between the institutions of *wypowiedzenie* and *odstąpienie* in the Polish law and its application to obligational relationships of a permanent character, compare: E. Rott-Pietrzyk [in:] M. Stec, *System Prawa Handlowego. Prawo Umów handlowych, Vol. V,* Warszawa 2017, pp. 605 *et seq.*

291 See: F. Zoll, *Rękojmia. Odpowiedzialność sprzedawcy w świetle znowelizowanych przepisów kodeksu cywilnego,* Warszawa 2018, p. 225.

of concluding the contract (which often occurs in practice), there is a possibility that the buyer will demand the dissolution of the contract (*unieważnienie, Nichtigkeit*)[292] if it falls within the scope of extortion. Under Polish law, if one of the parties – taking advantage of the forced circumstances, infirmity or inexperience of the other party – in exchange for his performance, accepts or reserves for himself, or for a third party, a performance whose value at the moment of concluding the contract blatantly exceeds the value of his own performance – the other party may demand a reduction in his performance, or an increase in the performance due to him (Article 388 KC). Where both prove to be excessively difficult, he may demand the invalidation of the contract. Thus, in order to claim extortion under Polish law, two conditions have to be met: the glaring disproportion between the performance of both parties and the existence one of the following situations: forced circumstances, infirmity or inexperience of the other party. Additionally, the party taking advantage of this situation has to act consciously. Whereas the disproportion of the performance of both parties is easy to prove due to its objective character and the possibility to refer to the market value, the Court has to examine very carefully the second prerequisite of extortion, i.e. whether this disproportion was combined with forced circumstances, infirmity or inexperience of the other party.[293] The referential system of German law sets similar prerequisites in order to qualify a certain contract as extortion, but qualifies the inequality of the performance between the parties more strictly, and sets out that the contract is invalid from the beginning.[294]

So, in the event that the seller knew about the defect and was therefore aware of the lower value of the horse, but failed to inform the buyer about it, it is worth considering whether or not the situation could be qualified as **extortion.** Ac-

---

292 See, with reference to this institution under both Polish and German law: M. Gutowski, *Nieważność czynności prawnej*, Warszawa 2017, pp. 71–73 and the court rulings cited therein.

293 See a recent ruling of the Polish Appelation Court in Katowice, where the Court admitted that one of the parties used the inexperience of the other party and acted obviously against the fair dealing principle, although the case related to a loan note (*weksel*), which is under Polish law independent from *causa:* SA Katowice, ruling from 6.2.2018 – I ACa 907/17. Nevertheless, the difficulties with judicial establishment, whether the prerequisite of forced circumstances has been met has been proven in numerous Polish Supreme Court rulings, see e.g.: SN, ruling from 26.4.2007 – II CSK 24/07 and SN, ruling from 19.9.2013 – I CSK 651/12, where the Court did not admit extortion due to the fact that at least one of its prerequisites has not been met. On the other hand, the Polish Supreme Court stated also in another case that, even if the party had acted with absolute awareness and consciousness, in "normal" circumstances and without the impossibility to rationally evaluate the situation, certain situations may still qualify as forced circumstances, see: SN, ruling from 24.11.1998 – I CKN 667/97. The qualification as forced circumstances seems, therefore, to constitute the most difficulties in its interpretation, and should always be evaluated taking into account the specifics of each case.

294 See: § 138 BGB.

cording to Article 388 KC and § 138 BGB, extortion is a situation where the value of one party's performance grossly exceeds the value of the second party's performance. However, there is also a second condition to be met – the affected party must be inexperienced, infirm or placed in forced circumstances where the situation will be used by the other party for its own profit.

Although it might be difficult to imagine such a situation in forced circumstances, as horses should be concerned as luxury goods[295] and nobody would buy them – or any other animal – while in a forced position, the purchase of an expensive animal by an inexperienced person is much more likely. However, German law recognizes the presumption that the seller had fraudulent intent if the performances of both parties are unequal to a particularly glaring extent.[296] This presumption can be disproven in the special circumstances of a sale agreement, though speculation or the emotional affection of the buyer are not thought to be sufficient reasons.[297] This was also the situation in the case described above, where the buyer bought a mare for his daughter based on the choice of the horse, mainly on the basis of the personal positive attitude of his daughter to this particular horse. Although the mare turned out to have several health issues after its purchase, and although the Court dismissed the claim due to the limitation period of warranty claims, it did consider the applicability of § 138 BGB, referring to extortion. Even though the Court stated that the buyer was not inexperienced, and therefore the conditions to qualify the actions of the seller as extortion were not met, it confirmed that the speculation or emotional affection of the buyer are not sufficient reasons to raise the price of the horse so significantly that the performances of both parties are unequal to a particularly glaring extent.[298] When applying the decision of the German Court to the Polish provisions of civil law, the outcome should be the same. Especially given that Polish law does not recognize the presumption that the seller had fraudulent intent if the performances of both parties are unequal to a particularly glaring extent. Nevertheless, it is an interesting assumption that the German court OLG Düsseldorf made in its discussed ruling from 9 November 2004 (21 U 140/01), namely by confirming that, although the estimate of the price of a horse has to be based on objective criteria, it is natural that the emotional affection of the buyer will always be an issue when "purchasing" an individual, living creature.

295 See: BGH, ruling from 7.12.2005 – VIII ZR 126/05 (LG Bautzen).

296 See, for example: BGH, ruling from 19.1.2001 – V ZR 437/99, where the court underlined that such a presumption can be taken into account, even if the seller did not know about the disproportion of the value.

297 So decided also the German in the case: OLG Düsseldorf, ruling from 9.11.2004 – 21 U 140/01.

298 *Idem.*

An interesting case would constitute a situation where the performances of both parties are unequal to a particularly glaring extent due to a long-lasting emotional bond between the buyer and the animal. One can imagine a situation where a horse that was particularly liked by the teenager disappears from the stable where she learned how to ride a horse and is found by her after many years. In the event that the actual owner would take advantage of the knowledge of the emotional bond the girl has with the horse and raises its price inaccurately with reference to the market value of the horse, then that action would qualify as extortion. Thus, the emotional bond between a human and an animal is something that cannot be put somewhere in the letter of the law, but constitutes a situation that could be compared to forced circumstances as referred to in Article 388 KC and § 138 BGB. Since the German Civil Code recognizes the presumption that the seller had fraudulent intent of the performances of both parties are unequal to a particularly glaring extent,[299] the outcome of the speculated case under German law is more easy to determine. Nevertheless, the Polish courts should also qualify such actions of the seller as extortion due to the contents of Article 388 KC – even without the existence of such a presumption. However, benefiting from experience of the German courts should take place very carefully. Hence, identity of a legal rule is not a guarantee of the same understanding of it in disparate legal systems.[300] Although the Polish and German legal systems are bound by the same European legal acts aimed at the harmonization of law[301] and share the same legal foundations[302], the doctrinal solutions developed within the German tradition may be misleading. Nevertheless, I consider experience of the German jurisprudence as an interesting lesson, which may somewhat inspire the Polish jurisprudence.

The speculation of scenarios constituting extortion with reference to sale contracts having an animal as the object could go even further, e. g. to a situation where a seller, claiming that it is willing to sell the horse for slaughter, whereas in fact he does so only to motivate people interested in saving the horse's life to

299 See, for example: BGH, ruling from 19.1.2001 – V ZR 437/99, where the court underlined that such a presumption can be taken into account even if the seller did not know about the disproportion of the value.

300 E. Rott-Pietrzyk, F. Zoll [in:] M. Jagielska, E. Macierzyńska-Franaszczyk, E. Rott-Pietrzyk, F. Zoll, G. Żmij (eds.), *Limits of Harmonisation and Convergence…*, p. 44; H. Honsell, *Die rhetorischen Wurzeln der juristischen Auslegung*, ZfPW 2016, p. 125.

301 With reference to similarities and differences in the Polish and German legal systems and the applicability of provisions of law of one European country to a certain factual situation in a different European country, see: M. Jagielska, E. Macierzyńska-Franaszczyk, E. Rott-Pietrzyk, F. Zoll, G. Żmij (eds.), *Limits of Harmonisation and Convergence…*; G. Falkner, O. Trein, M. Hartlapp, S. Leiber (eds.), *Complying with Europe. EU Harmonisation and Soft Law in the Member States*, Cambridge 2005.

302 See also: S. Frankowski (ed.), *Introduction to Polish Law*, p. 38.

collect as much money as he demands if they want to avoid killing the horse. Although the situation seems to be abstract, the practical information gained confirms that the situation happens and is not rare. Nevertheless, the latter scenario would probably be qualified as extortion under both the German and Polish legal systems, only in the event that the price of the horse would be unequal to a particularly glaring extent to the value of a horse (even if sold for slaughter). Thus, since animals are *de lege lata* neither treated as legal persons nor as a different legal category, and humans are also not treated as guardians of their interests,[303] the individual motivation of a person wanting to buy a horse in order to save him from slaughter would not be important to qualify it as extortion or not. Therefore, horse sellers often misuse the sale of horses for slaughter by selling them for higher prices than they would receive in slaughterhouses (and even before paying for a necessary veterinary examination, proving whether its meat may be consumed at all), since they are aware that animal rights' organizations would try to buy them anyway. As long as the legal situation of animals does not change, and as long as the price of the horse does not exceed its market value, the probability of success of a claim for extortion does not seem high enough to file it, sadly such situations are unavoidable.

Obviously, extortion may also apply to the situation, where the buyer sold an animal for a blatantly low price. Whereas establishing the price is left to the discretion of the parties, the situation is different in cases where the buyer used the seller's forced circumstances. This could happen, for example, in case where a creditor (who is a passionate horse rider or a dog or cat breeder, especially interested in a certain breed) insists on collecting the debtor's animal as a *datio in solutum*,[304] knowing that this animal is currently on sale for a significantly higher price, but there are no buyers willing to pay that amount at the moment.[305] Such a situation may even escalate to a threat[306] in the event that the creditor claims that he will demand execution from the debtor's estate if the debtor does not agree to his conditions. Another situation that could qualify as extortion is

303 I do not believe that this will change within the next few centuries, see more with reference to animals kept for slaughter in: M. Lubelska-Sazanów, *Prawne regulacje dotyczące transportu zwierząt na terenie Unii Europejskiej* [in:] B. Błońska, W. Gogłoza, W. Klaus, D. Woźniakowska-Fajst (eds.), *Sprawiedliwość dla zwierząt*, Warszawa 2017; M. Rudy, A. Rudy, P. Mazur, *Ubój rytualny w prawie administracyjnym,* Warszawa 2013. Compare also: T. Pietrzykowski, *Recenzja książki M. Rudego, A. Rudego, P. Mazura, Ubój rytualny w prawie administracyjnym, Warszawa 2013,* Prokuratura I Prawo 2014, Issue 3, pp. 162–167.

304 See: Article 453 KC, § *365 BGB. The institution of datio in solutum has also been mentioned in the subchapter above.*

305 Although the inability to find a buyer willing to pay a certain price for the object offered for sale may refer to any object of the obligation, it has a specific meaning in animal sale, due to the fact that personal affection plays a significant role in animal sale. See: OLG Düsseldorf ruling from 16.04.2002 – 21 U 140/01.

306 Article 87 KC, § *123 BGB.*

where an experienced rider counsels a less experienced rider to sell a horse, stating that it does not have certain abilities or is losing its market value due to a certain health condition, and offers help in making the sale, whereas his allegations are not true and the horse's owner is inexperienced. In this case, it is the seller, who may demand an increase in the performance due to him, i. e. the payment of a price difference between the price of a sold animal and its market value.[307] He could also demand the invalidation of the contract, but only where the payment of the price difference would be excessively difficult.[308]

2.4. Applicability of specific types of sale contracts to animals

2.4.1. Animals as specific objects of sale on approval

Under both the Polish and German legal systems, it is common to transfer the ownership of animals using the construction of a specific type of sale contract. A perfect solution for an animal acquirer is **sale on approval.** Therefore, this contract appears quite often in the sale of horses, whereby the horses acquired for sport, or generally for riding purposes, are usually **tested in advance.** Although the test ride occurs usually in the place where the seller keeps the horse and consists of one or more test riding hours, it is also possible to sell a horse on the condition that the buyer will approve the sale within a certain amount of time. If the buyer does not approve the animal after a certain amount of time, he returns it and receives the money back. The sale contract is not concluded.[309] Nevertheless, in a situation where an animal meets the expectations of the buyer, the contract is concluded at the moment, when the parties to the contract achieve a consensus in reference to the conclusion of the contract. Since, under Polish law, the applicability of Article 592 KC occurs by the means of a suspensive condition,[310] in the situation where the buyer returns an animal and receives the money back, this effect occurs *ex tunc.* Thus, the acknowledgment that the good is "good" constitutes solely the delivery of a condition, which is obligatory to consider the contract as definitive, whereas the conclusion of the contract oc-

307 In this case, the seller may also refer to an error that was caused by his contracting party, and evade the legal effects of his declaration of intent, see: Article 84 KC, § *119 BGB.*

308 See also the Polish Supreme Court in the case: SN, ruling from 20. 5. 2010 – V CSK 387/09.

309 With reference to Polish law, see: K. Haładyj [in:] K. Osajda (ed.), *Kodeks cywilny. Komentarz. Tom IIIB,* pp. 231–234; with reference to the German law, see: H. Westermann [in:] H. Westermann (ed.), *Münchener Kommentar zum BGB, Vol. III,* München 2016, § 454, side number 4, *BeckOnline (last visited: 12. 3. 2018).*

310 See: J. Jezioro [in:] E. Gniewek, P. Machnikowski (eds.), *Kodeks cywilny. Komentarz,* Warszawa 2017, p. 1253. K. Haładyj [in:] K. Osajda (ed.), *Kodeks cywilny. Komentarz. Tom IIIB.* p. 233.

curred already before.[311] According to the Polish Supreme Court, the acknowledgment that the good is approved does not have any importance for the seller's liability for defects, and the only aim of this reservation is to give the buyer the possibility to check whether the good is free from defects.[312]

This solution is used mostly for the sale of horses at a middle price level, where the buyer resides some distance from the place where the seller keeps the horse. The parties decide on the conclusion of a contract based on a construction similar to sale on approval when the buyer wants to be sure that the horse's character meets his needs and skills, and the seller prefers the option of a few days of uncertainty in exchange of an increased probability that an undecided buyer will not claim that the horse has a defect in the future. Therefore, deciding on this kind of contract can be rewarding for both parties to the contract. What is more – when referring to the hypothesis of animals having their own interests – this solution would also be in the animal's interest (if an animal's interests were acknowledged by legal doctrine[313]), since it is never positive for an animal to change the place of living and the caretaker after creating a bond with him. Animals also create emotional bonds and it is wiser when an animal owner that bonds with an animal is sure about his intention to care for the animal for a longer period of time.

As already mentioned, according to the majority of the representatives of the Polish doctrine, under Polish law the contract is concluded at the moment when the parties to the contract achieve a consensus with reference to the conclusion of the contract, but this occurs under a suspensive condition that the animal meets the expectations of the buyer,[314] thus upon the buyer's approval of the animal, or within a certain time limit. In the event that no time limit for the buyer to approve the purchase of an animal is established, the seller is entitled to set a time limit if the buyer hesitates with the approval of the purchase. In this case, the contract is concluded when the time limit passes.[315] The buyer does not have to explain his motives for not giving approval – this issue is left to his discretion. During the test time, the buyer has the possibility to observe the horse and be

311 See: K. Haładyj [in:] K. Osajda (ed.), *Kodeks cywilny. Komentarz. Tom IIIB.* p. 233. Nevertheless, some representatives of the Polish doctrine suggest that the buyer's acknowledgment that the good is "good" is similar to acceptance of an offer, see: M. Safjan [in:] K. Pietrzykowski (ed.), *Kodeks cywilny. Komentarz*, p. 356.

312 So: SN, ruling from 18.6.2010 – V CSK 433/09.

313 The term of "animal interests", though it does not exist in the legal doctrine, is experimentally used in this book, so that the final conclusions can be made with reference to whether such "animal interests" should be legally acknowledged.

314 So: K. Haładyj [in:] K. Osajda (ed.), *Kodeks cywilny. Komentarz. Tom IIIB.* p. 233; J. Jezioro [in:] E. Gniewek, P. Machnikowski (eds.), *Kodeks cywilny. Komentarz*, p. 1253. Compare: M. Safjan [in:] K. Pietrzykowski (ed.), *Kodeks cywilny. Komentarz*, p. 356.

315 Compare similar solutions under Polish and German law: § 455 BGB and Article 592 KC.

certain that the horse is accurate to the claimed skills.[316] Taking into account that the sale on the approval under Polish law is considered by the doctrine to be concluded before the final approval, the buyer bears the risk for any deterioration in the horse's condition or illnesses that are caused to an animal before he approves it. However, under German law the risk is passed to the buyer first after the approval of the horse, therefore it is in the seller's interest to construct a detailed agreement concerning the buyer's (tester's) liability for any deterioration in the horse's condition or illnesses that are caused to the horse during the its stay at the buyer's location. Thus, the consequences are defined differently under Polish and under the referential system of German law. Under Polish law, according to Article 591 KC, it is the horse owner's right to demand damages for any deterioration in the horse's condition or the appearance of an illness. Claiming the rights arising from Article 591 KC is independent from the possibility to claim reimbursement based on general rules applicable to contractual relationships.[317] Under German law, there is no regulation that would correspond with Article 591 KC. Therefore, under German law, the deterioration of the horse's condition during its stay at the buyer's place occurs at the risk of the seller.[318] Nevertheless, defining that the animal's owner is entitled to reimbursement in such case is also in the interest of the animal, whose health condition will more likely recover when the party who is at fault for the deterioration of its health pays for its medication. Therefore, the legal solution chosen by the Polish legislator seems – probably accidently – to better serve the wellbeing of the animal.

It is also possible to conclude a sale contract while **reserving the possibility to exchange the animal being object of this contract for a different one.** This solution might be useful for the sale of horses in similar circumstances to where contracts based on the construction of sale under approval are useful. However, a contract reserving the possibility to exchange the horse occurs only if the seller is able to provide a different animal in exchange[319] (e.g. a breeder). Although nowadays there are no specific provisions concerning this institution in Polish and German Civil Codes,[320] it is still applicable. Usually this reservation is made in connection with setting a certain time limit in which to exercise this right. Although there are no specific rules according this matter, it is presupposed, that

316 M. Sommer, *Der Pferdekauf*, pp. 80–81.

317 K. Haładyj [in:] K. Osajda (ed.), *Kodeks cywilny. Komentarz. Tom IIIB*, p. 231.

318 See: M. Sommer, *Der Pferdekauf*, pp. 80–81.

319 *Idem*, pp. 81–82.

320 However, this type of sale contract existed in the BGB before the reform and there are no obstacles to make such a reservation in a sale agreement also now. Compare: H. Westermann [in:] H. Westermann (ed.), *Münchener Kommentar zum BGB, Vol. III*, München 2016, § 454, side number 1, *BeckOnline (last visited: 12.3.2018).*

– unless the parties agree otherwise – the exchange can occur only once. It is not clear whether the buyer may choose the replacement animal himself.[321] Under Polish law, this reservation may be treated as a specific provision in a sale contract or as a mixed contract. This solution may also be in the animal's interests, so that it is not neglected by its owner as being not capable to meet his expectations (in sport or just, generally, as a companion on the same activity level or experience level as the owner is) and may instead return to its previous stable or another place, where its previous owner raised it.

The kinds of sale presented under this subchapter have to be distinguished from the fact that, in the event of **partial payment of the horse's price**, the seller usually reserves the right to retain ownership of the horse until the buyer pays the full price. This situation was dealt with in one of very few Polish cases referring to obligations with an animal as the object of a contractual obligation ruled on by the Polish Supreme Court.[322] In this case, the buyer and the seller concluded a contract to buy a horse, reserving the ownership right of the seller until the full price is paid for the horse. Thus, the parties agreed, that 10 % of the price would be paid when concluding the contract, and the rest within the next few months. Unfortunately, before the full price was paid, the horse died due to a blockage in its artery. The Court stated that the possession of a horse had already passed to the buyer, and at that moment all benefits and burdens connected within happened were at the risk of the buyer. Thus, the fact that the ownership over a horse was suspended under the condition that the buyer pays the full price of the horse was independent from the date of the risk passing to the buyer, i. e. the time when the horse was handed to him. Therefore, according to the Court, the buyer was forced to pay the full price of the horse despite its death.

2.4.2. Animals as specific objects of sale while reserving the right to repurchase

Another type of contract applicable to animals is **sale while reserving the right to repurchase.**[323] This variation of sale contract is regulated in both Polish and German Civil Codes and might be useful in contracts involving animals. Sales while reserving the right to repurchase are applicable in market practice mainly when selling a beloved animal for a price lower than its market value in order to provide it a loving new home, which is more important for the seller then the possibility of earning money through the sale of the animal. The use of this institution, although not especially attractive to the buyer, is often balanced by

321 See: H. Westermann [in:] H. Westermann (ed.), *Münchener Kommentar zum BGB*, BGB § 454, side number 4, *BeckOnline (last visited: 12.3.2018).*

322 SN, ruling from 25.9.2014 – II CSK 664/13.

323 See: Article 593 KC and § 456 BGB.

an occasional purchase for an unusually low price.[324] It is also common that including a provision setting out the possibility of buying an animal back in the contract is connected with more specific conditions of when such a situation occurs, e.g. by including in the contract a provision that the previous owner of the animal is entitled to repurchase it if the buyer does not take enough care for its health and appearance. Although such circumstances are always difficult to prove by the party who wants to buy the animal back, due to lack of standardized degrees of taking care for animals, the lack of care and beauty treatments, like regularly taking a dog to a groomer, etc., may sometimes constitute sufficient grounds to state that the buyer does not take enough care over the animal.[325] In contradiction to Polish courts – the German ones have already acknowledged insufficient care over an animal as a reason to repurchase an animal – nevertheless, the relevant provision has to be included in the contract (therefore, under the freedom of contract principle, I would advise the inclusion of such provisions in all contracts concerning animals). A judicial ruling concerning this issue can be found in the decision of the regional court in Fulda (Germany), where the seller of a dog alleged that the dog was not being sufficiently well taken care of, especially due to lack of grooming. Although the Court did not admit that the dog was insufficiently taken care of in the case at hand, it stated that the seller's conditions were defined sufficiently enough to exercise the right to repurchase the animal, and acknowledged it as legally binding.[326]

A similar provision should be included in a contract for the lease of an animal for breeding purposes.[327] This kind of contract is usually concluded in cases where a breeder sells a purebred dog or cat to another person for a low price, with the reservation that they will still be able to lease the animal for dog shows and breeding purposes (where such contract is usually concluded in analogy to "sale-and-lease-back" contracts used in corporate civil law relations[328]). In such cases, it is reasonable to include in the contract a provision that the animal may be taken back at the seller's demand in case certain objective criteria applies (such as not taking enough care for the appearance of the animal).

324 To learn more about this type of sale contract under German law, see: W. Weidenkaff [in:] O. Palandt, *Beck'sche Kurz-Kommentare: Palandt Bürgerliches Gesetzbuch mit Nebengesetzen*, München 2015, pp. 692–695; Under Polish law see also: J. Jezioro [in:] E. Gniewek, P. Machnikowski (eds.), *Kodeks cywilny. Komentarz*, Warszawa 2017, pp. 1254–1255; M. Safjan [in:] K. Pietrzykowski (ed.), *Kodeks cywilny. Komentarz*, pp. 356–358.

325 See: LG Fulda, ruling from 18.09.1992 – Az.: 1 S 108/92 (note that the case comes from the time period before the reform of the German Civil Code of 2002, though this does not have a significant impact on the described facts of the case).

326 See: LG Fulda, ruling from 18.09.1992 – Az.: 1 S 108/92.

327 Compare: Subchapter IV.2.5. of this book.

328 Compare: Finanzgericht Münster, ruling from 11.12.2014 – 5 K 3068/13 F, where the German Court explained the idea and practicality of the "sale-and-lease-back" institution.

The Polish Civil Code provides that a contract of sale while reserving the right to repurchase can only be made for the time period of five years,[329] whereas the German Civil Code provides for a three-year period for movables.[330] Due to the respective applicability of provisions referring to movables to animals arising from § 90a BGB and Article 1 of the Polish Animal Protection Act, the same applies to sale contracts having an animal as its object while reserving the right to repurchase.

The idea of repurchasing an animal seems to be most empathic and understanding to the emotions of the animal's owner, and the animal itself, from among all the types of sale contracts, and is the only institution in the sale law provisions in the Polish and German Civil Codes that would allow for collecting the animal back in the event of its maltreatment by the present owner. I suggest that it should be considered to include a provision in the Polish Civil Code stating, for example: **"The seller has the right and obligation to take an interest in the animal's health and general condition after transferring the ownership to the buyer, whereas the buyer is obliged to enable the seller to see the sold animal in order to check on its living conditions, unless the frequency of these checks exceed the moral standards of a given society. In the event that the animal turns out to be maltreated, its previous owner/ the seller is entitled to issue a claim to repurchase this animal."**

The solution presented above is a solution already used in the case of animal adoption agreements.[331] Thus, adoption agreements usually include provisions indicating that the organization providing the animal for adoption (i. e. its previous owner) retains the duty to take care of the fate of the animal and has a basic control over whether the actual owner fulfils the animal's substantial needs. This way it can ensure that it does not sell a particular horse for slaughter, or allow the use of an ill, "retired" horse for intense rides. The inclusion of such provisions *de lege lata* into contracts – or *de lege ferenda* in legislature – is the only legal solution that acknowledges the emotional bond between the previous owner and the animal, and allows for a change in the ownership of an animal in the event that its or its owner's interests (consisting in the wellbeing of the animal) are not being met by the present owner. In my opinion, since ownership of an animal is connected with the duty to take care of it (which could be considered as a passive right of an animal), it should be obligatory for the previous owner to check on the condition of an animal (though the frequency should not exceed the moral standards of a given society, or be disruptive for the

329 See: Article 593 § 1 KC.

330 See: § 462 BGB.

331 See: Subchapter III.2.4.1 of this book ("Contracts transferring ownership of a good in reference to animals other than a sale contract – Donation").

present, as well as for the previous owner) previously owned by him, and should react if he observes that it might be mistreated. Nevertheless, as already mentioned – changes in the Polish Civil Code may also be substituted by the voice of the doctrine and jurisprudence, which could concern the admissibility of a claim to repurchase an animal, and possibility to check on its living conditions as compliance with general clauses included therein.

2.4.3. Animals as specific objects of sale with a pre-emptive right

The abovementioned type of sale contract has to be distinguished from **the pre-emptive right,**[332] which states that the previous owner of an animal can re-purchase it from the current owner, though only in the event that the current owner decides to sell the animal.[333] Thus, he is the one who decides about the moment of sale; the previous owner only has priority to decide whether he wants to buy the animal before other potentially interested buyers have an opportunity to decide on this matter. In the case of selling the animal without informing the party entitled to the pre-emptive right, one has to cover damages.[334] However, as damages in this case might be difficult to assess, it is advisable to establish a contractual penalty for this course of events.[335]

2.5. Contracts aimed at the transfer of property with reference to animals other than a sale contract

2.5.1. Donation

Although a donation agreement with reference to animals does not usually raise many practical questions, it often serves as a prototype for agreements considered to be more "problematic", namely as a **prototype for adoption agree-**

332 Compare Article 596 KC and § 463 BGB. With reference to Polish law, see: J. Jezioro [in:] E. Gniewek, P. Machnikowski (eds.), *Kodeks cywilny. Komentarz*, Warszawa 2017, pp. 1256–1259; M. Safjan [in:] K. Pietrzykowski (ed.), *Kodeks cywilny. Komentarz*, pp. 362–369; with reference to German law, see: W. Weidenkaff [in:] O. Palandt, *Beck'sche Kurz-Kommentare: Palandt Bürgerliches Gesetzbuch mit Nebengesetzen*, pp. 695–700.

333 With reference to the legal character of the pre-emption right under Polish law, see: J. Górecki, *Umowne prawo pierwokupu*, Kraków 2000, pp. 65–98.

334 See: J. Górecki, *Umowne prawo pierwokupu*, pp. 225–241. With reference to damages in accordance with the contracts transferring ownership of an animal, see: Subchapter III.3. in general.

335 With reference to types of contractual fees and the possibility to claim damages based on different liability regimes in Polish law, see: E. Łętowska [in:] E. Łętowska (ed.), *System Prawa Prywatnego, Vol. V, Prawo zobowiązań – część ogólna*, pp. 196–199.

ments used nowadays by several organizations and animal shelters.[336] Those agreements are usually qualified as mixed types of contracts with a predominance of donation.[337] The qualification as such results in the applicability of provisions concerning donation agreements to adoption agreements, including those referring to the warranty rights described in § 524 I BGB and Article 892 KC. Thus, both the Polish and German Civil Codes set out that a "donor" is liable for defects in a good only if they have been fraudulently concealed. The idea that the warranty rights are patterned on the legal regulation of donation rather than of sale expresses the will and interest of the parties concluding an adoption agreement. Although the German doctrine has addressed this legal problem with reference to the German legal system, its considerations under the Polish legal system would consist of the same foundations, since both the Polish and German Civil Codes include similar provisions referring to donation.[338] Therefore, although some judicial rulings in Germany have qualified such contracts as safekeeping,[339] I agree with J. Wertenbruch and would qualify such contracts as mixed contracts based on the provisions of a donation agreement (under both the Polish and German legal systems).[340] Thus, understanding the intent of the parties and achieving their intentions at the time of concluding the contract is one of the fundamental principles of contract law and should not be abandoned in any case.

Looking further at the referential system of German law, the situation where the intent of the parties is to gratuitously transfer ownership to close family members (ownership of plots in the case at hand) has also been qualified by the court as a prevalent indicator to qualify the contract at hand as a mixed contract with predominance of donation in an old German case from 1982, recalled by J.

336 See examples of adoption agreement forms in Poland: Zwierzęca Przystań in Piła, http://zwierzecaprzystan.pl/wp-content/uploads/2017/01/UMOWA-ADOPCYJNA-PSA.pdf (last visited: 3.1.2018); Wzajemnie Pomocni Foundation http://www.wzajemniepomocni.pl/images/umowa.pdf; http://www.schroniskoazorek.pl/kontakt/wzor-umowy-adopcyjnej, (last visited: 3.1.2018); and in Germany: Hundevermittlung Herzensache e.V., http://www.hundevermittlung-herzenssache.com/.cm4all/uproc.php/0/FORMULARE/Adoptions-Vertrag.pdf?cdp=a; https://auslandstierschutz.jimdo.com/infos-tierschutz/muster-tierabgabevertrag/ (last visited: 3.1.2018).

337 See remarks to the transfer of the ownership against a very little amount of money, which is to be qualified as a mixed contract: J. Wertenbruch, *Die Besonderheiten…*, p. 2070.

338 However, it should be always kept in mind that the identity of a legal rule is not a guarantee of the same understanding of it in disparate legal systems. Compare: E. Rott-Pietrzyk, F. Zoll [in:] M. Jagielska, E. Macierzyńska-Franaszczyk, E. Rott-Pietrzyk, F. Zoll, G. Żmij (eds.), *Limits of Harmonization and Convergence…*, p. 44; H. Honsell, *Die rhetorischen Wurzeln der juristischen Auslegung*, ZfPW 2016, p. 125.

339 See: AG Krefeld, ruling from 1.9.2006 – 7 C 255/06 and its appellation: LG Krefeld, ruling from 13.4.2007 – 1 S 79/06.

340 See: J. Wertenbruch, *Die Besonderheiten…*, p. 2070.

Wertenbruch in his article.[341] Thus, BGH in its case IV a ZR 185/80,[342] stated that the previous intent of both parents expressed in their common will to equally and gratuitously divide their estate between their two sons determined the nature of the transfer of ownership to these sons despite the lease and usufruct relations that have arisen in the last years of life of the father of the family (one of the two bequeathers) and one of his sons, when he needed his help and presence after his wife's death (the second of the two bequeathers).

Nevertheless, in cases concerning animal adoption agreements (i. e. getting[343] an animal from an animal shelter), the German court qualified these contracts as safe-keeping. Namely, in case – 7 C 255/06 ruled by AG Krefeld on 1 September 2006 and its appeal (case 1 S 79/06) ruled by LG Krefeld on 13 April 2007, the adoption agreement set out that the animal shelter was not liable for situations where the previous owner claims the return of the animal (in the case of a found animal), and if he did so within six months from finding the animal, the party having this animal in custody was obliged to return it. Additionally, the adoption contract also contained other clauses typical for adoption agreements, such as the duty to take care over an adopted animal bẏ feeding it, covering veterinary costs, etc. The contract also explicitly stated that the party adopting the animal has no warranty rights against the animal shelter. Nevertheless, a party adopting a dog in the case at hand claimed the reimbursement of veterinary costs incurred with reference to medical operations of the dog's aching hip, basing its claim on findings that the parties concluded a sale contract. BGH did not admit the claim of the adopting party, stating that this was not a sale contract and so the reimbursement of medical costs is not justified. However, since the dog was found, the court acknowledged the common findings of the parties that the transfer of ownership over this animal occurs first after six months, and therefore qualified this contract as safe-keeping.

Although the German courts of both instances qualified adoption contracts as safe-keeping and not donation in the case described above,[344] this does not exclude the possibility of qualifying such contracts as mixed contracts with a predominance of donation. Thus, the main issue of the cases ruled by German courts in Krefeld was not the question, on which basis occurred the transfer of ownership, but why the warranty rights were not applicable in the case at hand and how to deal with the problem of 6 months term, since the previous owner was eligible to claim extradition of the dog. In my opinion this contract could just easily be qualified as donation concluded under a condition (suspensive or

341 *Idem.*
342 BGH, ruling from 23.09.1981 – IV a ZR 185/80 (Köln).
343 I do not use the term "transfer of ownership" on purpose – please read further.
344 AG Krefeld, ruling from 1.9.2006 – 7 C 255/06 and its appellation: LG Krefeld, ruling from 13.4.2007 – 1 S 79/06.

subsequent – depending on further details of the case). However, I believe that the conclusion made by the court in the case at hand was the easiest way to solve this case at that moment under those conditions. Nevertheless, the outcome would have been different if the dog at hand had not been found, or if the six months had already passed. In that case, the court would have no other choice than to qualify this contract in accordance with one of my proposals. The most logical solution would be to qualify the contract at hand as a mixed contract with a predominance of donation[345] concluded under a suspensive condition, and I believe that this is also how Polish courts would solve this case. However, there are no Polish court rulings referring to adoption contracts – probably because of the low value of the subject of the case, and still very low interest in raising claims that concern animals (not to mention that in the rural areas of Poland it is still not common to operate on animals that are ill – especially if these are not purebred animals or they would no longer be useful on the farm after the operation). Nevertheless, as already mentioned at the beginning of this subchapter, both the Polish and German Civil Codes include similar provisions referring to donation. Therefore, considerations of the legal problems connected with the construction of donation contracts under both legal systems are on the same foundations. However, it should be always kept in mind that the identity of a legal rule is not a guarantee of the same understanding of it in disparate legal systems.[346] Still, in this case I believe that, the outcome of cases presented under the German legal system should be the same as if they were resolved by Polish courts.

Concerning **donation agreements** generally, there is one characteristic feature that gains special interest with reference to animals. Namely, both the German and Polish Civil Codes recognize the possibility of a donating party vesting in the benefiting party **a duty to perform a specified act or omission** while not making any person a creditor (*polecenie*, *Auflage*).[347] This institution is very useful for organizations that train dogs for visually impaired people, or for animal shelters. The idea of a complimentary transfer of ownership of an animal, with a reservation that the benefiting party is obliged to take care of the animal, is often the best legal base for organizations specializing in animal protection to pass the dog or cat to the new owner. A commonly used reservation is also an obligation of the benefiting party who is visually impaired to accept the fact that

345 So also: J. Wertenbruch, *Die Besonderheiten…*, p. 2070 (with reference to qualification as mixed contract with predominant of donation).

346 E. Rott-Pietrzyk, F. Zoll [in:] M. Jagielska, E. Macierzyńska-Franaszczyk, E. Rott-Pietrzyk, F. Zoll, G. Żmij (eds.), *Limits of Harmonization and Convergence…*, p. 44; H. Honsell, *Die rhetorischen Wurzeln der juristischen Auslegung*, ZfPW 2016, p. 125.

347 Compare: Article 893 KC and § 525 BGB.

the dog retires at a certain age and can no longer be used as a guide dog.[348] The possibility to terminate (*odstąpienie, das Rücktritt*) a donation and get the animal back in the event that the benefiting party fails to follow the reservation, or in the event of a displayed ingratitude against the donating party, makes the donation agreement even more attractive.[349] This applies not only to animal shelters and organizations passing animals to new owners, but also to riders who want to leave their horses for a deserved retirement at somebody else's ranch/stable. As mentioned in the previous subchapter, I would at least consider including a provision in the Polish Civil Code that animals can only be donated on the condition that the new owner takes sufficient care of the animal. In that case, the previous owner would still have a duty (and a right to do it, at the same time – depending on the perspective) of care for the fate of the animal, and has a basic control over whether the actual owner provides for the animal's substantial needs. Such a provision could contain, for example, the formula: "**The donor has the right and obligation to be interested in the animal's health and general condition after transferring the ownership to the recipient, whereas the recipient is obliged to enable the donor to see the donated animal in order to check its living condition, unless the frequency of these controls exceeds the moral standards of a given society.**" However, the possibility to check on animal's living conditions may also come from the doctrine and jurisprudence, which should qualify the behavior of a donor as compliant with general clauses included in the Polish Civil Code (especially in Articles 56 and 354 KC).

2.5.2. Barter

According to both Article 604 KC and § 480 BGB, the rules applicable to sale contracts are respectively applicable to barter agreements. Although this type of contract does not apply very often in reference to animals due to its specific nature,[350] and therefore will not be described in as much detail as in reference to sale contracts,[351] there is one issue worth mentioning in this matter. Namely, in practice it is quite often to include in a sale contract an additional provision setting out that the buyer keeps the right to exchange an animal (usually a

348 See, for example: rules applicable for passing guide dogs by the Organisation "Vis Maior", last visited: 21.1.2016 from the website; http://fundacjavismaior.pl/dzialania/psy-przewodniki/zostan-wlascicielem/.

349 Compare: Article 895 KC, Article 898 KC, § 527 BGB, § 529 BGB.

350 Except for the already mentioned situation, which is often practiced, i.e. an exchange of ponies among young riders who need to have a horse suitable for their height and weight.

351 However, look at the characteristics of the warranty with reference to barter agreements in section 3.

horse[352]) for a different one within a certain (usually short) period of time.[353] In this case, the German judiciary again provides an example of the judicial acknowledgment of such practices, whereas the Polish courts have not published any case referring to these issues (therefore – probably they did not rule on such matters). Nevertheless, due to the similarity of the structure of the Polish and German civil law provisions, the German jurisprudence in the cases presented in this book is usually based on the same legal foundations that exist in the Polish Civil Code, and therefore there Polish courts could profit from the experience of German jurisprudence. However, taking advantage of the experience of the German courts should take place very carefully.[354] Although the Polish and German legal systems are bound by the same European legal acts aimed at the harmonization of law[355] and share the same legal foundations,[356] the doctrinal solutions developed within the German tradition may be misleading. Still, I believe they may constitute (at least to a limited degree) an inspiration for the Polish courts. At the very least, in the situation described in this subchapter, the qualification of a contract should be the same.

Thus, the Court of Appeals in Stuttgart (Germany) stated in 2003 that, in cases where the parties agreed that a purchased horse can be exchanged (though not due to an individual subjective decision of the buyer, but only when objective criteria are met, e.g. an inability by the buyer's daughter to ride a horse due to its disobedience), this provision should not be qualified as a sale contract with a postponed effect of effectiveness, nor as a contract of sale on approval.[357] According to the opinion of the court, the possibility to exchange a horse constitutes a provision that additionally entitles the buyer to demand the conclusion of a barter contract with the seller in case any objective criteria apply. Thus, in

352 However, the right to exchange an animal within a certain time period may, for practical reasons, also be reserved in adoption agreements concerning dogs or cats taken from animals shelters, see the subchapter above. Thus, it corresponds with the idea that an adopted animal should rather find a familly that will be able to grant its basic needs, and not a family that is not able to deal with an animal with behavioral problems. Thus, such a situation may lead to this animal's later return to an animal shelter with greater trauma than before.

353 See: OLG Stuttgart, ruling from 27.10.2004 – 3 U 198/03.

354 So also: E. Rott-Pietrzyk, F. Zoll [in:] M. Jagielska, E. Macierzyńska-Franaszczyk, E. Rott-Pietrzyk, F. Zoll, G. Żmij (eds.), *Limits of Harmonization and Convergence…*, p. 44; H. Honsell, *Die rhetorischen Wurzeln der juristischen Auslegung*, ZfPW 2016, p. 125.

355 With reference to similarities and differences in the Polish and German legal systems and the applicability of provisions of law of one European country to a certain factual situation in a different European country, see: M. Jagielska, E. Macierzyńska-Franaszczyk, E. Rott-Pietrzyk, F. Zoll, G. Żmij (eds.), *Limits of Harmonisation and Convergence…*; G. Falkner, O. Trein, M. Hartlapp, S. Leiber (eds.), *Complying with Europe. EU Harmonisation and Soft Law in the Member States*, Cambridge 2005.

356 See also: S. Frankowski (ed.), *Introduction to Polish Law*, p. 38.

357 See: Article 592 KC and § 454 BGB.

such cases, the sale contract between the parties remains unaffected and the buyer keeps all the warranty rights arising from the sale contract.

Therefore, although barter contracts are not frequently concluded with reference to animals, it is much more likely that this type of contract will be concluded as a result of a previously concluded sale contract between the same parties (if an accurate additional provision is included in the sale contract). Whether such a provision will result in the qualification of a contract as a contract of sale under approval or as a provision allowing the buyer to demand the conclusion of a barter contract in the future, depends on the facts of each case.

2.5.3. Contracts of delivery of pre-contracted agricultural produce (*umowa kontraktacji*)

Another agreement that might result in the transfer of property of an animal is a **contract of delivery of pre-contracted agricultural produce** (*umowa kontraktacji*). This contract, recognized by Polish law (but not by German law) is based on the principle that an agricultural producer undertakes to produce and to deliver to the pre-contracting party a specified amount of agricultural produce of a determined kind, and the pre-contracting party undertakes to collect these products within the time limit agreed on, pay the price agreed on and perform any specified additional performance (if the contract or specific provisions provide for a duty to render such performance).[358] The specific performance might be, in this case, a provision of one of the following: the possibility to acquire certain means of production and to obtain financial aid, agrotechnological and zootechnical aid, pecuniary bonuses and non-cash bonuses.[359] There are no obstacles to applying the construction of a contract of delivery of pre-contracted agricultural produce to animals (usually in the meaning of a troop of animals, e.g. production of chickens, porkers), though it is more connected with plant production.[360] Thus, investors would prefer to conclude sale contracts for a certain number of living chickens, rather than to wait until they are born, without the certainty that the required numbers of animals will be ready to collect at a certain time. Therefore, the practical usage of contracts of delivery of pre-contracted agricultural produce with reference to animals is rather marginal, and therefore will not be presented in a more detailed way in this book.

358 See Article 613 KC.

359 Article 615 KC.

360 With reference to the object of a pre-contracted agricultural produce, see: Polish Court of Appeals in Gdańsk: SA, ruling from 12.2.2013, V ACa 1043/12, defining the object of a pre-contracted agricultural produce agreement.

3. Results of the improper performance of contracts aimed at the transfer of property with reference to contracts having an animal as the object

3.1. Legal foundations of the seller's liability in connection with the sale of animals

Under both the Polish and German legal systems, the liability of the seller may arise on several foundations. The first of them is liability for *culpa in contrahendo,* which refers to disloyal actions undertaken by the contracting party before the conclusion of the contract. The liability for *culpa in contrahendo* on the side of the horse's potential buyer arises if he does not act in accordance with the duty to negotiate with care, and hides his fraudulent intent when negotiating the acquisition of the animal.[361] Whereas such liability could arise with reference to any animal (e.g. taking the time and effort of a dog breeder by visiting him numerous times to obtain information about a whelp that he never really intended to buy, but wanted only to receive some inside information on breeding methods, business contacts, etc., in order to be able to start breeding as a business activity himself), it is most likely to occur with reference to the sale of horses. Thus, when selling a sport horse, it is a commercial standard that the potential buyer/rider will try the horse before buying it, very often several times and sometimes even by taking part in competitions. As a creature up for sale, the horse is not able to jump high obstacles every day (or rather should not be allowed to do that, in order to keep his health condition in an undetriorated state and to avoid contusions). Therefore, training sessions on a horse with the intent to try it before buying should be scheduled carefully so that the horse does not become stressed or over tired. It is typical that a horse's owner wants to avoid too many riders trying a horse without having a serious intent to buy it, leading to irregularities in its training schedule under its current rider. Therefore, a situation where a rider pretends to want to buy a horse, where the real intention is to prevent a competitor from trying a horse, would definitely not constitute negotiations with care, but would go against various fair dealing principles, in particular the principles of social co-existence[362] and good faith. Nevertheless, it is even more likely that a competitor could try to insist on taking a horse for a competition in order to see how it will react under stress and in a different place,

361 Compare: regulation of the *culpa in contrahendo* liability in German (see: M. Wojtas, *Studien zum ausländisches und internationalen Privatrecht: Haftung für culpa in contrahendo*, Tübingen 2017, pp. 29–55) and Polish law (see: M. Wojtas, *Studien zum auslandisches und internationalen Privatrecht: Haftung fur culpa in contrahendo*, pp. 55–73).

362 Article 56 KC.

where the actual intent is not to buy the horse, but to take part in a certain competition (especially if he wins a prize). During such a prolonged process of "trying" a horse, many accidents can happen. Thus, it is not only the risk of damage to the horse as a result of taking part in a competition,[363] but also the risk that the rider and the horse will not cooperate well enough and the outcome of the competition (which is available to the public) will result in making the sale of the horse more problematic in the future. If the potential buyer had fraudulent intent from the beginning of negotiations, the liability for *culpa in contrahendo* applies.[364] The possibility to breach the duties arising from Article 72 § 2 KC[365] may also arise on the side of a seller who, for example, negotiates the sale of an animal that he has no real intention of sellling, despite the buyer declining other offers for the duration of negotiations.[366] Nevertheless, the liability for *culpa in contrahendo* does not constitute a separate object of considerations in this book, due to its relatively low applicability in reference to the conclusion of contracts involving animals. Additionally, I did not consider it as the most suitable solution for the purpose of this book to collect all the hypothetical situations that may create such liability in a separate subchapter due to the different character of this liability under Polish and German law, and the lack of sufficient jurisprudence in this matter.[367]

Where it concerns different liability regimes in general, in situations where the contract has already been concluded, the buyer – in the event of the improper performance by the seller – may base his claim on general provisions referring to

363 In such situations, the general rules of liability for damage apply (liability *ex delicto*), thus there is a causal link between a potential rider riding the horse and the horse's owner's financial damage. See: Article 415 KC and § 823 (1) BGB.

364 Compare Article 72 § 2 KC, § 311 (2) BGB.

365 Compare: § 311 (2) BGB; G. Hohloch G., *Culpa in contrahendo in private international law*, Problemy Prawne Handlu Zagranicznego 2000, Issue 19/20.

366 With reference to the scope of applicability of Article 72 § 2 KC, see: M. Krajewski [in:] E. Łętowska (ed.), *System Prawa Prywatnego, Vol. V, Prawo zobowiązań – część ogólna*, p. 846.

367 Nevertheless, if there is possibility that such liability arises as a result of certain behavior of the parties to one of the contracts mentioned in this book, this issue is considered respectively here (for example, see: Subchapter IV.3.2 referring to agency contracts). With reference to *culpa in contrahendo* under Polish law, see especially: M. Krajewski [in:] E. Łętowska (ed.), *System Prawa Prywatnego, Vol. V, Prawo zobowiązań – część ogólna*, pp. 835–957; A. Machnicka, *Przedkontraktowe porozumienia – umowa o negocjacje i list intencyjny. Studium prawnoporównawcze*, Warszawa 2007; P. Machnikowski, *Odpowiedzialność przedkontraktowa – jej podstawy, przesłanki i funkcje* [in:] M. Pazdan, W. Popiołek, E. Rott-Pietrzyk, M. Szpunar (eds.), *Europeizacja prawa prywatnego*, Vol. I, Warszawa 2008; M. Gutowski, *Konwersja umowy stanowczej w przedwstępną wobec zmian kodeksu cywilnego*, PiP 2004, Issue 11; R.L. Kwaśnicki, R. Lewandowski, *Culpa in contrahendo w prawie polskim oraz niemieckim*, Prawo Spółek 2002, Issue 5; Gwiazdomorski J., *Umowa przedwstępna w kodeksie zobowiązań*, Czasopismo Prawnicze i Ekonomiczne 1936, Issue 30 (with reference to the previously binding version of the Polish Civil Code).

standards of contractual performance[368] (liability *ex contractu*, contractual liability)[369] or on the warranty regime[370] (the claim could also be based on guarantee of the seller, though this institution is not applicable to animals[371]). Since contractual liability is a liability regime based on the obligor's fault,[372] it is more difficult to file a successful claim under this regime – thus, the obligee has to prove the obligor's faulty behavior. On the other hand, liability arising on warranty (and guarantee as well) provisions is based on the risk factor, which leads to a specific liability for the quality of performance.[373] In order to find the seller liable for a defect in an animal basing the claim on a warranty regime (the same case refers to guarantee, though it is not applicable with reference to animals) it is necessary only to prove that the defect in an animal existed already at the time of purchasing an animal and the buyer was not aware of it. Moreover – in the event that the buyer is a consumer – after the reform of the Polish Civil Code in 2014, the lawmaker confirmed that, where the defect shows within a year (not within six months, like before the reform),[374] there is a presumption that the defect already existed at the time of purchase.[375] Therefore, if an animal turns out to be defective, it is much more likely that the buyer will file the claim based on a warranty regime, which is independent from the seller's fault, knowledge or intent.[376] However, whereas the warranty regime under German law also sets out payment for damages, in order to receive the same outcome under Polish law, the Claimant has to prove the seller's fault in order to file a concurring claim basing

368 Compare: Article 472 KC and § 242 BGB.

369 See: Articles 471 et seq. KC and § 280 et seq. BGB.

370 See: Articles 556 et seq. KC and § 433 et seq.BGB.

371 With reference to guarantee, see also: See: Subchapter III.3.3. ("Applicability of the institution of guarantee as to the quality of the good to animals" of this book. Since the animal's sale market is very unique, due to the inability to foresee future behavior and the health condition of a sold animal, which is dependent on many factors, it would be unreasonable for a seller to issue a guarantee document for a sold animal.

372 See, with reference to Polish law, but which applies to German law as well: K. Zagrobelny [in:] E. Gniewek, P. Machnikowski (ed.), *Kodeks cywilny. Komentarz*, pp. 997–998.

373 See, with reference to Polish law, but which applies to German law as well: J. Jezioro [in:] E. Gniewek, P. Machnikowski (ed.), *Kodeks*, pp. 1172–1173.

374 F. Zoll, *Rękojmia. Odpowiedzialność sprzedawcy w świetle znowelizowanych przepisów kodeksu cywilnego*, pp. 45–46; 71.

375 *Idem*; P. Stec [in:] B. Kaczmarek-Templin, P. Stec, D. Szostek (ed.), *Ustawa o prawach konsumenta. Kodeks cywilny (wyciąg). Komentarz*, Warszawa 2014, p. 410.; J. Janeta [in:] M. Namysłowska, D. Lubasz, *Ustawa o prawach konsumenta*, Warszawa 2015, pp. 435–437. See also the ruling of the ECJ: ECJ, ruling from 11 September 2014, C-112/13 p. 2241.

376 However, under German law, if a defect is deceitfully hidden, the buyer may ask for a price reduction or the termination (*odstąpienie, Rücktritt*) of the contract without giving the seller time to cure. Under Polish law, the seller's awareness of a defect can increase his liability, but does not affect the remedies that the buyer may choose. See: M. Lubelska-Sazanów [in:] M. Jagielska, E. Macierzyńska-Franaszczyk, E. Rott-Pietrzyk, F. Zoll, G. Żmij (eds.), *Limits of Harmonisation and Convergence…*, pp. 196; 200–201.

it on the contractual regime (in this case, a cummulation of provisions covering warranty liability and contractual liability arises).[377]

As we can observe, the fact that an animal is the object of performance in the contractual obligations significantly impacts not only the scope of the seller's liability, but also defines liability regimes on which the buyer may base its claims. Thus, due to a specific nature of animal's defects, most claims are based on warranty regime. Animals, as living creatures, constitute a unique object of a contractual obligation. Therefore, in the market practice, not only are guarantee provisions not applicable to animals, but it is also very difficult to prove the seller's fault in bringing up the animal's defect while basing the claim on the contractual liability regime. This is because defects in living organisms are incomparably more complicated than in the case of regular things. Sciences like medicine and biotechnology are still developing new methods for the prevention, detection and treatment of physical defects in an animal. Therefore, the qualification of defects in reference to animals applies with a higher level of tolerance in reference to its health conditions,[378] whereas details of these considerations are presented in the respective subchapters of this book below.

3.2. The warranty regime with reference to animals as specific objects of obligations

3.2.1. Definition of a defect with reference to animals as specific objects of obligations

Although the referential system of German law contains very similar regulations referring to the warranty[379] for sold things as Polish law, the German Civil Code underlines its significance by mentioning already in the definition of a sale contract the duty to transfer ownership of a good that is free from defects.[380] The Polish legal system, on the other hand, includes all provisions concerning warranty in a separate subchapter.[381] The most significant change, which has

377 With reference to cumulative claims based on a warranty regime and contractual liability under Polish law, see: J. Jezioro [in:] E. Gniewek, P. Machnikowski (eds.), *Kodeks*, p. 1174.

378 BGH, ruling from 18 October 2017 – VIII ZR 32/16.

379 The author uses the term "warranty" in the meaning of liability for defects in a good (not an additional guarantee document, which may, but does not have to be provided by the seller), in German: *Gewährleistung*, in Polish: *rękojmia.*

380 See: § 433 BGB.

381 Polish Civil Code in the version promulgated on 23.4.1964, last version: J L No. 16, item 93 as amended. Since then, it became controversial whether the warranty rights still create a different regime of liability under Polish law, or whether the warranty rights are also based on contractual liability (Article 471 KC). See: F. Zoll, *Rękojmia. Odpowiedzialność sprzedawcy*, Warszawa 2018, pp. 1–7.

been introduced to the Polish and German Civil Codes as a result of the implementation of Directive 1999/44/EC, was the removal of provisions referring to a different legal act applicable to warranty issues with reference to certain types of animals.[382] Since then, the warranty regime concerning all types of animals has been unified in both countries.[383]

The most important issue with reference to warranty issues in contracts aimed at the transfer of property of animals is the definition of **a defect.** Before the reform of 2002[384] in Germany, and 2014[385] in Poland, there was a different legal act[386] wherein the legislator explicitly described what constituted a defect in accordance to horses and some other types of animals. There were several illnesses and behavioral changes that were on the list of an animal's defects, and only the appearance of those listed defects led to the seller's liability.[387] Currently,

382 All references to animals in the Polish Civil Code disappeared with the implementation of the Act on Consumer Rights on 30 May 2014 (J L of 2014, item 827). The amendment of the Polish Civil Code brought many changes affecting the sale of animals, especially concerning the seller's warranty for any defects. The formerly binding Minister's Act on the Seller's Responsibility for Defects in Certain Types of Animals from 7 October 1966 (J L No. 43, item 257 as amended) is no longer applicable, and so, since the end of 2014, all rules concerning defects in things became also applicable to animals. The same situation happened more than ten years before in Germany, where the Emperor's Order concerning major defects and warranty terms for the trade of livestock from 27.3.1899, J L Part III, item 402–3, lost its legal binding force on 1.1.2002.

383 With the reform, the warranty regime in both legal systems became also unified with reference to consumer contracts ("B2C") and other contracts ("B2B" or "C2C"). This does not mean that there are no longer special provisions to be used for consumer contract – it merely means that these provisions are now in the same place (Polish and German Civil Codes – BGB and KC), where provisions are applicable to all types of contracts.

384 Germany repealed special provisions applicable to animals in the implementation of Dir. 1999/44EC already in 2002; see: the German Civil Code in the version promulgated on 2.1.2002, J L of 8.1.2002, part I, No. 2, item 2787, as amended. See also: N.F. Marx Fallstricke in Pferderechtsprozessen seit Abschaffung des Viehgewährleistungsrechts, NJW 2010, No. 39, pp. 2839–2845.

385 The amendment of the Polish Civil Code as a result of the implementation of Directive 2011/83/EU of the European Parliament and of the Council of 25 October 2011 on consumer rights and reimplementation of Dir. 1999/44EC occurred in 2014 with the introduction of the Polish Act on Consumer Rights from 30 May 2014 (J L of 2014, item 827); see: Polish Civil Code in the version promulgated on 23.4.1964, last version: J L No. 16, item 93 as amended.

386 See: the formerly binding Polish Minister's Act on the Seller's Responsibility for Defects in Certain Types of Animals from 7 October 1966 (J L No. 43, item 257 as amended), which lost its legal binding force on 1.1.2015, and the German Emperor's Order concerning major defects and warranty terms for the trade of livestock from 27.3.1899 (J L (Bundesgesetzblatt) Part III, item 402–3), which lost its legal binding force on 1.1.2002.

387 To learn more about the qualification of an animal's defects and about the buyer's warranty rights under the Polish and German law before the reforms, see: M. Sommer, *Der Pferdekauf* and M. Lubelska-Sazanów, *Odpowiedzialność z tytułu rękojmi za wady fizyczne przy sprzedaży zwierząt*, Transformacje Prawa Prywatnego 2015, No. 4, pp. 21–42.

there is no legal definition of a defect in an animal. This means that all defects that may appear with reference to animals are to be treated equally and individually.

Before the Polish Civil Code reform of 2014 (the law was signed on 30 May 2014 and came in force on 25 December 2014), Article 556 KC contained a more detailed description of the character of liability for a defect and a definition of a defect itself, whereas after the reform the definition of a defect was moved to Article 556[1] KC, and Article 556 KC changed its content. After the reform of 2014, Article 556 KC is more concise, confirming only the fact of the seller's liability for a defect by naming it with a fixed term (*rękojmia*). The newly introduced Article 556[1] KC contains a quite comprehensive listing of factual situations that may lead to liability for a defect. Thus, after the 2014 reform, the definition of a defect provides that a good is defective: if the good – and respectively also an animal – does not have the characteristics it was supposed to have, taking into account the purpose of its purchase; if it lacks characteristics about which the seller assured the buyer; if it is not suitable for the purpose that the buyer informed the seller about when concluding the agreement and the seller did not mention this; or if it has been handed to the buyer as incomplete.[388]

In German law, the definition of a defect recognizes three types of defects: if the good – and respectively also an animal – lacks the characteristics that were established by the parties in the contract; if it is not suitable for the purpose for which the buyer wanted to use it according to the contract; or if it is not suitable for ordinary use foreseen for a certain type of good (animal).[389] As we can observe, the definition of defects is different in both legal systems, but leads in most situations to similar legal solutions, namely to recognizing the ordinary characteristics of an animal of a certain type, and the purpose for which it has been purchased, or for which it is usually used as defect free.[390]

The changes introduced to the Polish Civil Code in 2014[391] were, in particular, meant to serve the implementation of Directive 2011/83/EU of the European

388 See: the exact wording of Article 556[1] KC.

389 See: § 434 BGB.

390 See: SN, ruling from 17.2.2005 – I CK 568/04. The Polish Supreme Court decided that, in order to claim the buyer's warranty rights, a good does not necessary have to be defective in regard to its basic use. Namely, if the seller made declarations according to additional characteristics of this good, he should take into account the consequences of this. Therefore, the content and the scope of the seller's declarations have an impact on his contractual risk.

391 The novelisation of the Polish Civil Code occured by the introduction of the Polish Act on Consumer Rigths of 30 May 2014 (J.L. of 2017, item 683). The Polish Act on Consumer Rights contained provisions changing the Polish Civil Code in its Article 44, and repealed the previously binding Polish Act on the Protection of Certain Rights of Consumers and on Liability for Damage Caused by Dangerous Products of 2 March 2000 (J.L. of 2000, Vol. 22,

Parliament and of the Council of 25 October 2011 on consumer rights. However, the Polish legislator decided to use this as an opportunity to reimplement Directive 1999/44/EC of the European Parliament and of the Council of 25 May 1999 on certain aspects of the sale of consumer things and associated guarantees. F. Zoll understands the changes made in the Polish Civil Code in 2014 as the Polish lawmaker implementing the German *Erfüllungstheorie*,[392] i.e. as a legislator's confirmation of the fact that the Polish Civil Code follows the "remedy theory", according to which the seller's liability for a defect constitutes a specific type of liability for the wrongful performance of the obligation.[393]

Since defects in reference to animals always appear in the form of illnesses or behavioral problems,[394] the judicial rulings referring to this problem do not usually concern provisions that are specific for national legal orders, but rather refer to the general problem of interpretation of the term "defect" and its respective applicability to animals. Therefore, most of the German judicial rulings referring to animal defects would lead to the same solution under the Polish letter of the law. Additionally, both of these legal systems follow the "remedy approach", which has been expressed in Directive 2011/83/EU.[395] This means

item 271) and the Polish Act on Special Rules on Consumer Sales and Amending the Civil Code of 27 July 2002 (J.L. of 2002, Vol. 141, item 1176).

392 The discussion about the legal character of the liability for defects has been the subject of vigorous discussion in Germany, where it resulted in the establishment of two main theories: *Erfüllungstheorie* and *Gewährleistungstheorie*. Whereas the representatives of the first theory understand liability for defects as a certain type of contractual liability, the representatives of the second one believe that this establishes a different regime of liability. Thus, according to *Gewährleistungstheorie*, the creditor loses his rights arising in case of the wrongful performance in the moment when he accepts the performance of the obligation. See: F. Zoll, *Rękojmia. Odpowiedzialność sprzedawcy*, Warszawa 2018, pp. 1–7; J. Schaper; R. Kandelhard, *Leistungsstörungen und Gewährleistungsrecht*, NJW 1997, Nr 13, p. 836; H. Westermann [in:] H. Westermann (ed.), *Münchener Kommentar zum BGB, Vol. III*, München 2016, § 433, side number 3, *BeckOnline*.

393 See: F. Zoll, *Rękojmia. Odpowiedzialność sprzedawcy*, pp. 1–7; 101–103. For a different view, see: M. Tulibacka, K. Haładyj [in:] K. Osajda (ed.), *Kodeks cywilny. Komentarz. Tom IIIB*, p. 99, who underline that the warranty regime is separate from the regime of contractual liability and liability *ex delicto*. J. Jezioro stresses also differences in the liability for a defect from other liability regimes, by signaling that it is an objective, independent liability based on the principle of risk, see: J. Jezioro [in:] E. Gniewek, P. Machnikowski (ed.), *Kodeks*, p. 1174. See also: R. Trzaskowski [in:] J. Gudowski (ed.), *Kodeks cywilny. Komentarz. Zobowiązania*, Vol. IV, p. 263.

394 It is very important to mention that there is also the possibility of a legal defect existing. However, the definition and procedure connected with claiming legal defects do not differ at all in the case of animals and in the case of other types of things. Therefore, the problem of legal defects will not be described further in this book.

395 This "remedy approach", expressed in Directive 2011/83/EU, has its roots in the United Nations Convention on Contracts for the International Sale of Goods from 1980 (CISG, Vienna, 11 April 1980, Treaty Document Number 98–9 (1984), UN Document Number A/CONF 97/19, 1489 UNTS 3; http://www.uncitral.org/pdf/english/texts/sales/cisg/V10569

that the types of defects that appear in reference to animals can be described together in accordance to both legal systems.

It is important to appreciate that there are different psychological features to be expected from animals bought for different purposes. For example, it is unreasonable to expect a dog that has been bought for a family with children, or for an elderly person, to have the same features as a guard dog. In the same way, a horse that is being bought for an amateur horse rider would not be expected to have the same characteristics as a horse bought for an experienced rider. In these cases, the arrangements made between the contracting parties in the pre-contractual stage and the purpose for which an animal could be used, expressed either by the buyer or by the seller, are significant. These features trigger several expectations in reference to an animal on the side of the buyer and may indicate the foundations for a future claim.[396]

In some cases, **the qualification of an animal's defect** might be problematic. For example, this may occur in a situation where a horse that is purchased for sport purposes does not achieve the sporting results that were expected by the buyer. In other words, this is a question as to whether a certain feature can be qualified as a defect with reference to a sport horse and not in reference to a recreational horse. In such a situation it is also questionable whether an animal that has been sold as a sport horse is failing to achieve certain sporting results because of its inherent lack of ability, or whether it is an effect of the wrong training programmer introduced by the new rider. Expensive animals sold for sport or breeding purposes are luxury items and their buyers are entitled to have high expectations in reference to their pupils. However, in order to qualify an animal's feature as a defect, the crucial factors are: the purpose of its purchase,

97-CISG-e-book.pdf), whereas its effect can also be observed in UNIDROIT Principles of International Commercial Contracts (UPICC, published by International Institute for the Unification of Private Law, Rome; http://www.unidroit.org/english/principles/contracts/principles2010/integralversionprinciples2010-e.pdf), in the Draft Common Frame of Reference (DCFR, https://ec.europa.eu/info/policies/justice-and-fundamental-rights_en), in the Principles of European Contract Law (PECL, prepared by the Commission on European Contract Law, 2000, http://frontpage.cbs.dk/law/commission_on_european_contract_law/Skabelon/pecl_engelsk.htm) and in the Proposal for a Regulation of the European Parliament and of the Council on a Common European Sales Law (CESL, COM (2011) 635, https://eur-lex.europa.eu/legal-content/EN/TXT/?uri=CELEX%3A52011PC0635).

396 Compare the judgement of the Polish Court of Appeals in Cracow: SA, ruling from 16.4.2013, I ACa 235/13 and the judgement of German Supreme court: BGH, ruling from 9.1.2008 – Az. VIII ZR 210/06. In the German case, the parties established different criteria for the quality of the good by stating that the horse was supposed to be used in a certain way, i. e. as a dressage horse. Even though the subject of a Polish case was not an animal, the court based its judgement on similar foundations. It stated that when considering a defect in a good, the functional criteria should be used before the normative criteria – i. e. the technical use of the good. It means that the value and the usability of a good depend on its normal use, as long as the parties did not establish a different criteria.

pre-contractual information and the provisions of the sale contract.[397] Thus, defects consisting in a horse's schooling deficits[398] constitute the biggest group of defects reported by buyers. In reference to this type of defects, it is important to accurately define the legal character of testing a horse (*Probereiten, jazda testowa*). If the buyer overlooks or wrongly interprets a deficit while testing a horse, his actions are treated as grossly negligent. In other words, in such a case the buyer is considered to be acting without due care, and his unawareness excludes his material defect rights, this qualifies as positive knowledge about a defect. The same effect is achieved if the buyer acknowledges a horse's deficit in schooling, but ignores it, thinking that the deficit can be corrected throughout his riding skills, for example.

In addition, illnesses and physical defects are to be evaluated individually. What happens if it turns out after a certain time that an animal is injured in such way that it does not impact its capability to be ridden for now, but is very likely to impact it in the future?[399] Such cases have to be approached very carefully – for example, a simple diagnosis of decreased vision in a sport horse can lead to different results. The impact that decreased vision has on a particular horse depends not only on the grade of the defect, but also on the behavioral characteristics of this horse. Namely, there are many cases where a horse that is blind in one eye (or even lost an eye completely) was able to achieve very good sporting results.

In Germany, there is a comprehensive jurisprudence concerning several types of animal defects. The substantive defects, i. e. defects that have been found relevant for exercising warranty rights by the German courts are:[400] sarkoids, tumors, summer eczema,[401] periodic inflammation of the eye by horses,[402] heart

397 See, for example, an old, classical, Polish Supreme court case: SN, ruling from 11.8.1978 – III CRN 151/78, where a cow did not give enough milk, which did not constitute a defect under the Polish law before the 2014 reform (it would constitute a defect only if the seller had given assurances about the existence of a certain feature). Under the applicable law, the cow would be qualified as defective if the buyer had merely mentioned the intended purpose of the purchase of the cow while concluding the contract.

398 A comprehensive description of the legal character of horse's deficits in schooling can be found in: S. Brückner, C. Kochhan, *Die klassische Ausbildung des Pferdes – Basis für die langfristige Zufriedenheit des Käufers*, Piaffe 1/2011, pp. 34–47.

399 Compare the court rulings in the cases below (concerning the illnesses: spat, chip and "*kissing-spines*"): LG Münster, ruling from 20.7.2007 – 10 O 240/06; BGH, ruling from 18.12.2002 – VIII ZR 123/02; OLG Celle, ruling from 31.5.2006, 7 U 252/05.

400 B. Oexmann, *Sachmangel Pferdekauf – von der Kasuistik zur Typologie*, last visited: 20.1.2016 from the website: http://www.oexmann.de/pferderecht/2/publikationen/jahr/2007/monat/01; Adolphsen, *Tierkauf* [in:] B. Dauner-Lieb, W. Langen, *BGB Schuldrecht. Nomos Kommentar*, p. 1974.

401 BGH, ruling from 29.3.2006, VIII ZR 173/05; OLG Hamm, ruling from 1.7.2005 – 11 U 43/04.

402 BGH, ruling from 7.12.2005 – VIII ZR 126/05.

defects,[403] chronic bronchitis, overbite, chronic colic, gastritis, defects in masculine and feminine genitalia,[404] "*cushing-syndrome*", paralysis of nerves, several defects of the spinal column,[405] bones and limbs,[406] equine hoof cancer, laminitis, equine navicular disease, soil nailing, lack of some prophylactic vaccinations, as well as vaccinations against rabies and parasites. Whereas some of these cases have been cited in the footnotes, it is not necessary to present the content of all of them comprehensively in this book. Hence, the medical ambiguities of each of these cases are not that important for presenting the legal peculiarities connected with the qualification of an animal's health conditions as a defect. Therefore, only the most famous and – in my opinion – most important German rulings referring to animal defects are explained in the further part of this book. At this point, as a general remark, it is necessary to present the most recent position of the German Supreme court on the qualification of animal conditions as defects. Thus, in 2017 the German Supreme court acknowledged that there is a higher level of tolerance with reference to the health condition of animals.[407] In case VIII ZR 32/16 from 18 October 2017 the Court examined the situation where a horse, after in-depth medical examinations, turned out to suffer pain caused by medical changes in its spine. According to the decision of the Court, this particular factual situation did not qualify as a defect, since horses, as living creatures, may show a broader scope of deviation from the norm with reference to their health condition. One can never predict what will be the final visible reaction of the horse on the changes visible on an x-ray image.[408] On the other hand, it is also possible that there is no visible reason for a horse's pain, but such pain may even lead to the inability to use this horse. This case has a significant importance when defining the existence of defects with reference to animals, and due to its novel character it should always be taken into account when referring to such situations. Therefore, it will also be referred to in the further part of the book.[409]

403 OLG Schleswig, ruling from 13.12.2005 – 3 U 42/05.

404 OLG Hamm, ruling from 27.08.2008 – 11 U 143/05; OLG Düsseldorf, ruling from 2.4.2004 – 14 U 213/03.

405 OLG Celle, ruling from 31.05.2006 – 7 U 252/05.

406 LG Lüneburg, ruling from 16.03.2004 – 4 O 322/03; OLG Hamm, ruling from 15.10.2004 – 19 U 75/04; OLG Koblenz, ruling from 12.09.2005 – 12 U 1047/04; OLG Stuttgart, ruling from 08.02.2006 – 3 U 28/05; OLG Düsseldorf, ruling from 2.4.2004 – 14 U 213/03.; LG Münster, ruling from 10.12.2004 – 10 O 716/03; OLG Frankfurt a.M., ruling from 17.7.2006 – 18 U 96/05.

407 BGH, ruling from 18.10.2017 – VIII ZR 32/16.

408 With reference to the importance of x-ray images for of the horse's seller's liability, see: Subchapter III.3.2.8 of this book ("Peculiarities of the sale of horses – the importance of pre-contractual information, medical examination and x-ray images as basis for the horse's seller's liability").

409 *Idem.*

In Germany such cases have not only been subject to hypothetical speculations, as in the Polish doctrine, but have been the subject of numerous judicial decisions.[410] The comparison between the Polish attitude (solely doctrinal hypothetical speculations) and the German attitude (practical knowledge based on judicial decisions) shows the faultless inexperience of Polish jurisprudence in matters of animal defects. Therefore, it is always advisable to take into account the German jurisprudence and take a lesson from the experience of our neighbor.

Benefiting from the experience of German jurisprudence is a useful method that the Polish courts could – in my opinion – take advantage of. This has probably never be done by the representatives of Polish doctrine referring to the issue of animal defects, since, according to the Polish doctrine, in order to decide whether a certain defect is substantive or not, the buyer's point of view should be taken into account.[411] M. Goettel states that, due to the fact that it is a specific object of obligations, it is reasonable to qualify an animal's defects using subjective criteria. He indicates that certain defects are always to be treated as substantive, irrespective of the subjective purpose of purchasing the animal and calls them disqualifying defects,[412] adding that serious and incurable illnesses or deformations of the legs should always to be treated as such.[413] Whereas I agree with the second part of the previous sentence, the first part of it is a more complicated issue.

Namely, the German attitude to qualifying defects is different. This difference in attitude can be observed, for example, using the example of a German case ruled by the German Supreme Court (BGH) in 22 June 2005, where the claimant claimed damages for a purchased dog that turned out to have extensive problems with bowed legs.[414] This problematic health issue led to an expensive operation exceeding the purchase price of the dog and causing the animal pain that had to be cured by constant visits to a veterinary doctor's. The German Supreme Court in the case at hand admitted that the solution proposed by the seller (the exchange of the dog, or its return against reimbursement of its purchase price) was not possible due to the personal bond that had arisen between the dog and the new owner, and the only warranty right that could be performed was payment of

410 See: the cases cited above.

411 See: W. Katner, [in:] W Katner (ed.), *System Prawa Prywatnego, Vol. IX, Prawo zobowiązań – umowy nienawzwane*, Warszawa 2015, pp. 1118–1130; C. Żuławska, [in:] G. Bieniek and others (ed.), *Komentarz do Kodeksu Cywilnego. Księga trzecia. Zobowiązania*, Vol. II, Warszawa 2011, p. 77.

412 M. Goettel, *Sytuacja zwierzęcia w prawie cywilnym*, Warszawa 2013, p. 137.

413 *Idem*. The same attitude can be found in the German doctrine, see e.g.: H. Westermann, *Zu den Gewährleistungsansprüche des Käufers*, pp. 342–343.

414 See: the case of a bow-legged dog, BGH, ruling from 22.6.2005 – VIII ZR 281/04 (LG Oldenburg).

damages. In the end the German Court did not accept the claim as the dog's breeder was not able to foresee the existence of such defect, his good will to exchange the dog and the lack of the seller's fault or negligence. However, what is most important with reference to this paragraph of the book, the Court evaluated the defect according to objective criteria. Most of the representatives of German doctrine admit that defects should be evaluated according to objective criteria, examining whether a specific feature has been put into the contract, and whether an average animal could have such a defect.[415] The same applies to the understanding of a defect under Polish law after the 2014 reform.[416]

In Germany, where the horse-riding is a much more popular sport, and the average yearly income of German citizens is around four times higher than that of Polish citizens,[417] there are numerous judicial cases referring to warranty issues arising from contracts having animals as their subject, and they usually concern horses. In Poland, on the other hand, it is difficult to find any judicial cases referring to warranty rights arising on the side of an animal acquirer. There are several reasons for this situation. Primarily, Germany is known throughout Europe and the world for its riding techniques, for horse competitions and for the sale of high quality sport horses. Therefore, for many years there was a possibility to develop a rich jurisprudence in that matter. In Poland, the cases that could lead to granting warranty rights on the side of the animal acquirer qualify in most cases into one of two groups. Either they did not concern large amounts of money and were therefore considered as "not worth going to court" or – in rare cases like the sale of expensive Arabian horses – any arising problems were resolved personally between the contracting parties or were the subject of confidential arbitration proceedings, since the courts are known not to have sufficient experience in these matters. Nowadays, although the Polish market has grown with reference to the sale of purebred animals, such cases referring to the most expensive animals on the market, i.e. horses, do not end up in the courts, because most of the purchases are made in Germany, Austria, the Netherlands or

415 This concerns also abnormalities in the physique of an animal, such as deformations of legs or spine structure anomalies, which might become subjects of warranty claims as well; see: H. Westermann, *Zu den Gewährleistungsansprüche des Käufers*, pp. 342–343. See also: BGH, ruling from 7.2.2007 – VIII ZR 266/06, which shows that the court does not apply standards of a perfectly healthy and horse in order to qualify a defect, but a standard of a horse of an average quality. See also: Adolphsen, *Tierkauf* [in:] B. Dauner-Lieb, W. Langen, *BGB Schuldrecht. Nomos Kommentar*, p. 1973. Differently, criticising the judgement of the court: E. G. von Westphalen, *Der BGH auf der Suche nach dem Normpferd*, ZGS 2007, pp. 168–171.

416 See: F. Zoll, *Rękojmia. Odpowiedzialność sprzedawcy*, p. 93.

417 As of 2014 – the data comes from the 2014 survey made for European Commission, see: Eurostat website (last visited 9.012018): http://ec.europa.eu/eurostat/web/labour-market/earnings/database.

other European countries. In these cases, the parties decide on arbitration or file claims in different courts[418] with jurisdiction in the particular case. In the end, contracting parties in Poland are mostly afraid to file claim under Polish law because of the lack of jurisprudence in these matters. This problem might be partially resolved by patterning judicial decisions ruled by Polish judges on German decisions referring to similar facts of a particular case. Hence, a "side mission" of this book is to examine whether the German legal solutions, and the legal reasoning on which they are based, may constitute inspiration for the Polish jurisprudence. As far as cases referring to animal law are concerned, given that the Polish jurisprudence has less experience than its German neighbor, the answer with reference to the qualification of defects is positive. Thus, I take the view that the solutions presented by the Polish doctrine should rather be based - at least at some point, due to the many similarities between these two legal systems[419] - on the practical experience of German courts. It seems to be a more inspiring solution than being based on hypothetical speculation leading to other results.

3.2.2. General overview of the buyer's warranty rights with reference to contracts aimed at the transfer of property of an animal

With reference to liability for defective things, the main conceptual difference between Polish and German law concerns the relationship between the general rules on non-performance and the specific rules.[420] Thus, the Polish Civil Code does not have a rule like § 437 BGB, linking liability for defective things with the general rules on breaches of obligation. What is more, the Polish Civil Code provides an autonomous system of remedies linked to the liability for defective things.[421] Although these are mostly the same remedies as those provided in the

418 According to Article 4 of Rome I Regulation (Regulation (EC) No. 593/2008 of the European Parliament and of the Council of 17 June 2008 on the law applicable to contractual obligations, OJ 177, 4. 7. 2008, pp. 6–16;), a contract for the sale of things is governed by the law of the country where the seller has his habitual residence.

419 E. Rott-Pietrzyk, F. Zoll [in:] M. Jagielska, E. Macierzyńska-Franaszczyk, E. Rott-Pietrzyk, F. Zoll, G. Żmij (eds.), *Limits of Harmonisation and Convergence...*, p. 44; H. Honsell, *Die rhetorischen Wurzeln der juristischen Auslegung*, ZfPW 2016, p. 125. Compare: the considerations included in Subchapter IV.3.2. ("Agency contracts having an animal as their object".

420 See: E. Rott-Pietrzyk, F. Zoll [in:] M. Jagielska, E. Macierzyńska-Franaszczyk, E. Rott-Pietrzyk, F. Zoll, G. Żmij (eds.), *Limits of Harmonisation and Convergence...*, p. 59.

421 J. Jezioro [in:] E. Gniewek, P. Machnikowski (ed.), *Kodeks*, pp. 1158–1159; M. Tulibacka, K. Haładyj [in:] K. Osajda (ed.), *Kodeks*, pp. 128–133; E. Habryn - Chojnacka [in:] M. Gutowski (ed.), *Kodeks*, p. 427 and 435.

German Civil Code (the right to repair and replacement, termination[422] and price reduction),[423] the right to damages is regulated differently.[424] Namely, damages are provided as a genuine remedy in case of a defective performance.[425] Thus, the right to full damages is regulated by reference to the general system of non-performance.[426] This is because the Polish Civil Code does not have a rule like § 437 BGB, linking liability with general rules on breaches of obligation.[427]

According to the Polish Civil Code, the buyer has four **remedies in the event that the purchased animal turns out to be defective:**[428] replacement of the "defective" animal with a different animal that is free from defects; the removal of the defect by the seller (if the defect is curable, which might be questionable in the case of animals); a price reduction and the termination of the contract (*odstąpienie, das Rücktritt*).[429] The German Civil Code provides the buyer with similar remedies, though the content of § 437 BGB also sets out the buyer's right to demand damages or the reimbursement of futile expenditure.[430] This does not mean that the Polish law does not recognize this remedy, but under Polish law the Buyer's right to claim damages in addition to other warranty remedies is structured differently. According to Article 566 KC, the buyer may claim damages additionally to his demand of a price reduction and the termination of the contract. However, he may also claim damages while basing this claim on a regime other than the warranty regime (especially if the warranty rights have already expired), namely the contractual liability of the seller.[431] In the end, the

422 With reference to the term "termination" used in referene to the warranty regime, it should be always identified with the definitione of *odstąpienie, das Rücktritt* in the Polish and German law.

423 See: I. Saenger [in:] R. Schulze, H. Dörner, I. Ebert, T. Hoeren, R. Kemper, I. Saenger, K. Schreiber, H. Schulte-Nölke, A. Staudinger (eds.), *Bürgerliches Gesetzbuch. Handkommentar*, Baden-Baden 2016, *Bürgerliches Gesetzbuch. Handkommentar*, BGB § 437 Side numbers 1–30, *BeckOnline (last visited: 12.3.2018).*

424 Compare: E. Rott-Pietrzyk, F. Zoll [in:] M. Jagielska, E. Macierzyńska-Franaszczyk, E. Rott-Pietrzyk, F. Zoll, G. Żmij (eds.), *Limits of Harmonisation and Convergence…*, p. 29.

425 Article 566 KC.

426 Article 566 last sentence and Article 574 last sentence KC.

427 Markesinis, Unberath, Johnston, The German Law of Contract – A comparative Treatise, Oxford 2006, p. 379.

428 Compare: Article 560 KC and § 437 BGB.

429 As already mentioned above, with reference to the term "termination" used in referene to the warranty regime, it should be always identified with the definition of *odstąpienie, das Rücktritt* in the Polish and German law.

430 With reference to the buyer's right to damages under German law, see: S. Hofer, *Der Schadenersatzanspruch des Käufers bei Sachmängeln – Grundsätze, Wertungen und Konstruktionen*, Archiv für die civilistische Praxis (ACP) 2001, Issue 2/201, pp. 275–292. Compare: U. Huber, *statt der Leistung*, Archiv für die civilistische Praxis (ACP) 2010, Issue 3–4/210, pp. 320–353.

431 The German legislator has used exactly the same solution in § 437 BGB, where he sends the reader back to the provisions of contractual liability regime.

buyer has similar possibilities to claim damages under both legal systems.[432] Thus, under Polish law the buyer has the rights expressed in Article 560 KC (replacement of the "defective" animal with a different animal that is free from defects; the removal of the defect by the seller (if the defect is curable, which might be questionable in the case of animals); a price reduction and the termination of the contract). He may also claim damages based on Article 566 § 1 KC and Article 574 KC (whereas in the last case the claim is not based on warranty rights, but this right is based on general provisions referring to the contractual obligation – Article 574 KC).[433] This confirms, in my opinion, that the warranty regime has in fact melted (in a certain extent) with the regime of contractual liability, as F. Zoll acknowledges (see also, more comprehensively, below).[434]

The first two remedies are to be used in both legal systems as a priority, as according to § 1 of Article 560 KC, the buyer may not terminate the contract (in the meaning of *odstąpienie/das Rücktritt*) if the seller immediately replaces the defective thing with a good free from defects, or if he immediately removes the defects in the good. Under Polish law, the right to terminate a contract is exercised by the buyer's statement of intent.[435] The buyer does not have to give any period of time to enable the seller to cure the defect. It is the seller's right to cure the defect in order to avoid the termination of the contract.[436] What is more, he has to do it immediately in order to keep the contract in motion. Under German

432 With reference to the contractual and warranty regime in Polish law: see below. Most of the Polish doctrine is of the opinion that the warranty regime is based on the principle of risk. See: M. Podrecka, *Rękojmia za wady prawne rzeczy sprzedanej*, p. 24; A. Brzozowski [in:] K. Pietrzykowski (ed.), *Kodeks cywilny. Komentarz. Article 450–1088. Vol II*, Warszawa 2013, p. 244. However, there are also different opinions to be found, see e. g.: W. Katner, [in:] J. Rajski (ed.), *System Prawa Prywatnego, Vol. VII, Prawo zobowiązań – część szczegółowa*, Warszawa 2011, p. 134, who states that the fact that the buyer's warranty rights are independent from the seller's knowledge and fault is not sufficient to state that the warranty regime is based on the principle of risk. He agrees that it is a liability based on objective criteria, though this does not mean that the seller undertakes the risk of defects appearing, but merely acknowledges his liability for their appearance.

433 See: F. Zoll, *Rękojmia. Odpowiedzialność sprzedawcy*, pp. 79–80.

434 See: Thus, according to F. Zoll, Articles 566 § 1 and 574 KC *in fine* refer to the provision covering the contractual liability in general, i. e. to Article 471 KC. Comprehensively with reference to this issue: F. Zoll, *Rękojmia. Odpowiedzialność sprzedawcy*, pp. 173–176.

435 K. Haładyj, M. Tulibacka [in:] K. Osajda (ed.), *Kodeks cywilny. Komentarz. Tom IIIB*, pp. 125–135; A. Brzozowski [in:] K. Pietrzykowski (ed.), *Kodeks cywilny. Komentarz*, Warszawa 2015, pp. 315–318; J. Jezioro, [in:] E. Gniewek, P. Machnikowski (eds.), *Kodeks cywilny. Komentarz*, Warszawa 2014, pp. 1195–1203; J. Antoniuk [in:] B. Kaczmarek-Templin, P. Stec, D. Szostek (ed.), *Ustawa o prawach konsumenta. Kodeks cywilny (wyciąg). Komentarz*, pp. 425–433.

436 Before the 1996 amendment of the Polish Civil Code, the buyer was not entitled to terminate the contract if the seller has merely declared that he will cure the defect, see: the Polish Civil Code in the version of 1996.

law, curing a defect is also a remedy to be used as a priority, although its legal construction is slightly different.[437] Namely, the seller has a limited number of attempts to repair the good or to exchange it for a new one.[438] Thus, under the German legal system, a repair is deemed to have failed after a second unsuccessful attempt.[439] This is a clear difference in comparison to the Polish Civil Code, where the buyer is entitled to terminate the contract if the good has already been replaced or repaired[440] – so, according to the Polish legal system, a repair is deemed to have failed after a first unsuccessful attempt. Afterwards, the buyer may terminate a contract without waiting for the seller to repair or exchange the good (even though the Polish Civil Code provides that he has to do it immediately, according to the Polish legal system).[441]

Whereas the Polish and the German Civil Codes provide the buyer with the same four remedies, the German Civil Code also recognizes the option of the buyer's right to demand damages or the reimbursement of futile expenditure, as expressed in § 437 BGB.[442] E. Rott-Pietrzyk and F. Zoll underline that this does not mean that Polish law does not recognize this remedy, but that the buyer's right to claim damages in addition to other warranty remedies is structured differently.[443] Namely, according to Article 566 KC, the buyer may claim damages in addition to a demand for a price reduction and the termination of the contract. However, he can also claim damages basing this claim on a regime other than the warranty regime, namely the contractual liability of the seller, which leads to the same outcome as in case of basing a claim on § 437 BGB. Thus, the buyer has similar possibilities to claim damages under both legal systems, and can claim damages basing this claim on a regime other than the warranty regime

437 See § 440 BGB.

438 C. Höpfner [in:] B. Gsell, W. Krüger, S. Lorenz, J. Mayer (ed.), *Beck-online Grosskommentar BGB*, München 2015, § 440, side numbers 17–23.

439 According to § 440 sentence 2 BGB: "A repair is deemed to have failed after the second unsuccessful attempt, unless in particular the nature of the thing or of the defect or the other circumstances lead to a different conclusion."

440 Compare: Article 560 KC.

441 K. Haładyj, M. Tulibacka [in:] K. Osajda (ed.), *Kodeks cywilny. Komentarz. Tom IIIB*, pp. 125–135; A. Brzozowski [in:] K. Pietrzykowski (ed.), *Kodeks cywilny. Komentarz*, Warszawa 2015, pp. 315–318; J. Jezioro, [in:] E. Gniewek, P. Machnikowski (eds.), Kodeks cywilny. Komentarz, Warszawa 2017, pp. 1195–1203; J. Antoniuk [in:] B. Kaczmarek-Templin, P. Stec, D. Szostek (ed.), *Ustawa o prawach konsumenta. Kodeks cywilny (wyciąg). Komentarz*, pp. 425–433.

442 See: S. Hofer, *Der Schadenersatzanspruch des Käufers bei Sachmängeln – Grundsätze, Wertungen und Konstruktionen*, Archiv für die civilistische Praxis (ACP) 2001, Issue 2/201, pp. 275–292. Compare: U. Huber, *statt der Leistung*, Archiv für die civilistische Praxis (ACP) 2010, Issue 3–4/210, pp. 320–353.

443 E. Rott-Pietrzyk, F. Zoll [in:] M. Jagielska, E. Macierzyńska-Franaszczyk, E. Rott-Pietrzyk, F. Zoll, G. Żmij (eds.), *Limits of Harmonisation and Convergence...*, p. 29.

in the event that the warranty rights have already expired.[444] Nevertheless, the structure of these claims under Polish law again raises concerns as to whether the warranty regime should still be considered as a separate liability regime, different to contractual liability.[445]

3.2.3. The applicability of seller's right to cure animals

The buyer's right to demand the removal of a defect is rarely used with reference to animals. Thus, a defect that is caused by an illness or by an animal's inability to be used for a certain purpose (e.g. a horse bought for a rider to take part in jumping competitions with a certain height of obstacles;[446] a cow bought in order to bring milk;[447] a dog bought for breeding purposes[448]) can never be removed with any certainty.[449] The German judiciary has proven this in several cases, e.g. in the previously mentioned case, where the claimant claimed damages for a purchased dog that turned out to have extensive problems with bowed legs.[450] This problematic health issue led to an expensive operation exceeding the purchase price of the dog and caused the animal pain, which had to be cured by frequent visits to a vet. The German Supreme Court, in the mentioned case, admitted that, in view of the fact that the medical operation did not succeed in solving the dog's medical defect and the solution proposed by the seller (exchanging the dog or reimbursing the purchase price in return for the dog) was not possible due to the personal bond that had arisen between the dog and the

444 With reference to the contractual and warranty regime in Polish law, see below. Most of the Polish doctrine is of the opinion that the warranty regime is based on the principle of risk. Otherwise, in order to constitute liability based on *culpa in contrahedndo*, the party must be at fault for the improper performance of the contractual obligation. See: M. Podrecka, *Rękojmia za wady prawne rzeczy sprzedanej*, p. 24; A. Brzozowski [in:] K. Pietrzykowski (ed.), Kodeks cywilny. Komentarz. Article 450–1088. Vol II, Warszawa 2013, p. 244. However, there are also different opinions to be found, see: W. Katner, [in:] J. Rajski (ed.), *System Prawa Prywatnego, Vol. VII*, p. 134, who claims that the mere fact that the buyer's warranty rights are independent from the seller's knowledge and fault is not sufficient in order to state that the warranty regime is based on the principle of risk. He agrees that it is liability based on objective criteria, though this does not mean that the seller takes on the risk of defects appearing, but merely acknowledges his liability for their appearance.

445 See: F. Zoll, *Rękojmia. Odpowiedzialność sprzedawcy*, pp. 1–7; 101–103. For a different view, see: M. Tulibacka, K. Haładyj [in:] K. Osajda (ed.), *Kodeks cywilny. Komentarz. Tom IIIB*, p. 99, who underlines that the warranty regime is separate from the regime of contractual liability and liability *ex delicto*.

446 OLG Düsseldorf, ruling from 16.04.2002 – 21 U 140/01.

447 SN, ruling from 11.8.1978 – III CRN 151/78.

448 BGH, ruling from 22.6.2005 – VIII ZR 281/04 (LG Oldenburg).

449 This has also been confirmed by the German Supreme court in the case: BGH, ruling from 22.6.2005 – VIII ZR 281/04 (LG Oldenburg).

450 See: the case of the bow-legged dog, BGH, ruling from 22.6.2005 – VIII ZR 281/04 (LG Oldenburg).

new owner, the only warranty right that could be performed was the payment of damages. The Court confirmed in its statement that medical defects in animals can almost never be removed with any certainty. This was also the outcome, for example, in the German Supreme court in the case: BGH, ruling from 9 January 2008 – Az. VIII ZR 210/06, which concerned a dressage horse with a defect caused by an unsuccessful castration. The buyer based the claim on the improper belief that the horse was a gelding, which is easier and better to use in dressage, and so demanded a 50 % reduction in price. The Court admitted the buyer's right in this case, since the removal of the defect was doubtful and risky to the horse's health, therefore it was justified that the seller was refused the opportunity to cure by allowing for medical interference. Medical operations are always connected with a certain risk to the animal's health. Since the German court in the case at hand stated that "the horse did not have the characteristics established between the parties" – it used the same wording that is used in the Polish Civil Code.[451] What is more, under Polish law[452] the buyer is also not entitled to terminate the contract if the seller cures the defect by exchanging the defective good for a new one, or by removing the defect. Whereas there is only a slight difference with reference to German law (consisting in the amount of possible attempts of the seller to cure the defect),[453] there is no reason why the Polish court would insist on curing the defect in such case. Therefore, the outcome in judicial reasonings concerning these matters should be the same under Polish law, and medical defects in animals under Polish law should also in most cases be qualified as incurable with a 100 % certainty.[454]

Nonetheless, there are situations when **the removal of a defect is possible,** also with reference to animals – e.g. when the illness of an animal or its bad condition can easily be cured by a short and simple intervention from a veterinary doctor, or by introducing a certain diet.[455] This is also the case under German law, where the buyer has to determine a specified period of time for the

451 According to Article 556[1] KC, one of the ways in which a product might be found defective is "*the lack of characteristics about which the seller assured the buyer.*"

452 Article 560 § 1 KC.

453 However, in German law, the seller has two attempts to cure the defect. According to § 440 sentence 2 BGB: "A repair is deemed to have failed after the second unsuccessful attempt, unless in particular the nature of the thing or of the defect or the other circumstances lead to a different conclusion."

454 Compare: a description of the same German case with more comprehensive references to Polish law: M. Lubelska-Sazanów [in:] M. Jagielska, E. Macierzyńska-Franaszczyk, E. Rott-Pietrzyk, F. Zoll, G. Żmij (eds.), *Limits of Harmonisation and Convergence…*, pp. 44–51.

455 Compare: H. Westermann: H. Westermann, *Zu den Gewährleistungsansprüche des Käufers*, pp. 342–348.

seller to cure the defect.[456] Firstly, in the event that the seller does not react during the term given by the buyer, he may cure the defect himself and demand damages from the seller.[457] Under Polish law after the reform of 2014, the seller has to react promptly (where "promptly" is to be understood as "shortly and without delay, but not immediately")[458] and cure the defect, if he wants to prevent the buyer from terminating the contract.[459]

A problem that may appear in connection with the seller's attempt to cure a defect is the place of its performance. As already mentioned, the transportation of animals is always connected with a certain risk, which turns out to be even bigger if an animal is sick. As the provisions applicable to warranty claims do not provide any additional regulation concerning the place where the defect is to be removed, the provisions concerning the general rules for contractual relationships, i.e. § 269 BGB and Article 454 KC apply. So, as long as this issue is not defined otherwise in the parties' agreement, the nature of the obligation will determine the place. Therefore, it is much more effective to carry out the medical treatment on the animal in the location of the buyer, where it does not necessarily have to be his residence, but could also be the stable where the horse is being kept, or a veterinary clinic that is one of the closest to the place, where the animal is being kept by the owner. This solution is also more economical for the seller.[460] What is more, if the place of performance is defined in the contract as the place of the seller, but the facts of the case lead to the conclusion that it will be more reasonable not to transport an animal to the seller's place, the seller is obliged to return the costs of transportation to the veterinary doctor to the buyer.[461] In the end, it is important to bear in mind that hiring a veterinary doctor is still the duty of the seller, and he has to order the medical visit, regardless of the place where the treatment is to be performed.

The seller's right to cure is usually treated more as a theoretical option with reference to obligations that concern animals specified as to its identity.[462] Thus, the removal of a defect is rarely possible and the owner's emotional bond with an

456 See: F. Faust [in:] H. Bamberger, H. Roth (ed.), *Beck-online Grosskommentar BGB*, München 2015, § 437, side number 17–21; C. Berger [in:] R. Stürner (ed.), *Jauernig, Kommentar zum BGB*, München 2015, § 437, side number 4.

457 However, there are some exceptions, like emergency cases, where the intervention of a veterinarian is needed immediately. See more in the text below.

458 See: Polish Supreme Court: SN, ruling from 10.1.2002 – II CKN 564/99.

459 K. Haładyj, M. Tulibacka [in:] K. Osajda (ed.), *Kodeks cywilny. Komentarz. Tom IIIB*, pp. 125–135; J. Jezioro [in:] E. Gniewek, P. Machnikowski (ed.), *Kodeks cywilny. Komentarz*, Warszawa 2014, pp. 1203–1204; J. Rajski [in:] J. Rajski (ed.), *System Prawa Prywatnego. Volume VII. Prawo zobowiązań-część szczegółowa*, Warszawa 2011, pp. 140–142.

460 See also: J. Wertenbruch, *Die Besonderheiten…*, pp. 2065–2066.

461 So also stated the German Supreme court: BGH, ruling from 13.4.2011 – VIII ZR 220/10.

462 See: M. Goettel, *Sytuacja zwierzęcia w prawie cywilnym*, p. 143; J. Wertenbruch, *Die Besonderheiten…*, p. 2065.

animal usually creates an obstacle for its exchange for a different animal of the same kind as well. Although in the past German courts accepted the exchange of the good for a different one as a remedy used also in reference to animals specified as to its identity,[463] the exchange can only be taken into account if it occurs in accordance with the parties' contractual agreement (which does not happen very often).[464] Interestingly, the German courts consider the possibility of exchanging the animal or not without reference to the fact whether the seller is in possession of animals for exchange at the moment. Thus, in a case[465] concerning two cart-horses that were "tried" with a positive effect before the purchase, but turned out to be unsuitable to draw a cart a few days after the conclusion of the contract, the German court of second instance in Koblenz admitted the possibility of exchanging the animals. The buyer alleged that one of the horses had been traumatized due to an accident that occurred at the seller's place between the time he tried the horse and when he collected the horses. Although the Court did not state whether the horse's condition constituted a defect, and whether the horses were actually traumatized due to the seller's negligence, it confirmed that the seller may try to cure the defect also by exchanging the horses. The Court undoubtedly took into account the short time (two days) that passed before the buyer learned about the horses' condition, and therefore took into account the exchange of horses due to the likely insufficient amount of time to create a bond between the animals and their new owner.

On the other hand, in a case ruled by the Court OLG Frankfurt a. M.[466] the Court denied that the exchange of the horse was possible. In that case, the buyer bought a horse for his daughter with an additional right to exchange this horse for a different one within a year. After less than a month, the purchased horse turned out to have medical defects (osteophytes in the joints), and therefore the buyer returned it without any objection from the seller. Nevertheless, although the buyer tried three different horses, none of them was suitable for his daughter. In addition, none of them were qualified by the seller as being equal to the horse

463 See: the repeatedly mentioned case of a bow-legged dog, where the seller offered an exchange of a defective dog, but the Court – although it dismissed the claim – confirmed that this remedy should not be taken into account against the will of the buyer, due to its bond with the dog: BGH, ruling from 22.06. 2005 – VIII ZR 281/04 (LG Oldenburg). The German Supreme court has also confirmed the possibility to exchange a good specified as to its identity many different times, see (although with reference to used cars): BGH, ruling from 7.6.2006 – VIII ZR 209/05; BGH, ruling from 29.11.2006 – VIII ZR 92/06.

464 Compare two rulings of the German courts described below, where the court has admitted (OLG Koblenz, ruling from 23.4.2009 – 5 U 1124/08) and denied (OLG Frankfurt a. M., ruling from 1.2.2011 – 16 U 119/10) the applicability of the remedy of an exchange for a different good with reference to animals.

465 OLG Koblenz, ruling from 23.4.2009 – 5 U 1124/08.

466 OLG Frankfurt a. M., ruling from 1.2.2011 – 16 U 119/10.

originally purchased (i. e. the purchase price was not the same at the price of the returned horse). The Court acknowledged that the purchase of the first horse was not accidental and took place after several rides in order for the buyer's daughter to try the horse, where the buyer had to undertake three journeys of 70 km from his home. Therefore, although the contract set out the possibility to exchange the horse, and although there were several horses proposed by the seller for exchange, the Court admitted that the exchange was not possible for the same price.

The outcome of the two cases described above under Polish law could not be different if the facts of the case were the same. Thus, the seller's remedy to cure the defect due to the exchange of an animal is possible only if this was already agreed in advance between the parties, and the bond allows for this, or there is insufficient time to create a strong bond.[467] Although this is not clear in the provisions of the Polish Civil Code, it is a general logical schema that could be applied by the Polish courts in cases similar to those ruled by German courts and described in this paragraph, regardless of differences between these legal systems.

The exchange of an animal is only possible if the seller is able to provide a different animal of the same kind (and value[468]) and if the parties have agreed on this matter in advance. The sale of animals is a special case, as not only objective factors, such as age, size and color play a role, but – especially – emotions and an overall impression, and so the possibility to exchange an animal will very rarely correspond with the will of the parties.[469]

On the other hand, this remedy could constitute a more admissible option for the buyer in reference to obligations in kind.[470] Thus, qualifying an obligation with an animal as its object as an obligation in kind is usually connected with the purchase of an animal whose purpose is limited to a certain period of time, e. g. poultry or another group of animals purchased for slaughter.[471] However, even in this situation an exchange of an animal for a different one may not always be effective. The exchange of a sick animal may not rule out the danger connected with infecting other animals in the herd. Nevertheless, this remedy could be used with reference to small mammals like rodents, which are purchased in pet stores.[472]

467 As it was the case in the case described above: OLG Koblenz, ruling from 23.4.2009 – 5 U 1124/08.
468 Compare: the case described above: LG Frankfurt a. M., ruling from 1.2.2011 – 16 U 119/10.
469 See also: J. Wertenbruch, *Die Besonderheiten…*, pp. 2065–2066.
470 *Idem*, p. 2066.
471 See also: M. Sommer, *Der Pferdekauf*, pp. 56–57.
472 M. Lubelska-Sazanów, *Odpowiedzialność z tytułu rękojmi za wady fizyczne przy sprzedaży zwierząt*, Transformacje Prawa Prywatnego 2015, No. 4, pp. 21–42.

With reference to animals – as living creatures – special circumstances, like the symptoms of an illness or suspicious behavior may always appear. Sometimes the condition of an animal raises doubts as to whether it is possible to wait for the seller to accept a cure; sometimes this is also the last thing on the buyer's mind when confronting a case of emergency. Such cases are subject to medical examination immediately, which is also in accordance with animal protection laws.[473] Therefore, in these situations the buyer is entitled to demand reimbursement from the seller.[474] Such cases are exceptions, allowing an immediate assertion of a claim for damages justified by special circumstances.[475] The same solution (although the issue has not been undertaken by the Polish jurisprudence or doctrine) is correct also under Polish law. However – under Polish law – the buyer does not need to set a term in which to cure the defect, as it is in the seller's interest to cure the defect immediately if he wants to avoid the situation, where the buyer uses a different remedy.[476] Therefore there is no comprehensive case law in that matter.

3.2.4. Applicability of warranty rights to the continuous medical treatments of animals

The procedure connected with warranty rights raises many further questions. One of them is the question of how to handle a case when **the removal of a defect in a good turns out to be a multistage process**, e. g. the continued treatment of a dog. Is the buyer obliged to inform the seller about this fact and expect him to remove a defect after he undertakes only the necessary measures (the emergency measures)? In other words, if the first stage of the medical treatment is undertaken by the buyer, does the further cure have to be continued by the seller?[477]

In a German case[478] concerning the situation of a serious threat to a dog's health, the German Supreme court justified the buyer undertaking the first stage of treatment. In the case at hand, the buyer purchased a terrier whelp from the seller, which suffered from a life-threatening kind of diarrhea shortly after the purchase. The sickness was cured at the buyer's veterinary doctor and resulted in expenses exceeding the purchase price of the dog. The Court stated that changing the veterinary doctor after undertaking the first stage of treatment,

473 See also: J. Wertenbruch, *Die Besonderheiten…*, p. 2068.
474 *Idem*, p. 2068.
475 See: § 281 (1) BGB.
476 See: Article 560 KC.
477 With reference to this problem, see: M. Lubelska-Sazanów [in:] M. Jagielska, E. Macierzyńska-Franaszczyk, E. Rott-Pietrzyk, F. Zoll, G. Żmij (eds.), *Limits of Harmonisation and Convergence…*, pp. 223–227.
478 BGH, ruling from 22.6.2005 – VIII ZR 1/05 (LG Bielefeld).

and then starting the treatment again somewhere else (where the seller would take the dog while performing his right to cure), would be unreasonable. Therefore, continuing the dog's medical treatment at the veterinary doctor chosen by the buyer was also justified by the court. Thus, a change would probably increase the costs of the treatment, which confirms that the costs of the treatment were reasonable and accurate. It is also questionable whether the buyer may demand a price reduction or terminate the contract without giving the Seller enough time to cure the defect (as it occurred in the German case at hand). According to § 440 BGB, the buyer has the possibility to ask for a price reduction or to terminate the contract without setting the seller a time to attempt a cure.[479] Such a situation occurs when the seller explicitly rejects the opportunity to cure.[480] The Buyer may also ask for a price reduction or terminate the contract without setting the Seller a time in which to attempt a cure, if the defect has been deceitfully hidden. There is no justification for such behavior, and therefore no reason to give the seller a "second chance".[481] This problem does not appear under Polish law,[482] as there is no need to set a certain period of time for the seller to cure the defect. Thus, according to Article 560 KC, the buyer is not entitled to terminate the contract only if the seller immediately cures the defect by exchanging the defective good for a new one or by removing the defect. However, the cure of the defect cannot constitute a significant impediment for the buyer.[483] What is more, according to the Polish legal system – as already mentioned several times in this Dissertation[484] – a repair is deemed to have failed after the first unsuccessful attempt. Afterwards, the buyer may terminate the contract without waiting for the seller to repair or exchange the good (although he has to do it immediately under Polish law). However, the seller is still able to counteract the buyer's choice of a price reduction or the termination of the

479 See also the decision of the German Supreme court: BGH, ruling from 22.6.2005 – VIII ZR 1/05 (LG Bielefeld).

480 See the exact wording of § 440 BGB, according to which it is not necessary to give the Seller time to cure the defect if the seller has refused to carry out both kinds of cure, or if the kind of cure that the buyer is entitled to receive has failed or cannot reasonably be expected of him.

481 So also decided the German Supreme court in the case: BGH, ruling from 9.1.2008 – Az. VIII ZR 210/06, which concerns the purchase of a horse named Diokletian. When the buyer realised that Diokletian had a defect caused by an unsuccessful castration, he demanded a 50 % reduction in price. The buyer based the claim on the wrongful belief that the horse was a gelding, which is easier and better to use in dressage. Unfortunately, the horse behaved more like a stallion, which made him less useful at this sport. What is more, the seller knew about the horse's behaviour in advance, therefore the seller argued that he has fraudulently kept the information secret.

482 See; Article 560 KC.

483 J. Jezioro [in:] E. Gniewek, P. Machnikowski (ed.), *Kodeks cywilny*, pp. 1195–1196.

484 See: Subchapter III.3.2.2. of this book.

contract. What is more, the seller can also decide how he will counteract - he can replace the defective goods or repair them. In accordance with the Polish sales law, if the buyer is a consumer, he has even more possibilities. Thus, according to the second paragraph of Article 560 KC, he may also demand that the defective good be exchanged instead of accepting its repair proposed by the seller (unless this would be impossible for the seller or would cause him unreasonable costs). Since, with reference to waiting for the seller to cure the defect, the provisions of the Polish Civil Code seem to be even more favorable to the buyer than the ones included in the German Civil Code, the outcome of the German case referring to a whelp suffering from diarrhea would probably be similar under Polish law. Nevertheless, since - at the time of writing this book - most of the accessible judgements concerning Article 560 KC concern the previously applicable law,[485] there are no similar judiciary rulings to compare.[486]

3.2.5. Reduction in price and termination of contract with reference to contracts aimed at the transfer of property of an animal

The reduction of price and termination of the contract are secondary remedies, though their applicability is much more suitable for the sale of animals. When assessing which of these two remedies is more suitable in a certain case, the intent of the parties and type of defect are to be taken into account.[487] According to the Polish Supreme court,[488] the buyer may not demand a price reduction[489] if

485 The amendment of the Polish Civil Code as a result of implementing Directive 2011/83/EU of the European Parliament and of the Council of 25 October 2011 on consumer rights and the reimplementation of Dir. 1999/44EC occurred on 25.12.2014 with introduction of Polish Act on Consumer Rights from 30 May 2014 (J L of 2014, item 827); see: Polish Civil Code in the version promulgated on 23.4.1964, last version: J L No. 16, item 93 as amended.

486 Compare: M. Lubelska-Sazanów, *Identification of the case-problem (BGH verdict of 22.06.2005 - VIII ZR 1/05)and German law* [in:] M. Jagielska, E. Macierzyńska-Franaszczyk, E. Rott-Pietrzyk, F. Zoll, G. Żmij (eds.), *Limits of Harmonisation and Convergence…*, p. 227.

487 However, there are also different opinions. See: M. Goettel, *Sytuacja zwierzęcia w prawie cywilnym*, p. 145, who represents the opinion that the applicability of the remedy consisting in reduction of price of an animal is difficult, since an estimation of the diminished value is impossible with reference to animals.

488 Resolution of the Polish Supreme Court (*Uchwała Sądu Najwyższego*) of 21.3.1977 - III CZP 11/77, OSNCP 1977, No. 8, item 132, Legalis.

489 According to the legal status applicable until 2015, and according to the Resolution of the Polish Supreme Court (*Uchwała Sądu Najwyższego*) of 21.3.1977 - III CZP 11/77, OSNCP 1977 (No. 8, item 132, Legalis), the termination of a contract was considered as an unfettered right (*Gestaltungsrecht*), whereas three other warranty rights of the buyer were considered to have the legal character of claims. According to part of the doctrine, after the amendment of the Polish Civil Code in 2015, this qualification is still valid, see: J. Widło, *Rękojmia za wady fizyczne w świetle nowelizacji Kodeksu cywilnego*, Monitor Prawniczy 4/2015, pp 177–186. However, most of the representatives of the Polish doctrine qualify a

he is not able to show the proportional difference between the price of a defective good and a good of the same kind that is free from defects. Although there were previously no doubts that this is not possible with reference to animals,[490] now the situation has changed. The growing interest in the market of purebred animals and sport horses has caused its broad accessibility and enabled an estimation of their prices. Additionally, if a horse is being purchased for sport purposes, it is not difficult to estimate its price on the market according to the horse's age, experience and prognosis for future progress. Therefore, excluding the applicability of this remedy will only be reasonable in the event that the defect permanently prevents the expected use of the animal. Nevertheless, this does not apply to animals coming from shelters, etc., where an estimation of price is not possible. The problem of estimating a proportional price reduction does not appear in these cases, as these animals are usually purchased in exchange for a very low amount of money or are donated.[491]

Thus, the right to terminate a contract and the right to claim damages constitute a list of remedies that are preferred by the buyer. The reason for this situation might be seen in the specific object of the obligation, namely an animal specified as to its identity, purchased for a certain purpose and chosen because of its certain, unique features.[492] In many cases, the emotions of the buyer will play such a significant role that he might be willing to keep an animal in spite of its defects. In the end, a claim for damages frequently turns out to be the best solution for the buyer. However, it must be underlined that damages may also be claimed in addition to other remedies, such as a demand to cure the defect or lower the price. Thus, the liability based on a warranty regime does not prevent the possibility of basing a claim on contractual liability as well.[493]

Under German law, the right to claim damages, based on §§ 437 (3), 280, 281 and 283 BGB is the remedy used most frequently. In particular, § 284 BGB positively answers the question whether it is also possible to demand damages

---

reduction in price as an unfettered right after the amendment of the Polish Civil Code in 2015: J. Jezioro[in:] E. Gniewek, P. Machnikowski (eds.), *Kodeks cywilny. Komentarz*, p. 1195–1202; K. Haładyj/M. Tulibacka [in:] K. Osajda (ed.), *Kodeks cywilny. Komentarz. Tom IIIB*, pp.125–135. See also, *more comprehensively*): F. Zoll, *Rękojmia. Odpowiedzialność sprzedawcy*, pp. 1–7; M. Pecyna, *Ustawa o sprzedaży konsumenckiej*, Warszawa 2004, pp. 197–198; J. Widło, *Rękojmia za wady fizyczne w świetle nowelizacji Kodeksu cywilnego*, Monitor Prawniczy 4/2015, pp. 177–186.

490 See: M. Goettel, *Sytuacja zwierzęcia w prawie cywilnym*, p. 145; J. Adolphsen, *Tierkauf* [in:] B. Dauner-Lieb, W. Langen, *BGB Schuldrecht. Nomos Kommentar*, p. 1981.

491 With reference to animals coming from shelters, etc., where an estimation of price is not possible, see more: this subchapter, above.

492 See: M. Goettel, *Sytuacja zwierzęcia w prawie cywilnym*, pp. 144–145.

493 M. Lubelska-Sazanów, *Odpowiedzialność z tytułu rękojmi za wady fizyczne przy sprzedaży zwierząt*, Transformacje Prawa Prywatnego 2015, No. 4, pp. 21–42.

for costs that have been voluntarily incurred by the buyer. This provision concerns reimbursement paid instead of performing an obligation.[494]

In the case of the termination of a contract, general rules apply. Thus, the buyer has to return all profits – including any that have already been consumed.[495] That will rather not be the case, if an animal was ill and, therefore not useful. Thus, reimbursement for the reduction in an animal's value and the costs of the animal's recovery are more interesting issues. The entitlement to receive such reimbursement may arise if the buyer does not take enough care of the defective animal, e.g. neglects the quality and amount of the animal's food, or does not prevent a sick animal from contracting other illnesses. Such situations do not occur frequently, but if they do, then the seller is entitled to receive reimbursement based on the rules applicable to the termination of a contract.

3.2.6. Monetary damages and excessive costs with reference to exercising a warranty right in the case of animals as specific object of obligations

The problem with **setting a limit of damage** that the seller is obliged to cover in the case of an ill animal arises not only in connection with the buyer's right to cure,[496] but also with his right to claim damages for the costs incurred.[497] Such costs can occur, for example, in a situation where it turns out that the costs incurred during an emergency visit at a veterinary clinic were caused by a pre-existing defect in the purchased animal.[498] Under German law, the seller has to reimburse the costs that were directly incurred by the buyer, along with any costs that arose as a result of it.[499] Under Polish law, the seller would be obliged to return the costs described as *damnum emergens* and *lucrum cessans*.[500] The construction of an entitlement to receive damages as a *lucrum cessans* very often leads to similar solutions as the application of the German institution of *Man-*

494 A similar legal solution can be achieved by applying Article 363 KC. See: B. Lanckoroński [in:] K. Osajda (ed.), *Kodeks cywilny. Komentarz. Tom IIIA*, pp. 180–190.

495 Compare: § 346 (1) BGB and Article 566 KC. See also: H. Westermann, *Zu den Gewährleistungsansprüche des Käufers*, pp. 342–348.

496 See: Article 480 KC, § 281 BGB.

497 Under German law, an entitlement to the reimbursement of such costs can arise on base of §§ 812 or 251 BGB, under Polish law this right would rather be based on Article 480 KC, though there are no obstacles to base it on the regime of groundless enrichment, i.e. on Article 405 KC.

498 See, With reference to German law: J. Wertenbruch, *Die Besonderheiten…*, p. 2068. Compare, with reference to Polish law: Article 480 KC.

499 To learn more about "*Mangelschäden*" and "*Mangelfolgeschäden*" see: W. Weidenkaff [in:] O. Palandt, *Beck'sche Kurz-Kommentare: Palandt Bürgerliches Gesetzbuch mit Nebengesetzen*, München 2015, p. 667.

500 See: B. Lanckoroński [in:] K. Osajda (ed.), *Kodeks cywilny. Komentarz. Tom IIIA*, pp. 180–190.

gelfolgeschäden,[501] but can absolutely not be used as a substitute for it. The German courts have already accepted claims for damages that comprised of costs incurred for keeping a horse from the time of its purchase until the time of its return.[502] H. Westermann presents examples of reimbursements where the courts awarded buyers with damages of up to several thousand Euro, which are to be treated as average reimbursement for keeping a defective horse for several months until the time of its return.[503]

The wording of § 439 (3) BGB and Article 560 § 2 KC introduce the term of **excessive costs**, which is the main source of doubts in reference to the removal of defects in an animal.[504] An exact interpretation would require an estimation of the market value of the animal and could lead to inhumane results.[505] However, legal acts concerning animal protection do not allow an owner to leave its animal in a condition causing pain or suffering. Therefore, the restitution of an animal to its healthy condition should not be restrained because of the fact that the owner will only be able to receive damages in the amount that does not exceed the value of the animal.[506] In this matter, there is no difference whether the seller is obliged to return veterinary costs in the form of damages or in the form of payment for the removal of the defect. This liability, resulting from the obligation to cover damages occurred as a result of keeping an animal,[507] is transferred to the seller where an animal he sold turns out to be defective (i.e. ill). The possibility to euthanize an animal can be used only as a last resort, where there are no other means to reduce its pain and suffering.[508] Therefore, the definition of excessive costs with reference to medical treatments of animals must be understood to the extent that the costs of an animal's veterinary treatment are not excessive as long as they do not exceed an amount that a reasonable owner of an animal would be willing to spend.[509] The German judiciary has confirmed that

501 H. Westermann presents an example of *Mangelfolgeschaden* as an inability to sell a horse with a certain defect for the price of a horse without this defect. The same facts of the case would also cause an entitlement to receive damages described as *lucrum* cessans. See: H. Westermann, *Zu den Gewährleistungsansprüche des Käufers*, pp. 342–348.

502 LG München, ruling from 9.9.2004 – 26 O 1241/02.

503 H. Westermann, *Zu den Gewährleistungsansprüche des Käufers*, pp. 342–348. LG Braunschweig, ruling from 26.3.2004 – 4 O 118/04; OLG Düsseldorf ruling from 2. 4. 2004 – I - 14 U 213/03.

504 See also: F. Zoll, *Rękojmia. Odpowiedzialność sprzedawcy*, pp. 319–320.

505 See: J. Wertenbruch, *Die Besonderheiten…*, p. 2068.

506 Compare: § 1 of the German Act on the Protection of Animals from 24.07.1972 (J.L. 2006, p. 1206, item 1313 with further amendments) and Articles 5 and 9 of the Polish Act on the Protection of Animals from 21.8.1997 (J.L. 2014, item 856).

507 See: § 833 BGB and Article 431 KC.

508 §§ 1 and 4 of the German Act on the Protection of Animals and Article 6 of the Polish Act on the Protection of Animals.

509 See also: J. Wertenbruch, *Die Besonderheiten…*, p. 2068.

unreasonable costs can occur, for example when it is known from the very beginning that a defect in an animal cannot be completely removed, and a costly treatment would only lead to different defects. Such a situation occurred in the case of the already mentioned bow-legged dog, whose operation was not effective, since it only removed a cosmetic defect, but caused a need to make regular medical visits relieving animal's pain.[510] If removing a defect exceeds the costs that a reasonable owner of an animal would be willing to spend for a treatment, the buyer can still decide to perform the treatment and then ask the seller for a partial reimbursement of the costs of treatment, covering, for example, half of the costs incurred by the animal's owner.[511]

In the case of consumer contracts, the buyer is always able to shift the burden of proof to the seller, under § 476 BGB and Article 556^2 KC. This issue is connected with a general principle of civil law[512] providing that the person who claims a defect has the burden of proving not only its existence, but also the fact that the defect already existed before the good was purchased. However, in the case of consumer sales, if a defect arises then, during the first six months (German law) or one year (Polish law), the burden of proof shifts from the consumer proving that the defect existed before the purchase, to the seller proving that the defect did not exist before the purchase.[513] The German legislator introduced a further provision stating that this facility to consumers is not applicable if the presumption is incompatible with the nature of the thing or of the defect. The Polish legislator clearly did not consider the sale of animals when establishing these rules, and so did not adjust the provisions of the contract of sale for the sale of animals, introducing a legislation even worse than the German legislator (who has yet still been blamed by many German authors for not comprehensively adjusting the provisions of contract of sale in the German Civil Code to take into account the sale of animals when the Emperor's Order concerning major defects and warranty terms for the trade of livestock from 27 March 1899[514] lost its legal binding force on 1 January 2002).[515] Setting a one-year period of time during which the burden of proof is shifted to the seller (i.e. in favor of a consumer) without providing any exceptions is a very aggravating provision for horse sellers and should be evaluated negatively. The solution

510 BGH, ruling from 22.6.2005 – VIII ZR 281/04 (LG Oldenburg).

511 See also: J. Wertenbruch, *Die Besonderheiten…*, p. 2069.

512 Compare: Article 6 KC.

513 Compare: the wording of §476 and Article 556^2 KC.

514 German Emperor's Order concerning major defects and warranty terms for the trade of livestock from 27.3.1899 (J L (Bundesgesetzblatt) Part III, item 402–3.

515 See: J. Adolphsen, *Tierkauf* [in:] B. Dauner-Lieb, W. Langen, *BGB Schuldrecht. Nomos Kommentar*, pp. 1970–1971; P. Rosbach, *Pferderecht*, p. V – Vorwort; J. Adolphsen, *Die Schuldrechtsreform…*, pp. 203–208.

chosen by the Polish legislator may suppress the progress of equestrian sports in Poland, as well as the economics of the sale of horses. However, the solution chosen by the German legislator seems, on the contrary, to meet the requirements of equestrian sports and the sale of animals generally, where the characteristics of an animal as a living and feeling creature that is subject to constant changes has to be taken into account. In this case, the German legislator clearly based the provisions of sale contracts to animal sales, taking his knowledge from the experience of German jurisprudence.[516] This is an example where the Polish legislator should pattern legal solutions on his German neighbor. Thus, making a slight difference consisting in adding one more sentence to Article 556^2 KC could change a lot in reference to its applicability to animal sales.

The Polish judiciary has not yet provided any examples of the applicability of rules at hand.[517] The German courts, having more possibilities for practical rulings concerning the legal exception included in § 476 BGB, have already established some case law on that matter.[518] So, for example, in case of the allegedly traumatized cart-horses described earlier, the defect arising shortly after purchase and possibly due to a course of events (accident) that occurred shortly before the collection of the horse by the buyer – was qualified as existing before the purchase.[519] German courts usually also qualify the horse sickness recognized as "spat" – due to its nature – as existing before the purchase.[520] Thus, illnesses that need a certain amount of time to show up are usually qualified as already existing at the time of purchasing the animal.[521] Taking into account the similar provisions in the German and Polish Civil Codes, and the greater experience of the German judiciary, the defects in the cases described in this

516 Despite the critical opinions mentioned above referring to the removal of the Emperor's Order concerning major defects and warranty terms for the trade of livestock from 27.3. 1899 from the legal order without comprehensively adjusting the provisions of the German Civil Code to the sale of animals, see: J. Adolphsen, *Tierkauf* [in:] B. Dauner-Lieb, W. Langen, *BGB Schuldrecht. Nomos Kommentar*, pp. 1970–1971; P. Rosbach, *Pferderecht*, p. V – Vorwort; J. Adolphsen, *Die Schuldrechtsreform…*, pp. 203–208.

517 The provision of Article 556^2 KC has been fairly recently introduced to the Polish Civil Code in December 2014, but already existed in a different legal act, namely the Polish Act on Consumer Rights. However, its provisions did not apply to the sale of animals, as at this time there were special rules applicable to this type of sale.

518 See e.g.: OLG Koblenz, ruling from 23.4. 2009–5 U 1124/08; BGH, ruling from 11.7.2007 – VIII ZR 110/06 (LG Krefeld); LG Münster, ruling from 20.7.2007 – 10 O 240/06; AG Herne, ruling from 6.10.2003 – 5 C 85/02. The probability that the defect already existed before the risk was passed to the buyer is usually higher in cases of changes in the skeletal system, e.g. "chips" in the sale of horses.

519 OLG Koblenz, ruling from 23.4.2009 – 5 U 1124/08.

520 See cases: LG Münster, ruling from 20.7.2007 – 10 O 240/06; OLG Stuttgart, ruling from 8.2. 2006 – 3 U 28/05.

521 H. Westermann, *Zu den Gewährleistungsansprüche des Käufers*, pp. 342–348.

paragraph should also be qualified as existing before the purchase on the basis of Article 556^2 KC.

3.2.7. Animals as used goods?

Although the issue of whether an animal should be treated in a certain factual situation as a used good or not is important under Polish law only in reference to the possibility to shorten the term for acknowledging a defect under the warranty regime (Article 568 § 1 KC). The German jurisprudence and legal literature used to show vigorous interest in this issue, especially in the last decade.[522] Due to the original characteristic of this problem, not undertaken by the Polish scholars until now (which is also justified by its marginal applicability), I believe that it is worth briefly mentioning.

In the German legal system there is a theory whereby animals should always be qualified as used goods because – as living creatures – they are being "used" from the moment they are born,[523] though this theory has yet to gain much popularity. Thus, most of the representatives of the German doctrine,[524] as well as most of the German judicial rulings,[525] indicate that the qualification as a used animal is dependent on the purpose for which a certain animal has been purchased. Therefore, a horse bought for riding will be treated as a used animal if it has already been ridden, and a dog (or any other animal) bought for breeding will be treated as a used animal if it has already been inseminated in the past.[526] It is worth mentioning that the jurisprudence already had to deal with this problem before the reform of the German law of obligations – at that time, the courts

522 See, e.g. with reference to the German doctrine: J. Eichelberger, *Von neuen und gebrauchten Tieren – Zur Anwendbarkeit des § 475 Abs. 2 BGB auf den Tierkauf*, ZGS 2007, No. 98, pp. 98–101; U. Büdenbender [in:] B. Dauner-Lieb, W. Langen, *Anwaltkommentar BGB*, Bonn 2005, p. 1444; H. Westermann, *Zu den Gewährleistungsansprüche des Käufers*; J. Wertenbruch, *Die Besonderheiten des Tierkaufs bei der Sachmängelgewährleistung*, NJW 2012, No. 29, pp. 2065–2144. With reference to the German jurisprudence, see e.g.: OLG Düsseldorf, ruling from 2.4.2004 – I-14 U 213/03; BGH, ruling from 24.2.2010 – VIII ZR 71/09 (OLG Köln); BGH, ruling from 3.7.1985 – VIII ZR 152/84 (OLG Köln), NJW-RR 1986, 52; OLG Schleswig, ruling from 13.12.2005 – 3 U 42/05. All of these sources are referred to more comprehensively in the footnotes below.

523 S. Lorenz [in:] H. Westermann (ed.), *Münchener Kommentar zum BGB, Vol. III*, München 2016, § 474, side number 16a, *BeckOnline*; see also: OLG Düsseldorf, ruling from 2.4.2004 – I-14 U 213/03.

524 See most of the representatives of the doctrine: H. Westermann, *Zu den Gewährleistungsansprüche des Käufers*, pp. 342–348; J. Wertenbruch, *Die Besonderheiten des Tierkaufs bei der Sachmängelgewährleistung*, pp. 2065–2144.

525 See also the German Supreme Court: BGH, ruling from 24.2.2010 – VIII ZR 71/09 (OLG Köln), where the court stated that a six-year old horse is to be treated as a used good as it had already been ridden before.

526 Compare: P. Rosbach, *Pferderecht*, p. 70.

indicated that living fish (using the example of trout[527]) and young animals (here: foals[528]) – from the time when they are taken away from its mother – are to be treated as used goods.[529] Nevertheless, there are also authors who criticize the general applicability of provisions describing a good as used or new (§ 475 (2) BGB) to animals at all.[530] I agree with the last of these presented theories, since I am of the opinion that animals should be granted a position putting them at least somewhere between objects and subjects of obligations, though they should definitely not be treated as a regular good, which could be described as used or not. Therefore, although this issue is only addressed in German law, in my opinion the provisions referring to used goods – especially the exclusion of the warranty for used goods sold at public auctions – should not apply to animals in any case. Consequently, in cases where an animal is sold on a basis of a consumer contract, all the notions that serve to strengthen the consumer's position under Polish and under German law should apply.

3.2.8. Peculiarities of the sale of horses – the importance of pre-contractual information, medical examination and x-ray images as the basis for the horse's seller's liability

According to German doctrine, an animal's **medical examination,** made by a veterinary doctor when concluding the contract, gains a great deal of significance with reference to the definition of an animal's expected quality, which becomes part of the parties' agreement. It concerns not only a detailed examination made by a veterinary doctor when buying a horse for high level sport competitions, but also the purchase of any other animal (e.g. almost every kennel includes a provision in the sale contract stating that the buyer has a certain amount of time in which to examine the condition of a cat or dog). One should also bear in mind that in some cases even a detailed examination may not prevent certain defects in an animal from arising in the future, e.g. **genetic defects.** In such cases, the liability of the seller depends on his carefulness, namely whether he has taken all the necessary steps that he should have taken in order to avoid a genetic defect in the whelps in his breed. Thus, if he neither acted negligently nor had intent to cause damage to the buyer, there is no legal basis to

527 BGH, ruling from 3.7.1985 – VIII ZR 152/84 (OLG Köln), NJW-RR 1986, 52.

528 OLG Schleswig, ruling from 13.12.2005 – 3 U 42/05 (the facts of the case come from October 2002, thus several months before the reform was imposed).

529 Compare: S. Lorenz [in:] H. Westermann (ed.), *Münchener Kommentar zum BGB, Vol. III,* § 474, side number 16a, *BeckOnline (last visited: 12.3.2018).*

530 See: J. Eichelberger, *Von neuen und gebrauchten Tieren – Zur Anwendbarkeit des § 475 Abs. 2 BGB auf den Tierkauf,* pp. 98–101; U. Büdenbender [in:] B. Dauner-Lieb, W. Langen, *Anwaltkommentar BGB,* p. 1444.

hold him liable for an animal's defect.[531] The German Supreme Court confirmed this position in its case VIII ZR 281/04 referring to a dog with a problem with excessively bowed legs[532] leading to several negative consequences, like the need to undergo medical operations and the need to regularly undergo pain-relief therapy consuming high expenses. Among other things, this problematic health issue led to an expensive operation exceeding the purchase price of the dog and caused animal pain that had to be cured by constant visits to a veterinary doctor. The German Supreme Court in the case at hand admitted that the solution proposed by the seller (to exchange the dog or accept back the dog and re-imburse the purchase price) was not possible due to the personal bond arisen between the dog and its actual owner, and the only warranty right that could be performed was the payment of damages. Although the German Court did not accept the claim due to the inability by the dog breeder to foresee the existence of the defect, his good will to exchange the dog and the lack of the seller's fault or negligence. Therefore, in the case at hand, the Court did not grant damages to the dog's owner and stated that the breeder is not liable for genetic defects in a sold animal if he did not act with intent or with negligence when choosing and pairing the parents of this sold animal. At this point, it is worth mentioning that, whereas a veterinarian's examination of the whelps' parents is usually necessary in order to undertake steps preventing these whelps from displaying genetic defects, these veterinary doctors are usually also not held liable for negligence in their medical examination of these dogs – thus in biology there is never a 100 % guarantee that the descendants of a certain couple of animals will be healthy. Therefore, just as in the case of a veterinary doctor as in the case of a breeder, the condition that has to be met in order to hold any of them liable for a genetic defect is negligence.

Nevertheless, as the wording of the German Civil Code[533] emphasizes an agreed quality, the question to consider is whether the veterinary examination influences the content of the parties' agreement, or maybe even the validity of the parties' agreement at all. It is also important to answer the question whether a mistake made by a veterinary doctor, when examining an animal or when putting the results of the examination to the protocol, interferes with the parties' agreement in terms of the quality of the purchased animal too. It is significant to separate these two issues, as it is unacceptable for an incorrect veterinary report to influence the parties' agreement according to the quality of the purchased

531 See: BGH, ruling from 22.6.2005 – VIII ZR 281/04, where the German court stated that the breeder is not liable for genetic defects in a sold animal if he did not act with intent or with negligence when choosing and pairing the parents of this sold animal.

532 The facts of the case have already been mentioned in Subchapter III.421. of this book ("Definition of a defect with reference to animals under German and Polish civil law").

533 Compare: § 434 (1) BGB.

animal.[534] Thus, it might be necessary to prove who was in the contractual relation with the veterinary doctor, and whether the other party may claim damages as a result of this contract.[535] The court in Germany decided that, in the event of the parties' agreement in accordance with the veterinary examination, a sale contract is concluded on the understanding that the good condition of animal will be proven in the report.[536] In the case at hand, the parties agreed on the purchase price of a horse, though the horse was still supposed to be examined by a veterinary doctor. Whereas the medical examination led to doubts with reference to its ability to be used for rides and as a dressage horse, the potential buyer decided himself not to purchase it. After a year, the seller of the horse ordered its medical examination and – as it did not prove any health issues – he claimed payment of the previously agreed price for the horse against its handing over. Whereas the court of first instance admitted the claim, the OLG Köln stated, as pointed out above. Thus, it cannot be expected that the buyer would purchase a horse in a case where there are reasonable (based on a medical examination performed by a veterinary doctor) doubts concerning its health condition. However, in the event where the medical examination shows a positive outcome, so that, according to the fair-dealing principle, the buyer's decision with reference to purchase of the horse should be positive, the sale contract is deemed to be concluded. Thus, in this case the German court qualified this contract as a sale concluded under the condition that the medical examination proves that animal's health is in a good condition. As the Polish legal system regulates the construction of sale under a condition similarly to the German legal system,[537] the outcome – in the event that the problem would be resolved by a Polish court – should be the same.

534 See: H. Westermann, *Zu den Gewährleistungsansprüche des Käufers*, p. 342.

535 In German law, this type of contract for work ((*umowa o dzieło, Werkvertrag*) and services concluded by the seller of an animal but performed for the buyer, is to be treated as a contract with a protective effect on a third person, which differs from the construction of *pactum in faworem tertii*; compare: A. Kober [in:] B. Gsell, W. Krüger, S. Lorenz, J. Mayer (ed.), *Beck-online Grosskommentar BGB*, München 2015, § 634, side number 273. In the Polish doctrine, the possibility of the buyer claiming warranty rights with reference to a veterinary doctor who was hired by the seller would be possible only through the construction of *pactum in favorem tertii*; compare: W. Popiołek [in:] K. Pietrzykowski (ed.), *Kodeks cywilny. Komentarz*, Warszawa 2015, pp. 1294–1301.

536 OLG Köln, ruling from 24.6.1994 – 20 U 11/94. The court underlines also that, if the diagnosis makes the future use of an animal doubtful, the seller may not demand the performance of a contract based on an opinion of a different veterinarian who would prove that the first diagnosis was wrong.

537 See: Subchapter III.2.4.

Nevertheless, one should take into account the fact that too broad an interpretation of this ruling is also not acceptable.[538] Namely, the buyer must prove the existence of a certain defect in order to waive his duty to conclude the contract – if the defect is not major, the buyer might also make use of his warranty rights and, for example, demand that the price be lowered in the event of a defect that is not curable, but does not significantly impact the purpose of purchasing the animal.[539] However, it is clear that the buyer's choice to conclude the sale contract is dependent on the results of the medical examination, therefore this choice is to be made first after the examination.[540] The reason for this is also the exclusion of the seller's liability in case the buyer knew about the defect.[541]

Most of the German doctrine and jurisprudence confirm that **the pre-contractual examination of an animal influences the content of the parties' agreement.** Namely, the results of the medical examination are to be treated as a contractual estimation of quality of a purchased animal in the meaning of § 434 BGB.[542] Thus, this fact not only has consequences for the sale contract, but also consequences for the liability of the veterinary doctor. However, the parties can also estimate the further characteristics of the sold animal in a contract in order to be able to qualify the possible lack of examination as a defect. On the other hand, the parties may also agree that only the characteristics included in the protocol of the medical examination of an animal constitutes the foundations for the future qualification of defects. A foundation for the future qualification of defects might also be included in the contractual provision stating (taking a horse as an example) that "the horse is sold as inspected and tested".[543] There is no doubt that these legal considerations are, in practice, mostly used for the sale of horses, which can be observed using the example of German doctrine, where almost all consideration about the sale of animals refer to horses.[544]

538 With reference to contracts with veterinary doctors, see: Subchapters: IV.1.2.5., IV.2.5., IV.3.5.

539 See: H. Westermann, *Zu den Gewährleistungsansprüche des Käufers*, p. 342; compare: BGH, ruling from 22.6.2005 – VIII ZR 281/04 (LG Oldenburg).

540 Adolphsen, *Tierkauf* [in:] B. Dauner-Lieb, W. Langen, *BGB Schuldrecht. Nomos Kommentar*, p. 1978.

541 *Idem*, compare: § 442 BGB and Article 557 § 1 KC.

542 There are no strong significant disagreements in the doctrine in this matter. See: H. Westermann, *Zu den Gewährleistungsansprüche des Käufers*, pp. 342–348, Adolphsen, *Tierkauf* [in:] B. Dauner-Lieb, W. Langen, *BGB Schuldrecht. Nomos Kommentar*, p. 1978; P. Rosbach, *Pferderecht*, p. 5.

543 So also decided the German court in the case: LG Braunschweig, ruling from 26.3.2004 – 4 O 118/04.

544 See, for example: P. Rosbach, *Pferderecht*; J. Wertenbruch, *Die Besonderheiten…*, pp. 2065–2144; J. Eichelberger, M. Zentner, *Tiere im Kaufrecht*, JuS 2009, p. 2012; H. Westermann, *Zu den Gewährleistungsansprüche des Käufers*, pp. 342–348; J. Adolphsen, *Tierkauf* [in:] B.

In the German case ruled by OLG Stuttgart on 8 February 2006,[545] the buyer purchased a horse for his daughter for high dressage competitions (M, S class) for a price of 150,000 Euro. During its training, the horse's walk turned out to be "uneven", which led to medical consultations on the horse's condition and resulted in the diagnosis that the horse has an arthritic condition in the hock, recognized as "spat". According to § 442 BGB, it is the seller's duty to inform the seller about any health problems that the sold animal has or had before, and he cannot avoid liability as long as he knew about a certain medical condition. In this case, the seller tried to justify his actions, stating that "he was sure that he had informed the buyer that this medical examination had gone in the direction of spat illness" during the allegedly promising medical examinations undertaken in the seller's stable by a veterinary doctor. The Court found the seller reliable and ruled for the reimbursement of price and further costs to the buyer, based on its ruling on the opinion of an expert confirming the horse's illness. Recognition of the seller's obligation to provide necessary information to the buyer has often been proven by the German judiciary, e.g. with a ruling of the Court LG Darmstadt,[546] according to which the seller is obliged to provide comprehensive information concerning the operation of the horse, if the buyer is asking for a reason for its thickened leg. The outcome in both cases would probably be the same when basing the ruling on Polish law. Thus, Article 546 KC obliges the seller to inform the buyer about all important legal and factual issues concerning the purchased good – or respectively – the animal (whereas this information duty is even more strictly defined with reference to consumer sale in Article 546[1] KC).

However, the seller's duty to provide all necessary information referring to the sold animal is limited to the extent of the seller's knowledge. Therefore, if the seller is not an expert, the information that he passes to the buyer depends on the statements made by a veterinarian during his medical examination of an animal. Above all, it is not acceptable for the seller to conceal information about the illnesses that the horse had before, and which he obviously knows about. It is worth mentioning that a previous illness that has been completely healed might not be of much importance when selling a leisure horse, but it certainly would gain significance when selling a horse that is planned to be used for sport purposes, like dressage or jumping.[547] Nevertheless, it is very rare to receive such detailed information from the seller, and therefore buyers should concentrate on

Dauner-Lieb, W. Langen, *BGB Schuldrecht. Nomos Kommentar*, pp. 1969–1992; H. Müller, *Gewährleistung beim Tierkauf* [in:] L. Aderhold, B. Grunewald, D. Kingberg, W. Paefgen (ed.), *Festschirft für Harm Peter Westermann zum 70. Geburtstag*, Köln 2008, *pp. 517–534.*

545 See: OLG Stuttgart, ruling from 8.2.2006 – 3 U 28/05.

546 LG Darmstadt, ruling from 22.4.1998 – 21 S 263/97.

547 See also: H. Westermann, *Zu den Gewährleistungsansprüche des Käufers*, pp. 342–348.

the expected characteristic of the purchased animal and the purpose for which it is being bought while ordering its medical examination.

It is also questionable whether it is possible for the buyer to lose its warranty rights because of his knowledge or negligent oversight of an animal's defect. Namely, the buyer's knowledge of a defect, or its oversight due to gross negligence, may lead to an exclusion of his future warranty rights in both analyzed systems, namely: § 442 (1) BGB and Article 557§1 KC. However, in order to establish that the buyer was aware of the defect, it is not enough for the buyer to know about a certain characteristic that constitutes a defect. It can be assumed that the buyer knew about a defect if he knew that this defect leads to a deviation from an established characteristic of an animal, and that it prevents its use for a certain purpose. Thus, animals – as living creatures – are subject to constant changes and their qualification as fit for a certain purpose is very often based on individual preferences. Therefore it is difficult to define whether the buyer was aware of a defect in an animal. However, under German law the exclusion of warranty is also possible in cases of a gross negligence,[548] and such a situation is much more probable.[549] In such cases, warranty rights might be excluded. Nevertheless, this does not apply if the seller has fraudulently hidden the defect or set a quality guarantee.[550]

The issue of information that the horse seller is obliged to provide with reference to the existence of an animal's possible defects is usually connected with the horse's x-ray images. The German veterinary medical council has established an **x-ray images guide**[551] that is to be treated as recommendations for their interpretation, qualification and description. In order to evaluate an x-ray image, there are four classes of qualification: class I encompasses results with no negative changes and changes, that can be classified as anatomical variations; class II encompasses results that do not differ significantly from the ideal condition and where the probability of their clinical appearance is lower than 3 %; class III encompasses results that differ from the ideal condition and a probability of their clinical appearance is between 5 and 20 %; class IV encompasses results that differ significantly from the ideal condition, where the probability of their clinical appearance is more than 50 %.[552] The same classes of x-ray visible

548 Compare the content of § 442 (1) BGB and Article 557§1 KC.

549 See the second part of the § 442 (1) BGB.

550 See: H. Westermann, *Zu den Gewährleistungsansprüche des Käufers*, pp. 342–348. The guarantee is to be understood in the meaning of § 443 BGB and Article 577 KC. However, note that guarantee provisions are not generally applicable to animals. See: Subchapter III.3.3.

551 Known as RöLF, last visited: 20.1.2016 from the website: http://www.bundestieraerztekammer.de/downloads/btk/leitlinien/RoentgenLeitfaden_2007.pdf.

552 J. Adolphsen, *Tierkauf* [in:] B. Dauner-Lieb, W. Langen, *BGB Schuldrecht. Nomos Kommentar*, pp. 1974–1975.

changes is also applied by veterinary doctors in Poland,[553] though it does not constitute a recommendation of the Polish veterinary medical council, and is rather to be treated as a practical solution used by Polish veterinarians in order to correspond with European standards.[554] Nevertheless, it must be underlined that the guide does not constitute legally binding rules – neither in Germany nor in Poland. The authors of the guide have used the term "guide" on purpose, in order to qualify it as a recommendation, not as legally binding rules. Therefore, although the x-ray images guide is cited by courts on a regular basis, the judges are not authorized to qualify the buyer's decision not to make x-ray images before the purchase of a horse as negligence.[555] It was also established that the fact that the market reacts by lowering the price of a horse classified to a certain class according to the x-ray images guide does not equate to the supposition that the horse cannot be used for its usual purpose,[556] thus does not constitute a defect,[557] which has been proven by the German judiciary. In the German case ruled by OLG Stuttgart on 8 February 2006,[558] the buyer purchased for his daughter a horse for high dressage competitions (M, S class) for a price of 150,000 Euro. Although the horse was qualified to the I/II class of x-ray class (ideal/norm condition), it turned to have an illness called "spat". Despite the horse's x-ray images being qualified into a certain class, the German Court did not take for granted that the horse was healthy at the time of its purchase, but based its ruling on an independent expert who stated that the illness had to have been visible, thus known to the seller already before the purchase.

The opposite situation was subject of the German Supreme Court in the already mentioned case VIII ZR 32/16.[559] In this case, the buyer bought a dressage horse for 500,000 Euro explicitly stating that the purpose of the horse is to

553 See: chart with classes for qualification of x-ray images, presented in: M. Zimmerman, S. Dyson, R. Murray: *Comparison of radiographic and scintigraphic findings of the spinous processes in the equine thoracolumbar region*, Vet. Radiol, Ultrasound 2001, No. 52, pp. 661–671, cited after: R. Henklewski, A. Florczyk, W. Kinda, *Punktowa skala w radiograficznej ocenie zdjęć rentgenowskich u koni z bolesnością grzbietu*, Życie weterynaryjne 2013, No. 88 (10), pp. 880–883.

554 *Idem.*

555 See also: J. Adolphsen, *Tierkauf* [in:] B. Dauner-Lieb, W. Langen, *BGB Schuldrecht. Nomos Kommentar*, p. 1975.

556 With reference to the relations between a party's error and warranty rights see e.g.: M. Grochowski, *Zbieg norm w zakresie rękojmi za wady rzeczy sprzedanej oraz błędu i podstępu (Zagadnienie prawne)*, Monitor Prawniczy 2012, No. 19, pp. 1048–1050; J. Adolphsen, *Tierkauf* [in:] B. Dauner-Lieb, W. Langen, *BGB Schuldrecht. Nomos Kommentar*, p. 1975.

557 BGH, ruling from 18.12.1954 – II ZR 296/53.

558 See: OLG Stuttgart, ruling from 8.2.2006 – 3 U 28/05. The case has been described in a more detailed below, see: Subchapter III.3.2.8 ("Peculiarities of the sale of horses – the importance of pre-contractual information, medical examination and x-ray images as the basis for the horse's seller's liability").

559 BGH, ruling from 18.10.2017 – VIII ZR 32/16.

take part in high-class sports competitions. Before taking the horse, the buyer made "significant medical examinations" in one of the horse clinics, but did not prove any defects in the horse. Nevertheless, a few months later the buyer had problems with the health and rideability of the horse and decided to have it checked again by a veterinary doctor. Since this medical examination revealed big changes in the x-rays of the horse's legs, the buyer claimed a horse's defect and demanded the horse's price back against returning the horse itself. However, the Court stated that only changes to the x-ray damages of the horse's legs are not enough to state that a horse has a defect, since it is not expected that the horse will always be in ideal condition. What is more – according to the Court – it is not unusual that, after passing the risk to the buyer, an animal is in a different state of health than at the time of its purchase. Such differences from the "ideal norm" do not constitute a defect according to the Court. Since, under Polish law, the x-ray classes serve solely as recommendations and are not binding – just as it is in Germany – the conclusions of the German Supreme Court could be also taken into consideration by the Polish doctrine and jurisprudence when ruling in cases referring to similar facts of the case (nevertheless, the judge should always keep in mind that even the identity of a legal rule does not mean the same understanding of it in disparate legal systems).[560] In this case, the legal comparative argument – which the courts may take advantage of when justifying rulings – may gain a lot of value.

The German court's decisions presented above prove that x-ray images are not enough to establish the existence of a horse's defect or its lack. Solely a different state of the horse, making the contractually agreed use of a horse impossible, may be defined as a defect. Nevertheless, the first of the cases referred to above proves that lowering the class of x-ray images when selling a horse does not allow the seller to avoid liability. This attitude of German judges should also be transferred into Polish courts when solving cases referring to animals, where the facts of the case refer to medical condition and are usually unclear. However, it should be noted that the doctrinal solutions developed within the German tradition may be misleading. Nevertheless, I consider experience of the German jurisprudence as an interesting lesson, which may somewhat inspire the Polish jurisprudence.

560 E. Rott-Pietrzyk, F. Zoll [in:] M. Jagielska, E. Macierzyńska-Franaszczyk, E. Rott-Pietrzyk, F. Zoll, G. Żmij (eds.), *Limits of Harmonisation and Convergence…*, p. 44; H. Honsell, *Die rhetorischen Wurzeln der juristischen Auslegung*, ZfPW 2016, p. 125. Compare: the considerations included in Subchapter IV.3.2. ("Agency contracts having an animal as their object").

3.3. Applicability of the institution of guarantee as to the quality of the good to animals

Note that **warranty,** in the meaning of this subchapter, should be distinguished from the seller's **guarantee as to the quality of the good** (*die Garantie, gwarancja jakości*).[561] Such a guarantee should be understood as a contractual relationship between the seller and the buyer concerning the seller's declaration concerning the quality of a sold good and its acceptance by the buyer.[562] However, guarantee in this meaning does not have any practical applicability to the sale of animals. Thus, animals are specific objects of obligations and – although the provisions concerning movables are applied respectively to contracts involving animals – they cannot be treated as such. As living creatures, their health condition, genetic predispositions and character is always individual and the future development of these factors can never be predicted. Therefore, as the seller's guarantee is an optional instrument occurring with reference to sale contracts within the boundaries of the freedom of contract,[563] it is impossible for a seller to declare a guarantee in reference to a sold animal's quality. Thus, it would be unreasonable for a person selling a living creature, whose future development depends on many conditions to undertake an independent declaration concerning the future quality of a sold animal.

561 Compare: Article 577 KC and § 443 BGB.

562 See: Z. Radwański [in:] Z. Radwański (ed.), *System Prawa Prywatnego, Prawo cywilne – część ogólna, Vol. II,* Warszawa, 2008, pp. 177–178; Z Radwański, J. Panowicz-Lipska, *Zobowiązania – część szczegółowa,* Warszawa 2015, p. 46; E. Łętowska, *Prawo umów konsumenckich,* Warszawa 2002, p. 247 l; W. Czachórski (ed.), *Zobowiązania – Zarys wykładu,* Warszawa, 2012, p. 403. With reference to the contractual qualification of a contractual guarantee of the seller as a contractual provision, concluded by the parties on the basis of the freedom of contract principle (and not a simple declaration of one party to the sale contract), see: J. Krawczyk, *Haftung fuer Garantieerklaerungen im deutschen und polnischen Zivilrecht,* Konstanz 2015, pp. 97, 109. As to the same qualification in the German Civil Code, see: J. Krawczyk, *Haftung fuer Garantieerklaerungen im deutschen und polnischen Zivilrecht,* p. 109.

563 See: J. Krawczyk, *Haftung fuer Garantieerklaerungen im deutschen und polnischen Zivilrecht,* p. 97. With reference to the freedom of contract principle, see: H. Schulte-Nölke [in:] *Common European Sales Law – Commentary*; E. Rott-Pietrzyk, *Commercial Agency Contracts and Freedom of Contract* [in:] T. Drygala, B. Heiderhoff, M. Staake, G. Zmij (ed.), *Private Autonomy in Germany and in Poland and in Private European Sales Law,* Munich 2012, pp. 15–34; M. Lubelska-Sazanów, *The "Principle of No Freedom of Contract": A Post-Modern Version of the Freedom of Contract Principle?,* [in:] M. De Maestri, S. Dominelli (ed.), *Party autonomy in European private (and) international law, Vol. II,* Rome 2015, pp. 15–31.

3.4. Results of the improper performance of contracts aimed at the transfer of property of an animal other than the sale contract

3.4.1. Donation

The results of the improper performance of contracts aimed at the transfer of property are significantly different in the case of **donation contracts.** Thus, this is the only contract described in this chapter that in its *essentialia negotii* concerns the performance of only one of the contractual parties.[564] The complimentary transfer of ownership results in the dilution of liability of the donor. As already mentioned, according to Article 892 KC and § 521 BGB, the donor is liable for defects in a good only if he fraudulently concealed these defects. What is more, he is liable for defects resulting from the improper performance of a contract, or its non-performance, only if the defect has been caused with intent or by gross negligence.[565] In practice, a problem that often occurs in reference to a donation involving living animals is the issue of transferring ownership to a minor. As donation is a contract that only brings a benefit to the donee, the acceptance of a person with at least limited legal capacity (in the meaning of Article 15 KC and §§ 104, 106 BGB)[566] is usually sufficient for the legal validity of this type of contract (i. e. acceptance of a legal advisor is not necessary).[567]

However, in the case of donating an animal, where ownership is always combined with undertaking obligations, the case is different. These obligations do not consist in being obliged to perform a duty against the other contractual party, but it means an obligation against the gifted animal – the obligation to take care after it. Therefore, in the case of donating an animal to a person with limited legal capacity, the fact that an animal is a specific object of obligations has far-reaching consequences resulting in the inapplicability of Article 17 KC and § 107 BGB to this type of contract. Thus, although the animal being a specific object of obligations does not change the qualification of a contract as donation (at least *de lege lata* – as long as animals are still owned just as regular things, without adjusting the provisions of the Polish Civil Code to its specific character, contracts for the gratuitous transfer of ownership of an animal are still qualified as

564 See: Article 888 KC and § 516 BGB.

565 See: Article 891 § 1 KC and § 521 BGB.

566 Note, that the scope of persons limited in legal capacity is different under Polish and German law: whereas both legal systems qualify persons in a state of pathological mental disturbance that prevents the free exercise of will (unless the state is, by its nature, a temporary one) as limiting its legal capacity, the age defining legal capacity is different. So, whereas Polish law requires that a minor is 13 years old in order to have limited legal capacity, the German law grants limited legal capacity to anyone who is seven years old.

567 In Polish law, this rule may be indicated in Article 17 KC, whereas in German law this rule is included directly in § 107 BGB. See: D. Looschelders, *Schuldrecht. Besonderer Teil*, p. 106.

donation contracts), provisions referring to animals apply respectively, taking into account its specific nature as a living creature. This specific object of obligation results mainly in the fact that people are obliged to take care of animals, whereas this duty is based not only on moral rules applicable throughout the EU,[568] but also on the provisions of the Polish and German Animal Protection Acts and other specific administrative rules applicable in Poland, Germany and the EU as a whole.[569] Therefore, in the case of transferring of property of an animal, a donation contract loses its complimentary character due to two kinds of duties arising with the acquisition of an animal. Firstly, these are duties consisting in taking factual care of an animal, e. g. feeding, grooming, walking, riding, milking and any others depending on the type of animal acquired. Secondly, these are monetary duties, since keeping an animal always indicates costs that a person limited in legal capacity may not be able to cover. Thus, all animals have to be fed, which constitutes a primary cost, and all animals have to attend to at least occasional veterinary examinations. In addition, they often need accessories for walking them, riding them or adjusting the territory to their needs. The biggest costs probably concern horses, which have to be kept in special conditions outside of places where its owners live (usually connected with high costs), not mentioning the costs of any training and persons taking care of the regular needs of the horse (grooms, etc.).[570] In addition, if the donation concerns an animal like a horse, then taking care of it is also connected with the need to conclude contracts with other people (e. g. pension contracts, contracts with blacksmiths, etc.) and with the need to spend large amounts of money in order to keep this animal in good condition. Summing up, in my opinion, the donation of an animal (any animal – a dog or even a hamster – is also connected with obligations earned by the donee) cannot be concluded without approval from the legal counsellor of a person with limited legal capacity.

568 See: Subchapter II.3.1. of this book.

569 See: the Polish Animal Protection Act from 21. 8. 1997; German Animal Protection Act from 24. 07. 1972 and – due to the fact that this issue has been broadly referred to in Chapter II.3.1. of this book ("The bridge between the law of obligations and animal ethics" – "Animal law in the EU") – at this point, see only such EU regulations as: Council Regulation (EC) No. 1/2005 of 22 December 2004 on the protection of animals during transport and related operations, and the most important primary source of law of the EU, Article 13 of the TFEU referring to animals and introduced by the Treaty of Lisbon.

570 Compare the German case: OLG Hamm ruling from 25. 11. 2015 – 12 U 62/14, where the contract consisting in keeping the horse in a stable contained also duties like riding the horse, training it and granting it the necessary movement.

3.4.2. Barter

Concerning improper performance, the contract changing ownership of an animal that is regulated most similarly to the sale contract is the **barter agreement.** Thus, Article 604 KC and § 480 BGB establish the respective applicability of provisions concerning sale contracts to barter agreements. Therefore, in the case of the improper performance, the buyer is free to claim any of the warranty rights provided in Article 560 KC and § 437 BGB.[571] The claim that causes most legal problems is a claim for a price reduction. The German doctrine,[572] as well as the German horse market, has tended to resolve this problem by allowing the difference in value to be offset with monetary means, whereas the Polish doctrine does not allow for this legal solution and such a solution could only be applied as a result of a settlement between the parties.[573] Thus, according to some Polish doctrine representatives, a claim for a price reduction is possible only where the obligation that would eventually be reduced can in fact be reduced in that way,[574] whereas other representatives of the Polish doctrine represent the opinion that a claim for a price reduction is impossible in the case at hand.[575] In any case, it should be remembered that neither group representing the opposing attitudes presented in the Polish doctrine were referring to barter contracts with animals as their object. The German court confirmed, in the case 21 U 140/01,[576] that animals are specific objects of contractual obligations and there is no other living creature looking the same, with the same health condition, height, character, capabilities and – most importantly – the same emotional bond with its owner as the one being the object of a particular warranty claim.[577] Taking the example of sport horses, it is much more likely to find a different animal that will fit the rider's needs and offset its difference against the market value of the primary bought horse, than to find a horse with the same market value (which is

571 Compare the BGH court ruling, where the Court stated that in barter agreements – just as in the case of sale contracts – the parties are entitled to damages (moreover, the court stated that, in the case of a disease demanding a medical operation, the acquirer of a horse was entitled to undertake medical actions before informing the other party while retaining his warranty rights unaffected): BGH, ruling from 07.12.2005 – Az.: VIII ZR 126/05 (NJW 2006, 988).

572 See: D. Looschelders, *Schuldrecht. Besonderer Teil*, Munchen 2012, p. 99.

573 See: W. Olejniczak [in:] J. Rajski (ed.), *System Prawa Prywatnego, Vol. VII*, pp. 271–272.

574 *Idem.*

575 See: M. Safjan [in:] K. Pietrzykowski (ed.), *Kodeks cywilny. Komentarz*, p. 383.

576 See: the previously mentioned German case, where the Court compared purchase of a living, constantly progressing horse taking part in sport competitions on a certain level to the purchase of a piece art, where the affection of the buyer is a very important factor, but the future progress of the artist and the price of his paintings depend on many details and are not predictable: OLG Düsseldorf, ruling from 16.04.2002 – 21 U 140/01.

577 *Idem.*

always dependent on many factors and is difficult to establish in case of bartering an animal) that will fit the rider. Therefore, since the provisions referring to the buyer's warranty rights are similar under Polish and German law due to far-reaching unification of consumer law thanks to Directive 2011/83/EU of the European Parliament and of the Council of 25 October 2011 on consumer rights, and since German jurisprudence and doctrine has been proven to have more experience in barter agreements referring to horses, I suggest that the possibility to offset the difference in value of animals being objects of barter contracts against monetary means should also become a part of Polish law.

3.4.3. Delivery of pre-contracted agricultural produce

Although the provisions concerning sale contracts also apply to **contracts for the delivery of pre-contracted agricultural produce** (*umowa kontraktacji*), they apply only if the defect is significant.[578] This would mostly be the case if the producing party provided animals that could not be used for meat production. However, where the producing party is not at fault for the inability to produce contracted products, both parties are solely obliged to return everything that they received when preparing to perform their contractual duties.[579] Nevertheless, as already mentioned, this issue remains outside of the scope of this book.

578 Compare: Article 621 KC.
579 See: K. Zaradkiewicz [in:] K. Pietrzykowski (ed.), *Kodeks cywilny. Komentarz*, p. 403.

IV. Service contracts

1. General characteristics of service contracts with reference to contracts having an animal as their object

1.1. General remarks

In order to provide clear structure and terminology in the legal analysis of how having an animal as a specific object of obligations determines the conclusion, performance and non-performance of service contracts, it is necessary to briefly introduce the basic differences in the legal regulations referring to service contracts. Namely, the qualification of service contracts[580] reveals significant differences in the legal structure of service contracts (*umowy o świadczenie usług, Dienstleistungsverträge/ Dienstverträge*)[581] under Polish law and under German law, used as referential legal system in this book. Thus, this term is understood as a group of contracts concerning the performance of any services (not connected with transfer of rights). There is no normative definition of a service contract in the Polish Civil Code – this term is used only in Article 750 KC with reference to undefined service contracts.[582] However, the German Civil Code includes a definition of a service contract in § 611 BGB stating that a service contract (*umowy o świadczenie usług, Dienstleistungsverträge/ Dienst-*

580 Service contracts are to be understood as a group of contracts having performance of any services as the object (*Umowy o świadczenie usług, Dienstleistungsverträge*) defined in the German law under § 611 BGB, whereas a mandate contract is to be understood as a certain type of service contracts, defined in the Polish law under Article 734 § 1 KC (*Umowa zlecenie*).

581 With reference to an understanding of service contracts in comparative law and model law, see: E. Rott-Pietrzyk [in:] M. Pazdan, (ed.), *System Prawa Prywatnego, Vol. XX B, Prawo prywatne międzynarodowe*, Warszawa 2015, pp. 109–113; F. Zoll [in:] W. Popiołek (ed.), *System prawa handlowego. Międzynarodowe prawo handlowe, Vol. IX,*, Warszawa 2013, pp. 1179 et seq.

582 With reference to the content of Article 750 KC and its meaning, see below in this subchapter.

verträge) is a contract, where "one person who promises a service is obliged to perform the services promised, and the other party is obliged to grant the agreed remuneration."[583] Service contracts, in the meaning of both German and Polish legal systems, should be differentiated from the definition of a mandate contract under Polish law (*umowa zlecenia*), which is regulated in Article 734 § 1 KC. According to the Polish Civil Code, a mandate contract foresees "the performance of a specific juridical act for the principal."[584] The provision of Article 734 § 1 KC does not have its equivalent in German law (with reference to the contract regulated in § 662 BGB – *Auftrag* – see the next sentence), and § 611 BGB does not have its equivalent in Polish law (with reference to the term "service contract" used in Article 750 KC only in reference to undefined contracts – see below). Thus, although § 662 BGB defines the scope of a contract included therein (*Auftrag*) similar to that of a mandate contract in the meaning of Article 734 KC, and many translations refer to this contract also as mandate,[585] § 662 BGB is included outside of the scope of service contracts from § 611 BGB[586] due to its gratuitous performance of judicial acts, which constitutes a significant difference to the definition of mandate contract under Polish law.[587]

The German Civil Code does not separate the definition of a mandate contract in the meaning of Article 734 KC from that of service contracts referred to in § 611 BGB. The German normative definition of a service contract covers the performance of factual and juridical actions (legal acts), which means that it covers both mandate and other contracts, whereas the Polish Civil Code includes only a very narrow definition and detailed regulation of a mandate contract as covering the performance of juridical acts.[588]

583 See: K. Schreiber [in:] R. Schulze, H. Dörner, I. Ebert, T. Hoeren, R. Kemper, I. Saenger, K. Schreiber, H. Schulte-Nölke, A. Staudinger (eds.), *Bürgerliches Gesetzbuch. Handkommentar*, pp. 870–877; R. Müller-Glöge [in:] M. Henssler (ed.), *Münchener Kommentar zum BGB, Vol. IV*, München 2012, § 611, side numbers 1–42, *BeckOnline (last visited: 12.3. 2018)*.

584 See: Article 734 KC in the translation of T. Bil, A. Broniek, A. Cincio, M. Kiełbasa (consulted with G. Dannemann, S. F. Fischer, F. Zoll), *Kodeks cywilny, Civil code*, Warszawa 2011, pp. 327–328.

585 See also: the translation of the German Civil Code provided online by the website *Gesetze im Internet* provided by the German Federal Ministry of Justice: https://www.gesetze-im-internet.de/englisch_bgb/englisch_bgb.html#p2908 (last visited: 18.1.2018).

586 The German legal system recognises five types of service contracts (*Dienstleistungserträge*): service contract (*Dienstvertrag*), contract for work (*Werkvertrag*), mandate (*Geschäftsbesorgungsvertrag*), agency contract (*Maklervertrag*) and safekeeping agreement (*Verwahrungsvertrag*). See: W. Braun, *Geschäftsverträge*, Stuttgart 2007, p. 777.

587 Compare: Article 735 § 1 KC.

588 As already mentioned, the Polish Civil Code does not define a service contract and uses this term used solely in Article 750 KC with reference to undefined service contracts. See: L. Ogiegło [in:] J. Rajski (ed.), *System Prawa Prywatnego, Vol. VII*, pp. 556–584. See: M. Lubelska-Sazanów, *The meaning of service contracts with reference to animals under Ger-*

What is more, under Polish law, all service contracts that are not defined as a certain type of contract in the Polish Civil Code, and which provide performance of factual services, are qualified as "undefined contracts" (Art 759 KC). This qualification occurs as result of the fact that such contracts are not covered by the mandate contract, under the definition inserted in Article 734 KC (as this definition refers only to performance of legal acts), nor by any different legal definition of a contract, where the performance of a party consists in undertaking any specific kind of action. Nevertheless, the service contract under both legal systems is understood as the performance of certain services against payment of an agreed remuneration.[589] The main common characteristic of the provisions of Article 734 KC and § 611 BGB is the lack of an agreed outcome.[590] Thus, the parties agree on a certain performance, but not for a certain result of this performance.[591]

---

man and Polish law [in:] P. Pinior (ed.), *Evolution of private law - new approaches*, pp. 121–130.

589 Compare: the definition of service contract in DCFR, Part C – Services, Section IV.C.-1:101: Scope, which defines service contracts as contracts under which one party, the service provider, undertakes to supply a service to the other party, the client, in exchange for a price and with appropriate adaptations, to contracts under which the service provider undertakes to supply a service to the client other than in exchange for a price (in particular contracts for construction, processing, storage, design, information or advice, and treatment). See: C. Von Bar, E. Clive, H. Schulte-Nölke et al., *Principles, Definitions and Model Rules of European Private Law – Draft Common Frame of Reference (DCFR), Interim Outline Edition*, Munich 2009. The full text of the DCFR from 2009 is available in pdf format at: http://ec.europa.eu/justice/policies/civil/docs/dcfr_outline_edition_en.pdf (last visited: 18.1.2018).

590 This is also what differentiates a service contract from a contract for work (*umowa o dzieło, Werkvertrag*); so, under German law: W. Braun, *Geschäftsverträge*, p. 779; under Polish law: P. Machnikowski [in:] E. Gniewek, P. Machnikowski (eds.), *Kodeks cywilny. Komentarz*, Warszawa 2016, pp. 1411–1413.

591 See, comprehensively on this matter: L. Ogiegło, *Usługi jako przedmiot stosunków obligacyjnych,* Katowice 1989; M. Barański, *Konstrukcja prawna umów o pośrednictwo*, Rejent 2010, Issue 9; B. Bladowski, *Umowa o dzieło i umowa zlecenia,* Warszawa 1987; E. Dobrodziej, *Prawa i obowiązki stron w umowach zlecenia i o dzieło*, Bydgoszcz 1993; E. Dobrodziej„ *Zatrudnienie na podstawie umów cywilno-prawnych. Aktualne przepisy. Wyjaśnienia, komentarze*, Bydgoszcz 2000; P. Drapała, *Prowadzenie cudzych spraw bez zlecenia. Konstrukcja prawna*, Warszawa 2010; Gawlik B., *Umowy mieszane – konstrukcja i ocena prawna*, Palestra 1974, Issue 5; W. Ludwiczak, *Umowa zlecenia*, Poznań 1955; Małysz F., *Kontrakty menedżerskie*, Służba Pracownicza 2012, Issue 8; M. Mrozowska, *Umowy o zarządzanie*, Państwo i Prawo 1996, Issue 5; I. Mycko-Katner, *Umowa agencyjna*, Warszawa 2012; J. Olszewski, A. Paszek, *Umowy o dzieło, agencyjne, zlecenia. Objaśnienia i wzory*, Warszawa 2000. Aside from the legal qualification of services, which can be found in Article 353 § 1 KC, the Polish doctrine recognises also a different differentiation that is accepted by the judiciary – the differentiations of the obligations into services of result and services of careful performance. See: E. Łętowska [in:] E. Łętowska (ed.), *System Prawa Prywatnego, Vol. V, Prawo zobowiązań – część ogólna*, pp. 196–199; K. Topolewski, *Przedmiot zobowiązania z umowy zlecenia*, Warszawa 2015, Chapter II.10.

The differentiation of service contracts into defined and undefined contracts (i. e., according to Article 750 KC – contracts on the performance of services not regulated by other provisions) in the Polish legal system constitutes another difference in reference to German law.[592] The defined contracts are those where the *essentialia negotii*, i. e. the definition of the parties, the object and the content of the parties' obligations, can be found in the Polish Civil Code or in a different Polish legal act.[593] However, the differentiation into defined and undefined contracts does not have to be limited to service contracts. The most recognizable undefined contracts under both Polish and German law are: franchise,[594] distribution, factoring, forfaiting and know-how contracts.[595] Although some of these contracts could be applicable to animals – at least in theory (e. g. in the case of a know-how contract, one could imagine the distribution of knowledge with reference to a special animal's training method; nevertheless, this would be rather qualified as a training contract) – this book does not refer to these types of contracts due to their marginal applicability to animals.

The reason for presenting the differences between defined and undefined contracts in the Polish legal system is the importance of understanding how to qualify certain service contracts under Polish law, and which rules to apply. Thus, Article 750 KC provides that the provisions applicable to mandate contracts, defined in Article 734 § 1 KC, are also applicable to all undefined service contracts.[596] Therefore, it is important to distinguish between a defined contract and an undefined one, as the referral from Article 750 KC combines two features of contracts and applies them to contracts that are not only **undefined**, but also refer to **services.**[597] These are contracts on the performance of services that – according to Article 750 – are not regulated by other provisions concerning obligational contracts (e. g. providing performance of one or more factual activities by the parties). Generally, contracts providing for the performance of a

592 Compare: M. Lubelska-Sazanów, *The meaning of service contracts with reference to animals under German and Polish law* [in:] P. Pinior (ed.), *Evolution of private law – new approaches*, pp. 121–130.

593 See: W. Katner, [in:] W Katner (ed.), *System Prawa Prywatnego, Vol. IX, Prawo zobowiązań – umowy nienazwane*, p. 7.

594 See: U. Promińska, [in:] W Katner (ed.), *System Prawa Prywatnego, Vol. IX, Prawo zobowiązań – umowy nienazwane*, pp. 858–883.

595 See: M. Romanowski, W. Kocot, A. Kappes [in:] W Katner (ed.), *System Prawa Prywatnego, Vol. IX, Prawo zobowiązań – umowy nienazwane*, pp. 289–359.

596 To learn more about the interpretation and scope of application of Article 750 KC, see: R. Morek, M. Raczkowski [in:] K. Osajda (ed.), *Kodeks cywilny. Komentarz. Tom IIIB*, pp. 757–776; L. Ogiegło [in:] K. Pietrzykowski (ed.), *Kodeks cywilny. Vol. II, Komentarz*, pp. 1411–1413; E. Rott-Pietrzyk, *Glosa do wyroku SN z 28. 10. 1999 – II CKN 530/98*, OSP 2000, No. 7–8, item C 118, pp. 393–396.

597 P. Machnikowski [in:] E. Gniewek, P. Machnikowski (ed.), *Kodeks cywilny. Komentarz*, pp. 1411–1413.

legal action are not covered by the scope of Article 750 KC, as they are regulated by special provisions applicable to these types of contracts (in particular commission or agency contracts), or by the more general provisions of the mandate contract from Article 734 KC. However, an undefined contract may also contain various elements that are typical for other defined contracts (in particular for contracts referred to by some representatives of the Polish doctrine as mixed contracts[598]).[599]

The respective applicability of provisions covering mandate contracts from Article 734 KC *et seq.*, according to Article 750 KC, means that these provisions can be applied in three ways. Firstly, they can be applied respectively without modifications,[600] secondly with proper modifications, or thirdly then might not be applied at all – depending on the content of a certain contract.[601]

The German doctrine also defines contracts that are not regulated in the German Civil Code or other German legal acts (*atypische Verträge*). However, under German law, these are never considered to be service contracts, as all service contracts (i.e. an obligation for one party to perform a legal or factual action) are covered by specific provisions covering specific types of service contracts, or by the general definition of service contracts included in § 611

598 Nevertheless, I follow the point of view introduced to the Polish doctrine by Z. Radwański, namely that there is no need to differentiate a group of contracts referred to by certain representatives of the legal doctrine as "mixed contracts". According to this theory, contracts that are not regulated by the civil law provisions are either undefined contracts or contracts, to which – due to their *essentialia negotii* – the provisions of a specific defined contract apply. See: Z. Radwański, *Teoria umów*, Warszawa 1977, pp. 241–242. See also: W. Katner [in:] W Katner (ed.), *System Prawa Prywatnego, Vol. IX, Prawo zobowiązań – umowy nienazwane*, pp. 13–14 and Subchapter IV.1.2.3. of this book.

599 P. Machnikowski [in:] E. Gniewek, P. Machnikowski (ed.), *Kodeks cywilny. Komentarz*, pp. 1411–1413. See also: M. Lubelska-Sazanów, *The meaning of service contracts with reference to animals under German and Polish law* [in:] P. Pinior (ed.), *Evolution of private law – new approaches*, pp. 121–130.

600 This does not mean direct application. It is still the respective applicability of certain law provisions, which means that these provisions regulate different factual situations than the facts of the case at hand (which are not covered directly by any civil law provisions of a certain legal system). However, due to certain characteristics of the factual situation regulated by law, deemed to be significant by the lawmaker, they are respectively applicable to the factual situation not regulated by law. See: J. Nowacki, *Odpowiednie stosowanie przepisów prawa*, PiP 1964, Issue 3, pp. 370–371.

601 With reference to a respective applicability of provisions concerning mandate contracts to "undefined" service contracts, see: SN, ruling from 28.10.1999 – II CKN 530/98, with an approving gloss of E. Rott-Pietrzyk, *Glosa do wyroku SN z 28.10.1999 – II CKN 530/98*, OSP 2000, No. 7–8, item C 118, pp. 393–396; J. Nowacki, *Analogia legis*, Warszawa 1966, p.141. Compare also with the examples shown in the publication: M. Lubelska-Sazanów, *Odpowiedzialność z tytułu rękojmi za wady fizyczne zwierząt*, Transformacje Prawa Prywatnego 4/2015, pp. 21–41.

BGB.[602] The difference between undefined contracts in the understanding of Article 750 KC and *atypische Vertäge* under German law constitutes a significant difference for the service contracts having an animal as their object. Thus, most service contracts having an animal as their object are qualified as undefined service contracts under Polish law (Article 734 KC in connection with Article 750 KC) and as defined service contracts under German law (§ 611 BGB). Under German law, the respective applicability of provisions covering different types of contracts to contracts described in the German Civil Code (i. e. *atypische Verträge*) occurs on the same basis - they may be applied respectively without modifications, with modifications or might not be applied at all. However, the provisions that are applied respectively may be provisions covering all types of contracts.[603]

The differentiation into defined and undefined contracts (also: *atypische Verträge*) derives from the fact that, due to the freedom of contract principle,[604] the parties are able to conclude contracts that are not defined by the provisions of civil law in Poland and Germany.[605] Under both laws, the existence of the freedom of contract principle is considered to be natural and is derived from

602 The German legal system recognizes five types of service contracts (*Dienstleistungsverträge*): service contract (*Dienstvertrag*), contract for work (*Werkvertrag*), mandate (*Geschäftsbesorgungsvertrag*), agency contract (*Maklervertrag*) and safekeeping agreement (*Verwahrungsvertrag*). See: W. Braun, *Geschäftsverträge*, p. 777. The Polish Civil Code also recognizes these types of contracts and qualifies them, as already mentioned, as defined service contracts. Thus, the only difference between the two legal systems can be observed with reference to undefined service contracts, which cannot be qualified as mandate contracts under Polish law, since they provide the performance of factual, rather than legal acts (according to Article 734 KC, the definition of a mandate contract refers only to performance of legal acts). This problem does not occur in German law, as service contracts (*Dienstvertrag*) covers the performance of both factual and legal acts.

603 Thus, the respective applicability of provisions covering different types of contracts to "undefined" contracts/ *atypische Verträge* leads to the same result under Polish and German law, compare: Subchapter IV.1.1. of this book. The difference between the respective applicability of provisions covering different types of contracts as "undefined" contracts/ *atypische Verträge* under Polish and German law is the fact that these "undefined" contracts under Polish law are service contracts providing performance of a factual action. Compare also: M. Lubelska-Sazanów, *The meaning of service contracts with reference to animals under German and Polish law* [in:] P. Pinior (ed.), *Evolution of private law - new approaches*, pp. 121–130.

604 In general to the freedom of contract principle, see: P. Machnikowski, *Swoboda umów według Art. 353(1) KC. Konstrukcja prawna*, Warszawa 2005. See also: E. Rott-Pietrzyk, *Commercial Agency Contracts...* [in:] *Private Autonomy...*, pp. 15–34; M. Lubelska-Sazanów, *The "Principle of No Freedom of Contract": A Post-Modern Version of the Freedom of Contract Principle?*, [in:] M. De Maestri, S. Dominelli (ed.), *Party autonomy in European private (and) international law Vol. II*, Rome 2015, pp. 15–31.

605 See also: W. Katner [in:] W Katner (ed.), *System Prawa Prywatnego, Vol. IX, Prawo zobowiązań - umowy nienazwane*, pp. 3–6.

Article 353^1 KC and – respectively – § 311 BGB.[606] The limits of the freedom of contract principle are set by the law and by content of fair dealing principles[607] (which under Polish law means the principles of social co-existence,[608] and under German law the values derived from the constitution and represented by society[609]). However, the extent of the parties' contractual freedom to conclude undefined contracts is usually limited by law.

Generally, there are at least three aspects of the freedom of contract principle in Europe.[610] Firstly, the parties are free to decide whether they want to conclude a contract or not; secondly, the parties may freely choose the business partner with which they want to conclude a contract; and thirdly, they may determine the content and aim of their contract. Most Polish scholars consider the freedom of form as a fourth aspect of this principle.[611] It means that the parties are also free to determine the form of their contract. The freedom of form and the freedom to make amendments to the contract create, together with the first aspects of the freedom of contract principle, a definition of the freedom of contract principle *sensu largo*.[612] However, there is also a definition of the freedom of contract principle in the *sensu stricto* sense, which gains importance in the context of the creation of undefined contracts and their differentiation from defined contracts. This principle is strictly connected with the parties' autonomy and expressed by the fact that the parties are free to determine the content and the goal of the contract themselves.[613] The importance of the freedom of contract principle is still a very current and practical issue, since the right to individually decide how to structure a certain contract and to freely agree on its terms, are the cornerstones of an open, market-oriented and competitive international economic order.[614]

606 See: M. Gehrlein [in:] H. Bamberger, H. Roth, W. Hau, R. Poseck (eds.), *Beck'sche Online Kommentare, BeckOK, BGB*, 45. Ed., München 2017, BGB § 311 side number 2.

607 Compare: § 134 and § 138 BGB. With reference to Polish law, see: W. Katner, [in:] W Katner (ed.), *System Prawa Prywatnego, Vol. IX, Prawo zobowiązań – umowy nienazwane*, p. 3.

608 Article 56 KC.

609 Under German law: "*Die Wertentscheidungen der Wirtschafts- und Sozialverfassung*", See: V. Emmerich [in:] W. Krüger (ed.), *Münchener Kommentar zum BGB*, § 311, side numbers 1–4, *BeckOnline (last visited: 12.3.2018).*

610 H. Schulte-Nölke [in:] R. Schulze, H. Dörner, I. Ebert, T. Hoeren, R. Kemper, I. Saenger, K. Schreiber, H. Schulte-Nölke, A. Staudinger (eds.), *Common European Sales Law – Commentary*, Baden-Baden 2012, p. 85.

611 S. Włodyka, C. Żurawska, *Zasady prawa gospodarczego prywatnego (handlowego)* [in:] *System Prawa Handlowego, Vol. 1*, Warszawa 2009, pp. 328–330; M. Safjan [in:] K. Pietrzykowski (ed.), *Kodeks cywilny., Komentarz*, Vol. I, pp. 1074–1084.

612 E. Rott-Pietrzyk, *Commercial Agency Contracts...* [in:] *Private Autonomy...*, p. 19.

613 *Idem.*

614 M. Lubelska-Sazanów, *The "Principle of No Freedom of Contract": A Post-Modern Version of the Freedom of Contract Principle?* [in:] M. De Maestri, S. Dominelli (ed.), *Party autonomy in European private (and) international law Vol. II*, Rome 2015, pp. 15–31; M. Bonell, *The*

Due to the composition of this book, the impact of an animal being an object of a contractual obligation has been divided into general remarks, performance and consequence of improper performance and non-performance on a particular service contract. Therefore, the first subchapter sets out general remarks referring to different kinds of service contracts having an animal as their object presented in this book (one after another), the second subchapter refers to the performance of these contracts, and the third subchapter refers to improper performance and non-performance of these kinds of service contracts having an animal as their object.

1.2. General characteristics of specific types of service contracts with an animal as their object

The service contracts that are most commonly used with reference to animals are both defined and undefined contracts. Service contracts, which due to their qualification as most commonly having animals as their object and, therefore, referred to in this book in separate sections are: commission contracts, agency contracts, teaching/training contracts and safe-keeping contracts. These types of contracts, together with other types of service contract that are not qualified as any of the contracts above, but are also briefly referred to in this book due to their less common applicability to animals, constitute foundations of this chapter and will be described in turn. This chapter, therefore, consists of analyses of the conclusion, performance and the consequences of improper and non-performance of these types of service contract in the Polish legal system and in the referential legal system of Germany, in cases where an animal is an object of the contract constituting a specific object of obligations.

Animals as specific objects of obligations have a significant impact on the content of a service contract. Due to the freedom of contract principle described in the subchapter above, parties are free to define the content of their contract[615] how they like, and therefore to adjust it to the nature and needs of the animals being its object. The specifics of these obligational relationships are described below. Whereas the content of the subchapter "General remarks" presents only an introduction to the service contracts referred to in this book, they are pre-

---

UNIDROIT Principles in Practice. Case law and Bibliography on the Principles of Commercial Contracts, New York 2006, second edition, p. 69; M. Lubelska-Sazanów, *The "Principle of No Freedom of Contract": A Post-Modern Version of the Freedom of Contract Principle?*, [in:] M. De Maestri, S. Dominelli (eds.), *Party autonomy in European private (and) international law, Vol. II*, Rome 2015, pp. 15–31.

615 Whereas the scope of the freedom of contract principle is much broader: see Subchapter IV.1.1.

sented more detailed in the subchapter concerning performance and non-performance of contracts divided into sections referring to specific types of these contracts.

1.2.1. Commission contracts having an animal as their object

According to Article 758 KC and § 383 of the German Commercial Code (HGB),[616] commission contracts (*umowa komisu, das Kommissionsgeschäft*) state that the commission agent undertakes the service of selling an animal (usually a horse) for the principal (i. e. the horse's owner). The agent acts in his own name, but on the principal's account, and performs its services professionally.[617] At this point, it is worth referring to an interesting explanatory chart of A. Kędzierska-Cieślak, which presents the problem of representation *sensu largo* and refers to the differences in legal relationships, where the party performing obligation acts in his own name and in the principal's name.[618] Thus, the commission agent is always acting as a business (whereas his contracting party, i. e. the principal/horse owner – not necessary).[619]

In order to avoid confusing the reader with the introduction of a new German legal act on undertaking commercial activities by at least one of the contracting parties,[620] it is necessary to make some general remarks concerning differences in the legal nature of the **commission contract** in Polish legal system and the system used as referential in this book, i. e. the German legal system. The main difference is connected with the different placement of provisions concerning commission contracts. Hence, in the German legal system these provisions can be found in the German Commercial Code, whereas in Poland they are in the Civil Code.[621] This situation is caused by a general European qualification of a commission contract as a commercial activity,[622] and the fact that the com-

616 The German Commercial Code [*Handelsgesetzbuch*] from 10. 5. 1987, J L of 18. 7. 2917, Part I, item 2446, as amended.

617 See, with reference to Polish law: J. Frąckowiak [in:] J. Rajski, (ed.), *System Prawa Prywatnego, Vol. VII*, pp. 729–731; A. Kędzierska Cieślak, *Komis (zagadnienia cywilnoprawne)*, Warszawa 1973, pp. 31 et seq. See, with reference to German law: I. Koller [in:] C. Canaris, M. Habersack, C. Schäfer, *Staub Handelsgesetzbuch Großkommentar*, Göttingen 2013, pp. 84–85. See more with reference to the conclusion of commission contracts, the qualification of parties and the content of their duties: Chapter IV.2.1.

618 See: A. Kędzierska Cieślak, *Komis (zagadnienia cywilnoprawne)*, p. 44 and its description on pages 45–47 (with another interesting chart on p. 46).

619 See: Subchapter IV.1.

620 See the act mentioned in the note below.

621 Compare: § 383–406 HGB.

622 See: J. Frąckowiak [in:] J. Rajski, (ed.), *System Prawa Prywatnego, Vol. VII*, p. 719; A. Kędzierska Cieślak, *Komis (zagadnienia cywilnoprawne)*, p. 31 et seq.

mission agent always acts as a business.[623] The German qualification of the commission agreement is typical of civil codes of countries that recognize a division of private law into commercial law and civil law. The qualification of a commission contract as a commercial activity justifies its regulation in the German Commercial Code. The Polish Civil Code does not recognize the differentiation of private law into the commercial law and the civil law. Therefore, the regulation of commission contract in the Polish legal system can be found in the Civil Code, although it is considered to be a commercial activity. This means that under Polish law as well, the commission agent always acts as a business, and the commission contract is treated as a commercial contract.[624] In both legal systems, the commission agent always acts in his own name, but on the principal's account,[625] the obligations and duties of the parties also remain the same.[626] Both legal systems qualify a contract as a commission contract only if the parties agree on remuneration for the commission agent.[627] However – unlike in the case of an agency contract – a commission contract under Polish and German laws requires commercial activity from only one of the contracting parties, i. e. on the side of a commission agent.[628]

Whereas the Polish Civil Code provides that only movables may be objects of commission agreements[629] (although some representatives of the doctrine accept that this provision applies also to securities[630]), the referential system of

623 As to the definition of a business, it is defined as a natural or legal person or an organisational entity that when entering into a legal transaction, acts in exercise of a trade, business or profession, see: § 12 BGB and Article 43[1] KC.

624 J. Frąckowiak [in:] J. Rajski, (ed.), *System Prawa Prywatnego, Vol. VII*, pp. 721–725, E. Rott-Pietrzyk [in:] *System Prawa Prywatnego, Vol. VII*, p. 632.

625 Compare: § 383 HGB and Article 765 KC.

626 With reference to Polish law, see: J. Frąckowiak [in:] J. Rajski, (ed.), *System Prawa Prywatnego, Vol. VII, Prawo zobowiązań – część szczegółowa*, pp. 736–746. With reference to German law, see: F. Häuser [in:] K. Schmidt, B. Grunewald (ed.), *Münchener Kommentar zum HGB, Vol. V*, München 2013, § 384, side numbers 1–79, *BeckOnline (last visited: 12. 3. 2018)*.

627 Otherwise, a contract is to be seen as an undefined contract *(atypischer Vertrag)*. See: J. Frąckowiak [in:] J. Rajski, (ed.), *System Prawa Prywatnego, Vol. VII*, p. 719. With reference to German law, see: I. Koller [in:] C. Canaris, M. Habersack, C. Schäfer, *Staub Handelsgesetzbuch Großkommentar*, Göttingen 2013, pp. 84–86.

628 Thus, the commercial nature of an agency contract is qualified with reference to both parties to the contract. See: E. Rott-Pietrzyk [in:] *System Prawa Prywatnego, Vol. VII*, p. 632.

629 See: Article 765 KC.

630 Some authors represent the opinion that the provisions regulating commission contracts are applicable to securities (directly or by analogy), See: J. Jezioro [in:] E. Gniewek, P. Machnikowski (eds.), *Kodeks cywilny. Komentarz*, pp. 1447–1450; A. Kędzierska Cieślak, *Komis (zagadnienia cywilnoprawne)*, pp. 55–57; J. Rajski [in:] J. Rajski, (ed.), *System Prawa Prywatnego, Vol. VII*, p. 723. However, A. Nowacki, does not mention this possibility: A. Nowacki [in:] K. Osajda (ed.), *Kodeks cywilny. Komentarz. Tom IIIB*, p. 848; L. Ogiegło [in:]

German law represents a very broad definition of a commission agreement and recognizes that not only movables, but also securities and any other actions undertaken by a commission agent may be the object of performance by a commission agent.[631] However, this issue does not affect the qualification of a contract having an animal as its object as a commission contract or not. Thus, the legal provisions applicable to movables, which are recognized as objects of commission contracts under both legal systems, Polish and German, are applied respectively to obligations having animals as their object.[632] Therefore, the sale of animals performed by a commission agent, acting as a business and in his own name, but on the account of a principal, in exchange for remuneration, will always be qualified as a commission contract – whether under Polish (Articles. 765–773 KC) law[633] or German (§§ 383–406 HGB).[634]

Commission contracts date back to the Middle Ages, where it arose as an answer to the needs of a growing commercial market.[635] A different, very important reason was the seller's desire or need (e.g. because of a lack of commercial contacts) to stay hidden from the buyer. Therefore, the institution of a commission agreement was founded in order to enable one seller to perform his business activities using the services and good name of a different seller.[636] This is exactly the same reason why the institution of a commission contract is also used today for the sale of horses. The lack of business contacts of inexperienced breeders and the buyers' trust in internationally known associations performing auction sales of most successful sport horses make this institution very popular in Germany.[637] The only successfully performed horse auctions in Poland are the

---

K. Pietrzykowski (ed.), *Kodeks cywilny, Komentarz*, Vol. II, pp. 704–705. The second approach seems to be more convincing.

631 See: § 383 HGB and § 406 HGB; F. Häuser [in:] K. Schmidt, B. Grunewald (ed.), *Münchener Kommentar zum HGB, Vol. V*, München 2013, § 384, side number 18; J. Rajski [in:] J. Rajski, (ed.), *System Prawa Prywatnego, Vol. VII*, p. 718.

632 § 90a BGB, providing that the rules applicable to the things are to be respectively applied to animals.

633 With reference to commission contracts in Polish law, see: A. Kędzierska-Cieślak, *Komis (zagadnienia cywilnoprawne)*, pp. 15–29 (however, with reference to a previously binding Polish Civil Code); J. Frąckowiak [in:] J. Rajski, (ed.), *System Prawa Prywatnego, Vol. VII*, pp. 711–761.

634 With reference to commission contracts in German law, see: F. Häuser [in:] K. Schmidt, B. Grunewald (ed.), *Münchener Kommentar zum HGB, Vol. V*, München 2013, §§ 383–406. K. Schmidt, *Handelsrecht*, Köln 2014, pp. 997–1057.

635 Compare: K. Schmidt, *Handelsrecht*, pp. 1002–1003.

636 J. Frąckowiak [in:] J. Rajski, (ed.), *System Prawa Prywatnego, Vol. VII*, p. 718.

637 The German breeds, like Hanoverian, Oldenburg and Holsteiner horses are known worldwide for their sport track records. Each of the breeds has its own association in Germany, and every year they hold horse auctions. For information about sport track records of horses of a certain breed and its auctions, see the websites of several breeding associations (last visited: 4.2.2016): http://www.hannoveraner.com/hannoveraner-verband/; http://oldenburger-pferde.net/; http://holsteiner-verband.de/.

once performed by the Arabian horses studs (Michałowice, Janów, Biała Podlaska),[638] though most horses[639] sold in these auctions are bred in the stud, therefore the institution of commission contracts does not apply in this case. Nevertheless, the sale of horses at auction, where the commission agent – through representing the horse's owner's interest in its own name, intermediates in the transfer of ownership – often takes place in the referential legal system of Germany. Therefore, the German common usage of commission agency construction to intermediate in the transfer of ownership on horse auctions justifies again the choice of the German legal system as a referential system referred to in this book. The Polish equestrian market could take advantage of the experience of Germany in the future, since at the moment there are no horse auctions organized, where the construction of commission agency would be used to intermediate in the transfer of ownership from the horse's owner to the bidder. Probably, the sale of horses in Poland is not currently popular enough to make holding these types of auctions profitable.

As already mentioned in the previous paragraph and in Subchapter III.2.2. of this book ("Consumer sale and related legal problems concerning B2B, B2C and C2C Contracts"), auction sales where the commission agent intermediates in the transfer of ownership are very popular for the sale of horses in Germany. Thus, the auction sale of horses in Germany occurs in two forms: either in the form of an auction performed by a certain horse stud selling its own horses, or in form of an auction organized by horse breeders associations, where the horses that are offered to the public are owned by different private principals. In this second type of auction, a commission agent intermediates in the transfer of ownership and all the provisions referring to commission contracts apply (since this issue refers solely to German practice, these provisions are regulated in §§ 383–406 HGB). In this case, the horse breeders associations usually sell horses owned by their members with engagement of a public expert auctioneer,[640] therefore the provisions of the German Civil Code providing for an exclusion of warranty for used goods sold at public auctions, which is respectively applicable to animals,[641] will apply. Nevertheless, as already mentioned in Subchapter III.3.2. of this book,

638 For more information, see: http://www.prideofpoland.pl/; http://www.janow.arabians.pl/.

639 There are no indications about a possibility of selling a horse from a private breeder using the institution of a commission contract in the auction rules, though this possibility cannot be excluded with any certainty and would probably be admitted in some exceptional cases (e. g. where it concerns the sale of an exceptionally promising horse from a private owner).

640 See, e. g.: BGH, ruling from 24. 2. 2010 – VIII ZR 71/09 (OLG Köln); typical rules of a horse auction performed by the Hanoverian horses association, last visited: 4. 2. 2016 from: http://www.hannoveraner.com/hannoveraner-verband/auktionen/auktionsarchiv/auktionen-2016/verdener-auktion-januar/auktionsbroschuere/.

641 See § 474 (1) BGB concerning the sale of used goods at public auctions and § 90a BGB, providing that the rules applicable to the things are to be respectively applied to animals.

I do not grade positively the applicability of provisions referring to used and unused goods to animals in German law, and do not suggest its eventual transition into Polish law.[642] Therefore, since they are not of importance for the Polish law, which is the primary legal system described in this book (whereas the German legal system serves solely as a referential one) and since their transition into Polish law would not be useful, this issue is not described in more detail in this book.

The structure of a commission contract is commonly used in animal markets. Thus, the trainer or breeder often appears as a person having many contacts and knowing the market from the "inside", and it is very likely that such people undertake additional economical activities, acting occasionally as commission agents. Even though commission contracts do not serve as a basis for conducting horse auctions in Poland, it is worth showing how the German legal system and practice deal with such auctions and be able to derive from this knowledge in the future.

1.2.2. Agency contracts having an animal as their object

According to Article 758 KC and § 84 HGB, in an agency contract (*umowa agencyjna, Handelsvertretungsvertrag*) a commission agent undertakes the obligation to mediate permanently within the scope of the activities of his enterprise, against remuneration, in concluding contracts with clients for the benefit of the business being the principal, or in concluding such contracts in the principal's name.

Agency contracts having an animal as their object are commonly used in the sale of horses due to its specific characteristics and usage in sport. Thus, where it concerns high-class horses that are prepared to take part in horse-riding championships at the highest level, or young horses with very promising pedigrees, its purchase is often carried out by commercial agents acting in the name and on the account of their principals. Thus, healthy and promising horses are not that easy to find and – as they are often being sought in different countries, or even different continents – their purchase would not be possible without an "insider" on the spot who knows all the local conditions very well. In addition, it is not enough to find a good horse, but the horse has to "fit" the rider, which means that not every healthy and promising horse will be suitable for each and every athlete. Taking all this into account, a commercial agent specializing in the sale of horses must have special connections in the equestrian society and a

642 However, it is undeniable that the issue of whether animals are used goods or not is still current in the German practice and jurisprudence, see e.g.: BGH, ruling from 24.2.2010 – VIII ZR 71/09 (OLG Köln).

longstanding practical knowledge in the field of horse sports in order to be able to find a suitable horse far away from its principal. Although there are no legal obstacles to using the legal institution of agency contract with reference to sale of other animals, such as purebred dogs, it is very rare. The institution of an agency contract might also be very helpful to achieve the idea of the wellbeing of an animal itself – thus, if the animal "fits" its owner and the owner is prepared for the duties connected with owning that specific type of animal, it is rather not probable that any of them could not be satisfied.

The regulation of a commercial agent in the German and Polish legal system (as well as in all EU states) is based on the Council Directive on the coordination of the laws of the Member States relating to self-employed commercial agents (Directive 86/653/EEC).[643] Although – due to the Directive 86/653/EEC – the provisions regulating the activity of a commercial agent are very similar in Germany and in Poland, in the German legal system these provisions can be found in the Commercial Code (HGB),[644] whereas in Poland they are in the Civil Code.[645] Thus, as has already been presented using the example of a commission contract in the Polish and German Civil Codes,[646] the qualification of an agency contract as a commercial activity justifies its regulation in the German Commercial Code (HGB).[647] As the Polish Civil Code does not recognize the differentiation of private law into the commercial law and civil law, the regulation of the agency contract in the Polish legal system can be found in the Civil Code, although it is considered to be a commercial activity. However, in the case of an agency contract, both parties are always professionals,[648] i. e. an agency requires both parties to a contract to perform commercial activity (unlike a commission contract – see the subchapter above).[649] According to the legal definition of agency, its specific nature consists in the permanent mediation of an agent against remuneration in concluding contracts with clients for the benefit of the

643 Council Directive of 18 December 1986 on the coordination of the laws of the Member States relating to self-employed commercial agents (86/653/EEC), OJ 382, 31. 12. 1986, p. 17–21; To learn more, see: E. Rott-Pietrzyk, *Agent handlowy…*, pp. 17–115.

644 Compare: § 84 – § 92c HGB.

645 See: Articles 758–764^{9} KC.

646 See: Subchapter IV.1.2.1. of this book.

647 However, note that in some European countries, the regulation of an agency contract can also be found in separate legal acts, e. g. in Finland, Belgium, Denmark, Greece, France, etc. See: E. Rott-Pietrzyk, *Agent handlowy…*, pp. 262–263.

648 However, the duties and responsibilities of both contracting parties are not always the same, see: E. Rott-Pietrzyk, *Ochrona przedsiębiorcy jako strony słabszej na przykładzie agenta handlowego* [in:] M. Boratyńska, *Księga Jubileuszowa ofiarowana Profesorowi Adamowi Zielińskiemu,* Warszawa 2016, pp. 701–724.

649 With reference to the commercial nature of agency, see: E. Rott-Pietrzyk [in:] *System Prawa Prywatnego, Vol. VII*, p. 632.

business being the principal, or in concluding such contracts in the principal's name.[650]

For the purposes of Directive 86/653/EEC, "commercial agent" means a self-employed intermediary who has continuing authority to negotiate the sale or the purchase of things on behalf of another person (the "principal"), or to negotiate and conclude such transactions on behalf of and in the name of that principal.[651] The German and Polish definitions of a commercial agent conform with the definition from the directive, but with one, substantial exception.[652] Namely, although Directive 86/653/EEC does not anticipate this, the most characteristic feature of an agency contract in both the German and Polish legal system is the fact that the commercial agent may perform his activities only on behalf of another business, which gives this contract a professional nature (a B2B – Business to Business Contract). Thus, although the content of Directive 86/653/EEC does not go that deep, the comparison of Article 758 KC with § 84 (1) HGB shows that the content of both provisions is very similar.

Agency contracts in which the agent undertakes an obligation to intermediate in the sale of horses have different contents, standards of performance and risk that the agent has to bear, and a different understanding of defects in the event of improper performance. Therefore, the fact that an animal is the object of the sale contract that the commercial agent undertakes to intermediate influences the conclusion, performance and improper performance of the agency contract. These differences arise from the fact that animals are living creatures, i. e. (under both Polish and German law) not things. Due to the methodology used in this book, further considerations referring to performance and non-performance of agency contracts can be found in Subchapters IV.2.2. and IV.3.2. of this book.

1.2.3. Teaching/training contracts having an animal as their object

The most frequent application of **service contracts having animals as their objects** can be observed with reference to contracts having the **training of an animal as its aim** (*umowa o trening zwierzęcia, der Trainingsvertrag*). However, in this case, the question arises: who is being trained – the animal or the owner?

---

650 Compare: Article 758 KC and § 84 HGB. See more with reference to the definition of an agency contract in the Polish legal system and other European countries' legal systems: E. Rott-Pietrzyk, *Agent handlowy…;* E. Rott-Pietrzyk, *Umowa agencyjna w prawie polskim a standardy europejskie*, Kwart. Prawa Pryw. 1998, z. 1, pp. 25–130.

651 See: Article 1.2 of the Council Directive of 18 December 1986 on the coordination of the laws of the Member States relating to self-employed commercial agents (86/653/EEC); see more: E. Rott-Pietrzyk, *Komentarz do Dyrektywy Rady nr 86/653 z 18 grudnia 1986 roku w sprawie harmonizacji praw państw członkowskich dotyczących niezależnych agentów handlowych*, Probemy Prawne Handlu Zagranicznego 2000, Issue 19/20, pp. 242–246.

652 Compare: § 84 HGB; Article 758 KC.

In fact, there are two types of contracts that have to be distinguished.[653] Thus, taking the example of horses: there are service contracts consisting in a trainer **teaching a rider** on his or her own horse (or on a horse left for him to ride by the owner)[654] and service contracts consisting in **training of the animal itself** (the trainer trains the animal as the horse rider).[655] The same applies to other animals, i. e. a trainer may train, for example, a dog's owner by instructing how to deal with the animal, but he may also train a dog himself at his place (where the "trainer's place" is used as the description of the place where he conducts his business, e. g. a certain stables or kennels, but it might also be his place of residence or an institution run by him).[656]

For contracts consisting in **teaching a rider on a horse by a trainer**[657] **or the owner of a different animal, by giving the rider instructions**, under Polish law these contracts are qualified as undefined service contracts, for which the provisions concerning mandate contract regulated in Article 734 KC apply respectively (in reference to the meaning of this term: see below).[658] Under German law, these contracts also qualify as service contracts, though they are covered by the general definition of service contract of § 611 BGB.[659] These contracts are

653 With reference to the legal qualification of training contracts under German law, see: J. Borggräfe, *Der Sporttrainervertrag*, Frankfurt am Main 2006, pp. 25–62.

654 There are no restrictions that would forbid any person from teaching horseriding, but in Germany, as in Poland, there are several courses offered that are acknowledged by equestrian organisations and can be attended only by trainers with certain skills and experience and, which finish with a obtaining a special title, see: Die Bundesvereinigung der Berufsreiter, *Welchem Reitlehrer kann ich trauen?*, St. Georg 2012, No. 11, pp. 64–69; PZJ, *Doszkalanie kadr instruktorsko-trenerskich – Warunki oraz tryb przyznawania i pozbawiania licencji szkoleniowca oraz certyfikatu instruktora szkolenia podstawowego PZJ*, available at: http://pzj.pl/sites/default/files/przepisy/doszkalanie_kadr_regulamin_2015_02_12.pdf (last visited: 13. 3. 2018).

655 Compare: regulations concerning the profession of a horse rider, downloaded from: the website "Pferd aktuell", available at: *http://www.pferd-aktuell.de/ausbildung/berufsaus bildung/berufsausbildung* and the website of PZJ available at: *http://www.pzj.pl/node/zawód-jeździec* (both, last visited: 4. 2. 2017).

656 Compare: W. Braun, *Geschäftsverträge*, p. 942.

657 With reference to the competences and certification of horse riding trainers in Poland, see: http://pzj.pl/sites/default/files/przepisy/doszkalanie_kadr_regulamin_2015_02_12.pdf. See also, with reference to the profession of horse rider in Poland and Germany: the website of PZJ available at: *http://www.pzj.pl/node/zawód-jeździec* (both, last visited: 4. 2. 2017) and the website "Pferd aktuell", available at: *http://www.pferd-aktuell.de/ausbildung/berufs ausbildung/berufsausbildung*.

658 See: Subchapter IV.1.1. of this book. With reference to teaching contracts and its recognition in Polish law, see: L. Ogiegło [in:] J. Rajski (ed.), *System Prawa Prywatnego, Vol. VII*, pp. 578–579 and with reference to German law, see: W. Braun, *Geschäftsverträge*, pp. 941–943. Compare also the decisions of Polish Courts of Appeals: SA Łódź, ruling from 19. 6. 2013, III AUa 1511/12; SA Gdańsk, ruling from 19. 3. 2015, III AUa 2736/13.

659 *Idem*. See also: W. Braun, *Geschäftsverträge*, pp. 942–943, who differentiates distance and stationary teaching contracts.

often described in the Polish and German doctrine and jurisprudence as teaching contracts,[660] though this is not a legal term. The doctrinal description of a contract as a "teaching contract" refers to the fact that the teaching process concerns mainly the rider/ animal owner. In case of a horse rider, he is the one who puts the trainer's advice into practice while riding the horse – no matter which of them is more experienced (the rider or the horse). However, the same applies to courses that are attended by dog owners who want to learn how to interact with their animals with the help of the trainer. Even, if the training of a dog involves some actions that are being done by the trainer himself, in my opinion these contracts still qualify as regular service contracts (regulated by § 611 BGB in the case of German law and unnamed in the case of Polish law) recognized by the doctrine as teaching contracts. Thus, the trainer's performance still consists mainly in sharing his knowledge in exchange for remuneration.[661] The outcome is also not directly dependent on the trainer, since it the client who has to be consistent and train at animal at home in order to achieve a certain result in reference to its animal's behavior. Additionally, both the owner and his animal have different personalities, capabilities and talents. These contracts are not subject to further considerations in this book, since the standards of its conclusion, performance and consequences in the case of its improper performance or non-performance do not vary from standards used with reference to contracts that do not have an animal as object of the training, e. g. music or language lessons.

On the other hand, there are service contracts that consist in **training the animal itself** (the trainer trains the animal as the horse rider[662] or as a person training the animal himself, without the owner's presence). In the event that the animal's owner is not nearby, the trainer's contractual obligation is much broader than in the event that the trainer only gives advice to the animal's owner, or interacts with the animal with its owner's help. In the case of these kinds of contracts, the trainer performs his contractual duty by teaching an animal a certain behavior (also by impacting the process of its body building, e. g. when

660 With reference to the contract's qualification as a teaching contract under Polish law, see: SA Łódź, ruling from 19. 6. 2013, III AUa 1511/12; SA Gdańsk, ruling from 19. 3. 2015, III AUa 2736/13 and under German law, see: M. Fuchs [in:] H. Bamberger, H. Roth (ed.), *Beck'scher Online-Kommentar BGB*, München 2015, § 611, side-number 26.

661 See, with reference to German law: M. Fuchs [in:] H. Bamberger, H. Roth (ed.), *Beck'scher Online-Kommentar BGB*, München 2015, § 611, side-number 26. With reference to the reliance between the remuneration and qualification of a contract as a service contract under Polish law: L. Ogiegło [in:] J. Rajski (ed.), *System Prawa Prywatnego, Vol. VII*, pp. 559–560.

662 Compare: regulations concerning the profession of a horse rider, last visited: 10. 2. 2016, *http://www.pferd-aktuell.de/ausbildung/berufsausbildung/berufsausbildung; http://www.pzj.pl/node/zawód-jeździec.*

training a sport horse), however he has to take care of the animal at the same time.[663] This type of contract may set out that the animal remains in the same place where it used to stay before (i. e. the stable, where the owner used to keep the horse until now), or that the animal is transferred to a place closer to the trainer, more convenient for him, or even owned by the trainer. The second option involves the trainer taking comprehensive care for an animal, i. e. concluding several contracts concerning the animal in its owner's name (e. g. an agreement to keep the animal in a stable/kennels by the trainer, contracts with blacksmiths, veterinary doctors, etc.), taking care for its feeding, keeping it in good health, taking responsibility for everyday decisions, which are all made by the trainer with reference to the animal being trained.

Therefore, **the subject of this subchapter are the service contracts** described above in the second place, **consisting in the trainer training the animal by himself**, without the owner, and referred to as **"contracts to train an animal"** in this book.

Contracts to train an animal have a very complicated structure because of the special regulation of the trainer's duties in reference to an animal. Under the referential system of German law, this contract can still be qualified as a service contract, as the definition of service contract under § 611 BGB allows the party undertaking the service to undertake factual and legal actions.[664] Thus, the trainer has to undertake both factual actions as well as legal actions, since the contract consists not only in training an animal (a factual action), but also in performing additional services. These additional services include additional factual actions, concerning taking care for an animal (performing other additional services such as grooming, feeding, lungeing, etc., i. e. also factual actions) but can also include legal actions like concluding contracts with other people who interact with the animal during its training (concluding contracts with the owner of the stable where the trainer keeps the horse, with the blacksmith, with the veterinary doctor, etc.). Therefore, whereas under German law the contract to train an animal (in the meaning as presented under this title) is covered by the scope of § 611 BGB, the Polish Civil Code regulation referring to service contracts consists only of the definition of a mandate (Article 734 KC), which solely refers to legal actions undertaken by the servicing party. Since the contract to train an animal consists of undertaking factual as well as legal actions, it qualifies as an undefined service contract under Polish law and the provisions concerning mandate contract, as regulated in Article 734 KC, apply respectively.

663 Compare: the facts of the case and the duties of the rider/trainer in the German case: OLG Hamm, *ruling from* 25.11.2015 – 12 U 62/14.

664 See: § 611 BGB.

With reference to Polish law, the reason for the problems connected with the legal qualification of contracts where the contractual obligations encompass different kinds of duties, such as those listed above, can be found in elements typically existing in market practice for such contracts. Namely, an undefined contract may contain various elements that are typical of several defined contracts,[665] and there are differing theories on how it should therefore be qualified. According to A. Brzozowski, one has to take a look at the most important type of services that the servicing party is offering, and this should serve as a determinant of the legal qualification of a contract[666] – whereas the elements that are typical for other defined contracts are applicable to this element of this particular contract as well.[667] Nevertheless, Z. Radwański and W. Katner represent the opinion that contracts not qualifying to any types of contracts defined in the Polish Civil Code should not be considered as "mixed contracts" (regarding this as a rather obsolete point of view),[668] but – simply – as undefined contracts, to which one of the following possibilities apply:

1) there are no provisions referring to any type of contracts defined in the Polish Civil Code that could be applied to this particular contract;
2) provisions referring to a certain type of contract defined in the Polish Civil Code may be applied to this particular contract;
3) provisions referring to a certain type of contract defined in the Polish Civil Code may be applied to this particular contract with certain modifications.[669]

665 Compare: M. Lubelska-Sazanów, *The meaning of service contracts with reference to animals under German and Polish law* [in:] P. Pinior, E. Zielińska, M. Żaba (eds.), *Evolution of private law-new approach*, Katowice 2016, pp. 121–130.

666 See: A. Brzozowski, J. Jastrzębski, M. Kaliński, W. J. Kocot, A. Skowrońska-Bocian, *Zobowiązania. Część szczegółowa*, Warszawa 2017, pp. 29–30. See also: P. Machnikowski [in:] E. Gniewek, P. Machnikowski (eds.), *Kodeks cywilny. Komentarz*, pp. 1411–1413. See also, according to German law: P. Rosbach, *Pferderecht*, pp. 111–115.

667 See: A. Brzozowski, J. Jastrzębski, M. Kaliński, W. J. Kocot, A. Skowrońska-Bocian, *Zobowiązania. Część szczegółowa*, Warszawa 2017, pp. 29–30; P. Machnikowski [in:] E. Gniewek, P. Machnikowski (eds.), *Kodeks cywilny. Komentarz*, p. 1412.

668 W. Katner [in:] W Katner (ed.), *System Prawa Prywatnego, Vol. IX, Prawo zobowiązań – umowy nienazwane*, p. 13; Z. Radwański, *Uwagi o umowach mieszanych*, ZNUJ 1985, Issue. 41, p. 105.

669 Z. Radwański, *Teoria umów*, Warszawa 1977, pp. 241–242; W. Katner [in:] W Katner (ed.), *System Prawa Prywatnego, Vol. IX, Prawo zobowiązań – umowy nienazwane*, pp. 13–14. See also: L. Ogiegło [in:] K. Pietrzykowski, *Kodeks cywilny, Komentarz*, Vol. II, pp. 669–670, who states that the provisions of Article 750 KC may not be applicable to contracts that qualify to a certain type of contracts defined in the Polish Civil Code, e.g. to safe-keeping contracts. With reference to the focal point of the contract in German jurisprudence, see: BGH ruling from 21.04.2005, Az.: III ZR 293/04, NJW 2005, 2008; with reference to Polish jurisprudence, see: the Court of Appeals in Gdańsk, ruling from 20.05.2016, III AUa 2125/15.

I absolutely agree with the views of Z. Radwański and W. Katner, presented above, especially since they are based on the idea of the respective applicability of civil law provisions,[670] used in several places in this book with reference to various provisions (i.e. with reference to the respective applicability of provisions covering things to animals and the respective applicability of provisions covering various types of contracts to undefined contracts).

In reference to the conclusion of teaching/training contracts, under both Polish and German law, the parties may conclude a contract to train an animal by any means.[671] It is often concluded by the implied conduct of the parties,[672] though a decision to conclude it in a written form is a wise choice. That way not only does a written contract constitute evidence that can be used in the event of possible future disputes, but it also clearly confirms the parties' contractual duties, their possibilities to end the contractual relation and deals with issues of liability. As the contract to train an animal is to be qualified as a service contract under both legal systems, the trainer is obliged to perform the contract with due care, and not simply achieve a specific result.[673] Thus, it is difficult to oblige a trainer to achieve a special result with reference to the animal's skills, e.g. although it might be possible to teach every dog to retrieve, there would have to exist a further definition of this skill (how quickly does the dog have to pick up the object, how close does he have to bring it back to the owner, how many times can he resist performing the command in order to still classify this skill as having been learned by the dog). The issue is even more complicated with sport horses, where the definition of a good jumping horse, or a correct performance of a flying change of leg by the dressage horse, is extremely subjective. However, there are no restraints on establishing additional remuneration for the trainer upon achieving a special result (like winning a certain competition on a trained

670 See: SN, ruling from 28.10.1999 – II CKN 530/98, with an approving gloss of Ewa Rott-Pietrzyk, OSP 2000, Nos 7–8, item C 118, pp. 393–396. J. Nowacki, *Odpowiednie stosowanie przepisów prawa*, PiP 1964, Issue 3, pp. 370–371 J. Nowacki, *Analogia legis*, p. 141.

671 See e.g.: K. Schreiber [in:] R. Schulze, H. Dörner, I. Ebert, T. Hoeren, R. Kemper, I. Saenger, K. Schreiber, H. Schulte-Nölke, A. Staudinger (eds.), *Bürgerliches Gesetzbuch. Handkommentar*, p. 873; J. Rajski [in:] J. Rajski, (ed.), *System Prawa Prywatnego, Vol. VII – część szczegółowa*, Warszawa 2011, p. 563. See also: M. Fuchs [in:] H. Bamberger, H. Roth (ed.), *Beck'scher Online-Kommentar BGB*, § 611, side-number 49 With reference to formal requirements in some professions.

672 M. Fuchs [in:] H. Bamberger, H. Roth (ed.), *Beck'scher Online-Kommentar BGB*, § 611, side-number 47.

673 W. Braun, *Geschäftsverträge*, p. 779; L. Ogiegło [in:] J. Rajski (ed.), *System Prawa Prywatnego, Vol. VII*, p. 572; P. Machnikowski [in:] E. Gniewek, P. Machnikowski (ed.), *Kodeks cywilny. Komentarz*, pp. 1411–1413; whereas the authors acknowledge the fact that service contracts are classified as contracts obliging the debtor to a careful performance (not a special result), but represent the opinion that this classification is misleading and should not be followed, or at least needs to be completed with some explanation.

horse), e.g. in the form of a bonus. However, obliging the trainer to perform a certain result as his main contractual duty would affect the legal nature of the contract. Thus, under German law, due to the broad definition of a service contract, encompassing both obligations of factual and legal nature, such a contract would not be classified as a service contract at all.[674] In this way, the lack of obligation to perform a certain result constitutes the most significant difference between a service contract and a work contract under German law.[675] Under Polish law, it would be disputable how to qualify such a contract, due to lack of any legal basis to qualify a mandate contract under Article 734 KC as a contract obliging only the careful performance of the service.[676] Nevertheless, since the standpoint that a person obliged to undertake legal actions under a mandate contract may not guarantee a certain result is widespread in the Polish doctrine,[677] the attitude that the person undertaking an obligation under a service contract is obliged to a careful performance is popular among the representatives of the Polish doctrine.[678] Still, this issue is much more complicated. Although a mandate does not offer any guarantee of its performance, it can also not be qualified as a contract obliging the party performing services only to offer its careful performance.[679] Summing up, in my opinion, the possible types of services provided in teaching/training contracts under the regulation of § 611 BGB and Article 750 KC (with reference to respective applicability of Article 734 KC) under the Polish and German legal systems is so broad that it cannot be qualified as an obligation to achieve a certain result. This is especially true, since

674 K. Schreiber [in:] R. Schulze, H. Dörner, I. Ebert, T. Hoeren, R. Kemper, I. Saenger, K. Schreiber, H. Schulte-Nölke, A. Staudinger (eds.), *Bürgerliches Gesetzbuch. Handkommentar*, p. 871; R. Müller-Glöge [in:] M. Henssler (ed.), *Münchener Kommentar zum BGB, Vol. IV*, München 2012, § 611, side numbers 22–26, *BeckOnline (last visited: 12.3. 2018).*

675 More with reference to this issue: *Idem.*

676 L. Ogiegło [in:] J. Rajski (ed.), *System Prawa Prywatnego, Vol. VII*, pp. 571–572. Compare also the decision of the Court of Appeals in Gdańsk: SA Gdańsk, ruling from 19.3.2015, III AUa 2736/13.

677 See: A. Machowska, *Koncepcja zobowiązań rezultatu i starannego działania i jej doniosłość dla określenia odpowiedzialności kontraktowej*, KPP 2002, No. 3, pp. 661 et seq. and other positions referring to contracts for work: W. Ludwiczak, *Umowa zlecenia*, Poznań 1955, p. 61; S. Wójcik, *Pojęcie umowy o dzieło*, SC, t. IV, 1963, pp. 110 et seq.; S. Wójcik, *Odgraniczenie umowy o dzieło od umowy o pracę i od umowy zlecenia*, ZNUJ 1963, No. 10, pp. 182 and 197; W. Siuda, Istota i zakres umowy o dzieło, Poznań 1964, p. 18; A. Brzozowski, *Odpowiedzialność przyjmującego zamówienie za wady dzieła*, Warszawa 1986, p. 20.

678 See, critically: L. Ogiegło [in:] J. Rajski (ed.), *System Prawa Prywatnego, Vol. VII*, pp. 571–572; see also: L.Ogiegło, *Usługi…*, pp. 207 T. Pajor, *Odpowiedzialność dłużnika za niewykonanie zobowiązania*, Warszawa 1982, pp. 293–294.

679 See: *Idem*, P. Machnikowski [in:] E. Gniewek, P. Machnikowski (eds.), *Kodeks cywilny. Komentarz*, pp. 1411–1413.

– as already mentioned – animals are living creatures and, therefore – just as in the case of human psychotherapy – a certain training result can never be guaranteed.

The trainer is obliged to perform the contract personally,[680] which constitutes an issue of prime importance for the animal's owner. Thus, the trainer's obligation to take care of an animal makes the contract to train an animal a relation strongly based on a mutual trust. In addition, the animal's owner needs to believe in the training methods used by a particular trainer, who has to undertake numerous decisions concerning the animal's training every day (i. e. the trainer's reaction with reference to a certain behavior of an animal, which is important for all learning processes and depend on the methods used by that particular trainer). Therefore, the possibility of subcontracting the animal's training, or any activities connected with taking care of the animal (grooming, lungeing, etc.), to another person is questionable and – according to some representatives of the doctrine – possible only if it is explicitly set out in the contract.[681]

Also under both Polish and German law, parties are free to establish the contract between them at their discretion. So, they can contain in the contract any provisions that are not against the law,[682] the nature of the obligation and the fair-dealing principle.[683] Therefore, it is very important to define the contractual obligations of the parties very carefully, especially with reference to contracts that are not described in the Civil Code, in the case of Polish law with reference to contracts to train an animal – even though there may be no legal requirement to do it.

Contracts to train an animal are a specific kind of contract that appear only in reference to contracts having the performance of services with an animal as the object of their contractual obligation. Thus, contracts to train an animal may not exist with reference to other things – one can only interact with living creatures.

---

680 See: Article 738 KC and § 613 BGB.

681 K. Schreiber [in:] R. Schulze, H. Dörner, I. Ebert, T. Hoeren, R. Kemper, I. Saenger, K. Schreiber, H. Schulte-Nölke, A. Staudinger (eds.), *Bürgerliches Gesetzbuch. Handkommentar*, p. 879; P. Machnikowski [in:] E. Gniewek, P. Machnikowski (ed.), *Kodeks cywilny. Komentarz*, pp. 1411–1413. See more in Subchapter IV.2.3. of this book ("Performance of service contracts with reference to contracts having an animal as their object" – "Teaching/training contracts having an animal as their object").

682 See: M. Fuchs [in:] H. Bamberger, H. Roth (ed.), *Beck'scher Online-Kommentar BGB*, § 611, side-number 55, who indicates that service contracts (together with contracts for work) are the largest group of contracts that are considered with reference to § 134 BGB.

683 With reference to the freedom of contract principle, see: E. Rott-Pietrzyk *Commercial Agency Contracts…* [in:] *Private Autonomy…*, pp. 15–34; M. Lubelska-Sazanów, *The "Principle of No Freedom of Contract": A Post-Modern Version of the Freedom of Contract Principle?*, [in:] M. De Maestri, S. Dominelli (eds.), *Party autonomy in European private (and) international law, Vol. II*, Rome 2015, pp. 15–31.

This means that it is a position that has to be mentioned in this book due to its subject matter. It is an example of a service contract that has arisen specifically to meet the needs of owners of animals, and where the main obligation of a contracting party requires interaction with an animal. However, it is also significant that – just as other contracts in which the contracting party undertakes an obligation to perform a service of which the object is an animal – it requires higher standards of performance than contracts in which the service provided by one or both of the parties does not concern a living animal. Thus, taking care of an animal consists of numerous duties, which are described in more detail below.[684]

1.2.4. Safe-keeping contracts having an animal as its object

The **safe-keeping contract** (*umowa przechowania, der Verwahrungsvertrag*) is the most commonly used contract with an animal as its subject, of all the contracts mentioned in Chapter IV of this book (apart from the training contract). However, despite its frequent use, it causes several problems with its legal qualification. According to Article 835 KC and § 688 BGB, a safe-keeping contract consists in the depositary's obligation to store a movable thing delivered to him by a depositor.[685] The problem with the legal qualification of contracts, where the contractual obligations cover many various kinds of duty, such as keeping a pet in a stable/kennels, taking care of it, feeding, grooming, exercising (taking a dog for a walk/letting the horse out onto a paddock by the stable), etc. make it a more complicated issue.[686] However, in my opinion, the contracts that concern keeping a dog (or any other pet) and taking care for it in kennels, or putting a horse into a stable and taking care of it will in most of the cases qualify as safe-keeping contracts. This qualification is visible in the organization and terminology of this book, and is consequently used below.[687]

---

684 See also: Subchapters: IV.2.4. and IV.3.4. referring to the performance and results of wrongful performance and non-performance of these contracts.

685 Unlike the German provision defining safe-keeping (§ 688 BGB), the Polish provision of Article 835 KC also contains the formula "in a non-deteriorated state", whereas the idea that the good should be kept in a non-deteriorated state under German law can be deduced from the content of § 694 BGB, providing that the depositor must compensate the depositary for any damage incurred by the depositary due to the quality of the thing deposited.

686 With reference to contracts where the contractual obligations encompass different kinds of duties, see: Subchapter IV.1.2.4 of this book and Z. Radwański, *Teoria umów*, Warszawa 1977, pp. 241–242; W. Katner [in:] W Katner (ed.), *System Prawa Prywatnego, Vol. IX, Prawo zobowiązań – umowy nienazwane*, pp. 13–14.

687 See: Subchapters: IV.2.4. and IV.3.4. referring to performance and the results of wrongful performance and non-performance of these contracts.

The qualification of contracts on keeping someone else's animal in a stable or in kennels is complicated under both legal systems, though the German jurisprudence and doctrine has already addressed this issue (and may serve as a role model for future claims arising out of the conclusion of such contracts under Polish law as well). An example of this comes from a case[688] concerning a claim to return a saddle kept as a pledge arising from the non-performance of a lease contract, the German court considered the issue whether the contract at hand, consisting in keeping a horse in a stable, was a lease contract or a contract already recognized in the German doctrine and jurisprudence as a "horse-keeping" contract. The court differentiated these two contracts by defining most important obligations of the party keeping the horse in each case, in accordance with the content of the contract and the intent of the parties. The Court qualified the contract subject of its judicial decision as being a lease, justifying this qualification by the fact that the horse was kept in an open space, without interference from the stable owner.[689] Thus, the main obligation of the party offering the paddock to a horse consisted in leasing this space, and did not contain other obligations consisting in taking care for a horse, such as feeding, grooming, paddocking, etc. However, the Court, when explaining the differences between the contract at hand and a horse-keeping contract, acknowledged that the so-called horse-keeping contract, which qualifies as safe-keeping contract, also mentioned other obligations, primarily being taking comprehensive care of the horse by performing additional services. Thus, generally, although the contract **to keep a horse in a stable** (*Umowa pensjonatowa dla konia, Pferdepensionsvertrag*) contains also elements of **a lease contract**,[690] the German courts have qualified a specific contract as such only where the obligation of the stable owner consisted solely in giving a stall in the stable or a paddock for use by the horse owner.[691]

Since, the idea of keeping the horse safe and healthy is most important for the horse owner in most cases, the contract with a stables (*Umowa pensjonatowa dla konia, Pferdepensionsvertrag*) should be qualified as **a safe-keeping contract** in my opinion.[692] However, it is important to bear in mind that a contract with a

688 See: Court of Appeals in Essen, ruling from 31.8.2007, 20 C 229/06, NZM 2008, 264.

689 The German Court of Appeals in Menden ruled differently, qualifying a contract to keep a horse in a stall as a lease as well. However, the ruling does not contain the Court's reasoning, due to the fact that the Court solely addressed the issue of its jurisdiction. See: Appeal court in Menden, ruling from 26.2.2007, 4 C 11/07, BeckRS 2007, 3278.

690 See: P. Rosbach, *Pferderecht*, p. 111–115.

691 See: Appeal court in Essen, ruling from 31.8.2007, 20 C 229/06, NZM 2008, 264; Appeal court in Menden, ruling from 26.2.2007, 4 C 11/07, BeckRS 2007, 3278. Compare: P. Rosbach, *Pferderecht*, pp. 111–115.

692 The same opinion is represented by the most representatives of the German doctrine, see: P. Rosbach, *Pferderecht*, pp. 111–115 and H. Sprau [in:] O. Palandt, *Beck'sche Kurz-Kom-*

stables – although it is a contract qualified as safe-keeping because of its focal point (taking care of an animal and its wellbeing) – it is still a contract with some specific elements of different types of contract. What is more, the applicability of the provisions concerning all types of contracts that could be applicable in the case at hand have to be made under the reservation that these provisions have to be applied respectively, taking into account the fact that an animal is a living creature, not a regular movable good.[693] This is also the reason why it is so important to carefully define the obligations of the parties to this particular contract, consisting in placing an animal into safe-keeping, in writing.

Safe-keeping contracts consisting in keeping a horse in a stable, or a dog in kennels etc. deserve a special place in this book due to the higher standard of performance, just as in the case of other contracts with an obligation to perform duties consisting in taking care of a living animal as its object. Whereas the legal provisions covering safe-keeping contracts –under both Polish[694] and German law[695] – refer solely to regular things, its respective applicability to animals with modifications is of special importance. Thus, the contractual obligation to keep a good (such as money, a piece of art, jewelry, furniture) safe, or to store it, does not require any action from the depositor. Contrast that to a safe-keeping contract with the obligation to keep an animal is the object, where the party keeping[696] the animal is required to undertake numerous continuous actions to keep[697] the animal safe and healthy.[698] In this way, taking care over an animal consists of numerous duties, as described in more detail below.[699]

mentare: Palandt Bürgerliches Gesetzbuch mit Nebengesetzen, p.1200 and commonly used also in Polish practice, see e. g.: the website of a horse pension "Country club" (last visited: 4. 2. 2017): http://www.countryclub.nowyfolwark.pl/Media/Files/umowa-pensjonatowa-country-club.pdf; Agnieszka Cwajna, *Możliwości wykorzystania prawa do wizerunku zwierząt w świetle prawa polskiego,* Equista 25. 2. 2016, available at: https://equista.pl/editorial/413/prawo-jak-powinna-wygladac-umowa-pensjonatowa (last visited: 20. 3. 2018). However, some authors qualify such contract under Polish law as an undefined contract, see e. g. Ł. Walter, *Umowa pensjonatowa-potrzebna czy nie?*, Konie i Rumaki 7/2012 (last visited: 4. 2. 2017): http://www.konieirumaki.pl/pl/umowa-pensjonatowa.

693 With reference to the applicability of the provisions of the Civil Code to animals, see: Subchapter IV.2.2. of this book.

694 Articles 835–845 KC.

695 §§ 688–700 BGB.

696 Whereas the term "to store" is more appropriate with reference to the safe-keeping of regular things, I choose to use the term "to keep" in this book, which fits much better the idea that one of the contracting parties is obliged to keep an animal of a different party safe and healthy.

697 *Idem.*

698 The term "to keep an animal safe and healthy" is not a legal definition, though it accurately defines the obligation of the depositor in cases where the object of safe-keeping is an animal. Thus, this is what I understand as respective applicability with modifications of the provision foreseeing "storing a good in a non-deteriorated state".

1.2.5. Other service contracts having an animal as their object

There are numerous different service contracts in which the contractual obligation may concern animals. However, their qualification does not raise as many legal problems as the service contracts mentioned in the separate subchapters above. Therefore, all these different types of contracts, which are worth mentioning (at least briefly) among other service contracts, are described all together in this subchapter. The service contracts having an animal as its object, which are in my opinion worth mentioning because of their common applicability are **contracts concluded with specialists like: veterinary doctor, groomer and a professional animal transporter.** The problem with these usually occurs in connection with liability issues concerning the problem of a person performing the contract being hurt by the animal. Under both the Polish and German legal systems, such cases are a source of tort liability of the animal's owner and constitute a concurring source of his liability, next to the contractual liability. Since this book refers solely to the conclusion, performance and the results of non-performance, as well as improper performance of contracts with an animal as the object of its contractual obligation, the tort liability arising in case, where one of the contracting parties gets harmed by an animal owned by the other contracting party, is not subject of this book, therefore it is not comprehensively presented herein.

Just as with the **contract to train** an animal, as described in Subchapters: IV.1.2.3, IV.2.3. and IV.3.3. of this book, **contracts with a veterinary doctor or groomer,** as well as a **contract for the transportation of animals,** qualify as service contracts under German law (§ 611 BGB) and as undefined service contracts under Polish law (Article 734 KC in connection with Article 750 KC). In reference to undefined service contracts under Polish law, provisions covering other contracts in which the *essentialia negotii* consist in similar obligations of the contracting parties apply respectively, where the respective applicability means that they may be applied respectively without modifications, with modifications or do not have to be applied at all.[700]

As far the **transportation of animals** is concerned, the main legal problem is compliance with state and international transportation requirements,[701] as well

699 See also: Subchapters: IV.2.4 and IV.3.4 referring to performance and the results of wrongful performance or non-performance of these contracts.

700 See: Subchapter IV.1.1. With reference to the direct application of legal provisions, see also: J. Nowacki, *Odpowiednie stosowanie przepisów prawa*, PiP 1964, Issue 3, pp. 370–371.

701 See, with reference to German regulations: § 6 of the Executive order concerning driving licences of 13 December 2010 [*Verordnung über die Zulassung von Personen zum Straßenverkehr/ Fahrerlaubnis-Verordnung – FeV*], J L of 13.12.2010, Part I, item 1980, as amended, later changed by Article 2 of the Executive order of 21 December 2016 (BGBl. I S. 3083). See, with reference to German regulations: Article 6 of the Polish Act on the drivers

as additional duties of the driver, who has to take care for living animals that he is transporting.

The most problematic and also most common contract among the contracts described in this subchapter is the one that an animal's owner concludes with a **veterinary doctor.** According to the German doctrine, there are two types of contracts that may be concluded with a veterinary doctor: a contract for a specific task (*umowa o dzieło, der Werkvertrag*) and a service contract.[702] The **contract for a specific task** is concluded when **a certain result** is expected, i. e. mechanical insemination of a horse,[703] or its medical examination in connection with a sale contract.[704] The German doctrine often deals with the issue of a medical examination of a horse when selling it,[705] and this problem has already been described in Subchapter III.3.2.8.[706] concerning sale contracts and other contracts changing the ownership of the things.

The Polish practice does not recognize **a medical examination of a horse** that occurs in connection with its sale as any special type of action undertaken by a veterinary doctor, and qualifies it simply as a regular medical examination or the medical treatment of a horse. Thus, a medical examination of a horse that occurs in connection with its sale (just as the mechanical insemination of a horse[707]) is qualified by the German doctrine as **a contract for a specific task (*umowa o dzieło, der Werkvertrag*)**, whereas all other contracts with a veterinary doctor, concerning medical examinations or treatment of an animal under different conditions, are qualified as service contracts.[708] Under Polish law, any treatment of a horse by a veterinarian is qualified as the performance of a service contract. The equestrian market practice in Poland does not differentiate these contracts into any special types. Therefore, the medical treatment of a horse always qualifies as an undefined service contract under Polish law and as a service contract in the meaning of § 611 BGB under German law. Therefore, the medical

[*Ustawa o kierujących pojazdami*] of 5 January 2011, J L of 2011, No. 30, item 151. Both regulations are based on the provisions of the Directive 2006/126/EC of the European Parliament and of the Council of 20 December 2006 on driving licences (Recast); OJ 403, 30. 12. 2006, pp. 18–60.

702 P. Rosbach, *Pferderecht*, pp. 180.

703 In this case, the contract for work (*umowa o dzieło, Werkvertrag*) is understood as a contract setting out a result of a succesful process of mechanical insemination, and not a succesful impregnation of the female. Thus, the impregnation composes of different causes and – in the event of failure – the veterinarian cannot be solely blamed for this state of facts. See: P. Rosbach, *Pferderecht*, p. 139.

704 P. Rosbach, *Pferderecht*, p. 139.

705 See, e. g.: H. Westermann, *Zu den Gewährleistungsansprüche des Käufers*, pp. 342–348; P. Wertenbruch, *Tierkauf und Sachmangel*, NJW 2012, No. 29, p. 2069; P. Rosbach, *Pferderecht.*

706 See: Subchapter III.3.2.8.

707 See: P. Rosbach, *Pferderecht*, p. 139.

708 *Idem.*

examinations or treatments that are described in this section are understood more broadly in reference to Polish law (any medical examination or treatment of a horse) than in reference to German law (only those treatments of a horse where the subject is not a medical examination in connection with a sale contract).

In reference to a **contract for breeding**, note that such a contract concluded by the owner of a female animal individual with the owner of a male animal individual would – under both Polish and German legal systems – not be qualified as a contract for a specific task (*umowa o dzieło, Werkvertrag*), but **as a service contract.** Thus, this was the judgement of the German court in Arnsberg considered under reference 2 O 18/08,[709] where – due to a mistake by the stallion owner's employee – a female horse was inseminated with the sperm of a different stallion than agreed in advance between the contracting parties. The breeder filed a claim against the stallion's owner and demanded damages, but the Court stated that the claimant in the case had not proved any real financial damage caused by a mistake on the respondent's side, and therefore did not grant him damages; it qualified the contract at hand as a service contract. The Court based its reasoning on the fact that the services offered by male animal's owner consisted in allowing its animal to inseminate the female animal owned by the other party to a contract, which should be understood as offering a certain service and not as offering a guaranteed result promised by the male animal's owner. This situation is different than in case of a medical examination of a horse. As the legal construction of service contracts in this matter[710] is similar under both the Polish and German legal systems, the German jurisprudence may be useful when interpreting Polish cases.[711] This is especially true in this case, since Polish law does not qualify any medical examination of a horse or its treatment as contract for a specific task. Thus, contract for breeding qualifies to service contracts under both the Polish and German legal systems.[712]

709 LG Arnsberg, ruling from 13.10.2009-2 O 18/08.

710 Thus, despite the fact that the German Civil Code includes a definition of a service contract in § 611 BGB, whereas the Polish Civil Code includes only the definition of a mandate and uses the construction of the respective applicability of provisions covering mandate to other undefined service contracts (Article 734 KC in connection with Article 750 KC), the construction of service contracts is similar under both legal systems.

711 See: Ruling of the European Court of Justice of 26.3.2009, C-348/07[1]; E. Rott-Pietrzyk [in:] M. Stec, *System Prawa Handlowego. Prawo Umów handlowych, Vol. V*, pp. 624–625, pointing at the European Commission Report of 1996, see: Commission report on the application of the Commercial Agents Directive (COM (1996) 364 final, 23.7.1996). See also: O. Sztejnert, *Świadczenie wyrównawcze dla agenta albo jaki wpływ na polskie orzecznictwo może mieć nowelizacja niemieckiego HGB*, MoP 2010, No. 14, pp. 806–909.

712 So also: E. Fellmer, P. Kiel, *Rechtskunde für Pferdehalter und Reiter*, Stuttgart 1984, pp. 147–148.

Another contract that is often used in reference to animals and which cannot be qualified as any of the contracts recognized by the Civil Codes of Germany and Poland is the **contract of participation in the horse usage** (*Reitbeteiligungsvertrag*). This contract constitutes an example of an undefined contract (*umowa nienazwana, atypische Vertrag*) under both the Polish and German legal systems, as it combines the features of tenancy/lease and the features of service contract.[713] However, I have decided to describe it in Chapter V as the contractual duties of the parties are very similar to those in a tenancy/lease contract for a horse.[714]

The broad applicability of many types of service contracts and their diversity justify its differentiation in this book. Due to the fact that these contracts may be concluded only with specialists performing their activities with reference to animals (veterinary doctor, groomer, professional animal transporter and breeder), they do not have its equivalents in the case where things (not animals) constitute the object of a contractual obligation. However, all these contracts have the same basis, consisting in interaction with an animal. On the other hand, they do not encompass as many additional duties consisting in taking care for an animal, as is the case with contracts having training of an animal as its object (except where an animal has to stay for a longer time in a veterinary clinic, for example, though in that event considerations referring to safe-keeping contracts having keeping an animal safe and healthy as its object presented above are applicable). Therefore, these contracts are only mentioned in this book to the extent that its specific character with reference to services addressed to animals differs from other considerations referring to service contracts having the performance of duties connected with animals as their object.

2. Performance of service contracts with reference to contracts having an animal as their object

2.1. Commission contracts having an animal as their object

Auction sales of horses have a very old tradition in the referential system of Germany, therefore the institution of commission contracts is likely used by

713 With reference to the qualification of contracts as undefined or mixed, see considerations included in Subchapter IV.1.1. ("General characteristic of service contracts with reference to contracts having an animal as their object" – "General remarks") and the literature cited therein: Z. Radwański, *Teoria umów*, Warszawa 1977, pp. 241–242. See also: W. Katner [in:] W Katner (ed.), *System Prawa Prywatnego, Vol. IX, Prawo zobowiązań – umowy nienazwane*, pp. 13–14.

714 See: Chapter V of this book in general, but especially in its Subchapter V.2.2.

horse sellers in this country. In cases where an auction is organized by horse breeders associations but the horses that are offered to the public are owned by different private principals, the horses listed in the catalogue are sold with intermediation of a commission agent.[715] Thus, in the German practice, the auction organizer acts as a commission agent, i. e. intermediates in the transfer of ownership acting in his own name but on the horse owner's account. The contract of sale is concluded at the time of accepting the bid. The contracting parties are the buyer and the organizer of the auction (i. e. the commission agent as an intermediary), where the latter is also the party who is liable for future warranty claims.[716] Thus, the term of a commission contract (*umowa komisu, das Kommissionsgeschäft*) is often used as a shortcut to all the obligatory relationships that compose the legal situation between the commission agent, the principal and the third person, namely the final acquirer of the horse, where – in fact – there are two contracts to be taken into account.[717] Firstly, this is a commission contract between the principal (i.e. the owner of the horse) and the commission agent, who intermediates in the sale of this horse. Secondly, this is a sale contract between the seller (i. e. the commission agent / auction organizer) and a third person (i.e. the acquirer of the horse). In the case of public horse auctions referred to in this subchapter, it is the breeding association that acts as the seller in reference to the buyer of the horse, and as a commission agent in reference to the horse's owner. Although referring to the actual situation of auctions, which are currently performed only in Germany, not in Poland, these legal remarks concern the legal composition of a commission contract under both legal systems.

The commission agent is a party to the commission contract and undertakes the service of selling the horse for the principal (i. e. horse's owner). In order to act as a commission agent, two requirements have to be met. Firstly, the agent has to act in his own name but on the principal's account and, secondly, the performing service has to be in the field of his business activity.[718] Thus, the commission agent always operates as a business.[719] Both these requirements are fulfilled by the horse breeders associations, which are the main performers of

715 With reference to types of horse auctions commonly taking place in Germany, see: Subchapter II.1.2.1. of this book ("Characteristic of specific types of service contracts having an animal as their object – Commission contracts having an animal as their object").

716 P. Rosbach, *Pferderecht*, p. 71.

717 See: A. Kędzierska-Cieślak, *Komis (zagadnienia cywilnoprawne)*, p. 9; pp. 31 et seq.

718 With reference to Polish law, see: A. Kędzierska Cieślak, *Komis (zagadnienia cywilnoprawne)*, pp. 31 et seq.; J. Frąckowiak [in:] J. Rajski, (ed.), *System Prawa Prywatnego, Vol. VII*, pp. 729–731. With reference to the German law, see: I. Koller [in:] C. Canaris, M. Habersack, C. Schäfer, *Staub Handelsgesetzbuch Großkommentar*, Göttingen 2013, pp. 84–85.

719 See: Subchapter IV.1.1. of this book.

horse auctions in Germany. The commission agent, possibly along with other business entities, are on one side of the commission contract. On the other side of the contractual obligation is the principal, who does not have to meet any formal requirements. This can be a natural person or a business entity. If the principal is a business, then the commission agent's duty to perform due diligence has less significance (the duty to act in accordance with good faith and fair dealing principle remains, though the extent of these duties with reference to a consumer is broader than to a business partner).[720]

The parties are free to establish the content of commission contracts at their discretion. The only restraints that may appear with reference to a commission contract are connected with the need to obtain licenses for certain types of services (though this does not apply to the sale of horses). The principle of freedom of contract allows the auction organizers to put their own terms and conditions into the auction rules (though there are several restrictions in these matters with reference to consumer contracts). These rules concern not only the sale contracts concluded with third parties, but also the commission agreements concluded with principals. Such terms and conditions are subject to the requirements included in respective provisions of the German and Polish Civil Codes concerning general conditions of contracts, standard forms of contracts and rules.[721] The German Supreme Court referred to unfair forms of contracts in a case under case reference VIII ZR 71/09.[722] According to the facts of this case – which is important in reference to unfair conditions and terms – the buyer purchased a horse at a public auction for €159,774.75, the terms of the auction were successfully announced to the public and contained a provision that the auction organizer and the horse breeders association are not liable for any condition of a horse that has not been agreed in the contract, and that the horse is sold "as seen and ridden". Since shortly after the purchase it turned out that the horse bought was cribbing, the buyer demanded reimbursement of the horse's price against its return, under his warranty rights. The German Supreme Court decided that, since – according to § 307 BGB – "provisions in standard business terms are ineffective if, contrary to the requirement of good faith, they give an unreasonable disadvantage on other party to the contract with the user",[723] the

720 On the due diligence duty of a commission agent under Polish law, see: J. Frąckowiak [in:] J. Rajski, (ed.), *System Prawa Prywatnego, Vol. VII*, p. 732.

721 See: §§ 305–310 BGB and Articles 384–385^4 KC, whereas some of them are applicable only to consumer contracts. To learn more with reference to German law, see: K. Schmidt, *Handelsrecht*, Köln 2014, pp. 977–981.

722 See: BGH, ruling from 24.2.2010, VIII ZR 71/09.

723 See: translation of the German Civil Code provided online by the website *Gesetze im Internet* provided by the German Federal Ministry of Justice: https://www.gesetze-im-internet.de/englisch_bgb/englisch_bgb.html#p2908 (last visited: 18.1.2018).

auction terms excluding warranty rights for defects not agreed in the contract are ineffective due to § 309, number 7, letter a) and b) BGB.[724] Thus, according to § 434 (1) BGB (containing the legal definition of defects), "The thing is free from material defects if, upon the passing of the risk, the thing has the agreed quality. To the extent that the quality has not been agreed, the thing is free of material defects, if it is **suitable for the use intended under the contract** (...))".[725] This exclusion of liability is possible due to the content of § 474 BGB, according to which the rules referring to consumer sale have a concomitant character to the general rules referring to a contract of sale. Due to the content of this provision, it is important to check the contents of unfair terms and conditions.

Under Polish law such a judgement could not be taken into account, due to the inability to modify the scope of warranty rights other than for the consumer's benefit (Article 558 § 2). Although the German court uses different means, it comes to similar conclusions – the scope of warranty rights may be modified only for the benefit of the consumer. In my opinion, this ruling was worth mentioning since the idea of selling privately owned and bred Arabian horses could constitute an interesting solution for the Arabian horse market in the future (especially now that the Polish Arabian horse auctions are starting to lose their prestige due to the political situation of Arabian studs in Poland).[726]

724 According to a translation of the German Civil Code provided online by the website *Gesetze im Internet* provided by the German Federal Ministry of Justice: https://www.gesetze-im-internet.de/englisch_bgb/englisch_bgb.html#p2908 (last visited: 18.1.2018): "7. (Exclusion of liability for injury to life, body or health and in case of gross fault) a) (Injury to life, body or health) any exclusion or limitation of liability for damage from injury to life, body or health due to negligent breach of duty by the user or intentional or negligent breach of duty by a legal representative or a person used to perform an obligation of the user; b) (Gross fault) any exclusion or limitation of liability for other damage arising from a grossly negligent breach of duty by the user or from an intentional or grossly negligent breach of duty by a legal representative of the user or a person used to perform an obligation of the user; letters (a) and (b) do not apply to limitations of liability in terms of transport and tariff rules, authorised in accordance with the Passenger Transport Act [Personenbeförderungsgesetz], of trams, trolley buses and motor vehicles in regular public transport services, to the extent that they do not deviate to the disadvantage of the passenger from the Order on Standard Transport Terms for Tram and Trolley Bus Transport and Regular Public Transport Services with Motor Vehicles [Verordnung über die Allgemeinen Beförderungsbedingungen für den Straßenbahn- und Obusverkehr sowie den Linienverkehr mit Kraftfahrzeugen] of 27 February 1970; letter (b) does not apply to limitations on liability for state-approved lotteries and gaming contracts".

725 See: translation of the German Civil code provided online by the website *Gesetze im Internet* provided by the German Federal Ministry of Justice: https://www.gesetze-im-internet.de/englisch_bgb/englisch_bgb.html#p2908 (last visited: 18.1.2018).

726 See, Polish and international press online articles: A. Gumowska, Newsweek Polska 10.4.2016, available at: http://www.newsweek.pl/polska/konie-arabskie-smierc-klaczy-shirley-watts-w-janowie-podlaskim,artykuly,383683,1.html; A. Smith, The Guardian 8.4.2016, available at: https://www.theguardian.com/world/2016/apr/08/purge-at-polands-renown

The parties have to describe the commission agent's obligations in details, i. e. the actions he is obliged to undertake in order to sell a horse (e. g. how and when he is planning to prepare and show the horse at the auction), the object of the contract (i. e. a certain horse), the commission agent's remuneration and the selling price of the horse. The price is usually established by putting into a contract the lowest price that would satisfy the seller.[727] Thus, the nature of a commission contract places the commission agent under a duty to achieve the price that would be most beneficial for the principal. This requirement does not raise any problems with reference to an auction sale, as the horses are always sold for the best price that has been offered.

The provision of a commission agent is usually expressed in form of a percentage of the horse's price, though there are no obstacles to establishing it differently. What is significant, the contract may not award the commission agent a provision consisting of everything above the minimal selling price. Thus, such a contractual provision would go against the idea of a commission contract, which is always connected with the commission agent's duty to conclude a sale contract that would be most profitable for the principal.[728] There are no requirements in reference to the form of concluding the commission contract. However, it is recommended to conclude a commission contract in writing as, after its conclusion, the principal remains the owner of a horse and the ownership of the horse is transferred – due to the intermediatory action of the commission of a commission agent – directly from the horse's owner to a third person, i. e. the acquirer of the horse.[729] As the horse's owners are usually not mentioned in the catalogue (unless they are also the breeders of the horse, though this does not indicate ownership), the principal's (i. e. horse owner's)

ed-stud-farms-pits-politicians-against-rich-and-famous; E. Bagłaj, *Polskiej potęgi hodowli koni arabskich by nie było, gdyby nie kilku ludzi, którzy kochali te zwierzęta*, Gazeta.pl 22. 11. 2016, http://weekend.gazeta.pl/weekend/1,15212 1,21011476,polskiej-potegi-konia-arabskiego-by-nie-bylo-gdyby-nie-wiedza.html (all of these links last visited: 20. 01. 2018).

727 One should bear in mind that the performance of a commission agent may occur as a sale or a purchase of a different good. However, with reference to the auction sale of horses, the obligation to sell a horse by the commission agent is much more common.

728 With reference to the character of the obligation of an agent under Polish law, see: J. Frąckowiak [in:] J. Rajski, (ed.), *System Prawa Prywatnego, Vol. VII*, pp. 734–735; A. Kędzierska Cieślak, *Komis (zagadnienia cywilnoprawne)*, pp. 61–65. With reference to German law, see: I. Koller [in:] C. Canaris, M. Habersack, C. Schäfer, *Staub Handelsgesetzbuch Großkommentar*, Göttingen 2013, p. 111.

729 There are usually no disputes with reference to ownership of the principal in the case of ordering a commission agent to sell a good. With reference to Polish law, see: J. Frąckowiak [in:] J. Rajski, (ed.), *System Prawa Prywatnego, Vol. VII*, p. 747. With reference to German law, see: K. Schmidt, *Handelsrecht*, Köln 2014, pp. 1036–1036. However, when ordering a commission agent to buy a good, the issue is more complicated, see with reference to Polish law: J. Frąckowiak [in:] J. Rajski, (ed.), *System Prawa Prywatnego, Vol. VII*, pp. 749–753 and with reference to German law: K. Schmidt, *Handelsrecht*, Köln 2014, pp. 1040–1041.

claims might be difficult to file in the event that there is no written commission contract. The inclusion of a *del credere* provision in the contract is also possible, though rarely used in the sale of horses because of a specific relation founded on trust, which is needed in order to entrust somebody a living animal.[730]

The last issue to mention in reference to the performance of a commission contract are the parties' additional duties in the event that the commission agent's service consists **in selling a horse** at auction (i.e. duties other than performing the service and paying the agreed remuneration). The commission agent's duty to act with the due diligence that is to be expected in his profession, as well as the duty to act in good faith and the duty of loyalty to the principal have already been briefly mentioned.[731] However, the most interesting duty is **the obligation to keep the horse safe and secure until its sale.** The performance of this duty does always cause some concern in reference to animals, as their actions – as living creatures – can never be predicted with certainty (special attention should be given to sale of stallions, as they are more prone to injury). Therefore, commission agents usually insure the horses and include the price of the insurance in the final auction price of the horse,[732] although they are not legally obliged to insure an object of the commission contract. The most important additional duty of a principal arising in reference to the horse's sale is the reimbursement of all expenses incurred by the auction performer (i.e. commission agent) in connection with his service.[733] This duty is connected with the nature of commission contracts, which usually set out the need to take an animal to the place where the commission agent runs his business.[734] This is

730 With reference to the character of the obligation of an agent under Polish law, see: J. Frąckowiak [in:] J. Rajski, (ed.), *System Prawa Prywatnego, Vol. VII*, pp. 734–735; A. Kędzierska Cieślak, *Komis (zagadnienia cywilnoprawne)*, pp. 61–65; E. Rott-Pietrzyk [in:] M. Stec, *System Prawa Handlowego. Prawo Umów handlowych*, Vol. V, p. 591 et seq. Compare: provisions referring to the *del credere* provision under German law: § 394 HGB.

731 To learn more about the duty of loyalty in reference to German law, see: K. Schmidt, *Handelsrecht*, Köln 2014, pp. 1001–1002.

732 See, for example: the rules of a horse auction performed by the Hanoverian horses associations, from: http://www.hannoveraner.com/hannoveraner-verband/auktionen/auktionsarchiv/auktionen-2016/verdener-auktion-januar/auktionsbroschuere/. Germany hosts over 25 different sport horse auctions and all the prominent breeding associations host their own auctions, See: Deutsche Reiterliche Vereinigung e.V. Fédération Equestre Nationale (FN), *A Guide through the German Equestrian World -equestrian sports and breeding in Germany*, available at: http://www.euroequestrian.eu/files/2/11/Horse_Sports_and_Breeding_Juli_2014.pdf (last visited: 3.3.2018).

733 See, with reference to German law: I. Koller [in:] C. Canaris, M. Habersack, C. Schäfer, *Staub Handelsgesetzbuch Großkommentar*, Göttingen 2013, p. 111.

734 See, with reference to commission contracts generally: K. Kruczalak, E. Rott-Pietrzyk [in:] M. Stec, *System Prawa Handlowego. Prawo Umów handlowych*, Vol. V, p. 701. With reference to the place of performance of the commission contract, see also, with reference to Polish law: J. Frąckowiak [in:] J. Rajski, (ed.), *System Prawa Prywatnego, Vol. VII*, pp. 738–

needed in order to be able to know the animal well enough to be able to show it properly at the auction (sometimes special training might also be necessary). As far as it concerns horses, these expenses are relatively high, and the amount of time when the horse is kept before its sale gains significant importance for the principal. Therefore, it is necessary to establish expenses for caring, feeding and keeping the horse, as well as the consequences of an unsuccessful attempt to sell it at the first auction in the commission contract. The horses are usually shown at auction under saddle, therefore the riding service has to be taken into account as well.[735]

The differences in the performance of commission contracts in cases where an animal (in particular, a horse) constitutes an object of a sale contract arising from this commission contract, requires different standards than the performance of a commission contract leading to the conclusion of a sale contract with regular things as its object. Thus, the duties and costs of a commission agent undertaking the obligation to sell a horse are diametrically different (i. e. higher) than in the case of a commission contract having an obligation to sell a different good as its object. In addition, the liability of a commission agent in the case of intermediating in the sale of an animal is different due to the duty to keep the horse safe and secure until its sale. Thus, it is impossible and against the needs of the horse to keep it – as a living creature, being flighty from its nature – motionless, and therefore also safe. Since the risk of keeping the horse safe and healthy is fraught with a high risk of failure, the costs of insurance are also much higher with reference to horses. Summing up, the commission agent undertaking the obligation to sell a horse undertakes higher risk, costs, liability, and has more duties connected with taking care for an animal, including the need to have special knowledge in the field of horses. Therefore, the commission contract where a horse is the object of a sale contract arising from this commission contract requires such diametrically different standards to the performance of a commission contract leading to the conclusion of a sale contract having regular things as its object, that these commission contracts turn out to have a different content – justifying a special place in the Polish legal order (or at least the Polish

739 and with reference to German law: I. Koller [in:] C. Canaris, M. Habersack, C. Schäfer, *Staub Handelsgesetzbuch Großkommentar*, Göttingen 2013, pp. 112–114.

735 It is also possible to show the horses in hand, though the auction performer (i. e. the commission agent) is obliged to show the horse in the best possible way in order to sell it for the best possible price. Therefore, sport and leisure horses are usually shown in a manner that expresses their best capabilities, i. e. being ridden by a qualified rider. Younger horses are shown in hand. Compare the information concerning showing horses at auctions on the websites of several breeding associations: http://www.hannoveraner.com/hannoveraner-verband/; http://oldenburger-pferde.net/; http://holsteiner-verband.de/ (last visited: 4.2. 2016).

legal doctrine that would specifically define how to apply provisions referring to commission contracts with modifications to animals).

2.2. Agency contracts having an animal as their object

As already mentioned, agency contracts under Polish and German law have a professional nature, which means that they can be concluded solely between businesses (i. e. it is a B2B Contract). According to § 12 BGB, the definition of a business consists of a natural or legal person or an organizational entity that, when entering into a legal transaction, acts in exercise of his or its trade, business or profession.[736] According to Article 43^1KC,[737] a business is a natural person, a legal person or an organizational entity referred to in Article 33^1 § 1 that conducts economic or professional activity on its own behalf.[738] Although the definitions of a business in Polish and German legal systems are not similar, the legal qualification of a business based on both of them has similar consequences. However, what is important when describing a contract of a professional nature (in the meaning of a type of a B2B transaction), are the consequences of a failure to comply with this legal prerequisite (i. e. what happens if one party to the contract does not act as a business). In such a situation, the contract cannot be qualified as an agency contract. If the principal does not conduct professional activity, according to Article 43^1KC, the regulations concerning agency contracts apply respectively.[739] If the agent does not act as a business, the case is more

736 With reference to the term "business activity" under German law, see: the paragraph below and J. Busche [in:] H. Oetker, *Handelsgesetzbuch. Kommentar*, München 2011, pp. 539; G. von Hoyningen-Huene [in:] K. Schmidt, *Münchener Kommentar. Handelsgesetzbuch*, München 2010, pp. 1140–1141.

737 With reference to the Polish definition of a business under Article 43^1 KC, see: E. Gniewek [in:] E. Gniewek, P. Machnikowski (ed.), *Kodeks cywilny. Komentarz*, pp. 89–92; M. Kępinski [in:] M. Gutowski (ed.), *Kodeks*, pp. 236–240; W. Katner, *Dylematy spójności Kodeksu spółek handlowych z Kodeksem cywilnym oraz Kodeksem rodzinnym i opiekuńczym – konferencja naukowa dla uczczenia 40lecia pracy naukowej Profesora Andrzeja Szajkowskiego w INP PAN (Warszawa, 23 września 2014 r.)*, Spółki handlowe jako przedsiębiorcy według Kodeksu cywilnego i Kodeksu spółek handlowych (dodatek MoP 7/2015), pp. 1013 et seq.; J. Jacyszyn, *Przedsiębiorca w regulacjach prawnych, cz. I*, EP 2015, No. 4, pp. 26 et seq.; M. Snitko-Pleszko, *Kodeks cywilny po nowelizacji. Cz. II. Konsument, przedsiębiorca, przedsiębiorstwo, gospodarstwo rolne, oferta, aukcja i przetarg*, MOP 2003, No. 10, pp. 474 et seq.

738 Note, that the definition in Article 43^1KC is broader than the definition of a business in the Polish Freedom of Economic Activity Act. See: Article 4 of the Polish Economic Activity Act of 2. 7. 2004 (J. L. 2004 No. 173 item 1807).

739 Note, that such a contract is not an agency contract, but an undefined contract, in case of which the lawmaker refers to provisions covering agency contracts. In this case, the provisions covering agency contract are respectively applicable. See: E. Rott-Pietrzyk [in:] S.

complicated, as there is no direct referral to any other regulation in the Polish Civil Code. According to Article 750 KC, the provisions applicable to mandate contract (*umowa zlecenia*) apply respectively.[740] However, as already presented under Subchapter IV. 1.1.[741] of this book, if an undefined contract contains elements that are typical for other defined contracts, the rules applicable to this kind of contract apply respectively.[742] Since respective applicability means that these provisions might be applied respectively without modifications,[743] with proper modifications or do not have to be applied at all – depending on the content of a certain contract[744]– this also concerns the respective applicability of provisions covering mandate contracts in the Polish Civil Code to a contract, in which the "agent" (thus, it is not an agent in the meaning of agency contract) does not act as a business. As a result, E. Rott-Pietrzyk proposes that, in the case where the "agent" in the case at hand does not act as a business, the rules concerning exclusive agency (Article 761 § 2 KC), the rules concerning provisions from the contracts concluded after the duration of the agency contract (Article 761^1 KC), the rules concerning compensatory benefits (Articles 764^3 – 764^8 KC) and the rules concerning the principal's obligation to pay an appropriate pecuniary sum for limiting the agent's competitive activity (764^6 § 3 KC) should all be omitted.[745] If neither of the parties to the contract are businesses, both solutions: the applicability of provisions concerning mandate (based on Article 750 KC) and the applicability of provisions concerning agency contracts respectively are to be considered. However, according to E. Rott-Pietrzyk, the first solution seems to be more appropriate.[746]

As far as it concerns the referential legal system of Germany, the agent also has to conduct a business (German: *das Gewerbe*), where this term is interpreted broadly and it does not make any difference in what nature the agent conducts

Włodyka, *Prawo Umów Handlowych, Vol. V*, Warszawa 2017, pp. 545–546. Compare: Article 764^9 KC.

740 *Idem*.

741 See: Subchapter IV.1.1. of this book.

742 See: SN, ruling from 28.10.1999 – II CKN 530/98, with an approving gloss of Ewa Rott-Pietrzyk concerning the applicability of Article 761 § 1 KC to a contract of a one-time agency: OSP 2000, No. 7–8, item 118; P. Machnikowski [in:] E. Gniewek, P. Machnikowski (ed.), *Kodeks cywilny. Komentarz*, pp. 1411–1413. Note that the respective applicability of provisions covering service contracts under Article 734 KC means that these provisions might be applied directly, with modifications or do not have to be applied at all – depending on the content of a certain contract, see: See: Subchapter IV.1.1. of this book.

743 This does not mean direct application. See: Subchapter IV.1.1. of this book. With reference to direct application of legal provisions, see also: J. Nowacki, *Odpowiednie stosowanie przepisów prawa*, PiP 1964, No. 3, pp. 370–371.

744 See: Subchapter IV.1.1. of this book.

745 E. Rott-Pietrzyk [in:] J. Rajski, (ed.), *System...*, pp. 636–637.

746 *Idem*, p. 637.

his business.[747] In the German literature, it is underlined that the agent has to conduct a business and act autonomously – otherwise, he is not to be treated as an agent, but rather as an employee.[748] Such a person, although is often called a commercial agent in practice, is not an agent in the meaning of § 84 HGB.[749]

The Polish and the German legal systems both set out two major types of agency contracts: one where the agent acts as **an intermediary,** and one where the agent acts as **a proxy.**[750] The main difference between an intermediary and a proxy is the fact that the intermediary undertakes only acts of a factual nature, whereas the proxy undertakes acts of a legal nature, acting in the principal's name and on his account.[751] The agent may also act as an intermediary and as a proxy, which qualifies as a mixed agency.[752]

However, it is important that, in both types of agency contracts, the agent needs to act for a principal on a **permanent basis.** Thus, intermediating in the sale of one particular horse would not constitute an agency agreement.[753] Such a situation – under Polish law – would rather be qualified as a commission contract – where the agent acts in his own name, but on the principal's account, or as a mandate contract – where the agent acts in principal's name and on principal's account.

In an agency, where the agent acts as an intermediary, he is obliged to undertake factual actions for a principal that aim and lead to creating a legal bound between a principal and a third person. Thus, he only intermediates, creates a certain state of facts for the principal.[754] Legal practice and doctrine define the actions that are undertaken by the agent in order to describe them as inter-

747 See: J. Busche [in:] H. Oetker, *Handelsgesetzbuch. Kommentar*, München 2011, pp. 519–521; G. von Hoyningen-Huene [in:] K. Schmidt, *Münchener Kommentar. Handelsgesetzbuch*, München 2010, pp. 1154.

748 In such case, the provisions of Employment law are applicable, not the provisions of the Commercial Code. See: J. Busche [in:] H. Oetker, *Handelsgesetzbuch. Kommentar*, München 2011, pp. 539; G. von Hoyningen-Huene [in:] K. Schmidt, *Münchener Kommentar. Handelsgesetzbuch*, München 2010, pp. 1140–1141.

749 See: G. von Hoyningen-Huene [in:] K. Schmidt, *Münchener Kommentar. Handelsgesetzbuch*, München 2010, pp. 1140–1141.

750 Note that in a commission contract – as opposed to an agency contract – the commission agent acts solely as an intermediary. Compare: Subchapter IV.2.1. See also with reference to Polish law: E. Rott-Pietrzyk [in:] S. Włodyka (ed.), *Prawo…*, p. 475. See also with reference to German law: J. Busche [in:] H. Oetker, *Handelsgesetzbuch. Kommentar*, München 2011, pp. 526–527.

751 See, with reference to the Polish law: K. Kruczalak, E. Rott-Pietrzyk [in:] M. Stec (ed.), *System Prawa Handlowego. Tom V, Prawo Umów handlowych*, p. 543.

752 *Idem.*

753 Under Polish law, in such a case the provisions applicable to service contracts from Article 750 KC apply. See: E. Rott-Pietrzyk, *Agent handlowy…*, pp. 268–269.

754 See: E. Rott-Pietrzyk [in:] J. Rajski (ed.), *System…*, p. 639.

mediating[755] and, **with reference to the sale of horses that would include:** networking; attending certain events where information concerning the sale of sport horses can be exchanged; finding the right horse (as a result of attending sporting competitions where such horses can be found or as a result of internet research based on the connections that have been made by an agent); organizing the possibility to try the horse; exchanging information between the horse's seller and the agent's principal; negotiating the price; constructing the sale agreement; etc. It is underlined that if the intermediary participates in any of those activities – as long as it leads to the conclusion of a contract of sale for a particular horse – is considered to be acting as an agent.[756]

For an agent to act as **a proxy**, it is necessary to grant a power of attorney to the agent.[757] The scope of the power of attorney depends on its content, but will rarely permit the purchase of a horse without consulting it with the principal. Thus, although it is common to grant the agent the right to purchase a horse for the principal, this right is usually withheld until the principal accepts the choice of the horse. In the market practice, this situation is caused by the fact that the competitors are often able to try the horse during competitions, which force them to make long distance trips (if the competitor buys a horse for itself, not the sponsor). However, after the decision is made, there are still medical examinations to be carried out. The competitor cannot allow himself not to take part in certain competitions or to skip training in order to arrange for transporting the horse and taking care of its medical examinations, negotiations with the seller, etc. That is why the type of agency contract where an agent acts as a proxy is often used in the sale of sport horses. In this case, the agent **takes care of:** medical examinations, negotiations and other formalities connected with the purchase of the horse and its safe transportation (Article 758 in connection with Article 760^1 KC), whereas the principal may take care for his stud and training of his own horses.

Concerning the conclusion of an agency contract in general (no matter whether the agent acts as a proxy or as an intermediary), the freedom of contract principle[758] applies to the content of the contract, and also to its form (the

755 See, with reference to Polish law, but with applicability to German law as well: E. Rott-Pietrzyk [in:] J. Rajski, (ed.), *System...*, p. 640–641.

756 *Idem.* See also, with reference to German law: J. Busche [in:] H. Oetker, *Handelsgesetzbuch. Kommentar*, München 2011, p. 527.

757 More about granting a power of attorney in agency contracts with reference to Polish law, see: E. Rott-Pietrzyk [in:] J. Rajski, (ed.), *System...*, pp. 642–654.

758 With reference to the freedom of contract principle in general, see: E. Rott-Pietrzyk *Commercial Agency Contracts...* [in:] *Private Autonomy...*, pp. 15–34; M. Lubelska-Sazanów, *The "Principle of No Freedom of Contract": A Post-Modern Version of the Freedom of Contract Principle?*, [in:] M. De Maestri, S. Dominelli (ed.), *Party autonomy in European private (and) international law, Vol. II*, Rome 2015, pp. 15–31; with reference to the freedom

contract may be concluded explicitly or *per facta concludentia*, and there are no form requirements for its conclusion). Most commonly it is concluded by an offer and its acceptance, as well as through negotiations between the agent and the principal.[759] In my opinion, the second manner has a broader practical meaning as the instructions concerning the horse that is being sought are always established individually, along with the conditions of payment and the actions undertaken by the agent.

At this point, it is necessary to take into account the criteria limiting the freedom of contract *sensu stricto* (Article 353^1 KC) with reference to an agency contract. These are: statutory law, the nature of the relationship and the principles of community life.[760] Concerning the criteria of statutory law, it is necessary to consider which of these statutory law provisions have an imperative or semi-imperative character. Thus, the parties are free to establish the content and aim of the contract in accordance with the freedom of contract principle only in the scope of semi-imperative legal provisions.[761] Concerning the criteria of the nature of the relationship and the principles of community life, these limitations may have a different scope if an animal is object of a contractual obligation. For example, in the case of an agency contract with reference to the sale of horses, the parties could not conclude a contract whereby, after the conclusion of a contract, the agent will keep the animal in a box at a certain stable, with the reservation that nobody is allowed to take care of the horse and to ride it before the principal/its new owner comes to collect the horse. Where such a provision would not provide any problems as long as the principal arrives on the same day, this precedence may very likely be interpreted as an obligation against the principles of community life, if the principal arrives later, for example, after a week.

With reference to the limitation of form, the Polish Civil Code, establishes **two limitations on the freedom of form principle** when establishing agency contracts:[762] in the case where the parties' agreement creates **a *del credere* obligation**

of contract principle under Polish law, see also: P. Machnikowski, *Swoboda umów według Art. 353(1) KC. Konstrukcja prawna.*

759 Other types of concluding a contract do not have much importance with reference to agency contract. See, with reference to Polish law: E. Rott-Pietrzyk [in:] J. Rajski, (ed.), *System Prawa Prywatnego, Vol. VII,* p. 654; E. Rott-Pietrzyk [in:] S. Włodyka (ed.), *Prawo Umów Handlowych, Tom V,* Warszawa 2014, pp. 85–99.

760 For more about the limitation in reference to the statutory law, see: E. Rott-Pietrzyk *Commercial Agency Contracts...*[in:] *Private Autonomy...*, pp. 15–34.

761 P. Machnikowski, Swoboda umów według Article 353(1) KC. Konstrukcja prawna, Warszawa 2005; R. Trzaskowki, Granice swobody kształtowania treści i celu umów obligacyjnych, Kraków 2005.

762 Thus, as already mentioned, most Polish scholars consider the freedom of form as a fourth aspect of this principle. See: Subchapter IV.1.1. of this book ("General characteristic of service contracts with reference to contracts having an animal as their object" – "General remarks"). See also: S. Włodyka, C. Żurawska, *Zasady prawa gospodarczego prywatnego*

of an agent, or where the parties' agreement sets **a limit on competitive activity**[763] of an agent. The first limitation should be reserved in writing as, if not in written form the agency contract will be deemed to have been concluded without this reservation. As to the limitation of an agent's competitive activity, this reservation has to be set out in writing or it is not valid.[764] The limitation on an agent's competitive activity is a condition that a principal may be likely to include in an agency contract aimed at finding a suitable horse for a high-level competitor. Thus, it is very possible that an agent seeking a horse for several competitors at the same level will have to decide which of them will have priority, in order to decide whether he is interested in trying a certain horse or not. On the other hand, a limitation on the agent's competitive activity may be very expensive for the principal, as finding the right horse may take several months.[765] Therefore, it is commonly practiced that an agent looks for horses prepared for a certain level of competitions, and then shows them to all his principals. The first of them who shows an interest in a certain horse, and is then willing to purchase it, has the priority to act this way. In most cases, an agent looking for horses or trying to find a buyer for its principal's horse also undertakes other occupational activities that help him build up a network of connections needed to act as an agent and to provide earnings on a daily basis. Thus, agents in this field are usually trainers in several horse-riding disciplines, horse breeders or competitors (which occupationally train horses as well).[766] However, it is also possible for an agent to act solely for a certain principal – such a situation may happen, for example, where a principal has a horse stud selling significant numbers of horses, which keeps an agent busy on a daily basis, and the contract may then limit any competitive activity of such an agent.

(handlowego) [in:] *System Prawa Handlowego, Vol. 1*, Warszawa 2009, pp. 328–330; M. Safjan [in:] K. Pietrzykowski (ed.), *Kodeks cywilny. Komentarz*, pp. 1074–1084.

763 According to Article 764[6] KC, the parties may limit the agent's activity of a competitive character during the period after the termination of the contract of agency. However, with reference to the *de lege ferenca* proposals in connection with the provisions referring to the *del credere* provision in Polish civil law, see: K. Topolewski, *Umowa agencyjna według Kodeksu cywilnego. Wybrane problem de lege ferenda* [in:] A. Olejniczak, J. Haberko, A. Pyrzyńska, D. Sokołowska, *Współczesne problemy prawa prywatnego,* Warszawa 2015, pp. 712–727.

764 See: Article 764[6] KC.

765 Note, that agency implies a permanent contract. Thus, although the competitor is looking for a perfect horse for the principal in a certain season, it does not mean that if the agent finds more horses that would be appropriate for the principal, he will not buy them. Therefore, also finding a horse that a competitor was looking for at a certain moment does not mean that the agency contract is terminated. Thus, competitors and breeders look for promising horses on a regular basis, and are ready to purchase new horses as soon they have any spare room in their stable.

766 Thus, it is common to take a certain horse in training and to act as an agent when selling it afterwards.

Moving to the duties of the parties to an agency contract,[767] one of most significant features of this type of contract is the **duty of loyalty.** In the Polish Civil Code, this duty is explicitly regulated in Article 760 KC, which makes it one of the most important obligations of an agency contract. Thus, this duty cannot be excluded by the parties to the agency contract and does not have any equivalent in the provisions of the Polish Civil Code concerning other contracts.[768] However, a general duty of loyalty could have been derived from the general provisions concerning obligations (i.e. Article 354 and Article 355 KC) already before Article 760 KC was introduced to the Polish Civil Code.[769] This duty both has a general character and concerns all the specific duties of the parties to the agency contract. Some Polish scholars define two dimensions of the agent's duty of loyalty.[770] The first concerns a duty of loyalty when fulfilling other contractual duties of the parties, and the second concerns an independent duty of loyalty. Generally, the second type of duty of loyalty in an agency contract is connected with confidential information that comes to the agent's knowledge while performing his duties.[771] However, where it concerns the sale of horses, the duty of loyalty in an agency contract is rather based on trust that all information concerning the horse's behavior and health that has come to the knowledge of then agent will not be concealed from the principal. The duty of loyalty equals also non-competition during the term of the agency contract.[772] Especially where it concerns agency in the sale of horses, acting in the interest of the other party to the sale contract, or in the interest of any other competitive entity, would certainly lead to the breach of the duty of loyalty.[773] Thus, it is very important for the agent to look for a horse that would be healthy, promising and suitable for the principal, without trying to fulfil the interest of the seller at the same time.

767 Compare: E. Rott-Pietrzyk [in:] S. Włodyka, *Prawo...*, pp. 99–114.

768 See: E. Rott-Pietrzyk [in:] J. Rajski, (ed.), *System...*, p. 662.

769 *Idem.* To read more about duty of loyalty, see also: E. Rott-Pietrzyk, *Agent handlowy...*, pp. 307–311; L. Ogiegło [in:] K. Pietrzykowski (ed.), *Kodeks cywilny, Tom II, Komentarz*, pp. 684–685.

770 With reference to the duty of loyalty in agency contracts in general, see: E. Rott-Pietrzyk [in:] M. Stec, *System Prawa Handlowego. Prawo Umów handlowych*, Vol. V, Warszawa 2017, pp. 567–569; J. Jezioro [in:] E. Gniewek, P. Machnikowski (ed.), *Kodeks cywilny. Komentarz*, pp. 1469–1470; P. Mikłaszewicz [in:] K. Osajda, pp. 807–808. See also: J. Pokrzywniak, *Obowiązek lojalności jako element stosunku zobowiązaniowego*, MoP 2003, No. 19, pp. 885 et seq.

771 See: E. Rott-Pietrzyk [in:] J. Rajski (ed.), *System...*, p. 662.

772 Note that the limitation on an agent's competitive activity after the termination of the agency agreement as a possibility of the parties to the agency contract has been regulated in Article 764^6 KC, whereas there are no provisions limiting *expressis verbis* the agent's competitive activity during the term of the agency agreement. This non-competition during the term of the agency contract has to be stipulated from Art 760 KC.

773 Except for a situation where an agent acts for more than one principal at once, see above in the previous paragraphs of this subchapter.

The German Commercial Code does not include a provision corresponding with Article 760 KC referring to a duty of loyalty in the agency contract, which constitutes a difference in comparison to the Polish legal system. However, that does not mean that the German legal system does not foresee such a duty with reference to a commercial agent. Thus, in the German legal system the duty of loyalty is described as the obligation to take care of the principal's interest and is included as an accessory obligation of an agent in § 86 HGB, among the other duties.[774]

According to both the Polish Civil Code, and the German Commercial Code, **other contractual duties of an agent** include: the duty to pass on all necessary information to the principal (e. g. about horses that he has found, the prices that he has negotiated, any proposals that he rejected, etc.), the duty to protect the interests of the principal, and the duty to follow the principal's instructions, where the last one applies only to instructions that are justified in a certain situation.[775] Although it is stressed that the commercial agent is not subordinate to the principal, this duty might look differently in an agency contract having the purchase of a horse as its subject (though this problem does not apply to an agency agreement concerning the sale of the principal's horse). Namely, defining the right horse for the principal is a decision of a very personal character and – in this particular case – the principal's instructions should be obeyed more than in case of any other commercial agency that does not concern the sale of animals. Nevertheless, the agent is not subordinate to the principal in the meaning that he may organize his activities by himself and he has his time at his disposal. Thus, the differences arisen in view of the fact that the agency contract concerns the sale of animals does not undermine the rule that commercial agent is independent and acts autonomously.

The **duties of the principal** generally encompass: the duty to pay the agent's remuneration,[776] the duty to allow the agent to check the amount of commission due to him,[777] the duty to pass the agent documents, information and give him notifications,[778] and the duty to reimburse the agent's expenses.[779] Taking into

774 Compare: J. Busche [in:] H. Oetker, *Handelsgesetzbuch. Kommentar*, München 2011, pp. 546–560.

775 Compare: L. Ogiegło [in:] K. Pietrzykowski (ed.), *Kodeks cywilny, Tom II, Komentarz*, pp. 685–686; I. Mycko-Katner, *Umowa Agencyjna*, Warszawa 2012, pp. 161–185; J. Busche [in:] H. Oetker, *Handelsgesetzbuch. Kommentar*, München 2011, pp. 546–560; G. von Hoyningen-Huene [in:] K. Schmidt, *Münchener Kommentar. Handelsgesetzbuch*, München 2010, pp. 1173–1187.

776 The duty to pay the agent remuneration constitutes one of the *essentialia negotii* of the agency agreement, see: Article 758 KC.

777 See: Article 761^5 KC.

778 See: Article 760^2 KC.

account agency contracts for the sale of horses, the documents and information that have to be passed to an agent concern rather the situation where the principal is selling a horse with the support of an agent. Thus, the seller of the horse is the one who has to provide all the information concerning the horse – its medical history, pedigree, behavior, etc., and potentially pass to the agent a copy of its passport, medical history, etc. The duty to give the agent notifications does not have that much importance in a situation where the parties agree that the agent receives remuneration expressed as a percentage of the price of the horse being sought or being sold. This is usually the case with the sale of horses.

The most problematic issue when commissioning the sale of a horse to an agent (which does not occur when commissioning an agent to find the right horse for the principal) is the manner of **calculating the agent's remuneration.**[780] Thus, according to Article 758[1] § 1 KC, if there was no agreement in this matter, the agent will receive remuneration. Obviously, an agent is entitled to receive the remuneration only if the sales contract is concluded as a result of his actions.[781] The remuneration may be pledged by a seller, by a buyer or by both of them, which depends on the parties' agreement with an agent. In accordance with Article 758[1] § 2 KC, this remuneration should correspond to the number of contracts concluded by an agent. According to Article 758[1] § 3 KC, if the contract does not specify the amount of the agent's remuneration, it should be estimated in line with commonly accepted remuneration in relationships of a given type and in the venue where the agent pursues his activities. In case it is impossible to determine the commission that way, the remuneration of an agent should be an appropriate amount taking into account all the circumstances directly pertaining to the performance of the acts mandated to him. In the case of intermediating in the international sale of horses, this amount should correspond with the time the agent spent on travelling back and forth to a client, and time spent in negotiations, but should also take into account the price of the horse and

779 A comprehensive description of duties of parties' to agency contract in Polish law can be found in: E. Rott-Pietrzyk, *Agent handlowy…*, pp. 306–325. Compare: L. Ogiegło [in:] K. Pietrzykowski (ed.), *Kodeks cywilny, Komentarz*, Vol. II, pp. 686–687; I. Mycko-Katner, *Umowa Agencyjna*, Warszawa 2012, pp. 185–203.

780 With reference to certain problems connected with calculating an agent's provision (regardless of the service provided by the agent) and the nature of provisions regulating this remuneration in Polish and European law (Directive 86/653), see: E. Rott-Pietrzyk, M. Grochowski, *Prowizja agenta w czasie trwania umowy (imperatywny czy dyspozytywny charakter regulacji i wynikające z tego konsekwencje)*, TPP 2018, Issue 4 (to be published).

781 More about the prerequisites for an agent to demand the remuneration: P. Schwerdtner, C. Hamm, Maklerrecht, München 2012, p. 99 (in German law); E. Rott-Pietrzyk, *Agent handlowy…*, pp. 328–329; E. Rott-Pietrzyk, M. Grochowski, *Prowizja agenta w czasie trwania umowy (imperatywny czy dyspozytywny charakter regulacji i wynikające z tego konsekwencje)*, TPP 2018, Issue 4 (to be published); P Mikłaszewicz [in:] K. Osajda (ed.), *Kodeks cywilny. Komentarz. Tom IIIB*, pp. 813–817 (in Polish law).

the time it took an agent to create a network of clients interested in the horses offered by his principals (and also sellers interested in cooperating with him, in cases where agency contract sets out intermediation in the purchase of a horse), as well as knowledge in these matters, which probably took years to develop.[782] The remuneration occurs in form of a commission and usually amounts to 10–15 % of the horse's price; there are no significant differences between the European Member States in this respect, as the market of horses used for sports at a certain, high level is international. It should be underlined once again here, that the referential legal system of Germany has not been chosen accidentally, since Germany is known to be the European leader in breeding and selling sport horses (this concerns especially horses used in disciplines like dressage or jumping) and – in practice – horse sellers in other countries, which do not have such a rich doctrine and jurisprudence as Germany, usually pattern their provisions on German standards. According to the German literature, the provisions of Title 10 of Part VIII of Book 2 (Law of obligations) BGB are also applicable to these types of contracts.[783] The Polish doctrine has not addressed this problem so far, and so the solution used in the German market practice should serve as a role model in this case.[784]

After the agency contract expires, an agent is still entitled to receive remuneration in two cases:[785] if the sales have been concluded as a result of his activities, or if they have been concluded with clients formerly obtained by the agent for such contracts.[786] The problem of contracts concluded as a result of an agent's activities or contracts concluded with clients formerly obtained by the agent (for the contracts of the same kind) often arises in a situation where the agent is a rider who takes horses for training and rides them in competitions. Namely, Article 761–761^7 KC and – respectively – §§ 87–87c HGB define when an agent receives remuneration, and in what manner it should be defined, but do not cover all the possible complications that may occur in the process of selling a horse.[787]

782 Compare: SN, ruling from 28.10.1999 – II CKN 530/98, with an approving gloss of Ewa Rott-Pietrzyk concerning the issues that the court should take into account when applying Article 761 § 1 KC to a contract of one-time agency: OSP 2000, Nos 7–8, item 118.

783 P. Rosbach, *Pferderecht*, p. 72.

784 See: Book No. 3 of the Polish Civil Code, part II, Title XXIII – Agency contract. More about the institution of an agency contract in Polish and international law: E. Rott-Pietrzyk, *Agent handlowy – regulacje polskie i europejskie*, Warszawa 2006, pp. 6–10, 17–24.

785 See: E. Rott-Pietrzyk [in:] S. Włodyka, *Prawo…*, pp. 504–507.

786 See: Article 761 KC and § 87 HGB; to the details see: E. Rott-Pietrzyk, M. Grochowski, *Prowizja agenta w czasie trwania umowy (imperatywny czy dyspozytywny charakter regulacji i wynikające z tego konsekwencje)*, TPP 2018, Issue 4 (to be published).

787 See more: E. Rott-Pietrzyk, *Agent handlowy…*, pp. 325–336.

The situation that causes most problems in the Polish and German practice is the case when it is not an agent but a third person that contacts the owner and expresses a willingness to purchase his horse. The question arises whether the contract has been concluded as a result of the agent's activities or not. Thus, although the client has not been formally obtained by the agent, it is the agent who has been showing and training the horse, which has a significant impact on the third person's offer to acquire it. In order to avoid such problems, it is recommended that the parties define all the details of the agency contract and conclude it in writing.

A *del credere* provision[788] is rarely included in agency contracts involving the sale of horses under Polish and German law, as the final conclusion of the contract with the client is a personal choice (of the client or of the principal – depending on who the buyer is), and it would be too much risk for an agent to guarantee that the contract will be finally concluded. In the end, the principal's duty to reimburse the agent's expenses does not raise many practical problems[789] and consists usually in the reimbursement of the agent's travel expenses. However, these expenses not only have to be connected with the agent's performance of the contract, but also they have to be justified, and the amount must not exceed the rate that is customary in the given relations.

Summing up, the duties of an agent have a much broader scope in case where the object of actions he is obliged to undertake is a living animal (compare Article 760[1] KC). This scope is even broader in cases where the agent acts as a proxy. Thus, he undertakes responsibility to make the decision of selling/buying a particular horse for the principal, and his actions may constitute the foundation for future warranty claims in case the horse does not "fit" the rider due to its character or lack of certain natural capabilities. Since the agent is obliged to loyalty,[790] he has to take into consideration several factors that may have an impact on the relationship between the horse and its rider in the future. This requires not only knowledge of horse sports, but also higher resistance to stress

788 With reference to the *del credere* provision under Polish law, see: I. Mycko-Katner, *Umowa Agencyjna,* Warszawa 2012, pp. 289–306; E. Rott-Pietrzyk [in:] J. Rajski (ed.), *System...*, pp. 672–677; E. Rott-Pietrzyk, *Agent handlowy...*, pp. 346–353; E. Rott-Pietrzyk [in:] S. Włodyka, *Prawo...*, pp. 504–507; L. Ogiegło [in:] J. Rajski (ed.), *System Prawa Prywatnego, Vol. VII*, pp. 692–693; K. Topolewski, *Umowa agencyjna według Kodeksu cywilnego. Wybrane problem de lege ferenda* [in:] A. Olejniczak, J. Haberko, A. Pyrzyńska, D. Sokołowska, *Współczesne problemy prawa prywatnego*, pp. 712–727. With reference to the *del credere* provision under German law, see: J. Busche [in:] H. Oetker, *Handelsgesetzbuch. Kommentar*, München 2011, pp. 571–579; G. von Hoyningen-Huene [in:] K. Schmidt, *Münchener Kommentar. Handelsgesetzbuch*, München 2010, pp. 1198–1207.

789 See more: E. Rott-Pietrzyk [in:] J. Rajski (ed.), *System Prawa Prywatnego, Vol. VII*, p. 671.

790 See: the paragraphs above referring to the contractual duties of the parties to agency contracts in cases where an agent is obliged to intermediate in the sale of a horse.

and better abilities to anticipate than where the agent intermediates in the sale of different things. Whereas an agent usually does not undertake surveillance of horses when acting for its principal (he does not have duties connected with taking care of a horse, which usually appear in reference to commission contracts),[791] he still undertakes more risk than an agent working in different markets. It is also a moral challenge for an agent to evaluate the results of medical examinations of a horse with this particular horse's talent and market value. The same applies to the situation, where an agent undertakes an obligation to sell a horse for his principal. In both cases the specific character of agency connected with the sale of horses consists also in the respective applicability of provisions covering sale contracts (especially warranty rights) in reference to animals. All these issues increase the standards of contractual performance expected from an agent intermediating in the sale of horses.

2.3. Teaching/training contracts having an animal as their object

As **a contract to train an animal** (*umowa o trening zwierzęcia, der Trainingsvertrag*) is not regulated in the Polish Civil Code (and therefore has to be qualified as an undefined contract under Polish law), and as the German Civil Code has a very broad definition of a service contract,[792] the duties of the parties should be defined very clearly in the contract. The provisions of the German and Polish Civil Codes applicable to service contracts apply respectively to this type of contract, though the extent of its applicability depends on the contractual description of the parties' duties.[793]

Beginning with the main duties of the contracting parties in teaching/training contracts, under both the Polish and German legal systems, the main duty of an animal trainer consists in training an animal, and the main duty of the principal consists in paying the trainer's remuneration.[794] The construction of a typical service contract under these legal systems provides that the servicing party is

791 Compare: the duties arising usually in the contractual obligations of a commission contract having the sale of an animal as the object in Subchapter IV.2.1. ("Performance of service contracts with reference to contracts having an animal as their object" – "Commission contracts having an animal as their object") of this book.

792 See: Subchapter IV.1.1.; Subchapter IV.2.3. of this book.

793 See, with reference to German law: M. Fuchs [in:] H. Bamberger, H. Roth (ed.), *Beck'scher Online-Kommentar BGB*, § 611, side-number 60. With reference to Polish law, see: R. Morek, M. Raczkowski [in:] K. Osajda (ed.), *Kodeks cywilny. Komentarz. Tom IIIB*, pp. 757–765; P. Machnikowski [in:] E. Gniewek, P. Machnikowski (ed.), *Kodeks cywilny. Komentarz*, p. 1413.

794 As to the qualification of a training contract as a service contract from § 611 BGB under German law, see: J. Borggräfe, *Der Sporttrainervertrag*, Frankfurt am Main 2006, pp. 25–62.

obliged to follow the principal's instructions when performing its duties.[795] However, it must be underlined that the German legal system recognizes service contracts of a very different legal nature. The lack of unification in this matter at a European level[796] has caused a situation whereby the definition of a service contract under German law is applicable to two types of contracts: **contract for employment (*umowa o pracę, der Arbeitsvertrag*) and free service contracts (*der freie Dienstvertrag*).** Most of the service contracts provisions are applicable to both types of these contracts, though there are also provisions that are applicable either to contracts for employment (*umowa o pracę, Arbeitsvertrag*) or to free service contracts.[797]

Under Polish law, the contracts for employment are comprehensively defined under the Labor code and create an independent legal regime.[798] These differences must be taken into account when defining the extent of the servicing party's obligation to follow the principal's instructions. A contract to train a horse would probably lose its practical sense if the trainer was dependent on the horse's owner in reference to instructions on how to train a horse (the same applies to training any other animals). Thus, an animal's owner decides to conclude a contract with a certain trainer because of his training methods, and he must then trust that they are effective, since it is very unlikely that the trainer will change the methods he has been practicing throughout his training career. In such a case, it is rather likely that the animal's owner will change the trainer by **terminating (*wypowiedzenie/die Kündigung*** – thus, it appears in reference to a contractual obligation having a permanent character) the contract, if it turns out that he does not appreciate the trainer's training methods. If this situation applies, the principal may always terminate the contract in accordance with the contractual provisions, and in this case he is obviously obliged to pay the trainer's remuneration until the end of the term of the contract, and the trainer is obliged to train the horse until the end of the term of the contract as well (nevertheless, the animal owner – due to his ownership right over the animal – may always take the animal from the trainer earlier, though this does not release him from the obligation to pay the trainer's remuneration in accordance with the contract). The animal owner is entitled to terminate the contract with immediate

795 Compare, with reference to German law: M. Fuchs [in:] H. Bamberger, H. Roth (ed.), *Beck'scher Online-Kommentar BGB*, § 611, side-number 35; and with reference to Polish law: L. Ogiegło [in:] J. Rajski (ed.), *System Prawa Prywatnego, Vol. VII*, pp. 570–571.

796 See, the comparative presentation of service contracts in the laws of different EU Member States and EU law on the example of agency contract: E. Rott-Pietrzyk [in:] M. Stec, *System Prawa Handlowego. Tom V, Prawo Umów handlowych*, pp. 527–538.

797 M. Fuchs [in:] H. Bamberger, H. Roth (ed.), *Beck'scher Online-Kommentar BGB*, § 611, side-numbers 2–4.

798 The Labour Code in the version promulgated on 26.6.1974, J L No. 24, item 141 as amended. Compare: M. Gersdorf, *Umowa o pracę. Umowa o dzieło. Umowa zlecenie*, Warszawa 1993.

effect only in the event that the trainer improperly performed his contractual obligation, e.g. by maltreating the horse or being grossly negligent when performing his contractual obligations. In this case, in accordance with Article 471 et seq. KC or § 280 BGB (liability *ex contractu*), the obligor has to cover the positive interest (*der Erfüllungsschaden,*[799] *pozytywny interes umowny*[800]) of the party who suffered a loss due to the trainer's improper and faulty performance of the training. Thus, if the horse has decreased in value, suffered pain or become injured, the animal's owner may also demand reimbursement of these damages.

However, regardless of the legal system applicable to the contract, since the obligation of the trainer refers to a living creature, the obligation to train an animal is inseparably connected with taking care of it. It is important to establish, for example, whether the trainer is obliged to perform these duties by himself, or whether he is allowed to use anybody's help. Thus, according to the German doctrine addressing the issue of teaching/training contracts, the obligation to perform a service personally does not apply to the same extent to accessory obligations[801] of the parties of a service contract.

Since the Polish Civil Code defines only a few service contracts (e.g. mandate,[802] agency contract,[803] and commission contract[804]) and applies the construction of the respective applicability of provisions covering mandate contract to undefined service contracts (Article 734 KC with Article 750 KC),[805] the provisions covering mandate contract under Polish law are the ones that should primarily be compared to the German construction. As it concerns the regulation of mandate under Polish law, the Polish doctrine does not distinguish between the main and accessory obligations of the parties to a mandate contract,[806] though it allows the party undertaking the general performance of the service (here: the trainer) to subcontract the performance of certain actions to a third party, – as long as it occurs under the servicing party's supervision.[807]

799 For more in context to this kind of damage with reference to German law, see: H. Brox/ W. Walker, *Allgemeines Schuldrecht*, pp. 331.

800 See: Article 361 KC; compare also the popular view among the Polish doctrine: W. Czachórski, *Zobowiązania. Zarys wykładu*, pp. 96–109.

801 M. Fuchs [in:] H. Bamberger, H. Roth (ed.), *Beck'scher Online-Kommentar BGB*, § 611, sidenumber 61.

802 Articles 734 et seq. KC.

803 Articles 758 et seq. KC.

804 Articles 765 et seq. KC.

805 This problem has already been addressed several times in this book, see in particular: Subchapter IV.1.1.; Subchapter IV.1.2.3. of this book.

806 Compare: Article 738 KC and § 613 BGB. See also: https://equista.pl/editorial/2120/prawo-wybrane-umowy-cywilnoprawne-cz.-iv-umowa-o-trening-konia-lub-jezdzca, (last visted: 26.6.2018).

807 See, with reference to Polish law: P. Machnikowski [in:] E. Gniewek, P. Machnikowski (ed.), *Kodeks cywilny. Komentarz*, pp. 1402–1403.

Under Polish law, the extent to which some of the trainer's obligations can be passed to a third party depends also on the practice used in a certain community or type of business, and can be freely established in the contract between the parties.[808] Thus, according to Article 738 KC and § 613 BGB, the trainer is obliged to perform the contract personally (especially since it is a relation firmly based on mutual trust). However, as the accessory obligations of the trainer are characteristic only to this specific type of service contract (distinguished in the horse market practice and accepted in the German jurisprudence and doctrine), the provisions of Article 738 KC and § 613 BGB have to be applied with modifications in order to achieve the aim of the contract. Namely, if the trainer was obliged to feed, walk/paddock, groom etc. an animal, he would not be able to perform his activity as a trainer with reference to more than just a few horses.

Therefore, in my opinion, the provisions of Article 738 KC and § 613 BGB have to be applied with modifications leading to the conclusion that the obligation to perform the contract personally refers to trainer's main obligations, i. e. to training the animal. Thus, it is possible to subcontract additional activities connected with taking care for an animal (grooming, lungeing, shoeing the horse, etc.) to another person, but only if that is explicitly foreseen in the contract.[809] Therefore, it is very important to comprehensively describe the obligations of the parties and to define which of them are main, and which of them are accessory obligations. It is also important to bear in mind that, under both the Polish and German legal system, the trainer is also liable if he used help of other people to perform his obligation[810] (in this case: the persons performing accessory obligations in reference to taking care for the horse). Although he may demand recourse afterwards, he is the one who will be held liable for the services that he was obliged to perform as a contracting party.

The factual services like **shoeing the horse, feeding it or performing its medical examinations** qualify under German law as accessory obligations of the trainer.[811] This implies that it would not be typical for a trainer to perform them himself – there are blacksmiths, groomers and veterinary doctors, who are qualified to undertake these services (nevertheless, a trainer may still perform additional activity by performing some of these services). However, services **like**

808 *Idem.*

809 See, with reference to German law: K. Schreiber [in:] R. Schulze, H. Dörner, I. Ebert, T. Hoeren, R. Kemper, I. Saenger, K. Schreiber, H. Schulte-Nölke, A. Staudinger (eds.), *Bürgerliches Gesetzbuch. Handkommentar*, p. 879; and with reference to Polish law: P. Machnikowski [in:] E. Gniewek, P. Machnikowski (ed.), *Kodeks cywilny. Komentarz*, pp. 1411–1413. See more in Subchapter IV.1.2.3. ("General characteristic of service contracts with reference to contracts having an animal as their object" – "Teaching/training contracts having an animal as their object") of this book.

810 See: Article 474 KC and § 278 BGB.

811 P. Rosbach, *Pferderecht*, pp. 90–6.

lungeing and grooming the horse in practice are performed by assistants, which should be taken into account when defining the contractual duties of the parties in teaching/training contracts under Article 354 KC and § 242 BGB. In order to avoid ambiguities, the parties should comprehensively define who is allowed to take care of the horse as the trainer's assistant. They may establish these contractual provisions generally (e. g. by providing that the trainer is allowed to use assistants when taking care of a horse) or in a more specific manner (e. g. by providing expressly which blacksmith should shoe the horse, whether the trainer is obliged to lunge the horse himself or not, what kind of feed the trainer should use when feeding the horse). It is also advisable to include in the contract some provisions describing the manner of contacting the animal's owner in an emergency.

Given that the Polish and German legal systems have generally the similar axiology (connected with the various European standards and similar legal culture),[812] the same or similar goals (i. e. the harmonization of the national law with European standards) and common legal foundations,[813] it would not be difficult to benefit from the experience connected with commerce in different EU countries (e. g. Germany), or their jurisprudence (in the case of similar legal foundations in similar facts of the case). Thus, it is reasonable to divide a trainer's obligations with reference to training a horse in the same way as acknowledged by the German system. This is justified especially by the fact that Germany is a country that is famous for horse sports and a pioneer in acknowledging contracts like the one under discussion, and the Polish practice uses it as a role model anyway.

The duties concerning actions other than training that must be undertaken when taking care of a horse will usually be accessory duties and – in my opinion – they should always be qualified as such, unless the parties established otherwise in the contract. However, it is also possible, that the trainer chosen by the horse's owner specializes in behavioral disorders and has been chosen by the horse owner in order to learn to deal with certain emotions, e. g. when going into a trailer, being tied up, etc. Then the performance of duties that are additional to the duty to ride the horse (in order to train him) changes into part of the main obligation, i. e. the general training of the horse. The same situation occurs when a dog is sent to a trainer in order to attend obedience training and the duty to

812 With reference to similarities and differences in the Polish and German legal systems and the applicability of provisions of law of one European country to a certain factual situation in a different European country, see: M. Jagielska, E. Macierzyńska-Franaszczyk, E. Rott-Pietrzyk, F. Zoll, G. Żmij (eds.), *Limits of Harmonisation and Convergence…;* G. Falkner, O. Trein, M. Hartlapp, S. Leiber (eds.), Complying with Europe. EU Harmonisation and Soft Law in the Member States, Cambridge 2005.

813 See also: *S. Frankowski* (ed.), *Introduction to Polish Law*, p. 38.

walk him not only constitutes an accessory duty, but turns into part of the general training. Therefore, I represent the opinion that all duties that are part of the general idea of the training process should be undertaken personally by the trainer and are to be treated as his main obligation. The best way to define how certain obligations are to be qualified is to describe them comprehensively in the contract.

A contract to train an animal consists in two kinds of duties – the main ones and the accessory ones not defined in either of the legal systems described here. The additional duties appear only in reference to contracts having a performance concerning an animal as their object and do not exist in reference to other things – one can only interact with living creatures. It is a service contract that is used in practice and should be acknowledged by the Polish doctrine due to the freedom of contract principle, and due to the broad doctrinal definition of service contracts in Polish law (especially the undefined service contract referred to in Article 750 KC). Although the performance of this contract has been addressed by German law, there are still several legal questions arising as a result of its performance. Since it requires higher standards of performance than contracts in which the service provided by one or both the parties do not concern a living animal, the division into main and accessory obligations of the trainer is unavoidable. Thus, taking care of an animal consists of numerous duties. The description of these duties and their legal qualification are necessary in this book, since they constitute the specific performance of the trainer when performing this contract.

2.4. Safe-keeping contracts having an animal as their object

Although the conclusion of **a safe-keeping contract** (*umowa przechowania, der Verwahrungsvertrag*) may occur by any means, with reference to animals it is difficult to imagine that it could happen *per facta concludentia.*[814] As the well-being of an animal is usually the most important value for its owner, it is rather unlikely that he would leave his animal without exact instructions for its safe-keeper. Moreover, not accurately defining the provisions of a safe-keeping contract having an animal as their subject would make it pointless for an animal owner to conclude such a contract at all (orally or under one of the forms provided in legal order, in particular in writing). Thus, leaving an animal under someone's custody without comprehensively defining the duties when taking care for an animal could, in some cases, not differ from leaving this animal

814 Compare, with reference to safe-keeping contracts: J. Napierała [in:] J. Rajski, (ed.), *System Prawa Prywatnego, Vol. VII*, pp. 765–766.

unattended.[815] Therefore, it is far more likely that safe-keeping contracts in reference to animals are concluded explicitly – orally or in writing, whereas the conclusion of any of such complicated contracts is always recommended in writing. Describing the contractual duties of the parties' in a comprehensive manner in the contract helps avoid future problems and properly establish the subject of a contractual agreement. Thus – although a contract is qualified as a safe-keeping contract, for which the *essentialia negotii* are defined in the German[816] and Polish Civil Codes,[817] it is never obvious what a "keeping in a non-deteriorated state" means in reference to an animal, unless explicitly stated in the contract. Thus, the wording of Article 835 KC, includes the specification that the good has to be kept in a non-deteriorated state, whereas the corresponding provision of German law in § 688 BGB only sets out the "storage" of the good. However, there are no concerns that the German legal system also combines the main contractual duty of the depositor with the obligation to protect the good from its devastation, deterioration and loss.[818]

The main obligation of a depositor is to keep the animal and the main obligation of a depositary is to pay the remuneration.[819] However, as the provisions referring to movables are applicable to animals respectively,[820] in this case they undoubtedly have to be used with modifications.[821] Thus – without even establishing the contractual obligations of the parties differently than in Article 835 KC and § 688 BGB – the provisions of a safe-keeping contract referring to movable things have to be modified in order for it to be applicable to animals in

815 Note that in cases where the obligation of a horse pension owner consisted solely in giving a box in the stable or a paddock for the use of the horse owner, the courts have qualified such a contract as a tenancy. See: Court of Appeals in Essen, ruling from 31.8.2007, 20 C 229/06, NZM 2008, 264; Court of Appeals in Menden, ruling from 26.2.2007, 4 C 11/07, BeckRS 2007, 3278. Compare: P. Rosbach, *Pferderecht*, pp. 111–115.

816 §§ § 688–700 BGB.

817 Articles 835–845 KC.

818 See, with reference to the duty to protect the good from its devastation, deterioration and loss in safe-keeping contracts: H. Sprau [in:] O. Palandt, *Beck'sche Kurz-Kommentare: Palandt Bürgerliches Gesetzbuch mit Nebengesetzen*, pp. 1200.

819 Note that the safe-keeping contract is not necessary remunerated, see: H. Sprau [in:] O. Palandt, *Beck'sche Kurz-Kommentare: Palandt Bürgerliches Gesetzbuch mit Nebengesetzen*, p.1200; J. Napierała [in:] J. Rajski, (ed.), *System Prawa Prywatnego, Vol. VII*, pp. 767. However, taking into account several additional duties of the depositor of an animal, it is difficult to imagine a gratuitous safe-keeping contract having an animal as its subject.

820 See: § 90a BGB and Article 1 of the Act on Consumer Rights on 30 May 2014 (J L of 2014, item 827), providing that the rules applicable to the things are to be respectively applied to animals.

821 With reference to the respective applicability of provisions concerning movable things to animals, see: above and J. Nowacki, *Analogia legis*, p. 141. Compare also with the examples shown in the publication: M. Lubelska-Sazanów, *Odpowiedzialność z tytułu rękojmi za wady fizyczne zwierząt*, Transformacje Prawa Prywatnego 4/2015, pp. 21–41.

the manner whereby the animal needs to be fed, taken care of, taken for a walk or to a paddock, etc. in order to be returned in a non-deteriorated state after the safe-keeping contract. Therefore, additional duties of the parties connected with the fact that the subject of a contract is an animal (not a movable good) are a natural consequence of the fact of the respective applicability of provisions concerning movable things to animals and their existence. However, it might still be unclear for the parties to the contract about which duties consisting in taking care over an animal are the main duties, and which of them are accessory. Thus, the comprehensive contractual definition of these additional duties of the depositor in the contract is still recommended and allows both parties to meet their mutual expectations.

The additional duties of the parties to a safe-keeping contract having an animal as its subject are broad and can be established differently. Namely, they can depend on the quality of the services offered and the price of the stables/kennels. In some cases, the use of the horse, in the meaning of riding/lungeing/taking the horse into the horse walker, may be qualified as the obligation of the depositor as well.[822] The German doctrine claims that the duties of the depositor that are vital for keeping the subject of safe-keeping contract (namely the animal in this case) in a non-deteriorated condition, like feeding the animal, are connected with the main obligation of the safe-keeper (i. e. "to keep the good").[823] Additional duties of the depositor, according to the doctrine, include letting the horse out into a paddock,[824] walking the dog or cleaning the boxes, and would also be treated as such. However, some commentaries treat all of these duties as the main duty of the depositor and combine it with the general duty to keep an animal.[825] The duties of the depositary in reference to the safe-keeping contract having an animal as its object are much more transparent than those of the depositor. Thus, the party leaving the horse in the stables or a dog in kennels etc. – as already mentioned – has to pay for the offered service.[826] Next to this main obligation of the depositary, there is also a duty to inform the depositor about any specific details, i. e. all the behaviors of an animal that the depositor should be informed about in order to ensure his and the animal's safety.[827] The de-

822 See, with reference to German law: P. Rosbach, *Pferderecht*, pp. 115.

823 See, with reference to German law: H. Sprau [in:] O. Palandt, *Beck'sche Kurz-Kommentare: Palandt Bürgerliches Gesetzbuch mit Nebengesetzen*, pp. 1200.

824 *Idem.*

825 See, with reference to German law: M. Henssler [in:] *Münchener Kommentar zum BGB*, München 2009, § 688 BGB side number 11, *BeckOnline (last visited: 12. 3. 2018).*

826 Although the safe-keeping contract is not necessary remunerated, taking into account the several additional duties of the depositor of an animal, it is difficult to imagine a gratuitous safe-keeping contract having an animal as its subject. Compare, with reference to German law: P. Rosbach, *Pferderecht*, pp. 117.

827 *Idem.*

positary is also obliged to cover all the costs and any damages incurred by the depositor, and to reclaim the good/animal[828] after the safe-keeping contract terminates.[829]

The qualification of duties of the depositor connected with the fact that the good being left for safe-keeping is an animal (like feeding the animal, letting the horse out onto a paddock, walking of the dog, cleaning of the boxes, etc.) as duties comprising on depositor's main duty or its qualification as depositor's additional duties is also important for the issue whether they can be delegated to third[830] persons. Thus, Article 840 KC and § 691 BGB explicitly state that the main obligation (i.e. safe-keeping of the good/animal) of the safe-keeping contract has to be done by the contracting party, and that this contractual obligation may not be delegated to a third person[831] (unless there are special circumstances that justify delegating the safe-keeping to a third person or changing the manner of the safe-keeping[832]). However, I represent the opinion that in this case – unlike in the case of a teaching/training contract described above[833] – the duties like feeding an animal, letting the horse out onto a paddock, walking the dog, cleaning the boxes, etc. should be qualified as duties comprising an depositor's additional duties. Thus, they do not comprise the general learning process as it occurs in the teaching/training contract and constitute accessory activities that allow an animal to be kept in a non-deteriorated condition. Therefore, these duties may be delegated to third parties in my opinion – at least, unless the parties agree otherwise in the contract.[834]

828 Whereas the depositor is entitled to reclaim the good/animal at any time before the termination of the safe-keeping contract, see: Article 844 § 1KC and § 695 BGB.

829 See, with reference to Polish law: J. Napierała [in:] J. Rajski, (ed.), *System Prawa Prywatnego, Vol. VII*, pp. 783.

830 See, with reference to German law: H. Mansel [in:] R. Stürner (ed.), *Jauernig, Kommentar zum BGB*, München 2015, § 611, side number 6.

831 See: Article 840 KC and § 691 BGB.

832 See: Article 838 and 840 KC, § 691 BGB. Compare, with reference to Polish law: J. Napierała, who indicates that even the mere exposure to deterioration equals infringement of the contractual duty to keep the thing/animal safe, See: J. Napierała [in:] J. Rajski, (ed.), *System Prawa Prywatnego, Vol. VII*, pp. 780.

833 See: above in this subchapter.

834 Thus, due to the freedom of contract principle, the contracting parties may establish the content of their contract at their discretion (within some legal boundaries), see: Subchapter IV.1.1. and the literature with reference to both the Polish and German legal systems and the freedom of contract principle: E. Rott-Pietrzyk *Commercial Agency Contracts…*[in:] *Private Autonomy…*, pp. 15–34; M. Lubelska-Sazanów, *The "Principle of No Freedom of Contract": A Post-Modern Version of the Freedom of Contract Principle?*, [in:] M. De Maestri, S. Dominelli (ed.), *Party autonomy in European private (and) international law, Vol. II*, Rome 2015, pp. 15–31. Therefore, the parties may conclude a contract that will no longer qualify as safe-keeping, but will consist in training an animal and lungeing it regularly by the trainer (e.g. due to the horse's back problems) as the trainer's main ob-

Note that under Polish law, according to Article 837 KC, if nothing else has been agreed between the parties, the good (or the animal, respectively) should be kept in a manner that results from its nature and from the circumstances. Although there is no such provision in the German Civil Code, the German doctrine establishes a similar principle and comes to similar conclusions.[835] This only confirms the idea that runs through this book, namely that the German and Polish legal systems are very close to each other in many ways, and could derive from each other the doctrine and jurisprudence.[836]

Just as in the case of a contract to train an animal, a safe-keeping contract having keeping an animals as its object consists in two kinds of duties – main and accessory, which are not defined in either of the legal systems described herein. Whereas the question of whether an animal is kept by someone else occurs in the form of a lease or by a safe-keeping contract has already been addressed by the German jurisprudence[837] and the doctrine,[838] this issue has not been the subject of Polish jurisprudence and doctrine. Therefore, based on the arguments presented several times in this book,[839] the Polish jurisprudence could take into consideration the experience of German courts in these matters (as a source of inspiration concerning the methodology of interpretation and application of particular provisions of KC, or as additional, comparative arguments in the justification of a court decision). Consequently, the safe-keeping contract of an animal, where comprehensive care over an animal is essential for its performance (thus, without feeding or cleaning the box/cage of a kept animal, it may suffer, get ill or even die) is significantly different than safe-keeping of a regular good, where the depositor is solely obliged to store the good. Hence, in fact, the depositor of a good is obliged to abide by something, whereas the depositor of an animal is obliged to undertake several actions in order to keep an animal safe and healthy (e.g. in a "non-deteriorated state"). Nevertheless – *de lege lata* –

ligations. In this case, under Polish law, the provisions of both Article 734 KC and Article 750 KC, and the provisions referring to safe-keeping contracts will apply respectively. Under German law, such a contract would still be covered by the scope of § 611 BGB.

835 See, with reference to German law, e.g.: P. Rosbach, *Pferderecht*, pp. 112–115; M. Henssler [in:] *Münchener Kommentar zum BGB*, München 2009, § 688 BGB side number 11.

836 A similar idea has been expressed in the monograph of M. Jagielska, E. Macierzyńska-Franaszczyk, E. Rott-Pietrzyk, F. Zoll, G. Żmij (eds.), *Limits of Harmonization and Convergence. Dissimilarities in Similarities of Polish and German Contract Law*, Warszawa 2018, pp. 44–45.

837 See, e.g.: Court of Appeals in Essen, ruling from 31.8.2007, 20 C 229/06, NZM 2008, 264; Court of Appeals in Menden, ruling from 26.2.2007, 4 C 11/07, BeckRS 2007, 3278.

838 See: P. Rosbach, *Pferderecht*, pp. 111–117.

839 See: M. Jagielska, E. Macierzyńska-Franaszczyk, E. Rott-Pietrzyk, F. Zoll, G. Żmij (eds.), *Limits of Harmonisation and Convergence…, pp. 29; 44;* G. Falkner, O. Trein, M. Hartlapp, S. Leiber (eds.), *Complying with Europe. EU Harmonisation and Soft Law in the Member States*, Cambridge 2005; S. Frankowski (ed.), *Introduction to Polish Law*, p. 38.

until special regulations referring to the performance of obligations having actions dedicated to animals as its object will be accepted by the Polish and German law and introduced therein, the only possibility left to the parties is to conclude a very detailed safe-keeping contract, containing specific provisions addressing the main and accessory duties of the parties.

2.5. Other service contracts having an animal as their object

All of the contracts described in this subchapter are characterized by a construction of duties typical for a simple service contract. Thus, one party who promises a service is obliged to perform the services promised, and the other party is obliged to grant the agreed remuneration.[840] Although there are no peculiarities in reference to the construction of these contracts, there are significant focal points connected with the accessory duties of the parties to these contracts.

As far as it concerns **contracts with a veterinary doctor**, the service contract is concluded at the moment when the animal owner instructs the veterinarian to undertake certain medical action - operation, medication, medical control, etc.[841] These services are characterized by a high level of responsibility lying on the veterinary doctor and the trust dedicated to him by the animal owner. These two features constitute a very significant secondary duty in this contractual relationship - the duty of loyalty. Thus, the veterinarian is obliged to perform promised services with the standard of due care required for his profession and in accordance with applicable law (including animal protection laws and the professional code for veterinarians).[842] Whereas the high responsibility and risk of a veterinary doctor can be compared to those undertaken by a regular (human) doctor, this contract is still unique due to its object. Thus, the object of the veterinary doctor's performance is an animal that has granted animal rights, but is owned by a human. It is very specific, and so, although the provisions covering things are respectively applicable to animals also in this case, this contract is more similar to a medical performance of a person with limited legal

840 See: § 611 BGB and Article 734 and Article 750 KC. For a more detailed description of the legal composition of this contract, see: Subchapter IV.1.1. of this book.

841 However, note that under German law the medical examination of a horse prior to its sale, insemination or construction of a medical opinion by a veterinarian constitute a contract for work, See: P. Rosbach, *Pferderecht*, p. 139. In accordance with Polish law, I would share this opinion with reference to the second two situations, but not the first one. Thus, the Polish horse market reality does not recognise the institution of a medical examination of a horse prior to its sale to the same extent as it occurs in Germany. See: Subchapter III.3.2.8.

842 See: P. Rosbach, *Pferderecht*, p. 139.

capacity (in the meaning of Article 15 KC and §§ 104, 106 BGB)[843] performed under a contract with his legal advisor. Nevertheless, it is still a service contract having an animal as the object of a contractual performance covered by the scope of § 611 BGB and an undefined service contract under Polish law (Articles 734 KC with 750 KC), where provisions referring to regular things apply respectively under both of the legal orders described herein.

Another service contract is **a contract for breeding** (which refers most commonly to horses, dogs and cats). In this contract, the male animal's owner is obliged to leave the animal at the disposal of the female animal's owner at certain periods of time (depending on the fertility of the female animal) and for a number of times scheduled in advance in the contract.[844] However, in most cases the female animal's owner is the one that brings the female animal to the male animal's owner's place. The contractual duties are different, depending on whether the female animal's owner supervises the process of insemination and looks after his own animal, or leaves his animal at the male animal's owner's place. Thus, in the second case the male animal's owner's secondary duties are very similar to the duties of a trainer in the case of leaving a trained animal at his place and his liability extends to numerous different situations.[845]

Another contract presented herein with reference to the standard of its performance is the **contract with a blacksmith** having a contractual obligation to shoe a horse (or trimming its hooves) as its object. The standard of due care required for a certain profession can also be expected from a blacksmith. Thus, in general (under both the Polish and German legal systems), he is obliged to act in accordance with the modern knowledge known for an average blacksmith (who is obliged to obtain the education and certification required for this provision) and should always take into account the horse's wellbeing when performing the services. The animal's owner is obliged to provide not only the agreed remuneration, but also care for the horse for the time when the blacksmith will perform his services, so that the horse does not constitute a threat to the blacksmith.[846]Whereas – since the blacksmith is obliged to perform a certain result (shoeing/ hoof trimming) – the German doctrine qualifies it as a contract for **a specific task (*umowa o dzieło, der Werkvertrag*).**[847]

The same solution could be transposed to the Polish doctrine by stating that, due to a similar definition of a contract for work under both the Polish and German Civil Codes, regulated in Article 636 KC and § 631 BGB, the attitude of the German doctrine should be approved by the Polish doctrine. However, the

843 Subchapter III.3.2.2. of this book.
844 See also: E. Fellmer, P. Kiel, *Rechtskunde...*, pp. 147–148.
845 See: Subchapter IV.2.3.
846 See, with reference to the German legal system: P. Rosbach, *Pferderecht*, pp. 180–181.
847 *Idem.*

Polish doctrine addresses the problem of qualification of a contract with the blacksmith rarely and in a very narrow scope, mentioning that it can either be concluded as a contract for a specific task or as a service contract.[848] Nevertheless, in my opinion, the horse's owner concludes a contract that could be described as a "contract to take care of the horse's hooves" than a contract for a certain work. The horse's owner usually does not expect a specific result, but trusts the blacksmith in reference to his experience and knowledge. Additionally, shoeing a horse/ trimming its hooves is not comparable to contracts setting out the creation of a certain piece of art, which are typically concluded in the form of a contract for work. Therefore, although P. Rosbach, author of the book *Pferderecht,* qualifies this contract as a contract for a specific task under German law, in my opinion this contract qualifies rather as a service contract – unless under Polish law.[849]

The contract that is perhaps subject to the largest number of EU laws of all the contracts presented in this book is the **contract for the transportation of animals.**[850] Nevertheless, most of the transportation laws refer to the non-commercial transportation of animals, or the scope is broader than the scope of animals covered by this book.[851] Therefore, the presentation of EU laws covering the transportation of animals is summarized here, but is comprehensive.

In general, the legislation of the EU Member States has undergone many changes since Regulation 1/2005 of the European Council[852] (Regulation 1/2005), covering all kinds of transport (road/rail/air/vessels) with reference to live vertebrate animals carried out within the Community came into force.[853] Regulation 1/2005 sets out many very specific legal requirements with reference to the arrangements for the transportation of vertebrates, but its detailed provi-

848 Compare: E. Liberda, *Odpowiedzialność kowali za wykonanie usługi,* Prawo i Konie 1.9. 2014, http://prawoikonie.com/odpowiedzialnosc-kowali-za-wykonane-uslugi/ (last visited: 13.3.2018), where the author qualifies the contract with a blacksmith as a contract for work or as a mandate contract (meaning, probably, the respective applicability of provisions covering mandate contracts to this service contract – see: Articles 734 and 750 KC).

849 Under Polish law, it is an undefined service contract, see: Articles 734 KC with 750 KC.

850 With reference to administrative rules and licences concerning drivers transporting animals under Polish law, see: K. Hantz, K. Żukowska, A. Grieger, *Wymagania stawiane środkom transportu przy przewozie żywych zwierząt,* Autobusy: technika, eksploatacja, systemy transportowe 2016, Issue 8/17, pp. 236–239.

851 Compare: S. Corson, L. Anderson, *Europe* [in:] M. C. Appleby, V. Cussen, L. Garces, L. A. Lambert, J. Turner, *Long* …, pp. 355–386.

852 Council Regulation (EC) No. 1/2005 of 22 December 2004 on the protection of animals during transport and related operations and amending Directives 64/432/EEC and 93/119/ EC and Regulation (EC) No. 1255/97.

853 With reference to the legal situation before the Council Regulation (EC) No. 1/2005 came into force, see: E. Berkowska, M. Gwiazdowicz, M. Sobolewski, *Transport zwierząt – prawo, praktyka, perspektywy,* Kancelaria Sejmu – Biuro Studiów i Ekspertyz, 4.2002, also available at: http://biurose.sejm.gov.pl/teksty_pdf/i-894.pdf (last visited: 20.3.2018).

sions concern mainly farm animals, i. e. cattle, pigs and horses (whereas it does not refer to pets like dogs or cats).[854] Therefore, the provisions imposing minimum standards for the wellbeing of animals during its transportation do not have any practical meaning for the transportation of animals owned by private individuals, who usually take care of the good quality of the transportation of their pupils (e. g. the height and width of boxes separating animals for each other, necessary stops to let the animal eat and drink, a prohibition on using violence against animals, etc.)[855] However, there is one issue that changed a lot when Regulation 1/2005 was imposed, i. e. the requirement that the personnel handling animals be trained or competent as appropriate for this purpose and carry out their tasks without using violence or any method likely to cause unnecessary fear, injury or suffering.[856] Thus, the duties of a party undertaking transporting services also cover the duty to feed/drink an animal and to look after it while being transported. The duties to feed/drink an animal and to look after it during the transportation constitute accessory duties in this case and may be delegated to the driver's assistants. After all, it does not make any practical difference who feeds the animals during their transportation, as the main obligation consists in their safe transportation. However, it is worth noting that such assistants are also obliged to attend training on how to carry out their tasks without using violence or any method likely to cause unnecessary fear, injury or suffering.[857]

In addition to ensuring at least the minimum standards of animal welfare during their transportation, one also has to bear in mind that transportation of animals is one of the main risk factors for the spread of animal diseases, as shown by cases of infection in non-endemic regions.[858] Therefore, the commercial movement of animals must comply with Directive 92/65/EEC.[859] Non-commercial movements of pet animals are subject to Regulations (EU) No 576/

854 See: M. Lubelska-Sazanów, *Prawne regulacje dotyczące transportu zwierząt na terenie Unii Europejskiej* [in:] B. Błońska, W. Gogłoza, W. Klaus, D. Woźniakowska-Fajst (eds.), *Sprawiedliwość dla zwierząt*.

855 Compare: Chapter V of the Appendix to the Regulation 1/2005.

856 See: Article 3 of Regulation 1/2005. See also: D. Broom, *Welfare of Livestock During Road Transport* [in:] M. C. Appleby, V. Cussen, L. Garces, L. A. Lambert, J. Turner, *Long Distance Transport and Welfare of Farm Animals*, pp. 157–181 with reference to factors that can result in poor welfare during animal handling and transport.

857 *Idem*.

858 L. Englund, J. Pringle, *New diseases and increased risk of diseases in companion animals and horses due to transport*, Acta veterinaria Scandinavica, sup. 100, pp. 19–25.

859 Council Directive 92/65/EEC of 13 July 1992 laying down animal health requirements governing trade in and imports into the Community of animals, semen, ova and embryos not subject to animal health requirements laid down in specific Community rules referred to in Annex A (I) to Directive 90/425/EEC, OJ 268, 14. 9. 1992, pp. 54–72.

2013[860] and No 577/2013,[861] and Directive 90/425/EEC[862] laying down rules relating to veterinary and zootechnical checks to be applied to live animals and products of animal origin for intra-Community trade. Regardless of whether the trade occurs commercially or not, as far as it concerns horses, in the European Union all of them need to have a horse passport,[863] which has to be carried on board during its transportation.

The EU laws have special importance in reference to animals, since the transportation of animals is the subject of extensive unification at EU level.[864] Therefore, most of the local laws (local in the meaning of German and Polish laws) were passed as a result of the implementation of EU laws.[865] Due to the summary nature of presenting the contracts in this subchapter, I refer mostly to EU laws, which refer to both the Polish and German legal systems.

The transportation has to proceed in a certain manner (slight and slow changes of speed and braking), taking into account the wellbeing of the transported animal. The other party to the contract is obliged usually to prepare the animal for transportation, i. e. provide a special transporting box (in the case of dogs or other smaller animals) or paddings (in the case of horses). Note that

860 Regulation (EU) No. 576/2013 of the European Parliament and the Council of 12 June 2013 on the non-commercial movement of pet animals and repealing Regulation (EC) No. 998/2003.

861 Commission Implementing Regulation (EU) No. 577/2013 of 28 June 2013 on the model identification documents for the non-commercial movement of dogs, cats and ferrets, the establishment of lists of territories and third countries and the format, layout and language requirements of the declarations attesting compliance with certain conditions provided for in Regulation (EU) No. 576/2013 of the European Parliament and of the Council Text with EEA relevance, OJ 178, 28.6.2013, pp. 109–148.

862 Council Directive 90/425/EEC of 26 June 1990 concerning veterinary and zootechnical checks applicable in intra- Community trade in certain live animals and products with a view to the completion of the internal market. OJ 224 , 18.08.1990, pp. 29–41.

863 Since 1.1.2016, there is a new regulation in this matter, see: Commission Implementing Regulation (EU) 2015/262 of 17 February 2015 laying down rules pursuant to Council Directives 90/427/EEC and 2009/156/EC as regards the methods for the identification of equidae (Equine Passport Regulation), OJ 59, 3.3.2015, pp. 1–53.

864 With reference to the sea transport of animals, see: R. T. Norris, *Transport of animals by sea,* Revue Scientifique et technique Office International des Episooties 2005, Issue2/24, pp. 673–681; C. J. C. Philips, *The Welfare of Livestock During Sea Transport* [in:] M. C. Appleby, V. Cussen, L. Garces, L. A. Lambert, J. Turner, *Long Distance Transport and Welfare of Farm Animals,* pp. 137–156.

865 See: § 6 of the Executive order concerning driving licences of 13 December 2010 (Verordnung über die Zulassung von Personen zum Straßenverkehr/ Fahrerlaubnis-Verordnung – FeV) (BGBl. I S. 1980), recently changed by Article 2 of the Executive order of 21 December 2016 (BGBl. I S. 3083) with reference to German regulations; Article 6 of the Act on Drivers (*Ustawa o kierujących pojazdami*) of 5 January 2011 (J.L. 2011 No. 30 item 151) with reference to the Polish regulations. Both regulations are based on the provisions of Directive 2006/126/EC of the European Parliament and of the Council of 20 December 2006 on driving licences (Recast).

loading a horse in a trailer may also cause problems in some cases and take up a lot of the driver's time. Therefore, it is important to define who is obliged to do that prior to concluding the contract. Although this is usually the duty of the animal's owner, some companies/individuals specializing in the transportation of horses provide such services and include them in their offer.

The contracts presented in this subchapter are specific not only due to its performance, covering duties consisting in taking care of an animal, which are very different (i. e. broader) in comparison to any contracts in which the object of a contractual performance is a regular good. The performance of these contracts is so complicated and not yet unified in practice – either Poland or in Germany – that it is difficult to define them clearly as service contracts (see: considerations referring to contracts with a veterinary doctor and a blacksmith presented above). Although a detailed presentation of all these contracts could be the subject of a separate book, and these contracts are only summarized herein, there is one common feature of all of them. Namely, all of them have a specific object of performance – an animal – which raises the standards required of its performance due to the large number of accessory obligations arising therefrom, and the broader scope of possible risks and consequences in the event of its improper or non-performance. Thus, whereas a regular good may become damaged or not, an animal, as a living creature, may suffer many different emotions and health conditions,[866] which might be dependent on the performance of the party providing a certain service or not, and which may lead to several legal consequences.

3. Results of the improper performance of service contracts with reference to contracts having an animal as its object

3.1. Commission contracts having an animal as its object

As already mentioned, the purchase of a horse from **a commission agent** is covered by regular provisions applicable to sale contracts. Therefore, it is not possible to address the problem of the improper performance of commission contracts (*umowa komisu, das Kommissionsgeschäft*) having an agent's obligation to intermediate in the sale of horses as an object without referring to sale contracts. Thus, the warranty for defects in reference to horses sold with a commission agent's support applies to the same extent as it applies in reference to a regular sale that occurs without engaging a commission agent. The only

866 See more in: N. G. Gregory, *Physiology and Behaviour of Animal Suffering*, Oxford 2004.

difference consists in the person who can be found liable for warranty claims. Namely, in the case of a sale where the commission agent – by representing the animal's owner interest in its own name – intermediates in the transfer of ownership, he is the person liable for warranty claims.

Thus, it is the commission agent who concludes the sale contract with the customer, who can be either a professional or not. Under both the Polish and German legal systems, the qualification of a contract as a commission contract requires only that the commission agent carry out commercial activity.[867] Therefore, in the event that the principal is not a professional, consumer rights apply by granting him protection with reference to his contracting partner – the commission agent (which must always act as a professional).[868] These general remarks covering consumer and professional relations (B2C and B2B) and warranty claims in reference to commission contracts refer to both the Polish and German legal systems.

Since commission contracts concluded between a commission agent and a principal are connected with sale contracts concluded between the commission agent and a third party (buyer),[869] the provisions covering liability for defects covering sale contracts, and respectively applicable to commission contracts, are significant in reference to the improper performance of a commission contract under both Polish and German law. However, where it concerns Polish law, a provision that can be found only in the Polish Civil Code and is quite unique in reference to other legal systems,[870] is the rule included in Article 770 KC.[871] According to this rule, the commission agent may exclude liability for latent physical defects or legal defects in the animal, if he informs the buyer about them before executing the contract. However, the exclusion of liability does not apply

867 J. Frąckowiak [in:] J. Rajski, (ed.), *System Prawa Prywatnego, Vol. VII*, pp. 754–758.

868 With reference to regulations protecting the consumer as a weaker party, see: Subchapter III.2.2. of this book.

869 With reference to the structure of legal relations in the commission contracts, see: Subchapter IV.2.1. of this book.

870 J. Frąckowiak [in:] J. Rajski, (ed.), *System Prawa Prywatnego, Vol. VII*, pp. 754–758.

871 This article was newly introduced to the Polish Civil Code in 2014, in an amendment as a result of the implementation of Directive 2011/83/EU of the European Parliament and of the Council of 25 October 2011 on consumer rights, amending Council Directive 93/13/EEC and Directive 1999/44/EC of the European Parliament and of the Council and repealing Council Directive 85/577/EEC and Directive 97/7/EC of the European Parliament and of the Council (OJ L 304 of 22.11.2011, p. 64) and reimplementation of Directive 1999/44/EC of the European Parliament and of the Council of 25 May 1999 on certain aspects of the sale of consumer things and associated guarantees (O.J. L 171, 07/07/1999, pp. 12–16) and Directive 2002/65/EC of the European Parliament and of the Council of 23 September 2002 concerning the distance marketing of consumer financial services and amending Council Directive 90/619/EEC and Directives 97/7/EC and 98/27/EC (OJ L 271 of 9.10.2002, pp. 16–24).

to defects about which the commission agent already knew, or could have easily learned. The reason for introducing this provision into Polish law was probably intended to grant the buyer some minimum level of protection at the time when all shops operating on the basis of commission contracts were trying to exclude their liability as far as possible.[872] It may be hard to determine whether the commission agent could easily have learned about the defects in the good. In reference to the sale of horses at professional auctions, the associations performing the auction order a detailed medical examination before showing a particular horse.[873] However, this provision can only be found in the Polish Civil Code, whereas the sale of horses on the basis of a commission contract is not very common in Poland.

The German Civil Code does not contain a regulation corresponding with Article 770 KC. § 474 (1) BGB, concerning consumer sales (i. e. applicable to B2C commission contracts) and structures the warranty regime in commission contracts differently than the Polish law. Thus, according to § 474 (1) BGB, the facilities that strengthen the buyer's position in relation to a more experienced contracting partner (like the invalidity of contractual provisions excluding the buyer's warranty rights, reversing the burden of proof that a defect existed at the time of concluding the contract for the first six months after the contract was concluded by the seller,[874] etc.[875]) are applicable to contracts of sale concluded with a consumer, as long as it does not concern the sale of used goods at public auctions. The problem of qualifying animals as used goods has been comprehensively presented in Subchapter III.2.2. Under Polish law, the warranty regime has been unified in accordance with used and new things, and does not introduce any differences with reference to sale at auction.[876] The issue of whether animals are used goods or not is therefore important only for the sale of animals under German law.[877]

872 See: J. Rajski [in:] J. Rajski, (ed.), *System Prawa Prywatnego, Vol. VII*, p. 755.

873 Compare: http://www.hannoveraner.com/hannoveraner-verband/auktionen/auktionsarchiv/auktionen-2016/verdener-auktion-januar/auktionsbroschuere/.

874 Whether the rules set out in § 476 BGB, reversing the burden of proof onto the business, are applicable to the sale of animals or not is controversial. The German doctrine recognises positive (H. Westermann, *Zu den Gewährleistungsansprüche des Käufers*, pp. 342–348; P. Wertenbruch, *Tierkauf und Sachmangel*, NJW 2012, No. 29, p. 2069) and critical opinions (J. Adolphsen, *Die Schuldrechtsreform…*, pp. 203–208; see also: LG Verden, ruling from 16. 02. 2005 – 2 S 394/03; OLG Oldenburg, ruling from 17. 06. 2004 – 14 U 41/04) concerning the applicability of § 476 BGB.

875 For more detailed effects of qualifying sale contracts as consumer sales on the warranty rights of the buyer see: Subchapter III.2.2. of this book.

876 *Idem.*

877 The issue of whether an animal is seen as a used or as a new good has been described comprehensively in Subchapter III.2.2.

Although the question of whether an auction is to be treated as a public auction is only an issue under German law, this problem raises many questions in the doctrine. Thus, in order to meet the intentions of the German legislator with reference to § 474 (1) BGB, a public expert auctioneer has the consumers' trust while performing his duties. As a public auctioneer, he gives a guarantee of the legal and appropriate performance of the auction, and that the description of the horse is grounded in fact.[878] Therefore, although the facilities connected with consumer sale are excluded, the exclusion of warranty does not necessary apply, if the auction rules infringe the law or the general principle of trust.[879]

There are further consequences connected with the improper performance of a sale contract for a horse in which an agent intermediates, though they do not affect the relation between the commission agent and its principal.[880] For example, the purchase of a horse at a public auction is concluded at the time of accepting the bid. If the buyer then declines to purchase the horse after making the offer, he may be held liable for the payment of the horse's minimum auction price as damages.[881] Nevertheless, what is most important for the buyer of the horse are the guarantee rights and the issue of their possible exclusion by the commission agent. However, the consequences for the buyer are to be treated as consequences for a third party to the commission contract. In this chapter of the book, they have been presented only partially, with a comprehensive description of the buyer's warranty rights being set out in Chapter III.3.2.2. referring to buyer's warranty rights with reference to contracts aimed at the transfer of property of an animal.[882]

Under both the Polish and German legal systems, a commission agent is obliged to carefully perform the contract, to the extent that can be expected from a professional running business activity in a certain field. Therefore, the principal's right to damages in the case of the improper performance or a non-performance of the commission service is to be evaluated taking into account the commission agent's specific knowledge, but also taking into account the impact of the principal's instructions on the possibility for the commission agent to

878 P. Rosbach, *Pferderecht*, pp. 71–72.

879 So also decided the court with reference to the exclusion of warranty for horses sold at auctions organised by a German breeding association and performed by a public auctioneer. As the auction rules did not meet the German Civil Code's requirements with reference to general terms and conditions, included in § 307 et seq. BGB, the court decided that the exclusion of warranty based on § 474 (1) BGB does not apply in the case at hand. Thus, the public auctioneer was not able to guarantee fair auction conditions that the buyer trusted in. See: BGH, ruling from 24. 2. 2010, VIII ZR 71/09.

880 This does not only concern guarantee rights.

881 E. Fellmer, P. Kiel, *Rechtskunde…*, p. 68.

882 To learn more about several types of sale contracts, see: Subchapter III.2.4.

perform service.[883] Thus, the commission agent cannot show, feed or keep the horse (or any different animal that is to be sold by the commission agent) in any manner that would be against the will of the principal. Sometimes the instructions of an inexperienced, but obstinate principal might be the reason for an unsuccessful attempt to sell a certain animal.[884] The general rules of the Polish and German Civil Codes concerning the consequences of the non-performance of obligations apply respectively.[885] The positive interest of the party who suffered damage due to the improper performance of its contractual partner consists in the need to cover the damage in the scope of *damnum emergens* and *lucrum cessans*. In the case of horses, this could be not only the costs of the medical treatment of a horse who suffered damage due to the improper performance of the contract by an agent, but also reimbursement for this horse's loss of value, or loss of money paid for sport competitions in which the owner or the owner's rider could take part, etc.

Under both Polish[886] and German law,[887] in order to secure claims for the commission and claims for the reimbursement of the expenses and advance payment given to the commissioning party, as well as for securing all other dues resulting from the commission mandate, the commission agent has a statutory right of pledge on the things that are the object of the sale on commission.[888] This is a problematic issue with reference to animals, taking into account the point of view of both parties to the contract. Thus, it is natural that, in case of **terminating a contract (*wypowiedzenie/die Kündigung*)**, the owner of an animal – e.g. a horse breeder – has an interest in taking the animal back as soon as possible. Thus, in this case the commission agent theoretically loses its interest in taking care for an animal, and the only motivation for taking care of it as he did when the contract was still in force is the moral one. In the case of a horse, it is very likely that the commission agent will not invest more in the animal by granting it everyday movement and regular trainings in the situation where his contracting party seems to have financial problems and will not be able to reimburse these costs as well. On the other hand, it is unlikely – in the event that an agent does not have its own stud or stable (which is rather rare) – that he will be willing to

883 With reference to Polish law, see: J. Frąckowiak [in:] J. Rajski, (ed.), *System Prawa Prywatnego, Vol. VII*, pp. 737; with reference to German law, compare: § 385 HGB; see also: I. Koller [in:] C. Canaris, M. Habersack, C. Schäfer, *Staub Handelsgesetzbuch Großkommentar*, Göttingen 2013, pp. 111.

884 In such a situation, the commission agent cannot be held liable in accordance with Article 471 KC and § 280 BGB.

885 See: Articles 471–486 KC and §§ 276–292 BGB.

886 See: Article 773 KC.

887 See: § 397 HGB.

888 Translation of Article 773 KC: *The Polish Law Collection*, Translegis, Legalis online. The translations correspond with the German provision § 397 HGB.

undertake the risk of keeping an expensive, energetic sport horse under his surveillance longer than it is required. Therefore, in where a commission agent is willing and has the opportunity to pledge on the horse, the law allows him to do so and – on the condition that he takes proper care of it – there is no reason to deny the application of Article 773 KC and § 397 HGB to commission contracts having the obligation to sell/buy an animal as their object. Nevertheless, the right to pledge on a good horse (or any different animal) applies with modifications, i. e. with respect to the specific nature of an animal as a living creature. In the event that an animal is maltreated or simply not taken care for in the matter that would allow the animal's health not to deteriorate, the animal's owner should be entitled to exchange the animal for a different object of a pledge. The owner could also insist on placing the animal under the care of a third party where he believes that it will be properly taken care for, whereas it will be kept there for another party by realizing the right to pledge. In this case, the costs of keeping the animal at the place chosen by its owner should not grossly exceed the costs of keeping the horse elsewhere. Obviously, the owner is obliged to reimburse the costs of keeping an animal somewhere else to the agent when collecting the animal back (just as he would be obliged to reimburse the costs of keeping the animal anywhere else).

3.2. Agency contracts having an animal as their object

As an agency contract (*umowa agencyjna, Handelsvertretungsvertrag*) is a contractual relationship of a permanent nature, the agent usually gains "inside" knowledge of the principal's business and – if his principal is an animal breeder or trainer – the secrets of his breeding and training methods. Since, in practice, the agent intermediating in the sale of horses is usually a trainer with a broad network of potential clients and travelling around to many different equestrian centers, it is very difficult for him not to breach his duty to loyalty.[889] Thus, a person training various competitors and intermediating for a principal at the same time must be very careful in order not to disclose information that was kept in secret by its principal, or the disclosure of which could have negative consequences for the principal.[890] In the event that such a situation occurs, the principal is entitled to damages and may base his claim on Article 471 ff KC or

889 With reference to the contractual duties of the parties to agency contract, see: Subchapter IV.2.2. of this book.

890 With reference to the duty of loyalty under Polish law, see: J. Pokrzywniak, *Obowiązek lojalności jako element stosunku obligacyjnego, MoP* 2003, No. 19, pp. 885 et seq. Note that German law does not express the duty of loyalty as directly as in the Polish Civil Code, see: Subchapter IV.2.2. of this book.

§ 280 BGB (liability *ex contractu*) – thus, the parties are obliged to perform their duties in good faith[891] and with due care.[892] In the situation where the agent does not undertake its obligation to intermediate in accordance with the principal's instructions, or does not pass on relevant information to the principal.[893] Note that these duties of an agent are regulated differently in the German Commercial Code, which foresees more independence of a commercial agent by obliging him to act in accordance with the principal's interest instead of following his instructions.[894] This slight difference may constitute problems in qualifying the improper performance of an agent under both Polish and German law. Nevertheless, the liability based on Article 471 ff KC or § 280 BGB (liability *ex contractu*) may also arise on the side of a principal in the event that he obstructs the work of the agent by delaying a decision on whether or not to conclude the sale contract with a third person (i. e. the client, potential buyer), or not providing necessary information or documents.[895] In this case, all damages that arise as a result of either party's faulty behavior have to be covered by him (this also encompasses a loss of clients, for the principal as well as for the agent – however only where the deal with them was already fixed in place and not only probable, and the contract was not concluded due to the improper performance of the contract by one of the parties).

Coming back to the agent's **duty of loyalty**, with reference to the remuneration of an agent, the problem that may arise is the insincerity of an agent. Thus, an agency contract is determined by the duty of loyalty expressed in Article 760^2 KC. Therefore, the insincerity of an agent, for example, undermines the sense of the contract, which is based on the foundation of trust.

This situation occurs when an agent hides the fact of taking a commission on selling a horse from the buyer (which is a much more problematic situation) or from the seller for a sale contract he is intermediating. Firstly, such a situation may lead to a conflict of interest when a riding instructor or a specialized trainer puts himself in a position to advise his pupil on whether a certain horse is suitable for his skills and needs on the one hand, and is motivated to obtain the promised commission on the other. The German doctrine recognizes two negative consequences that a horse-riding instructor may directly suffer if he hides from the buyer (and the student) the fact of receiving a commission from the seller. The riding instructor not only undertakes the risk of imposing criminal

891 See: § 242 BGB.
892 Compare: Article 472 KC.
893 Article 760^2 KC.
894 § 86 HGB.
895 Article 760^2 KC and § 86a HGB.

sanctions against him for a breach[896] of the duty of loyalty and to act in good faith – especially if the purchase of the horse results in negative consequences for the buyer. Thus, the buyer can also claim damages for the increased price of a horse.[897]

The problem of hidden commission appears also with the same consequences in a situation where there is an official agreement between the parties to an agency contract in reference to a commission of a certain amount, but this commission gets increased by another one that is hidden from the client.[898]

Hiding a commission from the buyer or the seller may result in further legal problems, which have to be taken into account when it comes to the termination of a sale contract. If an agency contract was concluded, it should not be problematic to regulate the hypothetical consequences of returning the horse. In a casual situation, the agent's commission should also be returned in such case.[899] However, if the commission was kept hidden and the agency contract was never formally concluded, then the buyer usually has serious problems with collecting the full price of the horse.[900]

Improper performance in case of an agency contract usually results in its termination. In addition to termination by giving notice[901] and termination by mutual agreement of the parties, in both Polish and German law there is also a possibility to terminate the contract with immediate effect. Thus, according to Article 764^2 KC, the agency contract may be terminated without observing any terms of notice in two situations: in the case of the non-performance of the duties by one of the parties in full or in significant part,[902] as well as in case of extraordinary circumstances.[903] The German Commercial Code defines the

896 Note that in this case the breach of duty is understood as improper performance of the contract.

897 See about the consequences of hiding the agent's commission from the buyer: P. Rosbach, *Pferderecht*, pp. 72.

898 P. Rosbach, *Pferderecht*, pp. 73.

899 See: Article 761^4 KC and § 87 a (2) and (3) (second sentence) HGB.

900 See: P. Rosbach, *Pferderecht*, pp. 73.

901 Article 764^1KC, § 89 HGB.

902 Whereas it does not make any difference in this reference whether the reason for the non-performance of duties is a result of circumstances at the fault of one of the parties or not. However, the reason for the non-performance of duties of a party to an agency contract is important in order to define whether the duty to compensate damages arises. See: E. Rott-Pietrzyk [in:] J. Rajski (ed.), *System…*, pp. 688; E. Rott-Pietrzyk, *Agent handlowy…*, pp. 359; also: I. Mycko-Katner, *Umowa Agencyjna*, Warszawa 2012, pp. 319.

903 In the Polish literature, there are various opinions concerning the nature of extraordinary circumstances that would justify the termination of an agency contract with immediate effect. See, for example, E. Rott-Pietrzyk, *Agent handlowy…*, pp. 359–363, who represents the opinion that the extraordinary circumstances in Article 764^2 KC may constitute circumstances at the fault of one of the parties, or not at the fault of any party to the contract, whereas I. Mycko-Katner claims that the term "extraordinary circumstances" may not

reason to terminate the agency contract without the observance of the terms of notice in § 89a HGB, defining it solely as "important reason".[904]

Although, in my opinion, it is not possible to dissolve (*odstąpienie, das Rücktritt*)[905] an agency contract with an *ex tunc* effect, as it is a permanent contractual relationship (*stosunek o charakterze ciągłym, trwałym*),[906] some Polish authors take such possibility into account.[907] This does not seem correct, however, as Article 764^2 KC and § 89a HGB, setting out the possibility to immediately terminate the agency contract have comprehensively displaced such an opportunity. What is more, representatives of the German literature do not have any concerns with reference to whether the dissolution of a contract is possible in that case, as the termination of an agency contract regulated in § 89a HGB seems to exhaust this problem comprehensively.[908] However, it is important to bear in mind that the termination of a contract is an exceptional measure. Thus, in the case of a non-performance of the contract, the parties should seek the proper performance of the contract as the primary option.[909]

Non-performance of contractual duties with reference to the agency contract should be defined individually[910] and consists above all in the disloyal behavior of one of the parties. Thus, concealing the conclusion of a contract with a client acquired by an agent, failing to cooperate with an agent, refusing to provide necessary information on the side of the principal and undertaking competitive activity (e. g. by hiding information concerning a horse that would be suitable for the principal from him, in order to propose its purchase to another rider in the first place – if the parties did not provide for this possibility in their

include circumstances at the fault of the party terminating the contract with immediate effect. See: I. Mycko-Katner, *Umowa Agencyjna,* Warszawa 2012, pp. 319–320.

904 Note that Directive 86/653/EEC does not regulate the termination of the agency contract with immediate effect. Article 16 of Directive 86/653/EEC provides merely that nothing in this directive will affect the application of the law of the Member States, where the latter provides for the immediate termination of the agency contract because of the failure of one party to carry out all or part of its obligations, or in case exceptional circumstances arise.

905 As I have already mentioned above, the term "termination" used with reference to an agency contract is always used as a translation of *wypowiedzenie/die Kündigung.*

906 I share the opinion of I. Mycko – Katner, *Umowa Agencyjna,* Warszawa 2012, pp. 328–336.

907 In favour of the possibility to dissolve (*odstąpienie, Rücktrit*) the contract in general are: E. Rott-Pietrzyk [in:] J. Rajski, (ed.), *System…*, pp. 685–687 and – with reference to Article 395 KC, defining the possibility to dissolve the contract in general – W. Popiołek [in:] K. Pietrzykowski, *Kodeks cywilny, Komentarz*, Vol. II, pp. 1306–1313. See also: J. Kufel, *Umowa Agencyjna*, Poznań 1977, pp. 78–79; E. Rott-Pietrzyk, *Wygaśnięcie umowy agencyjnej*, Rejent 1999, No. 9 (101), pp. 246–251.

908 Compare: J. Busche [in:] H. Oetker, *Handelsgesetzbuch. Kommentar*, München 2011, pp. 642–654; G. von Hoyningen-Huene [in:] K. Schmidt, *Münchener Kommentar. Handelsgesetzbuch*, München 2010, pp. 1312–1337.

909 See: Article 455 KC and § 271 BGB, specifying time of performance of contractual obligations.

910 See: I. Mycko-Katner, *Umowa Agencyjna,* Warszawa 2012, pp. 319.

agreement), the disclosure of the principal's know-how (which also covers the competition plans for the ongoing or the following year, if the principal did not allow for its disclosure), non-compliance with the principal's instructions – despite reminders (e. g. by taking up the principal's time by showing him many horses that obviously do not meet the principal's requirements from a horse), letting a third person undertake actions that are the agent's duty, sending late answers to clients waiting for an agent's offer, etc.[911]

Additionally, the party that suffered a loss as a result of the improper performance of a contract is entitled to receive damages under both the Polish and German legal system, according to Article 471 KC or § 280 BGB respectively (liability *ex contractu*). The German Commercial Code has additionally underlined the duty to reimburse damages caused by the non-performance of the contractual obligation of a party to the agency contract in § 89a (2) HGB (stating in its first paragraph the possibility to immediately terminate the agency contract). The provision of § 89a (2) HGB corresponds with § 628 (2) BGB and regulates the issue of damages in reference to the party receiving the notice, whereas it lacks any provision regulating damages payable to the party giving notice – which means they have to be based on §§ 280 (1) and 241 (2) BGB.[912]

Directive 86/653/EEC also sets out an additional remedy – **indemnity** for an agent (as a weaker party to the contract) who – during the term of the agency contract – solicited new clients or led to a substantial growth in turnover with already procured clients, and the principal still derives significant profits from the contracts with those clients. According to Article 764^3 KC[913] and § 89b HGB,[914] corresponding with Article 17 of the Council Directive of 18 December 1986 on the coordination of the laws of the Member States relating to self-employed commercial agents (86/653/EEC),[915] the agent is entitled to file an

911 Compare: I. Mycko-Katner, *Umowa Agencyjna,* Warszawa 2012, pp. 319–320.

912 See, with reference to German law: G. von Hoyningen-Huene [in:] K. Schmidt, *Münchener Kommentar. Handelsgesetzbuch,* München 2010, pp. 1336–1337.

913 Note that this remedy is not qualified as damages, in order for it to apply, it is not necessary for an agent to be damaged and for the principal to be faulty, thus it is independent from the reasons for the termination of an agency contract and has an objective character. See, with reference to Polish law: E. Rott-Pietrzyk [in:] M. Stec, *System Prawa Handlowego., Prawo Umów handlowych, Vol. V,* pp. 623–631.

914 With reference to the indemnity of an agent after terminating an agency contract (*Ausgleichsanspruch*), under German Law, see comprehensively: G. von Hoyningen-Huene [in:] K. Schmidt, *Münchener Kommentar. Handelsgesetzbuch,* München 2010, pp. 1338–1410.

915 See: Ruling of the European Court of Justice of 26. 3. 2009, C-348/07; E. Rott-Pietrzyk [in:] M. Stec, *System Prawa Handlowego., Prawo Umów handlowych,* Vol. V, Warszawa 2017, pp. 624–625, pointing at the European Commission Report of 1996, see: Commission report on the application of the Commercial Agents Directive (COM (1996) 364 final, 23.7. 1996). See also: O. Sztejnert, *Świadczenie wyrównawcze dla agenta albo jaki wpływ na*

indemnity claim if – taking all the circumstances into account (and particularly if the agent lost his commission from contracts concluded by the principal with these clients) – the considerations of equity call for that.

Note that the solution presented in Article 17 (2) of Directive 86/653/EEC has been called the "*German clause*", as § 89b HGB was used as a role model for this provision (similarly, Article 17 (3) of Directive 86/653/EEC is called the "*French clause*" because of the French law serving as an inspiration in this case).[916] Although the agent's right covered by Article 17 is rather not of great importance with reference to agency contracts covering sale contracts concerning animals, this ruling is worth mentioning due to the fact that the experience of the German jurisprudence with reference to indemnity claims may gain importance when interpreting national provisions implementing Article 17 (2) of Directive 86/653/EEC. Hence, the experience of the German jurisprudence is worth taking into consideration when interpreting Article 764^3 KC, which implements the "*German solution*" inserted in Article 17 (2) of Directive 86/653/EEC. Such importance was given to the experience of the German jurisprudence by the Commission Report of 1996, referring to the performance of Articles 17 and 18 of Directive 86/653/EEC.[917] The Report indicates that – with reference to establishing the amount of the agent's indemnity claim – the courts of other EU Member States should take into account the German jurisprudence experience in these matters.[918] In ECJ rulings concerning the agent's indemnity claim, the ECJ referred to the methodology of interpreting and applying Article 17 (2) of the Directive 86/653/EEC, as proposed in the Report.[919] This way, the ECJ referred indirectly to the experience of German courts. It is interesting that the ECJ – by referring to the *proper* methodology of interpretation and application of Article 17 (2) of Directive 86/653/EEC – was indirectly addressing the experience of the German courts concerning § 89b HGB (which is a model for the solution covered by Article 17 (2)).[920] Nevertheless, this way of reasoning should be

polskie orzecznictwo może mieć nowelizacja niemieckiego HGB, MoP 2010, No. 14, pp. 806–909.

916 European Commission Report of 1996, p. 6; see also E. Rott-Pietrzyk, Agent handlowy, p. 65.

917 European Commission Report of 1996.

918 See: Commission report of 1996 , pp. 2–4.

919 See, for example: the ECJ ruling from 23.3.2006, *Honyvem Informazioni Commerciali v. Marielle de Zotti*, C-465/04, pp. I-2902, I-2913; ECJ, ruling from 26.3.2009, *Turgay Semen v. Deutsche Tamoil Gmbh,* C-348/07, section 22 .See also: Opinion of Advocate General Poiares Maduro on case C-465/04 from 25.10.2005, sections 24, 27, 28, which had importance for jurisprudence of ECJ with reference to the establishment of methods of methodology of interpretation and application of Article 17 (2) of Directive 86/653/EEC concerning the agent's indemnity claim.

920 Compare: ECJ, ruling from 23.3.2006, *Honyvem Informazioni Commerciali v. Marielle de Zotti*, C-465/04, pp. I-2902, I-2913; ECJ, ruling from 26.3.2009, *Turgay Semen v. Deutsche*

considered very carefully. Hence, the Report referred solely the German jurisprudence before 1994.[921]

With this in mind, this fact and the method employed in the book *Limits of Harmonization and Convergence. Dissimilarities in Similarities of Polish and German Contract Law*, edited by M. Jagielska, E. Macierzyńska-Franaszczyk, E. Rott-Pietrzyk, F. Zoll, G. Żmij, the knowledge about the manner of interpreting and applying the law in Germany might also be useful with reference to obligations having an animal as their object (from the point of view of German legal practice and jurisprudence). However, the legal comparative argument must be used very carefully. Hence, even similar facts of a case may lead to different rulings in cases where the black letter rules of laws of different EU Member States are the same, and the identity of a similarity of legal rules is not a guarantee of the same understanding of it in disparate legal systems.[922] Although the Polish and German legal systems are bound by the same European legal acts aimed at the harmonization of law,[923] have the same goals (i. e. the harmonization of national law in accordance with European standards – but only where the EU has competence) and legal foundations,[924] it has always been a problematic source of inspiration. The reason for this is the fact that Polish private law was inspired not only by German law, but also by other legal traditions, especially French law. Therefore, I am aware that the doctrinal solutions developed within the German tradition may be misleading to some extent. The fact that the German method of legal reasoning has been generally (albeit sometimes seemingly only on the surface) adopted in Poland, does not change the fact that these two systems are in many aspects still very different from each other. However, this should not affect the conclusion that the experience of the German courts may be useful

Tamoil Gmbh, C-C-348/07, section 22. See also: Opinion of Advocate General Poiares Maduro on case C-465/04 from 25.10.2005, sections 41–45, which was important for jurisprudence of ECJ with reference to the establishment of methods of methodology of interpretation and application of Article 17 (2) of Directive 86/653/EEC concerning the agent's indemnity claim.

921 Compare E. Rott-Pietrzyk [in:] M. Stec, *System Prawa Handlowego. Prawo Umów handlowych*, Vol. V, Warszawa 2017, pp. 624–625; O. Sztejnert, *Świadczenie wyrównawcze dla agenta albo jaki wpływ na polskie orzecznictwo może mieć nowelizacja niemieckiego HGB*, MoP 2010, No. 14, pp. 806–809.

922 E. Rott-Pietrzyk, F. Zoll [in:] M. Jagielska, E. Macierzyńska-Franaszczyk, E. Rott-Pietrzyk, F. Zoll, G. Żmij (eds.), *Limits of Harmonization and Convergence…*, p. 44; H. Honsell, *Die rhetorischen Wurzeln der juristischen Auslegung*, ZfPW 2016, p. 125.

923 With reference to similarities and differences in the Polish and German legal systems and the applicability of provisions of law of one European country to a certain factual situation in a different European country, see: M. Jagielska, E. Macierzyńska-Franaszczyk, E. Rott-Pietrzyk, F. Zoll, G. Żmij (eds.), *Limits of Harmonization and Convergence…*; G. Falkner, O. Trein, M. Hartlapp, S. Leiber (eds.), *Complying with Europe. EU Harmonization and Soft Law in the Member States*, Cambridge 2005.

924 See also: S. Frankowski (ed.), *Introduction to Polish Law*, p. 38.

when ruling in similar cases based on similar regulations in Poland. It seems that the applicability of legal comparative argument in justifications of court rulings is underestimated, whereas I believe that it might be very useful. This does not only concern pure jurisprudence, i.e. similar rulings, it also concerns the awareness about methods of coping with certain legal problems in other countries. This is always an inspiring exploration in reference to the functionality of concrete legal solutions and – in my opinion – this has a certain value.

The tension between the similarity and proximity of the German and Polish legal systems creates a fascinating field for experimentation with the process of the harmonization and unification of law (*bilateral*), which has been – at least partially examined in the book *Limits of Harmonization and Convergence. Dissimilarities in Similarities of Polish and German Contract Law*, as well as in this book.[925]

According to Article 764^4 KC[926] and § 89b (3) HGB, the agent is not entitled to this indemnity remedy if he has caused the termination of a contract due to circumstances for which he is liable. With reference to special circumstances concerning different standards of performance when intermediating in the sale of horses, this could be the case if an agent did not take into account the interests of an animal, e.g. when scheduling the testing of a horse by various clients day after day, without taking into account its best interests, or in case, he was acting negligently when transporting the horse, etc. Other circumstances, such as insincerity or spreading bad opinions about the principal on the market may occur in the same scope as in the case of different things.

The agent's liability may also be increased by including a *del credere* provision in the agency agreement.[927] Whether such a provision would be a form of guarantee, or whether it is performance for the benefit of a third party, the

925 See: M. Jagielska, E. Macierzyńska-Franaszczyk, E. Rott-Pietrzyk, F. Zoll, G. Żmij (eds.), *Limits of Harmonization and Convergence…*, pp. 44–45.

926 Note, that this remedy is not qualified as damages, in order for it to apply, it is not necessary for an agent to be damaged and for the principal to be faulty, thus it is independent from the reasons for the termination of agency contract and has an objective character. See, with reference to Polish law: E. Rott-Pietrzyk [in:] M. Stec, *System Prawa Handlowego. Tom V, Prawo Umów handlowych*, pp. 623–631.

927 With reference to the *del credere* provision, see: I. Mycko-Katner, *Umowa Agencyjna*, Warszawa 2012, pp. 289–306; E. Rott-Pietrzyk [in:] J. Rajski (ed.), *System…*, pp. 672–677; E. Rott-Pietrzyk, *Agent handlowy…*, pp. 346–353; E. Rott-Pietrzyk [in:] S. Włodyka, *Prawo…*, pp. 504–507; L. Ogiegło [in:] J. Rajski (ed.), *System…*, p. 692–693; J. Busche [in:] H. Oetker, *Handelsgesetzbuch. Kommentar*, München 2011, pp. 571–579; G. von Hoyningen-Huene [in:] K. Schmidt, *Münchener Kommentar. Handelsgesetzbuch*, München 2010, pp. 1198–1207; K. Topolewski, *Umowa agencyjna według Kodeksu cywilnego. Wybrane problem de lege ferenda* [in:] A. Olejniczak, J. Haberko, A. Pyrzyńska, D. Sokołowska, *Współczesne problemy prawa prywatnego*, pp. 712–727.

parties would decide when concluding the contract.[928] However, undertaking such a responsibility by an agent is rare with the sale of horses, as it is a purchase of a highly individual character.[929]

In reference to an agent's right to a pledge on things (in this case, the animal) received in connection with the agency contract in order to secure the claims for the remuneration and for the reimbursement of the expenses and advance payments given to the principal under both Polish[930] and German law,[931] see the same issue with reference to commission contracts in the subchapter above[932].

The results of the improper performance of non-performance of an agent in the case where he intermediates in selling a living creature are similar as in case where he intermediates in selling a regular good, though they encompass a different scope of situations for which the agent may be held liable. Thus, an animal being a different object of an obligation raises the standards of its performance and – in the case of horses – places more risk on the agent of a failure to fit the horse to the rider.

3.3. Teaching/training contracts having an animal as their object

The regulation of liability resulting from the improper or non-performance of a service contract under both the Polish and German legal systems are based on a general understanding. Thus, a party may be held liable for damage that has been caused as a result of the improper or non-performance of its contractual obligation (contractual liability).[933] The improper performance or non-performance **of the trainer's duties** (*umowa o trening zwierzęcia, der Trainingsvertrag*) can be observed not only if the trainer did not train an animal at all, but also if it is visible that the training methods were not applied properly. This can be usually stated not only with the help of witnesses, who may admit that the trainer did not perform his duties as set out in the contract, but also after an examination of an animal or its skills by an expert. Although service contracts are, as a rule, not contracts where a party is obliged to perform a certain result,[934] a visible lack of any new skills learned by an animal, evaluated by an expert, may be treated, in my opinion, as evidence of the improper performance of a contract

928 J. Napierała [in:] A. Koch, J. Napierała, *Umowy w obrocie gospodarczym*, Kraków 2006, pp. 154–155.
929 See: Subchapter IV.2.2.
930 Article 763 KC.
931 § 88a HGB.
932 See: Subchapter IV.3.1.
933 See: Article 471 KC and § 280 BGB.
934 See more in Subchapter IV.2.3.

by the trainer. The situation is more complicated in cases where an inappropriately balanced training regime leads to an overtraining syndrome in horses (which is rather not possible in the case of obedience training in dogs, for example).[935] An overtraining syndrome in horses leads to possible contusions, back pain or behavioral disturbances, which may result in suspending the training for a longer period of time and prevent it from taking part in competitions. In this case, according to Article 361 KC and § 280 BGB,[936] the trainer is liable to cover not only the costs of medical treatment, but also cover reimbursement of the fact that the horse was not able to participate in the competitions that were already planned (however, only for those to which it was already qualified, not for those in which its attendance was only hypothetical). Hence, this is a natural consequence of a damage[937] caused to a horse, and therefore – indirectly – to the owner. A general foundation of a contractual liability is the regime of fault, though it is also possible to introduce provisions that would objectively define the liability of the parties in certain situations into the contract.[938]

If performing the service (training an animal) is impossible, the animal's owner may not demand the performance. This issue is regulated in Article 475 KC and § 275 BGB, whereas the German Civil Code regulates the possibility to refuse performance of a contract by a servicing party much more broadly. Hence, according to § 275 BGB, the obligor may refuse performance not only if it is impossible, but also in two different situations. Firstly, he may refuse performance to the extent that requires any expense and effort that – taking into account the subject matter of the obligation and the requirements of good faith – is grossly disproportionate to the interest in performance of the obligee. When it is determined which efforts may reasonably be required from the obligor, it must also be taken into account whether he is responsible for the obstacle to carry out the performance.[939] In addition, the obligor may refuse performance if he is to perform the performance in person, and when the obstacle to the performance of the obligor is weighed against the interest of the obligee in performance, the

935 Thus, an animal that is overwhelmed by obedience training becomes rather tired and cannot continue training (unless the trainer uses illegal training methods, doping, violence, etc).

936 More in the context of this kind of damage with reference to German law: H. Brox/ W. Walker, *Allgemeines Schuldrecht*, pp. 331.

937 See, with reference to Polish law: K. Zagrobelny [in:] E. Gniewek, P. Machnikowski (ed.), *Kodeks cywilny. Komentarz*, pp. 677–690.

938 See, with reference to Polish law: W. Katner [in:] M. Stec, *System Prawa Handlowego. Prawo Umów handlowych*, Vol. V, pp. 400–401. L. Ogiegło [in:] J. Rajski (ed.), *System Prawa Prywatnego, Vol. VII*, p. 572. Compare, with reference to German law: M. Fuchs [in:] H. Bamberger, H. Roth (ed.), *Beck'scher Online-Kommentar BGB*, § 611, side-number 90.

939 See: § 275 (2) BGB.

performance cannot be reasonably required of the obligor.[940] Thus, according to German law, the horse's owner would not be entitled to demand performance if the horse has defects that make it unable to learn certain skills (e.g. a sports injury that prevents the possibility of training the animal); if the horse turns out to be especially difficult to train and the training would consume much more time than the parties provided in the contract; if the trainer would suffer under a sporting injury that results in the fact that the training requires an effort that is grossly disproportionate to the interest in performance of the animal's owner.[941] Under Polish law, the solution would be the same according to the first situation (the post-contractual impossibility to perform the obligation)[942] and according to the other two situations – as long as they do not make the performance impossible, but grossly disproportionate – would probably have to be resolved by applying the *rebus sic stantibus* provision.[943] However, when applying the *rebus sic stantibus* provision, one must take into account the fact that the result might be different. Thus, in this case it is the court that decides how the performance of the parties should be adjusted to new, formerly unexpected conditions, and whether the contract should be dissolved or not. Whereas the German solution is more appropriate when taking into account the variety of possible components of service contracts, Polish law does not address the problem of gross disproportion so directly. Although the outcome under both legal systems – due to the applicability of the *rebus sic stantibus* provision – in most cases would probably be similar, the German Civil Code offers more possibilities without the need for an advance interpretation of its provisions and the use of respectively applicable provisions of law. It seems that § 275 BGB corresponds with the fact of the comprehensive regulation of service contracts by covering all of them with the scope of § 611 BGB. Whereas the provisions respectively applicable to undefined service contracts under Polish law are the provisions covering mandate contracts (Articles 734 and 750 KC), the *rebus sic stantibus* provision[944] seems to be another construction of the Polish Civil Code that does not directly address the problem of gross disproportion of the trainer's performance in comparison to the existing conditions under Polish law. The only difference between the solutions under both legal systems is, in my opinion,

940 See: § 275 (3) BGB.
941 Compare: M. Fuchs [in:] H. Bamberger, H. Roth (ed.), *Beck'scher Online-Kommentar BGB*, § 611, side-number 83.
942 Compare: Article 471 KC.
943 Article 357[1] KC. With reference to the initial impossibility to perform the obligation, see: M. Krajewski, *Pierwotna niemożliwość świadczenia – między dwoma rozwiązaniami*, [in:] A. Olejniczak, J. Haberko, A. Pyrzyńska, D. Sokołowska, *Współczesne problemy prawa prywatnego*, pp. 323–333.
944 Article 357[1] KC.

the ease of usage of these provisions. Thus, in the case of a ruling in a case referring to a teaching/training contract, which is the subject of this subchapter, the Polish court would have several difficulties to overcome. The first problem that would possibly arise in this case would probably be the problem of qualifying this contract as a service contract under Articles 734 and 750 KC. Secondly, the Polish court would have to deal with the applicability of the *rebus sic stantibus* provision to the facts of the case. Thirdly, the Polish court would have to deal with the lack of jurisprudence in this matter and the applicability of German rulings to Polish conditions in this matter. Whereas the German legal solutions in the case at hand seem to be simpler, the reason for this being the differences in the construction of both the Polish and German Civil Codes, in the end both legal systems will apply similar solutions. Thus, the only disadvantage of the Polish legal system seems to be lack of Polish jurisprudence in this matter. This means that the Polish court may – albeit very carefully – take advantage of the experience of German jurisprudence (e. g. in the scope of using the comparative element applied when explaining the court's reasoning when giving a certain ruling).[945] Hence, different solutions under both of the compared legal systems should not be treated as a competition between more or less appropriate legal constructions, but – due to similar legal foundations and legal culture – they could inspire each other to the extent of legal reasoning and the methodology of interpretation and the application of the law. This is especially true as Germany is a pioneer in legal practice in reference to the obligations connected with the horse market, and the sale of horses in general. Awareness of these circumstances and knowledge in this matter may be useful when resolving the legal ambiguities referring to these issues under Polish law.

The provisions concerning a **delay in performance** would rather not be applicable to the obligation to train an animal (so this obligation is rather to be understood as having been concluded for a certain amount of time, not until a certain result occurs), though it may be applicable to the animal's owner's obligation to pay the price. In such a situation, the trainer would be allowed to keep the horse until the owner pays the trainer's remuneration.[946] He would also be entitled to damages for the additional time of taking care of the animal, feeding and keeping him. However, in my opinion, this situation would not entitle him to continue the training in order to require a higher remuneration. Nevertheless, the trainer may also demand default interest on the main obliga-

945 See: Commission Report of 1996, see: Commission report on the application of the Commercial Agents Directive (COM (1996) 364 final) of 23. 7. 1996, especially pp. 2–4. Compare: the considerations included in Subchapter IV.3.2. ("Agency contracts having an animal as their object").

946 Compare, with reference to German law: M. Fuchs [in:] H. Bamberger, H. Roth (ed.), *Beck'scher Online-Kommentar BGB*, § 611, side-number 84; §§ 281 and 286 BGB.

tion that has already been performed (the training process, performed in accordance with the contract) from the animal's owner.[947]

In the event of the **improper performance** of the training, the animal's owner has no warranty rights under either the Polish or the German legal system, as the provisions applicable to an undefined contract like the contract to train an animal are those referring to service contracts. Thus, with reference to Polish law – as already mentioned – Article 750 KC provides that the provisions applicable to mandate contract defined in Article 734 § 1 KC are applicable to all undefined service contracts.[948] Therefore, it is important to distinguish between a defined contract and an undefined one, as the referral from Article 750 KC combines two features of contracts and applies to contracts that are not only **undefined**, but also refer to **services.**[949] These are contracts on the performance of services that – according to Article 750 – are not regulated by other provisions concerning obligational contracts. Therefore, it is a different case than, for example, in reference to a commission contract, which is a defined service contract under Polish law (Articles 765–773 KC) and its *essentialia negotii* refer to a sale contract. In that case, the warranty provisions covering sale contracts apply, though the party liable is different than in the case of a regular sale contract concluded without intermediation from a commission agent.[950] Under German law, the teaching/training contract having an animal as an object of the performance of one of the parties falls within the scope of § 611 BGB and, therefore – due to its qualification as a service contract – warranty provisions are not applicable in this case either. As a result, it is not possible to directly demand that the price of the whole training process be lowered (e.g. because of its inaccuracy and irregularity) or improved (by prolonging the time in order to give the trainer an opportunity to fix the problem). Although these two remedies are often used in practice, they cannot be based on warranty rights, as these are not warranty remedies applicable to service contracts. However, an animal's owner and the trainer may agree for on the animal being kept for a longer time at the trainer's place, or on paying a lower price for the training, but these actions will only be

947 See: § 288 and Article 481 KC.

948 To learn more about the interpretation and scope of application of Article 750 KC, see: R. Morek, M. Raczkowski [in:] K. Osajda (ed.), *Kodeks cywilny. Komentarz. Tom IIIB*, pp. 758–765; L. Ogiegło [in:] K. Pietrzykowski (ed.), *Kodeks cywilny. Komentarz*, Vol. II, pp. 1411–1413.

949 P. Machnikowski [in:] E. Gniewek, P. Machnikowski (ed.), *Kodeks cywilny. Komentarz*, pp. 1411–1413.

950 Compare: Subchapter IV.3.1. of this book.

the results of the parties' agreement, which was secondary to the damages that had to be paid by the trainer.[951]

In the case of a teaching/training contract having an animal as an object of the parties' performance, the fact that an animal is object of this obligation not only creates a specific service contract itself, but also influences the scope of damages in the case of the improper performance of its training. Thus, since damages in case of a contractual liability encompass the positive interest (*der Erfüllungsschaden,*[952] *pozytywny interes umowny*[953]) of the party who lost due to its contractual partner's improper performance of the training, this scope is diametrically different in the case of an animal. Whereas I have already pointed to the consequences of the overtraining syndrome in horses, this may result in several diverse consequences that – due to the fact that an animal is a living creature, i. e. a very complicated organism – may not be foreseen with reference to all possible situations. The most common consequence is the need to pay for the medical treatment of an animal that has been improperly trained (i. e. trained in a way that caused its health to deteriorate in reference to the *sine qua non* test in accordance with Article 361 KC and § 280 BGB). This medical treatment is not only the treatment of the condition that was directly caused by the failure in this animal's training, but also all of its consequences and other medical conditions arising therefrom. In case some payments with reference to the planned participation of an animal in certain sporting competitions or other trainings have already been made, these costs should also be reimbursed. In the event that the horse has already been scheduled to take part in some kind of event that was supposed to bring income for its owner, the income that the animal's owner has been deprived of should also be reimbursed by the trainer (*der Mangelfolgeschaden,*[954] *korzyści, które mógłby osiągnąć, gdyby mu szkody nie wyrządzono*[955]). Nevertheless, it is worth noting that – due to the freedom of contract principle – parties may establish different consequences of the improperly performed training of an animal, or define its meaning differently (other than in the case of a casual understanding of the term).

951 However, one has to bear in mind that damages are to be paid only in the event that the trainer was at fault for causing a certain damage (i. e. did not perform his duties properly or did not perform them at all).

952 More in the context of this kind of damage with reference to German law: H. Brox/ W. Walker, *Allgemeines Schuldrecht*, pp. 331.

953 See: Article 361 KC; W. Czachórski, *Zobowiązania. Zarys wykładu*, pp. 96–109.

954 Compare: § 284 BGB.

955 Compare: Article 361 § 2 KC.

3.4. Safe-keeping contracts having an animal as its object

From a practical point of view, the provisions of most importance with reference to the improper performance of **a safe-keeping contract** (*umowa przechowania, der Verwahrungsvertrag*) are provisions referring to contractual liability in the main part of the law of obligations, to be found in Article 471 KC and § 280 BGB. However, there is a significant difference in the understanding of qualification of contractual liability in German and Polish law. Liability *ex contractu* in the Polish and German legal systems, concerns the liability of a depositor in the event of the improper performance of a contract when acting with intent or negligence.[956] The depositor is also liable if he used the help of other people to perform his obligation[957] (although he may demand recourse afterwards, he is the one who will be held liable for the services that he was obliged to perform). The Polish legal system acknowledges only the term of general negligence, whereas the German law of obligation – acknowledges two types of negligence (*grobe und leichte Fahrlässigkeit*).[958] Thus, the animal may injure itself in many different manners, especially when in contact with other animals. Due to the scope of damage that has to be reimbursed in order to cover the positive interest of the animal's owner, the safe-keeper has to prepare himself for a range of situations. For example, where the horse injures itself on the paddock,[959] the safe-keeper would not only have to pay for the medical treatment of the horse, but also for all future health disturbances of the horse that arise in connection with this accident. Nevertheless, it should be underlined that – despite certain differences – under both the Polish and German legal systems, liability *ex contractu* is principally based on the principle of guilt.[960]

Therefore, it is very popular for stable owners in Germany to limit the depositor's liability. P. Rosbach suggests the **contractual limitation of liability to a higher level of negligence** (*grobe Fahrlässigkeit*) in each case,[961] which would lead to the same consequences to those set out in the Polish law of obligations

956 Compare: Article 472 KC and § 276 BGB.

957 See: Article 474 KC and § 278 BGB. Under both the Polish and German legal systems, the debtor is liable for the damage of a third person as for its own..

958 Compare: § 276 (2) BG. See: C. Grüneberg [in:] O. Palandt, *Beck'sche Kurz-Kommentare: Palandt Bürgerliches Gesetzbuch mit Nebengesetzen*, München 2015, p. 368.

959 See: the German case LG Aschaffenburg, 3 O 332/01 described several lines below.

960 To learn more about the principle of guilt with reference to Polish law, see e.g.: K. Zagrobelny [in:] E. Gniewek, P. Machnikowski (ed.), *Kodeks cywilny. Komentarz*, pp. 956–961; see also: W. Popiołek, who indicates that Article 471 KC includes a presumption that the improper performance of a contract or non-performance of a contract occurred as result of circumstances that are the fault of the debtor, see: W Popiołek [in:] K. Pietrzykowski, *Kodeks cywilny, Tom II, Komentarz*, pp. 41–52.

961 P. Rosbach, *Pferderecht*, pp. 117–120.

without its contractual modifications. However, according to both the German and Polish Civil Codes, the liability of the depositor cannot be limited in such a way that he would not be liable for causing the improper performance of the contract or its non-performance with intent.[962] I would recommend the contractual limitation of depositor's liability in any case, without regard to the applicable legal system. If this is not the case, the depositor's liability would definitely have a too broad scope of application and would very quickly lead the stable owners to bankruptcy. Thus, the German courts have admitted the depositor's negligence in several cases. This was the case in a ruling by the German court in Aschaffenburg,[963] where the animal's owner filed a claim against a stable owner whose employee acted negligently when taking two young stallions from the paddock. The court agreed with the claimant and stated that taking of two young stallions at once, only by holding them on halters was negligent. However, in a different case, where the claimant alleged that, due to the fact that the electricity on the fence dividing the horses' paddocks was not checked regularly every day,[964] the stable owner is obliged to pay him damages for a horse euthanized due to injuries, the court denied the stable owner's negligence. Thus, the horse had to be euthanized due to injuries suffered when he jumped over the fence to another horse, which left him very badly injured. Nevertheless, in this case the Court stated that a fence higher than 1.20 m (namely 1.28 and 1.32 m) was sufficient to assume that the stable owner had undertaken all necessary actions to keep the animals safe. Whereas such matters have not yet been addressed by the Polish courts, the evaluation of the scope of negligence should occur similarly as in the ruling ruled by German courts. Thus, the standards of keeping horses safe should be the same in both countries whose legal systems are described in this book. However, Germany does not only have a longer practice in keeping horses and providing horse shows, and is known worldwide for its breeds (e.g. Hannoveraner, Holstein horses), but also the German courts have a richer jurisprudence in this matters. Therefore, due to the fact that Polish and German legal systems are bound by the same European legal acts aimed at the harmonization of law[965] and share the same legal foundations,[966] the doctrinal solutions developed within the German tradition may be an interesting in-

962 Compare: Article 472 KC and § 276 (3) BGB.
963 See: LG Aschaffenburg, 3 O 332/01, cited after: P. Rosbach, *Pferderecht*, p. 116.
964 See: OLG Celle, 9 U 130/99, ruling from 26.1.2000.
965 With reference to similarities and differences in the Polish and German legal systems and the applicability of provisions of law of one European country to a certain factual situation in a different European country, see: M. Jagielska, E. Macierzyńska-Franaszczyk, E. Rott-Pietrzyk, F. Zoll, G. Żmij (eds.), *Limits of Harmonization and Convergence…*; G. Falkner, O. Trein, M. Hartlapp, S. Leiber (eds.), *Complying with Europe. EU Harmonization and Soft Law in the Member States*, Cambridge 2005.
966 See also: S. Frankowski (ed.), *Introduction to Polish Law*, p. 38.

spiration for the Polish courts. However – as already mentioned – using the experience of German courts should take place very carefully, due to the still transparent dissimilarities in both legal systems.[967]

In all these cases, an accident involving an expensive horse would constitute an obligation to pay damages on the side of a depositor if there was no contractual limitation of this liability. At this point, it is important to remember about the horse owner's duty to inform the owner of the stables or kennels etc. about the specifics of the animal, i. e. all behaviors of the animal that the depositor should be informed about in order to ensure his safety and the animal's. Thus, a situation where locating a barrow by the door of a horse's box in order to clean it out caused an accident and led to the horse's injury, would not be qualified as the depositor's negligence, since it is a generally practiced manner of cleaning boxes and it is not expected that a horse could jump through the barrow.[968] All the presented examples prove that it is very important to describe all the specifics of the animal – its value and details concerning the depositor's liability in the contract concerning the stables or kennels etc. However, one should bear in mind that, if the depositor (acting as part of his business activity) concludes contracts based on the same form with various animal owners, the provisions should be qualified as general terms and conditions, and special attention has to be paid to the unfair contract terms (*niedozwolone klauzule umowne/ missbräuchliche Vertragsklauseln*).[969]

In addition, the qualification of a contract with the stables, or putting the pet into kennels as a safe-keeping contract has its further consequences. Thus, it is remarkable that the depositor does not have a right of lien on the horse in the stable,[970] since Article 670 KC and § 562 BGB are not applicable in the case at hand as they only concern lease contracts. However, the depositor is entitled to make use of the *ius retentionis* regulated in Article 461 BGB and § 273 BGB, regulating the general right of the parties in the right of obligations consisting in

967 See: E. Rott-Pietrzyk, F. Zoll [in:] M. Jagielska, E. Macierzyńska-Franaszczyk, E. Rott-Pietrzyk, F. Zoll, G. Żmij (eds.), *Limits of Harmonization and Convergence…*, p. 44; H. Honsell, *Die rhetorischen Wurzeln der juristischen Auslegung*, ZfPW 2016, p. 125. Compare: the considerations included in Subchapter IV.3.2. ("Agency contracts having an animal as their object").

968 See: OLG Stuttgart, 2 U 242/93, cited after: P. Rosbach, *Pferderecht*, pp. 115.

969 The unfair contract terms in Europe have been unified according to the Council Directive 93/13/EEC of 5 April 1993 on unfair terms in consumer contracts. However, with reference to the German implementation of the Directive, see the verdict of the European Court of Justice of 23 April 2015 (ECJ 0 C-96/14) suggesting that § 307 BGB (referring to the definition of unfair contract terms) is incompatible with the directive.

970 See: P. Rosbach, *Pferderecht*, pp. 122–124.

the possibility to keep the subject of a contract as long as the harm caused by this good is not compensated.[971]

3.5. Other service contracts having an animal as their object

As liability in the case of non-performance or improper performance of all types of service contracts falls within the scope of § 611 BGB and Article 734 (*per analogiam*) in connection with Article 750 KC, it is also the case in reference to the types of service contracts described below. The parties to the service contract are not obliged to any particular result, and their performance is concentrated on the due diligence[972] of the party undertaking the obliged services, meaning that the most common means of compensation are damages. Thus, although some authors underline that it is possible to cure the improper performance of services in some cases (under both Polish and German law),[973] it is not always possible due to its nature, and, in some cases, loss of trust of the other party of the contract. Therefore, as already mentioned, parties to the service contract, whether under Polish or German law, have two possible claims: a claim for the performance of the contract, and a claim for compensation of damages.[974] The issues of the termination of the contract and the payment of damages have already been described comprehensively in subchapters concerning service contracts. Namely, the party that has suffered any loss as a result of the improper performance of a contract caused by the other party is entitled to receive damages based on Article 471 KC or § 280 BGB respectively (liability *ex contractu*). However, note that in reference to each profession, the obligee is expected to act with due diligence typical for his profession.[975]

It is also important to bear in mind that some contracts with veterinary doctors may fall under the scope of application of a contract for a specific task[976] (the same occurs in all cases of contracts with blacksmiths) and in these cases

971 See, with reference to the German legal system: P. Rosbach, *Pferderecht*, pp. 122–124.

972 The liability *ex contractu* in the Polish, as well as in the German legal system, sets out the liability of a depositor in the event of the improper performance of a contract when acting with intent or negligence, compare: Article 472 KC and § 276 BGB.

973 See, with reference to German law: H. Mansel [in:] R. Stürner (ed.), *Jauernig, Kommentar zum BGB*, München 2015, § 611, side number 16. With reference to the inapplicability of the warranty regime (*Rechtsmängelgewährleistung, rękojmia*) under Polish law, see: L. Ogiegło, *Usługi…*, pp. 222–224.

974 See, with reference to Polish law (but applicable also to German law in this matter):: L. Ogiegło, *Usługi…*, pp. 220–221.

975 With reference to the authority of a veterinary doctor, see: E. Fellmer, P. Kiel, *Rechtskunde…*, p. 118; P. Rosbach, *Pferderecht*, p. 156.

976 See: Article 627 KC and § 631 BGB.

different consequences of the improper performance of the contract apply.[977] In a case where contract with a blacksmith or with a veterinary doctor qualifies as a contract for a specific task (*umowa o dzieło, Werkvertrag*), according to Article 638 KC and § 633 BGB, the provisions concerning warranty rights of the subcontracting party (which neither the Polish nor the German legislator has foreseen in the case of service contracts) apply.

In case of the improper performance of all these contracts, the party at fault for the improper performance of the contract has to cover the damage arising from contractual liability (Article 474 KC and § 278 BGB) in the scope of *damnum emergens* and *lucrum cessans*.[978]

In the case of the improper performance in all of these contracts, it is also important that – according to Article 474 KC and § 278 BGB – the obligor is liable in the same scope in the case where he used the help of other people to perform his obligation. Although he is entitled to demand recourse afterwards, he is the one who will be held liable for the services that he was obliged to perform.

977 See, with reference to German law (but applicable also to Polish law in this case): E. Fellmer, P. Kiel, *Rechtskunde...*, pp. 116–120.

978 Compare: examples of the scope of covering damage arisen from the contractual liability in case of other service contracts in this subchapter.

V. Contracts for the use of someone else's things

1. General characteristics of contracts for the use of someone else's things having an animal as their object

1.1. General remarks

Contracts used most commonly in reference to an animal being an object of the contractual performance in contracts for the use of someone else's things in Poland and Germany are: **lease (*najem,*[979] *Mietvertrag*[980]), tenancy[981] (*dzierżawa,*[982] *Pachtvertrag*[983]) and loan for use contracts (*użytkowanie,*[984] *Leihe*[985]).**[986] As in Poland, the nomenclature used in practice improperly indicates the usage of a tenancy contract to the actual lease of animals,[987] these two types of contracts are described jointly, whereas loan for use contracts are described separately. Aside from the contracts regulated in the Polish and German Civil Codes named above, the practice observed between riders acknowledges also other contracts based on the mutual use of the same horse. The practice recognizes different names for this undefined contract (*atypischer Vertrag*) such as "mutual lease" (*współdzierżawa*) in Polish language, whereas the name that seems to be most accurate and exists in a noticeable number of legal or semi-legal works or papers

979 Articles 659–679 KC.
980 §§ 535–548 BGB.
981 Often translated into English also as usufructuary lease, see: https://www.gesetze-im-internet.de/englisch_bgb/englisch_bgb.html (last visited: 31.3.2017).
982 Articles 693–709 KC.
983 §§ 581–584 b BGB.
984 Articles 710–719 KC.
985 §§ 598–606 BGB.
986 Lease and tenancy are often used to describe the same kind of contract, though for the purpose of this book the naming of the described contracts applies as listed.
987 See, for example, the website of stables in Moszna, available at: http://moszna.pl/sprzedaz-koni/dzierzawa-koni-sportowych/ or the website of the newspaper "Gallop", available at: http://gallop.pl/zasady-dzierzawy-konia-umowa/ (both, last visited: 28.01.2018).

is the German name "*Reitbeteiligungsvertrag*", which translates most closely to "horse-sharing". Therefore, this contract is described in this subchapter under the name "horse-sharing".

The fact that in Poland, the lease of animals is often named tenancy rather than lease is probably done for historical reasons, when animals left for usage were mostly farm animals that were leased with the intention of collecting the benefits (unlike in Germany, where horse sports have a longer and deeper tradition).[988] Nevertheless, it is currently more common to consider an animal as the object of a lease contract, as animals nowadays are used not only to collect the benefits, but also for social purposes.[989] One can only assume that in some time in Europe, leasing dogs or cats for social reasons will also become common practice.[990] The reason for this situation is the fact that modern European society is focused on making high-flying careers, which may entail frequent changes of place of residence and long working hours. This leads to a reduction in the social networks of young people and crises of family life. These reasons, as well as the ageing of European society, is leading unequivocally to the situation when people will have to meet their social needs by renting animals for social purposes. Thus, old age, long working hours or a need to frequently move location are all reasons that stop people from buying their own animal, whereas basic human needs still have to be met. On the other hand, there are many homeless dogs and cats in animal shelters, and the idea of "renting" them or taking them short term in the form of a loan for use contract would be rewarding for both sides of the contract.

Under both the Polish and German legal system, the **construction of lease** can also be used with reference to keeping a horse in a stable, in the understanding

988 Compare, press reports referring to the facts and numbers describing the scope of horse sports in Germany: A. Sten-Ziemons, DW 20.7.2013, available at: http://www.dw.com/de/deutschland-einig-pferdeland/a-16911941; Deutsche Reiterliche Vereinigung, *Zahlen und Fakten (2016)*, available at https://www.pferd-aktuell.de/fn-service/zahlen-fakten/zahlen-fakten (last visited: 13.3.2018).

989 See the article describing the slowly evolving branch of commerce consisting in renting animals such as cows, pigs and chickens to collect their benefits in the idea of an "ecological trend of living": I. Güttel, *Ein Huhn fur drei Monate, bitte*, n-tv.de 24.4.2016, available at: http://www.n-tv.de/panorama/Ein-Huhn-fuer-drei-Monate-bitte-article17531341.html; B. Czekała, *Wypożyczalnia kur niosek, czyli australijski sposób na biznes,* 19.1.2016, available at: https://www.topagrar.pl/articles/aktualnosci/wypozyczalnia-kur-niosek-czyli-australijski-sposob-na-biznes/ (last visited: 24.8.2017).

990 See: news information about dogs being leased: P. Clarck, *I'm renting a dog*, Bloomberg, 1.3.2017, available at: https://www.bloomberg.com/news/features/2017-03-01/i-m-renting-a-dog; I. Güttel, *Ein Huhn fur drei Monate, bitte,* n-tv.de 24.4.2016, available at: http://www.n-tv.de/panorama/Ein-Huhn-fuer-drei-Monate-bitte-article17531341.html; V. Elliott, *Wypożyczalnia psów,* The times/Onet.pl 13.5.2008, available at: http://wiadomosci.onet.pl/kiosk/wypozyczalnia-psow/13mhm (last visited: 24.8.2017).

that the stable provides a minimum of services. Thus, I would qualify this contract rather as the lease of a horse's stall, than as a safe-keeping contract described in Subchapters IV.1.2.4, IV.2.2.4 and IV.3.2.4 of this book. In this case, the object of the contract is not an animal (as in the other contracts described in this subchapter), but the space that is used (occupied) by an animal and leased for this purpose by its owner/keeper.[991] However, in order to qualify a contract consisting in keeping a horse in a stable as a lease contract and not a safe-keeping contract, the staff of the stable should not provide any additional services, like taking the horse into a paddock, taking care of the horse in the event of a deterioration in its health condition, etc.[992] Nevertheless, if the need for additional services arises after the conclusion of a lease contract, and would be rather infrequent, there are no obstacles to conclude additional service contracts with specific individuals from the staff of the stable (or outside of the stable) on meeting the needs of the horse's owner. The conclusion of a lease contract with reference to keeping the horse in a stable is much more likely in the case of what are known as outdoor stables, where the horses are left unattended for the most of the time, they are not fed by the stable staff (since they feed themselves on the grass from the paddocks, and are not undergoing regular training that would demand more solid food for a horse) and the space that is being leased to the horse's owner is a large paddock, usually with a wooden construction/an "open stable" where the horses can find shade and feel safe during the night, which is for the mutual use for all the horses kept on the paddock. However, this kind of contract is not described in more detail in the further parts of this chapter, since its construction does not show enough specific differences in reference to a general lease of any other immovable property (as its subject is space, i.e. part of an immovable property, and not an animal). A contract for keeping a horse in a stable with additional services provided for the horse's owner, which constitutes a more complicated type of contract and should – in my opinion – not be qualified as a typical lease contract, is described in Chapter IV of this book under the title "safe keeping contracts".[993]

As for a **loan for use contract**, the construction of this type of contracts may, at first glance, not seem very useful nowadays. This is unfortunate as the loan for use is a widely underestimated contract in practice, although its construction is very attractive when it concerns using someone else's animals. Namely, monetary payment is not always the only reward that the party loaning an animal can receive (as it is in case of lease contracts). Sometimes, knowledge about an

991 The German courts have already qualified a contract on keeping a horse in a stable as such in some cases, see: AG Essen, ruling from 31.8.2007 – 20 C 229/06; AG Menden, ruling from 26.2.2007 – 4 C 11/07.

992 See, with reference to German law: P. Rosbach, *Pferderecht*, pp. 111.

993 See: Subchapters IV.1.2.4, III.2.2.4 and IV.3.2.4 of this book.

animal's wellbeing is an accurate and sufficient award. Therefore, the construction of a loan for use contract is frequently used among foundations whose statutory aims are focused on taking care for animals.

The features of a loan contract presented in Subchapter V.2.3. of this book make this contract very attractive as a contract for passing a guide dog to a visually impaired person by a foundation training these kind of dogs under both Polish and German law. The existence of the Polish Executive Act of the Ministry for work and social politics of 1 April 2010 regulating matters of issuing certificates confirming the status of an assisting dog[994] indicates that using dogs as guides for visually impaired people is a common practice, thus theoretical foundations that would serve as the basis for the legal practice in the area of using and acquiring guide dogs by visually impaired people are needed.[995] Some of the foundations specialized in training dogs for visually impaired people transfer the ownership of the dog by concluding a donation agreement,[996] whereas other foundations let the dog be used on the basis of an agreement with the visually impaired person on the legal construction of a loan for use contract, retaining the ownership of the dog for the foundation.[997] It seems clear that the construction of a loan for use contract, and its social character, are perfectly adjusted to the statutory aim of the foundation's existence.[998] In addition, handing over a dog based on a loan for use agreement allows more control over the animal's health condition and wellbeing by the foundation, and makes the

994 The Polish executive act of the Ministry for Work and Social Politics of 1.4.2010 on issuing certificates confirming the status of a guide dog *[Rozporządzenie Ministra Pracy i Polityki Społecznej z 1.4.2010 r. w sprawie wydawania certyfikatów potwierdzających status psa asystującego]*, OJ 64, item 399. The executive act has been issued as a result of the Polish Act on *Occupational and Social Rehabilitation and Hiring Impaired Persons of 27.08.1997 [Ustawa z 27.8.1997 r.* o *rehabilitacji zawodowej* i *społecznej* oraz *zatrudnianiu osób niepełnosprawnych], J.L. 1997, No. 123, item 776.*

995 To learn more, see: J. Knapińska, K. Madej, *Niepełnosprawny z psem*, "Służba Pracownicza" 2010/11, pp. 33–35.

996 See, e.g.: § 4.7 of the rules of the Polish Foundation Vis Maior, stating that a dog passed to a visually impaired person free of charge becomes that person's property, see: the website of the foundation Vis Maior, available at: http://fundacjavismaior.pl/dzialania/psy-przewodniki/zostan-wlascicielem/ (last visited: 3.03.2017).

997 This is more often the case in the German practice, see e.g.: the website of a foundation for visually impaired people *Stiftung Schweizerische Schule für Blindenführhunde*, http://www.blindenhundeschule.ch/fuehrhunde/ein-fuehrhund-fuer-sie.html; website of a foundation for visually impaired people *Stiftung Ostschweizerische Blindenführhundeschule*, https://o-b-s.ch/programm/einfuehrungslehrgang/ (last visited: 31.01.2018).

998 With reference to the social and economic function of the loan for use contracts and a free of charge benefit based on a willingness to help another party to a contract with reference to Polish law, see: A. Kaźmierczyk, *Umowa*, pp. 19–21; J. Górecki, [in:] K. Osajda, *Kodeks cywilny. Komentarz. Tom IIIB*, pp. 674–675.

process of taking it back much easier if there are any concerns on the side of the foundation.[999]

It is worth mentioning that the dogs used for working with impaired people are usually purebred dogs, chosen as being the most intelligent and being born as a result of a very fine and selective process of breeding involving animals with the most stable and balanced character. After schooling, trainers taking care for training the dogs and buying selected whelps, the foundation still bears the cost of living of an animal and allowing the trainer to work with it, often by making numerous payments – by bearing the costs of educational fees and veterinarian doctor's remuneration. Thus, the dogs passed to impaired people by the foundations are often subjects with significant monetary value, which can be estimated around several thousand Euros. Therefore, I do not agree with the thesis that the loan for use contract is not very useful in the legal practice and its subject is solely for objects with a lower monetary value. It is very probable that diminishing the importance of a loan for use contract by the legal practitioners is the reason why the foundations training dogs for impaired people avoid naming the loan for use contract by its proper name. As a result, they often construct contracts where the *essentialia negotti* mostly corresponds with the construction of a loan for use contract, but they call it, for example, a "contract for handing over a dog". However, a person interpreting this contract in the event of a legal dispute between the parties should qualify the contract according to its content, i. e. as a loan for use contract.[1000]

Aside from the contract for use of someone else's things involving animals mentioned above, it is also possible to conclude a contract for the gratuitous use of an animal and the collection of its benefits. However, such contracts should be qualified as undefined under both legal systems (*umowy nienazwane, atypische Verträge*)[1001] and the provisions applicable respectively in this case are provisions concerning lease and tenancy. The applicability of other contracts for the use of someone else's things involving animals is marginal.

999 The early termination of a loan for use contract may occur in case where the party using an animal uses the animal improperly or passes it to a third person without being authorised to do so by its owner, or forced to do that circumstances. See: Article 716 KC and §§ 604 (2) – (4) BGB. See, under Polish law: A. Kaźmierczyk, *Umowa*, pp. 67–70 and under German law: M. Häublein [in:] H. Westermann (ed.), *Münchener Kommentar zum BGB, Vol. III*, München 2016, BGB § 604 side numbers 2–4, *BeckOnline (last visited: 12. 3. 2018)*. Compare, with reference to Polish law: W. Popiołek [in:] K. Pietrzykowski (ed.), *Kodeks cywilny*, Vol. II, p. 630. To read more on this topic, see: Subchapter V.3.2. ("Results of the improper performance of contracts with reference to loan contracts having animals as their subject") of this book.

1000 With reference to the interpretation of statements of intent under Polish law (but also applicable to German law), compare: Z. Radwański, *Wykładnia oświadczeń woli składanych indywidualnym adresatom*, Wrocław/Warszawa/Kraków, 1992, pp. 85–94.

1001 With reference to undefined contracts in Polish and German law, see: Subchapter IV.1.1.

1.2. Differentiation between lease contracts and tenancy contracts in reference to contracts having animals as their object

Under both the Polish and the German legal system, the purpose of both types of agreement: **tenancy and lease**, is to give a thing – in this case an animal – to be used for a definite or indefinite period of time, where the other party is obliged pay the agreed rent.[1002] However, in the case of a tenancy contract, in addition to the ability to use the animal, the tenant also has the right to collect the benefits from the animal. The meaning of this differentiation is significant only for natural benefits of the animal. Thus, neither the German nor the Polish lawmaker excludes the possibility to collect civil benefits as part of a lease contract. This means that the collection of civil benefits from a good is possible within both types of contracts – lease and the tenancy contract – under both legal systems: Polish and German, whereas the right to collect natural benefits of a good is possible only under the tenancy contract.[1003] Therefore, the decision as to which contract is concluded depends on the purpose for which the animal is given to the lessee or tenant. The similarities between these agreements also justify the fact that they are both regulated in the Polish and German Civil Codes.[1004] Namely, in the regulation of a tenancy contract, the lawmaker refers the reader to the provisions concerning lease contracts.[1005]

Both agreements: lease and tenancy, are causal and reciprocal agreements where the performance takes place for consideration.[1006] Nevertheless, the differentiation of both contracts in the Polish and German Civil Codes indicates that there are significant differences between them. Although it is clear that the most significant criterion in this case is the aim of the contract, there are a few

1002 With reference to Polish law, see: J. Jezioro [in:] E. Gniewek, P. Machnikowski (ed.), *Kodeks cywilny. Komentarz*, pp. 1336–1340, 1342–1343. With reference to German law, see: W. Weidenkaff [in:] O. Palandt, *Beck'sche Kurz-Kommentare: Palandt Bürgerliches Gesetzbuch mit Nebengesetzen*, München 2015, p. 760.

1003 See more: J. Panowicz-Lipska [in:] J. Panowicz-Lipska (ed.), *System Prawa Prywatnego*, Vol. 8, *Prawo zobowiązań – część szczegółowa*, Warszawa 2011, pp. 12–14; A. Lichorowicz, [in:] *System Prawa Prywatnego*, Vol. 8, pp. 183–184.

1004 Compare: Article 694 KC and § 581 (2) BGB.

1005 See also: Zaradkiewicz [in:] E. Gniewek, P. Machnikowski (ed.), *Kodeks cywilny. Komentarz*, pp. 559–561; V. Emmerich, B. Veit [in:] J. von Staudinger (ed.), *J. von Staudingers Kommentar zum Bürgerlichen Gesetzbuch: Staudinger BGB – Buch 2: Recht der Schuldverhältnisse*, Berlin 2005, Vorbem zu §§ 581.

1006 With reference to Polish law, see: J. Panowicz-Lipska [in:] *System Prawa Prywatnego*, Vol. 8, p. 10; A. Lichorowicz, [in:] *System Prawa Prywatnego*, Vol. 8, pp. 183; G. Kozieł, [in:] A. Kidyba (ed.), *Kodeks cywilny. Komentarz*, Vol. III, *Zobowiązania. Część szczególna*, Warszawa 2014, pp. 449; H. Ciepła [in:] J. Gudowski (ed.), *Kodeks cywilny. Komentarz. Zobowiązania*, Vol.IV pp. 880–883,958–959; with reference to German law, see: M. Gehrlein [in:] H. Bamberger, H. Roth, W. Hau, R. Poseck (eds.), *Beck'sche Online Kommentare, BeckOK, BGB*, 44. Ed., München 2017, BGB § 535 side number 135.

other differences between lease and tenancy contracts. The first of them is the subject of the contract. Whereas the subject of the lease are things (or – respectively – animals), the subject of tenancy agreements may also be rights (also substantive rights in reference to animals).[1007] However, it is important not to create the construction of separate catalogues of things that can be either the subject of lease or the subject of tenancy based on the nature of the good[1008] (as happens, for example, in the case of an improper naming of a lease agreement of a horse as a tenancy).[1009] Another difference between these two types of contracts consists in the manner of defining and paying rent. In reference to lease agreements, rent should be paid in advance,[1010] whereas with tenancy the rent is payable in arrears,[1011] though this issue does not have a direct impact on the subject of the contract.[1012] In the case of a lease contract, rent has to be defined in monetary means, or by defining the parties' provisions of a different nature, whereas with tenancy the rent may also be defined as a fractional part of the profits of the animal being the subject of the contract between the parties.[1013] Due to the similar construction of lease and tenancy contracts under Polish and German law, all the considerations mentioned above refer to both legal systems.

1007 See, with reference to Polish law: H. Ciepła [in:] J. Gudowski (ed.), *Kodeks cywilny,* Vol. IV, pp. 958–963; K. Pietrzykowski, [in:] K. Pietrzykowski (ed.), *Kodeks cywilny*, Vol. II, p. 463 and with reference to German law: J. Harke [in:] R. Schulze, H. Dörner, I. Ebert, T. Hoeren, R. Kemper, I. Saenger, K. Schreiber, H. Schulte-Nölke, A. Staudinger (eds.), *Bürgerliches Gesetzbuch. Handkommentar*, § 581 side number 5, *BeckOnline (last visited: 12.3.2018).*

1008 See, with reference to Polish law: A. Lichorowicz [in:] *System Prawa Prywatnego*, Vol. 8, pp. 183–184.

1009 In cases where an animal that does not bring any benefits is the subject of the tenancy contract, this contract should be considered as lease. Similarly: K. Zaradkiewicz [in:] K. Pietrzykowski (ed.), *Kodeks cywilny*, Vol. II, p. 535. See, with reference to German law: J. Harke [in:] R. Schulze, H. Dörner, I. Ebert, T. Hoeren, R. Kemper, I. Saenger, K. Schreiber, H. Schulte-Nölke, A. Staudinger (eds.), *Bürgerliches Gesetzbuch. Handkommentar*, § 581 side number 11, *BeckOnline (last visited: 12.3.2018).*

1010 See: Article 669 KC and § 556b (1) BGB.

1011 However, under German law, according to § 581 (2) BGB, the provisions covering lease contracts are respectively applicable to tenancy contracts, unless §§ 582–584b BGB sets out a different result. Thus, §§ 582–584b BGB do not include provisions referring to the terms of payment of rent, but § 587 BGB (referring to tenancy of land) does. Therefore, in the event that an object other than land is the object of the tenancy agreement, the rent is payable at the beginning of the time period (just as in case of a lease) and the specific regulations referring to the payment of rent at the end of the term – under German law – refer only to the tenancy of land. Compare: Article 699 KC § 587 BGB.

1012 See, with reference to Polish law: H. Ciepła, [in:] G. Bieniek, H. Ciepła, S. Dmowski, J. Gudowski, K. Kołakowski, M. Sychowicz, T. Wiśniewski, C. Żuławska, *Komentarz do Kodeksu cywilnego. Księga trzecia. Zobowiązania*, Vol. 2, Warszawa 2011, pp. 448.

1013 With reference to Polish law, see: H. Ciepła, [in:] G. Bieniek, H. Ciepła, S. Dmowski, J. Gudowski, K. Kołakowski, M. Sychowicz, T. Wiśniewski, C. Żuławska, *Komentarz*, pp. 377, 436. With reference to German law, see: W. Weidenkaff [in:] O. Palandt, *Beck'sche Kurz-Kommentare: Palandt Bürgerliches Gesetzbuch mit Nebengesetzen*, pp. 833–834.

These differences are especially important when differentiating lease and tenancy agreements with an animal as its subject. Firstly – generally under both the Polish and German legal systems, the tenant has many more duties in reference to the subject of the contract, i. e. the animal. Thus, in accordance with Article 696 KC and (indirectly) with §§ 582, 582a BGB, he is obliged to make use of his contractual rights in accordance with the rules of proper management,[1014] whereas the lessee is only obliged to use the animal as the subject of a lease agreement in accordance with its purpose. The meaning of these duties and the differences between them will be described in the next subchapter referring to the performance of contractual duties in lease and tenancy contracts having an animal as their subject.

As already mentioned, when defining whether the contract at hand is a tenancy or lease, most important under both legal systems is the aim of the contract, i. e. how the animal is going to be used.[1015] With reference to lease, the Polish literature often points to an animal as a possible subject of performance of one of the contracting parties,[1016] whereas with reference to tenancy contracts, animals usually can be found in the form of a livestock connected with agricultural land (which is often the subject of a tenancy agreement).[1017] Differently, under German law, the wording of regulations covering tenancy contract is used mostly with reference to farms[1018] and areas of land,[1019] which is expressly indicated by the respective provisions of BGB. However, there are no doubts that an animal may be a single subject of a contract under both the Polish and German legal systems – lease as well as tenancy. Therefore, if an animal bringing natural benefits by its nature is left solely for use, then this animal constitutes the subject of a lease contract. In this case, the natural profits collected by the lessee are rather side effects of a lease contract, not its main aim (e. g. manure produced by

1014 The Polish literature points to the duty to make repairs necessary to keep the subject of tenancy in a non-deteriorated state, see e. g.: K. Zaradkiewicz [in:] K. Pietrzykowski (ed.), *Kodeks cywilny*, Vol. II, p. 546; J. Górecki, G. Matusik [in:] K. Osajda, *Kodeks cywilny. Komentarz. Tom IIIA*, pp. 606–609; compare, the attitude of the German literature: C. Wagner [in:] H. Bamberger, H. Roth, W. Hau, R. Poseck (eds.), *Beck'sche Online Kommentare, BeckOK, BGB*, 44. Ed., München 2017, BGB § 582 side number 9, *BeckOnline (last visited: 12. 3. 2018)*.

1015 With reference to Polish law, see: M. Goettel, *Sytuacja zwierzęcia w prawie cywilnym*, pp. 157.

1016 With reference to Polish law, see e. g.: J. Panowicz-Lipska [in:] *System Prawa Prywatnego*, Vol. 8, p 13. With reference to German law, see: C. Kern, *Pachtrecht. Das gesamte Pachtrecht mit Nebengebieten*, Berlin, 2012, pp. 466–495.

1017 With reference to Polish law, but without regard to any national legal system, see: See, e. g. A. Lichorowicz [in:] *System Prawa Prywatnego*, Vol. 8, pp. 191–192.

1018 See: e. g. the wording of §§ 582–583 BGB.

1019 §§ 585–597 BGB.

a leisure horse).[1020] It is also worth mentioning that in the case of a lease contract, it is possible to collect benefits by subleasing an animal. Thus, there are no obstacles to subleasing a leisure horse during the time when the lessee is not able to use it. What is important is the aim of the contract, i. e. whether the contract has been concluded typically for economic purposes, or solely in order to use an animal for hobbyist purposes (e. g. using dogs for social purposes, but also, for example, for their use in sled dog racing; using horses for leisure riding) or for medical purposes (using dogs as dog guides for people with vision loss; using horses for equine-assisted therapy).[1021]

Observation of the Polish practice shows that in the equine context, the nomenclature of a tenancy contract is overused. Most contracts involving the use of a horse by riding it against paying rent are lease contracts, not tenancy. Tenancy occurs most frequently with reference to farm animals used for economic purposes, like tenancy of dairy cattle; tenancy of hens, which lay eggs to be sold; tenancy of any kind of animals for breeding purposes.[1022] The problem of confusion between lease and tenancy contracts does not occur in the German practice, probably due to its rich literature in the field of horse sports law[1023] and horse sport tradition.[1024] However, in most cases it is still a lease, even if the tenant uses the horse to collect benefits, e. g. where a horse is used by a horse-riding instructor, who teaches people how to ride a horse with the use of this horse in exchange for monetary benefits. The same situation occurs where a husky dog, being owned by a private person, constitutes the subject of a tenancy contract whereby the tenant uses it on particular days to make up a dog team for a sled dog racing for monetary gain (like taking children for a ride against remuneration). However, according to some representatives of the doctrine, in

1020 With reference to Polish law, see: M. Goettel, *Sytuacja zwierzęcia w prawie cywilnym*, pp. 158.

1021 With reference to Polish law, see: M. Goettel, *Sytuacja zwierzęcia w prawie cywilnym*, pp. 157–158. With reference to German law, see: W. Weidenkaff [in:] O. Palandt, *Beck'sche Kurz-Kommentare: Palandt Bürgerliches Gesetzbuch mit Nebengesetzen*, pp. 760.

1022 With reference to tenancy of a herd under Polish law, see e. g.: K. Zaradkiewicz [in:] K. Pietrzykowski (ed.), *Kodeks cywilny*, Vol. II, pp. 537.

1023 Compare, e. g.: P. Rosbach, *Pferderecht*; J. Wertenbruch, *Die Besonderheiten…*, p. 2065–2144; J. Eichelberger, M. Zentner, *Tiere im Kaufrecht*, JuS 2009, p. 2012; J. Adolphsen, *Tierkauf* [in:] B. Dauner-Lieb, W. Langen, *BGB Schuldrecht. Nomos Kommentar*, pp. 1969–1992; H. Müller, *Gewährleistung beim Tierkauf* [in:] L. Aderhold, B. Grunewald, D. Kingberg, W. Paefgen (ed.), *Festschrift für Harm Peter Westermann zum 70. Geburtstag*, pp. 517–534.

1024 See: press reports referring to the facts and numbers describing the scope of horse sports in Germany: A. Sten-Ziemons, DW 20. 7. 2013, available at: http://www.dw.com/de/deutschland-einig-pferdeland/a-16911941; Deutsche Reiterliche Vereinigung, *Zahlen und Fakten (2016)*, available atL https://www.pferd-aktuell.de/fn-service/zahlen-fakten/zahlen-fakten (last visited: 13. 3. 2018).

these cases animals bring benefits based on a legal relationship and therefore should be qualified as tenancy contracts.[1025] Nevertheless, an animal in such a situation is rather treated as a tool, not as an object, which generates profits (such a situation could exist, for example, in a case where the lessor leaves the horse to his neighbor in order to plough his land).

Still, an issue worth consideration is the tenancy of an animal for sporting purposes. Under both the Polish and German legal systems, the key element in this scenario is again the answer to the question whether the animal brings benefits to the tenant. However, this all depends on a single case, namely whether and how often the rider wins competitions granting him monetary benefits. In the case of horse-riding, taking part in such competitions is usually very expensive and the prizes are granted to only a few competitors. What is more, in the worldwide horse sports practice, the competitors that win prizes are usually professional riders, who rarely ride on rented horses. Therefore, in reference to both Polish and German legal systems, the intent of the parties when concluding the contract is very important in order to define whether the animal is the subject of a tenancy or a lease contract.[1026] The parties should also agree on a certain manner of calculating the income that the animal is bringing to a tenant or to the owner. Thus, this issue may also be very important for defining the type of contract. Taking all the issues mentioned above into account, I represent the opinion that an animal being used for sport purposes, if nothing else has been agreed between the parties, is rather the subject of a lease contract, not a tenancy.[1027]

2. Performance of contracts for the use of someone else's things having an animal as their object

2.1. Performance of lease contracts and tenancy contracts in reference to contracts having animals as their subject

When determining which contract the parties intend to conclude – lease or tenancy – it is important to consider the contractual duties connected with each of those types of contracts. Thus, as already mentioned, it is significant that the lessee is only obliged to use an animal as the subject of a lease agreement in

1025 See: M. Goettel, *Sytuacja zwierzęcia w prawie cywilnym*, p. 158.

1026 The consequences of qualifying a contract as tenancy or lease are connected with the burden of proof and liability in case of the deterioration in health or death of an animal. This problem will be described further in Subchapter 3.

1027 Similarly, with reference to Polish law: M. Goettel, *Sytuacja zwierzęcia w prawie cywilnym*, p. 159.

accordance with its purpose (Article 662 KC, §§ 541, 543 BGB)[1028] whereas the tenant must maintain the inventory of animals in good condition and replace it to an extent that complies with the rules of proper management (Article 696 KC and § 582 a BGB).[1029] This means that – under both the Polish and German Civil Codes, the tenant should also strive to improve the animal's health condition,[1030] for example by providing better quality forage in order to increase the chances of winning competitions, animal exhibitions etc., but also in order to increase the amount of milk given by a cow.[1031] In comparison to these duties, the lessee is solely obliged to take care of routine treatments connected with the animal's current needs, like feeding, grooming, medicating minor scratches, vaccinations, veterinary check-ups, etc. Although services generating additional costs, such as the costs of a trainer or the services of a blacksmith may also arise in reference to the lessee – these costs are to be paid only in accordance with the lessee's own needs.[1032] As the duties of a lessee and a tenant are different, the duty to return expenditures also applies to a different extent in reference to expenditures made by a lessee and made by a tenant. Thus, a tenant may not ask for the return of costs of ongoing medications or medical operations of an animal if they are essential in order to keep the animal in a non-deteriorated health condition[1033] (taking into account that these actions were not the result of already existent "defects" in the animal's health; in this case, the provisions refer to the restitution for expenses incurred by the tenant as immediate actions needed to remove a defect so that it does not lead to animal's death). Thus, the right to

1028 Whereas Article 662 KC establishes it explicitly, §§ 541 and 543 BGB indicate it indirectly. See also, with reference to German law: W. Weidenkaff [in:] O. Palandt, *Beck'sche Kurz-Kommentare: Palandt Bürgerliches Gesetzbuch mit Nebengesetzen*, München 2015, p. 766. With reference to Polish law, see: K. Pietrzykowski [in:] K. Pietrzykowski (ed.), *Kodeks cywilny*, pp. 471–472.

1029 See also, with reference to Polish law: K. Zaradkiewicz [in:] K. Pietrzykowski (ed.), *Kodeks cywilny*, Vol. II, p. 546 and with reference to German law: J. Harke [in:] R. Schulze, H. Dörner, I. Ebert, T. Hoeren, R. Kemper, I. Saenger, K. Schreiber, H. Schulte-Nölke, A. Staudinger (eds.), *Bürgerliches Gesetzbuch. Handkommentar* I. Ebert, A. Schleuch [in:] R. Schulze, H. Dörner, I. Ebert, T. Hoeren, R. Kemper, I. Saenger, K. Schreiber, H. Schulte-Nölke, A. Staudinger (eds.), *Bürgerliches Gesetzbuch. Handkommentar*, § 582a side numbers 1–13, *BeckOnline*; A. Teichman [in:] R. Stürner (ed.), *Jauernig, Kommentar zum BGB*, München 2015, Anmerkungen zu den §§ 582–583a, side numbers 1–5, *BeckOnline (last visited: 12.3.2018).*

1030 Similarly: K. Zaradkiewicz [in:] K. Pietrzykowski (ed.), *Kodeks cywilny*, Vol. II, pp. 546; compare, with reference to German law: D. Schuhmacher [in:] M. Düsing, J. Martinez, *Beck'scher Kurzkommentare*, München 2016, BGB § 582a, side numbers 14–15, *Beck-Online (last visited: 12.3.2018).*

1031 See, with reference to Polish law: M. Goettel, *Sytuacja zwierzęcia w prawie cywilnym*, pp. 160.

1032 *Idem.*

1033 Compare under Polish law: A. Lichorowicz, [in:] *System Prawa Prywatnego*, Vol. 8, pp. 226–228.

receive the return of expenditures applies to a much broader extent where it concerns lease contracts. This issue is very important for the lease or tenancy of animals, which – as living creatures – often suffer due to various health problems requiring veterinary intervention and often impossible to predict.

In addition to lease or tenancy contracts concerning the using of animals (regardless of whether it concerns a lease contract on using a horse for sport purposes or a tenancy contract consisting in earning money by giving riding lessons with the help of the horse; or whether it concerns lease contracts consisting in an elderly woman using a dog for purely social purposes, or tenancy contracts consisting in using cows for increased monetary gains),[1034] it is also worth mentioning that animals used for mass entertainment may also constitute the subject of lease or tenancy agreements. Whereas wild animals may only be kept by specialized institutions under the surveillance of the state administration of each European Member State[1035] and they can only be used after a public administration body has granted consent, and under the surveillance of a veterinary doctor,[1036] the use of privately-owned animals is increasingly common. Such relations, under both Polish and German law, usually consist in using animals for entertainment purposes in the form of a tenancy contract. So animals used in commercial movies are usually animals that have already been filmed before – or at least properly trained by the owner for such purposes. A movie producer may decide to conclude a service contract with a specialized animal trainer using his own animals trained for "acting" purposes, in which case it is the trainer who actually provides the services, and his animals serve solely as a form of stage prop.[1037] However, if the movie producer is experienced in filming animals for entertainment purposes, and/or has appropriate staff trained in working with animals and experienced with working in a certain team, he may simply rent an animal selected from among those offered in tenancy offers by the owners and work with it in accordance with his own experience, and with help from specialized animal trainers chosen by him. In this case, the contract that is concluded between the owner of the animal and the movie producer should, in my opinion, be qualified as a tenancy contract. Thus, given that the animal is left at the movie producer's disposal and serves as a tool to earn

1034 All the examples of lease and tenancy contracts given in this sentence are described further in this chapter in a more detailed way.

1035 See: Article 17 and Article 18 of Polish Animal Protection Act from 21.8.1997. With reference to provisions allowing for keeping wild animals in EU, see: M. Lubelska-Sazanów, *The Wild Differences in Law when Trading in Wild Animals: a US and EU Perspective*, American Journal of Trade and Policy 2018, [S.l.], Vol. 4, No. 3, pp. 87–96, available at: https://journals.abc.us.org/index.php/ajtp/article/view/1040 (last visited: 1.3.2018).

1036 *Idem.*

1037 In this case, see: Subchapter IV of this book, concerning service contracts involving animals.

money by filming that particular movie – the animal's owner typically receives remuneration. As already explained in Subchapter V.1.2. of this book, the most significant criterion in this case is the aim of the contract, therefore a contract consisting in using an animal for strictly economic purposes (choosing the most visibly attractive and easily trained animal to minimize hours spent on filming and maximizing the profit from the movie) should be qualified as a tenancy contract with all the legal consequences.[1038] However, the conclusion of a tenancy contract consisting in using an animal for filming purposes raises many ethical and legal questions. Whereas it is nowadays indisputable (worldwide) that the animals do not have their own copyrights (especially the right to the protection of its own image),[1039] the idea of treating an animal as a movable good being owned by a human and treated as his property and, therefore seeing an animal as being eligible to be used in commercial movies in accordance with human needs does also not seem accurate nowadays.[1040]

These remarks lead to different questions, indirectly connected with the subject of this subchapter, namely whether it is legally allowed to use the image of somebody else's animals without the owner's consent. There are no legal provisions that would forbid this activity –under German or Polish law. However, such activity could eventually lead to unlawful acts under Polish and German law, if the animal owner would be able to prove that he suffered any damage caused by an unlawful course of events. Thus, such actions could, theoretically, be avoided solely by the institution set out in Article 415 KC and § 823 (1) BGB, pointing to the entitlement to receive damages as a result of damage caused by a photographer's actions. This could be the case where a professionally trained animal bringing benefits to its owner by using it in commercial shows or movies, would be used for somebody's else's (the photographer's or his principal's) benefit.[1041] The animal's owner could claim the re-

1038 See: Subchapter V.1.2. of this book.

1039 See: the case of the monkey who accidently took a "selfie" (whereas the qualification of whether the process of taking a picture was an accident has been disputed by animal protection organisations), where the US court stated the monkey does not own the rights to this picture, and Polish article referring to that case: M. Suchorabski, Gazeta Prawna 9.8.2014, https://serwisy.gazetaprawna.pl/prawo-autorskie/artykuly/815016,malpa-zrobila-sobie-zdjecie-kto-ma-prawa-autorskie-do-fotografii.html (last visited: 30.10.2019).

1040 See: Juliet Iacona, *Behind closed curtains: the Exploitation of animals in the film industry,* Journal of animal & natural resource law XII/2016, pp. 25–51.

1041 Compare: The opinion of other lawyers in this matters, e.g.: Agnieszka Cwajna, *Możliwości wykorzystania prawa do wizerunku zwierząt w świetle prawa polskiego,* Equista 25.2.2016, available at: https://equista.pl/editorial/1120/prawo-mozliwosci-wykorzystania-wizerunku-zwierzat-w-swietle-prawa-polskiego; Bartosz Grykowski, *Fotografowanie zwierząt,* W todze i bez togi 8.12.2001, available at: https://bartoszgrykowski.wordpress.com/2011/12/08/fotografowanie-zwierzat/; (last visited: 20.3.2018). The authors also point out the possibility to base a claim on competition law (by qualifying the

imbursement of the damage (i.e. *damnum emergens* and *lucrum cessans*) that has been caused due to the loss of profits for its animal used for commercial purposes for somebody else. In this case, prerogatives for the liability based on Article 415 KC and § 823 (1) BGB (as liability *ex delicto*) would be: the factual existence of the damage, the unlawful and faulty action of the photographer/filmmaker and a causal link between them.[1042]

Another issue worth considering is the problem of unnecessary enhancements under Polish and German law in case, where animal is the subject of lease or tenancy. Thus, according to Article 676 KC and §539 BGB, the owner may keep any enhancements made by a lessee or a tenant against the reimbursement of costs at the end of the contract.[1043] Although there are legal measures allowing for the removal of enhancements in both German and Polish Civil Codes (though the regulations set out slight differences),[1044] in most cases of enhancements made to animals the removal is impossible. Therefore, the only issue is whether the lessee/tenant is entitled to demand any reimbursement at the end of the contract. Enhancements with reference to animals are usually expenditures made in order to improve its health or productivity and – in my opinion – the lessee/tenant demanding the reimbursement would go against the rules of common sense. However, there is no regulation in reference to the situation where the owner has agreed to this enhancement, and therefore it is in the tenant's or the lessee's best interests to ensure there is a comprehensive agreement covering the settlement of any such potential expenditures.[1045]

A legal construction that is not a general rule in the law of obligations in either country, and therefore establishes a specific institution in reference to lease and tenancy, is regulated in Article 674 KC and § 542 BGB. These provisions set out the possibility to prolong a contract after the lease or tenancy is finished. This means that the legal relationship is prolonged, not started again as a new legal relation. This construction is especially advantageous in reference to animals, as

photographer's actions as an act of unfair competition), whereas such cases are difficult to find with reference to lease or tenancy contracts involving animals. Although the authors refer to Polish law, their considerations are universal also with reference to other European legal systems.

1042 See: F. Förster [in:] H. Bamberger, H. Roth, W. Hau, R. Poseck (eds.), *Beck'sche Online Kommentare, BeckOK, BGB*, 45. Ed., München 2017, BGB § 823, side-numbers 1–94.

1043 With reference to Polish law, see: K. Pietrzykowski [in:] K. Pietrzykowski (ed.), *Kodeks cywilny*, Vol. II, p. 487; with reference to German law, see: W. Weidenkaff [in:] O. Palandt, *Beck'sche Kurz-Kommentare: Palandt Bürgerliches Gesetzbuch mit Nebengesetzen*, München 2015, pp. 797–798.

1044 According to Article 676 KC, it is the right of the owner of a good (or respectively an animal) to demand the return to the previous condition of the good, whereas according to §539 BGB it is a lessee or a tenant who is entitled to remove the enhancement.

1045 Similarly, with reference to Polish law: A. Lichorowicz [in:] *System Prawa Prywatnego*, Vol. 8, p. 230.

the manner of taking care for them is usually already agreed between the parties and does not have to be discussed again – which would cause logistic problems with how to treat them before a new agreement is reached. It is also very useful especially in cases where the lease/tenancy contract has expired and the horse is still being used by the lessee/tenant and is still kept in a stable under a form of safe-keeping contract.[1046] Thus, under both the Polish and German legal systems, the owner of a stables does not have to make any efforts to contact the owner of a horse who has not been around for a while (since he was not using the horse), but if he observes that the previous lessee/tenant is still using the horse, he is entitled to expect him to pay remuneration for safe-keeping the horse used by him in the stables.[1047] One should also bear in mind that under both the Polish and German legal systems, in the case of a lease or tenancy, it is the tenant and the lessee who are liable for any damages and injuries caused by an animal.[1048]

The qualification as to whether the contract at hand is a lease or a tenancy takes on very significant meaning where an animal is the object of a contractual obligation as they are living creatures that are liable to suffer various health problems that require veterinary intervention and are sometimes impossible to predict. The fact that an animal is the object of a contractual obligation influences significantly the content of lease and tenancy contracts by raising the standards of its performance. This may be observed not only in the extent of the lessee's or tenant's contractual duties (due to the need to feed, walk or groom an animal, etc.), but also in the problem of reimbursement for the lessee's or tenant's enhancements. Thus, under both the German and Polish Civil Codes, removing an enhancement is mostly impossible in reference to animals, since enhancements in reference to animals are usually expenditures made in order to improve its health conditions or productivity. Therefore, demanding the reimbursement by the tenant or the lessee would often run contrary to the rules of common sense, which changes the situation of the parties to the lease or tenancy contract diametrically in comparison to a situation where a regular good is the object of their contractual obligation.

1046 See: Subchapters IV.1.2.3, IV.2.3., IV.3.3. referring to safe-keeping contracts.

1047 With reference to an implied unspoken extension of the lease contract, see: J. Jezioro [in:] E. Gniewek, P. Machnikowski (ed.), *Kodeks cywilny. Komentarz*, pp. 1312–1313.

1048 See also, with reference to German law, but applicable to Polish law as well: P. Rosbach, *Pferderecht*, pp. 127–130. Nevertheless, the issue of liability for damages and injuries caused by an animal shows significant differences in its construction under Polish and German law, which – due to its broad scope – are not presented herein in detail.

2.2. Performance of undefined/atypical contracts having the use of animals as their subject

The most popular atypical contract is the contract setting out the **mutual use** of the same horse by at least two people, where one of them is the owner. The aim of this contract, named for the purpose of this work as **horse-sharing**, is to meet the needs of both parties: the person who wants to independently[1049] ride the same horse on a recurring (cyclical) basis (the user), and the owner of the animal, who wants to save money or time by making the horse available to another (trusted) person according to a specific time plan agreed between the parties.[1050] The German literature also recognizes the possibility of several people using a horse, where the horse is their common property, as well as several people using a horse where the horse has a different owner who does not use it.[1051] Although the use of a horse in the form of a civil partnership agreement[1052] is legally possible under both the Polish and German legal systems, this type of contract is not applicable to animals in practice.[1053]

In the case of a "horse-sharing" agreement, the main duty of the horse's owner is to make the horse available to the user as agreed in the contract, whereas the main duty of the user is to ride and take care for the horse in accordance with the contract. As the idea of horse-sharing is to find a trusted person to ride on a certain horse and to spare the horse owner's time on one hand, and for the user to make a bond with one particular horse on the other hand, it is clear that the duties of the user encompass more than simply riding the horse. Thus, this particular relationship between the horse and rider is always connected with grooming the horse before and after the ride, preparing it properly for the ride and checking its health condition before and after the ride. It is also clear that the user of a horse – by agreeing to use it in accordance with the owner's instructions

---

1049 Whereas it is also possible to agree that the party using somebody else's horse will ride this horse under supervision of a certain trainer, or that this party may also train, e. g. dressage or jumping, on this horse with any trainer he finds suitable for this purpose.

1050 See also, with reference to German law, where these contracts are more often the subject of doctrinal considerations than in Polish law, see: M. Schneider, *Die Reitbeteiligung – Was man als Pferdebesitzer und Reiter zu Vertrag, Haftung und Versicherung wissen sollte!*, available at: http://www.mps-pferderecht.de/die-reitbeteiligung-was-man-als-pferde besitzer-und-reiter-zu-vertrag-haftung-und-versicherung-wissen-sollte.htm (last visited: 29. 1. 2018).

1051 Compare: E. Fellmer, P. Kiel, *Rechtskunde…*, pp. 149.

1052 See: Article 860 KC and § 705 BGB.

1053 At least with reference to the use of horses or pets. However, it is much more reasonable to apply this institution to farm animals that constitute part of a venture. See e. g. with reference to a large area of tenancy law applicable to the use of cows, namely the German and EU provisions referring to the milk contingent: C. Kern, *Pachtrecht. Das gesamte pachtrecht mit Nebengebieten*, pp. 466–495.

– also agrees to observe the rules governing use of the stables where the horse resides.

Under both the Polish and German legal systems, the right (which at the same time constitutes a duty) to ride a horse on particular days also entails ensuring the horse has the necessary daily exercise in case the user is not able to ride the horse on that day, e.g. by lungeing it, by taking the horse to the paddock (if allowed by the horse's owner) or by organizing another person to ride it on that day (exceptionally and only if agreed with the horse's owner). However, defining exactly what the user's duties are in connection with taking care for the horse is important for the issue of its liability for any damage caused by the horse. Thus, sharing a horse may be defined as riding it against remuneration or gratuitously.

The parties should also agree on what kind of equipment should be used for the horse.[1054] In the event that the user of the horse uses the horse owner's equipment (which usually entails expensive leather products), he is automatically obliged to take care of it (e.g. wash it after each use and use specialized liquids for preserving leather products) and is liable for any damage to it caused by his fault or by negligence. The same level of liability applies in reference to any potential injuries to the horse. Thus, accidents may always happen when working with horses, and the risk that the user of the horse or the horse is injured should not rely on the other party to the contract.[1055]

A side duty that is gaining significant importance in reference to this particular type of contract is the **duty to cooperate with the other party.** Thus, it is crucial for the successful performance of the contract to stick to the plan agreed upon when concluding the contract, and to ride the horse as scheduled. However, crucially in atypical, undefined contracts like sharing a horse – the parties have to define their duties very carefully, as there are no legal regulations that could be applicable in the case at hand. In accordance with the contractual duties to which the parties agree in their contract, the provisions referring to lease or loan for use may be applied respectively – depending on whether the horse is used gratuitously or against remuneration.[1056] Thus, the main difference between lease

1054 See, with reference to the German law: E. Fellmer, P. Kiel, *Rechtskunde…*, pp. 151–152.

1055 Compare: *idem*, pp. 152–153.

1056 With reference to the respective applicability of provisions covering various types of "undefined" contracts (*umowy nienazwane, atypische Verträgen*), according to the distribution contract (as an undefined contract under Polish law), to which the provisions covering agency contracts are applicable respectively, see: footnote No. 6. Compare also: SN, ruling from 28.10.1999 – II CKN 530/98, with an approving gloss of Ewa Rott-Pietrzyk, OSP 2000, No. 7–8, item C 118, pp. 393–396. This mechanism may also be used in reference to various contracts. Compare also, with reference to the respective applicability of the legal provisions: J. Nowacki, *Analogia legis*, p. 141. Compare also the examples shown in the publication: M. Lubelska-Sazanów, *Odpowiedzialność z tytułu rękojmi za wady fizyczne zwierząt*, Transformacje Prawa Prywatnego 4/2015, pp. 21–41; M. Lubelska-Saza-

contracts and loan for use contracts consists in the remuneration agreed for the usage of an animal, or the lack of any remuneration (i. e. under both the Polish and German legal systems, a loan for use contract implies the gratuitous usage of an animal).

As a detailed description of contractual duties in the contract is important in particular for the liability issues of the parties, it is advisable to the parties to conclude the contract in writing. As horse-sharing is not defined in the Civil Codes of Poland and Germany, a precise description of contractual duties and a well-prepared timetable agreed between the parties to the contract is key to the long-lasting co-operation between the parties and the well-being of the horse being its subject.[1057] The institution of confirming the conclusion of the contract may also be a solution in this case. Under Polish law, this issue in covered by Article 77^1 KC, though only in reference to B2B contracts. Differently, under German law, it is always (thus, not only between businesses) possible to confirm a contract that was deemed void due to the lack of formal requirements for its conclusion (§ 141 BGB).

Another atypical/mixed contract based on the idea of **co-ownership** (though **co-possessing** would probably be a better expression in this case) is the contract commonly concluded between a breeder of an animal that is exceptionally "promising" with reference to its future achievements at dog shows in its category, and its care-taker/possessor. In reference to the general features of such a contract, without reference to any particular legal system, the animal (usually a dog, though other types of animals may also be the subject of this contract) can either be co-owned by its breeder and its caretaker, with the reservation that it will be fully owned by its actual caretaker after giving birth a certain number of times, or it can be still owned by the breeder, whereas its caretaker keeps him at his place and in possession with the same reservation (that in the future the ownership of the dog will be passed to him). The main idea is to pass the animal to its caretaker – who might become the owner in the future – while the breeder keeps the right to control the animal's living conditions, show him at shows (or advise its caretaker how and where to do it), choose the breeding partners and – finally – has ownership rights to the animal's whelps. The caretaker/possessor is obliged to take care of the animal and its future whelps in accordance with the instructions given by the breeder, and to leave the animal available for shows/ breeding purposes on the dates given by the breeder. He also covers the animal's

---

nów, *The meaning of service contracts with reference to animals under German and Polish law* [in:] P. Pinior (ed.), *Evolution of private law – new approaches*, pp. 121–130.

1057 See also: M. Schneider in the article *Die Reitbeteiligung – Was man als Pferdebesitzer und Reiter zu Vertrag, Haftung und Versicherung wissen sollte!*, see: http://www.mps-pferderecht.de/die-reitbeteiligung-was-man-als-pferdebesitzer-und-reiter-zu-vertrag-haftung-und-versicherung-wissen-sollte.htm (last visited: 29. 1. 2016).

costs of living (though the potential costs of veterinary doctors may be shared, or the parties may agree on a different participation in costs). Although the breeder maintains most decision-making power as well as control over the life and fate of the animal, the parties may negotiate the conditions of the contract and not only adjust the dates of the shows/sexual intercourses of the animal, but also give more decisions to the caretaker. Such a contract brings a lot of incentives for both parties to the contract – whereas the incentives of the breeder are countable and easily visible, the incentives of the caretaker and future owner of the animal (in the case of female animals, the caretaker usually receives ownership over it after a certain number of births, whereas in the case of male animals it is possible that: either the animal will always be co-owned, or the breeder will retain the right to use it for breeding purposes throughout its life) are also significant. Namely, he can take possession of one of most promising purebred dogs/cats in the breed, and enjoy not only its company, but also the joy of having its little puppies around without being worried about their future fate (i.e. time-consuming talking with potential buyers, taking care for the good name of the breed and its recognition, worrying that the puppies will not find new homes and will live the rest of their lives at the cost of the caretaker etc.). Nevertheless, it is undoubtedly a contract that can only be concluded between people with a compassion for purebred animals and raising them. This contract – as with the other contracts presented in this subchapter – is also not defined under Polish or German law.

The contract consisting in keeping breeding rights of an animal by its owner and possessing it by its caretaker, depending on the provisions of a contract in each case, is either a contract based on the institution of co-ownership (in which case, under both the Polish and German legal systems, the provisions referring to sale contracts apply respectively, meaning that it is an undefined contract under both legal systems, and the caretaker/second person has acquired partial ownership rights to this animal), or its provisions make it more similar to a lease or loan for use contract (in which case the provisions referring to one of these contracts apply respectively).

However, the German practice[1058] and jurisprudence[1059] recognizes also a contract called "***Mietzucht***", which can be translated as "**lease for breeding**

1058 See e.g.: the website of a newfoundland breeder: http://www.neufieve.de/Frames/Eve/Welpen.htm; point 2.2 of the Regulation of the German Dalmatiner Breeding Club, available at: http://www.cdf-dalmatinerverein.de/dokumente/Zuchtordnung_Stand_2014.pdf (last visited: 24.8.2017); website of the Australian Cattle Dog Breeding Club in Germany: http://www.acdcd.de/images/pdf/Mietzuchtantrag.pdf (last visited: 24.8.2017).

1059 LG Fulda, ruling from 18.09.1992 – Az.: 1 S 108/92 (note that the case comes from before the amendment of the German Civil Code of 2002, though this does not have a significant

purposes" (a breeder sells a whelp on the reservation that this animal will be leased to the breeder for breeding purposes). The conclusion of such a contract usually occurs as a result of a process similar to a sale-and-lease-back process recognized in economic sciences.[1060]

This was also the situation in the case ruled by the German court in 1992, which considered the sale of a dog with the reservation that this dog will be left to the seller for use in horse-show performances and breeding purposes. The seller reserved the right to repurchase the dog in the event that it is not left for his usage for these purposes, or is not cared for properly (which was necessary for the dog's participation in the horse-shows mentioned before). The court described this contract as a sale-and-lease-back process. Whereas the lack of proper care over the animal was not proven, the court acknowledged the fact that the dog had not been left for the seller's purposes as agreed in the contract. Therefore, the court acknowledged the seller's right to buy the dog back. Although it is an old case, it is still appropriate and – due to the lack of any legal definition of lease for breeding purposes in either the Polish or the German Civil Code – also applicable to similar facts of the case under Polish law.[1061] This construction, consisting in passing possession and an obligation to take care over of an animal to another person while keeping some of the breeder's rights to the animal – although seems to be a legally complicated process – is a better solution than other undefined/atypical contracts described in this subchapter. Thus, co-ownership (especially between two unrelated people with different aims concerning the animal) always raises concerns due to the likelihood that it will lead to disputes between co-owners, and will cause problems with the performance of the contract. On the other hand, the construction of a mixed contract based on the gratuitous acquisition of a purebred animal (similar to a donation contract) or an allowance for keeping the breeder's dog as it was one's own (similar to a loan for use contract), but against the possessor's obligation to lease this animal to its breeder at the same time (similar to a lease contract) raises many problems of a legal nature. Namely, such a contract would have to be concluded in writing, in a very detailed and careful manner. However, it can always happen that situations not foreseen by the parties will occur. In such an event, the need to adjust provisions referring to other civil law contracts so that they could be applied respectively would cause too many legal problems and ambiguities. Therefore, the German idea of *Mietzuchtvertrag*, consisting in buying an animal on advantageous conditions against a reservation to lease it later to its previous owner

impact on the described facts of the case and legal constructions considered in these matters).

1060 See: LG Fulda, ruling from 18.09.1992 – Az.: 1 S 108/92.

1061 Compare: Ruling of the European Court of Justice of 26.3.2009, C-348/07, several times referred to in Chapters III and IV.

(breeder) seems to be a better solution. It clearly shows who the possessor is and who the owner is in which time periods and in which situations. In addition, it easily points to the civil law provisions that should be applied accordingly. Therefore, I believe that the Polish breeders – although rarely concluding the contracts described in this subchapter – should move away from the co-ownership idea[1062] and turn rather to a role model of a contract that would be based on the same principles as the German *Mietzuchtvertrag*. Under both the Polish and German legal systems, it is an undefined contract and the parties can decide how they describe their contractual obligations. The only reason why the Polish legal system does not recognize this kind of contract is due to the inexperience of dealing with such matters by the doctrine and jurisprudence, which, in turn, means that it does not get used in practice. Given the experience of the German courts and the method that is employed in the mentioned book *Limits of Harmonization and Convergence. Dissimilarities in Similarities of Polish and German Contract Law*, the knowledge about the German interpretation and application may also be useful with reference to obligations having an animal as their object from the German legal practice and jurisprudence. However, taking advantage from the experience of German jurisprudence always has to occur very carefully, since even similar facts of the case may always lead to different rulings.

From looking at the contracts presented in this subchapter, it is clear that the fact that an animal is an object of contractual performance, changes the standards of the parties' contractual performance so deeply that it is necessary to create new kinds of contracts in order to express these changes. Thus, this subchapter refers to undefined contracts that cannot be qualified as any of the contracts mentioned in the Polish and German Civil Codes, but were created by the practice answering the needs of the market. Although some of the contracts presented in this subchapter are still only recognized in German market practice, they are all considered to be undefined contracts. Therefore, the construction and usability of the contracts may be transferred directly to the Polish reality. Nevertheless, it is worth considering where the border is for the reasonable use of animals aimed at a symbiosis of human wealth and animal well-being, and where the borders of morality lie. Thus, contracts consisting in the co-ownership of an animal, or in the fact that the owner takes possession over an animal for just a few moments in order to inseminate it or show it at a show, may indeed serve the wealth of the human, but definitely not the well-being of the animal.

1062 Which can be found in practice in some breeds in Poland, see e. g. the website of a the breed "Z Peronówki": https://www.zperonowki.com/site/pl/node/582 (last visited: 24.8.2017).

2.3. Performance of loan for use contracts in reference to contracts having animals as their object

The loan for use contract, although it is not a common subject of doctrinal considerations under Polish or German law, it is a contract that is concluded by animal owners more often than contracts having other things as their subject. Some Polish authors claim that loan for use contracts – even those where the subjects are animals – gain importance solely between family members or friends,[1063] and its subject are usually things of lower value.[1064] I believe that the gratuitous nature of loan for use contracts is very useful in contracts concerning animals, where ensuring the wellbeing of an animal is often the most important issue for its owner. Therefore, the social function of loan for use contracts may have a wide scope of application with reference to contracts having animals as their object, which the authors claiming that the importance of loan for use contracts may be observed mainly between family members or friends did not consider.

Under Polish law, in order to determine the scope of the obligor's liability in the event of the improper performance of a loan for use contract, it is important to define whether this is a unilaterally or bilaterally obliging agreement. Whereas the German doctrine recognizes this contract as gratuitous without further consideration,[1065] under Polish law the qualification of a contract as unilaterally or bilaterally obliging is dependent on which criteria are taken into account. What is more, these considerations under Polish law have a different meaning in reference to contracts having an animal as their object, due to the greater number of duties arising from the obligation to take care of an animal. Thus, borrowing an animal may not be gratuitous in the event that the possessor has to undertake actions to provide this animal appropriate health and living conditions. Therefore, under Polish law, the first issue that should be considered is whether there is a duty to provide a set obligation or a duty to undertake any action that would justify qualifying the contract as bilaterally obliging.[1066] For

1063 See, with reference to Polish law: M. Goettel, *Sytuacja zwierzęcia w prawie cywilnym*, p 162.

1064 See, with reference to Polish law: M. Orlicki, Z. Radwański [in:] *System Prawa Prywatnego*, Vol. 8, p 259; alternatively: A. Kaźmierczyk, *Umowa użyczenia w polskim prawie cywilnym*, Warszawa 2008, p. 21; and also J. Górecki [in:] K. Osajda, *Kodeks cywilny. Komentarz. Tom IIIB*, pp. 674–675, who points at the increasing importance of loan for use contracts.

1065 Compare: W. Weidenkaff [in:] O. Palandt, *Beck'sche Kurz-Kommentare: Palandt Bürgerliches Gesetzbuch mit Nebengesetzen*, p. 911.

1066 See: M. Orlicki, Z. Radwański [in:] *System Prawa Prywatnego*, Vol. 8, pp. 257–258. However, most of the representatives of the Polish doctrine qualify a loan contract as a unilaterally obliging agreement., see e.g.: W. Popiołek [in:] K. Pietrzykowski (ed.), *Kodeks*

example, if a dog owner leaves a dog for few hours, or even days, in the house of a different family by its request, for example in order to check for an allergic reaction from one of the family members, or for the pleasure of children living there while the lender is travelling, it is difficult to define which of the parties to this loan for use contract benefits more. Of course, the parties could also consider concluding a safe-keeping contract, though this decision would be combined with more formalities and legal consequences for the parties, especially connected with the liability of the party taking care of the dog while the owner is absent. Nevertheless, in the example at hand, the informal nature of a contract, the fact that it is gratuitous and the motives of the parties indicate that their intention was rather to conclude a loan for use contract. The same arguments justify the conclusion of a loan for use contract in a situation where a party leaves a horse for the use of another party, so that the other party may ride it or use it on a farm. Thus, what is important in this case are the motives of the parties concluding the contract, and these simple examples show that there are many situations where concluding an informal and gratuitous loan for use contract may bring many benefits to animal owners. It is undisputable that both parties benefit and perform an obligation at the same time in the case illustrated by the example presenting a dog to an allergic child. One of the parties agrees to leave the dog for the use of another party, and the other party agrees to take care of it. Therefore, if the criteria chosen for the qualification of a contract as bilaterally obliging entail the duty to undertake any actions, the loan for use contract is definitely a contract that obliges both parties. Namely, all contracts having an animal as their object are combined with the duty to take care of this animal. This duty, in the case of a loan for use contract, is derived from Article 713 KC and § 601 (1) BGB, which point to the need to cover the costs of keeping the borrowed good in a non-deteriorated state by the borrower.[1067] Whereas the Polish Civil Code barely mentions animals,[1068] the German Civil Code does it definitely more often, e.g. in § 601 (1) BGB, where the lawmaker underlines that

cywilny, Vol. II, pp. 624–625; J. Górecki [in:] K. Osajda, *Kodeks cywilny. Komentarz. Tom IIIB*, pp. 676. Differently: A. Ohanowicz, J. Górski, *Zarys prawa zobowiązań*, Warszawa 1970, p. 82; A. Kaźmierczyk, *Umowa*, p. 15.

1067 See e.g.: A. Kaźmierczyk, *Umowa*, pp. 111; Z. Gawlik [in:] A. Kidyba (ed.), *Kodeks cywilny. Komentarz*, Vol. III, pp. 680–681;. J. Gudowski [in:] J. Gudowski (ed.), *Kodeks cywilny*, Vol. IV, pp. 1029–1030. See also: SN, ruling from 20.1.2010 – III CZP 125/09, OSNC 2010, No 7–8, item 108 and articles referring to this ruling: P. Drapała, *Glosa do uchwały SN z dnia 20 stycznia 2010 r., III CZP 125/09*, PiP 2012, Issue 2, p. 121; E. Lewandowska, *Glosa do uchwały SN z dnia 20 stycznia 2010 r., III CZP 125/09*, Studia Prawnoustrojowe 2012, Issue 17, p. 119, Z. Strus, *Przegląd orzecznictwa*, Palestra 2010, Issue 3, p. 233.

1068 The Polish Civil Code includes only one-off provisions of a more general nature, referring briefly to animals, whereas these provisions are not meant to serve the well-being of animals, see: Article 182 (but with reference to bees, which are not covered by the scope of this book), 424, 431, 432, 4491, 846.

in the case of **a gratuitous loan of an animal**, the borrower has to cover the costs of feeding it without limitation.[1069] This situation shows that the German legal system is much more open to the existence of animals as subjects of civil law agreements, and is facing challenges created by the legal practice. Among the Polish Civil Code provisions, the obligation to feed an animal without limitation could be derived from the content of Article 354 KC, referring to the obligor's duty to perform his obligation in accordance with its contents and in a manner complying with its socioeconomic purpose and the principles of community life, and if there are established customs in that respect, also in a manner complying with those customs. Thus – although not directly mentioned in the Polish Civil Code – in both legal systems the duty to take care of an animal constitutes an inseparable element of a contract foreseeing the use of an animal by another party, the extent of this duty depends on the type of contract that is concluded between the parties.[1070] Still, I believe that mentioning the obligation to feed an animal without limitation *expressis verbis* in Article 354 KC would underline the differences between animals and other goods constituting regular objects of obligations, and could serve its well-being. Thus, additionally underlining the different scope of duties arising in the case where an animal is an object of the obligation is also an important psychological factor to change the legal status of animals under the Polish legal system.

In reference to contracts having the use of an animal owned by somebody else as the object of their contractual obligation, the fact that the contractual obligation concerns a living creature, is very significant. Animals, as specific objects of contractual obligations, change so much in the construction of codexal contracts, such as lease, tenancy and loan for use, that it was necessary for the market practice to create numerous different undefined contracts expressing its needs. The possession over an animal changes the most in the case of loan for use contracts. Thus, it is impossible to talk about a gratuitous loan when borrowing an animal. The loan of an animal is never gratuitous due to the several duties connected with taking care for an animal, which its possessor undertakes. What is more, possession over an animal raises the possessor's risk due to all the possible health problems that the animal may suffer and due to the risk of the death of the animal. Therefore, the standard of keeping the animal in a non-deteriorated state, the need to make quick decisions concerning medical interventions and to make necessary enhancements in order to keep it healthy make contracts having the use of an animal owned by somebody else as the object of

1069 See: the content of § 601 (1) BGB.

1070 See: M. Lubelska-Sazanów, *Zwierzę jako przedmiot świadczenia w umowach o używanie rzeczy* [in:] M. Pazdan, M. Jagielska, E. Rott-Pietrzyk, M. Szpunar (eds.), *Rozprawy z prawa prywatnego: księga jubileuszowa dedykowana Profesorowi Wojciechowi Popiołkowi*, Warszawa 2017, pp. 728–739.

their contractual obligation quite unique and not adjustable to standards approved for the performance of any other kinds of contracts.

3. Results of the improper performance of contracts aimed at the transfer of property of things with reference to contracts having an animal as their object

3.1. Results of the improper performance of contracts in reference to lease and tenancy contracts having animals as their object

The most important issue in reference to tenancy and lease is **liability for defects.**[1071] Thus, the institution of warranty applies under both the Polish and German legal systems with reference to both of these contracts, although the warranty rights of the lessor are obviously different to that of a sale contract.[1072] If the rented/leased animal turns out to have defects,[1073] the owner's primary duty is to remove the defect. However, this is usually not possible in reference to animals as, if the defect concerns the character of an animal, it cannot be suddenly changed, and if the defect concerns health issues, its removal usually entails medication or treatment undertaken by a veterinary doctor. Both of these manners of removing animals' defects need time for the effect to be visible and – therefore – in most cases it results in the animal being of limited suitability for the agreed use.

In this case, the provisions of Article 664 KC, as well as Article 536 BGB, provide that the owner has to immediately undertake actions aimed at removing the defect, and that until the defect has been removed, the lessee/tenant may demand that the rent be reduced accordingly. It happens very often that the lessee or the tenant bonds with the animal that he is taking care of and does not have anything against still taking care for it during the time of a medication (or a different process aimed at the removal of the defect), as long as the remuneration for the lease/tenancy is reduced. However, the lessee's/tenant's possibility to claim for a reduction in the agreed payment for lease/tenancy does not apply if he was already aware of the defect when concluding the contract (therefore, the parties should explicitly agree that the rent is to be reduced, or waived entirely if

1071 Comprehensively with reference to an animal's defects: M. Lubelska-Sazanów, *Odpowiedzialność*, pp. 21–42.

1072 With reference to warranty rights concerning the sale contract, see: Subchapter III.3.2.2. of this book.

1073 With reference to the classification of defects in contracts involving animals, see: Subchapter III.3.2.1. of this book.

a defect is already visible when concluding the contract and affects the use of the animal).[1074]

Under Polish law, if the defect preventing the use of an animal is not removed by the lessor in an "adequate" period of time, or if it cannot be removed at all, then according to Article 664 KC, the lessee/tenant may terminate the contract with immediate effect, i. e. without abiding by the legally set termination notice periods. Before the defect is removed, he is not obliged to pay the rent and may demand the reimbursement of any rent paid in advance.[1075] Of course, whether to terminate the contract or not is the lessee's/tenant's choice, since it is also likely that he would still want to keep the animal for usage, despite its defects. Thus, this is very likely to happen if the bond between him and the animal is more important than the economic gains, therefore is rather applicable in reference to lease than to tenancy contracts. In this case, the parties are free to establish a lower rent payment, or even change the contract into loan for use.

Under German law, the warranty rights of the lessee/tenant entitle him not only to reduce the rent according to § 536 BGB, but also to receive damages according to §536a BGB. The legal measure to terminate the contract without needing to give the other party any additional period of time to cure the defect according to §543 BGB may be undertaken, assuming that the lessee/tenant has already informed the lessor about the defect and it was not removed,[1076] whereas this issue is regulated outside the provisions referring to warranty rights. Under Polish law there is a similar provision, but it is included in Article 664 § 2 KC, i. e. among the warranty rights, which seems to constitute a significant difference between the two legal systems. Thus, under both the Polish and German legal systems, the liability for defects based on warranty rights is independent from the fault of the lessor and his knowledge about the defects. For this liability to arise, it is not necessary to inform the lessor about the defects, as this liability has an objective character. The only important question to answer in order for this liability to arise is whether these defects limit or prevent the agreed usage of an animal. However, this can only be effective with reference to defects that cannot be removed by the lessor (e. g. the horse being absolutely unfit to be ridden by a rider due to its permanent and incurable health condition that was not known by the lessee/tenant before the conclusion of the contract and which already existed before that), thus – even though the warranty for defects has an independent and

1074 Article 664 § 3 KC, § 536b BGB.

1075 With reference to Polish law, see: A. Lichorowicz, [in:] *System Prawa Prywatnego*, Vol. 8, pp. 205–206.

1076 With reference to German law on the content and the effect of § 543 BGB, see: A. Willingmann [in:] K. Tonner, A. Willingmann, M. Tabb (eds.), *Vertragsrecht*, Köln 2010, pp. 941–942; V. Gahn [in:] M. Schmid, A. Harz, *Fachanwaltskommentar. Mietrecht*, Köln, 2012, pp. 349–364.

objective nature – in the case of a removable defect, it is logical that the lessor has to be informed about the defect in order to be able to remove it.[1077]

On the other hand, the termination of a contract based on § 543 BGB should be understood as a termination due to an important reason, not as a warranty right. Thus, in order to be entitled to use this right to terminate a contract, the fault of the other party is not needed, but can be taken into account – that is because the prerequisite to make this termination right effective is an important reason justifying it, and not an independent fact where the defect exists or not.[1078] Therefore, with reference to animal defects in lease and tenancy contracts, it is possible under German law that an animal will present a defect that is not serious enough to make an important reason to terminate a contract, but that defect will allow the lessee/tenant to demand a reduction in the rent. Alternatively, under Polish law, the mere existence of a defect, even if it does not make the use of an animal impossible (thus is not obviously qualified as an important reason to terminate the contract), makes it possible to exercise independent warranty rights.

As far as it concerns **damages**, there are no specific provisions in the Polish Civil Code included in the regulation of lease and tenancy contracts allowing for the payment of damages, whereas the German Civil Code provides this in § 536a BGB. The claim for damages could be based on general provisions referring to contracts in the Polish Civil Code, but they are not a part of the warranty regime under Polish law (as they are under German law, although the provisions referring to damages are also included independently in the general provisions referring to contracts).

The most problematic issue in reference to animals as the objects of lease and tenancy contracts is qualifying the animal's condition as a defect or not. Thus, once the defect is already recognized, it should also be defined whether it is a defect limiting the animal's usability for the agreed use and for collecting its benefits, or a defect making the use and collection of the animal's benefits impossible. Therefore, the legal possibility of terminating the contract in the case of a defect solely limiting the usage of an animal is acceptable in the case of a lease contract,[1079] but disputable in the case of a tenancy contract.[1080]

1077 Compare, with reference to Polish law; SO w Bydgoszczy, ruling from 23.10.2013 – VIII Ga 13/13. See also: J. Jezioro [in:] E. Gniewek, P. Machnikowski (ed.), *Kodeks cywilny. Komentarz*, p. 1302.

1078 See, with reference to German law: A. Willingmann [in:] K. Tonner, A. Willingmann, M. Tabb (eds.), *Vertragsrecht*, p. 941.

1079 See, with reference to Polish law: J. Jezioro [in:] E. Gniewek, P. Machnikowski (eds.), *Kodeks cywilny. Komentarz*, pp. 1302.

1080 Most of the representatives of the Polish doctrine deny this right on the side of the tenant, see e.g.: K. Zaradkiewicz, [in:] K. Pietrzykowski (ed.), *Kodeks cywilny*, Vol. II, pp. 558–559; A. Lichorowicz, [in:] *System Prawa Prywatnego*, Vol. 8, pp. 205–206; G. Kozieł, [in:]

Nevertheless, there are also defects that can easily be removed by the animal's owner. Examples of this would include, for example, 'unrideability' (there is a German term for this condition: *der Unreitbarkeit,* which might be translated into Polish as *niezdatność do jazdy*) of a horse, which occurs as an effect of the horse's inactivity for the few previous days and makes riding a usually calm horse dangerous for an inexperienced lessee/tenant.

The problem of unrideability was the subject of a German case under case reference 9 S 10/05,[1081] which – although it concerned the purchase of a horse – may be relevant in this case due to the type of defect with reference to the horse. Thus, in the case at hand, the buyer made use of his warranty rights claiming the unrideability of the horse. The Court confirmed that the existence of such a defect may result in the need to return the horse against the reimbursement of the purchase price due to the inability to remove the defect. In order to counteract the exercise of the warranty rights by the buyer, the seller was obliged to prove that the horse was unable to ride already at the time when it passed to the buyer. The Court justified its decision by the fact that this defect consisted in the horse's nature, and therefore could not be removed. The judicial decision of the German case at hand is also transferrable to Polish conditions. Thus, the qualification of physical defects occurs on the same basis under both Polish and German law.

However, the unrideability in the case of a horse that is used by another person might be curable in some cases. Thus, sometimes a horse that has been ridden for a long time (sometimes even years) by only one person – its owner or another lessee/tenant – shows unexpected reactions to a change of rider. In such cases, the owner may often remove the defect by riding a horse and taking care of it in the way that he – as the owner of this animal – knows will make him emotionally stable and calm again. Nevertheless, the unrideability of a horse may occur for many reasons[1082] (such as the general character of a horse or a pain in the back, which needs time and medication to pass) and in most cases the solution is not as easy as in the last example.

In the case of the lease or tenancy of an animal, neither the lessee nor the tenant bears the risk of *casus mixtus* in the event of the risk of an accident to an animal. Such additional liability occurs under both the Polish and German legal

A. Kidyba (ed.), *Kodeks cywilny. Komentarz*, Vol. III, p. 449. A. Lichorowicz indicates, however, that there previously used to be different opinion with reference to this issue: J. Krzyżanowski, [in:] *Kodeks cywilny, Komentarz*, Vol. II, 1972, p. 1456; A. Lichorowicz, [in:] *System Prawa Prywatnego*, Vol. 8, p. 205. The German doctrine does not underline such a differentiation, see e.g. W. Weidenkaff [in:] O. Palandt, *Beck'sche Kurz-Kommentare: Palandt Bürgerliches Gesetzbuch mit Nebengesetzen*, München 2015, pp. 894–900.

1081 LG Göttingen, ruling from 17.10.2005–9 S 10/05.

1082 Compare, with reference to German law, but applicable to Polish law as well: P. Rosbach, *Pferderecht*, pp. 257.

systems in reference to a loan for use contract as a courtesy relationship,[1083] thus there is no need for such regulation in reciprocal agreements like tenancy or lease. In this case, the lessor's liability is based solely on the principle of fault.

Another important issue is the liability for any damages or injuries that the leased animal may cause to its lessee or tenant. Thus, the lessee/tenant is the user of an animal in the meaning of Article 431 KC and § 834 BGB, which makes him responsible for its actions. Therefore, the owner of an animal cannot be held responsible for any damage caused by an animal when the lessee/tenant was using it (e.g. injuries caused to another dog or person by a dog who was under the supervision of a lessee/tenant, especially if he did not hold him on a leash; injuries caused to the lessor when falling off a leased horse, etc.)[1084] It is important to mention that, according to the jurisprudence of the Polish Supreme Court,[1085] a horse that is being used for riding is always to be understood as a "tool" in the hands of a human, thus the rider's liability should always be based on the liability *ex delicto* and the principle of fault of Article 415 KC and § 823 (1) BGB. Therefore, the liability for damage that has been caused by a horse that has been used by the lessee/tenant should be based on Article 431 KC and § 834 BGB respectively, which means that the lessor cannot be held liable for such damage. However, in a situation when an animal causes damage by itself, especially if it has shown some behavioral improprieties that were not reported by the lessor, then the lessor may obviously be held liable for the damage.

3.2. Results of the improper performance of contracts in reference to loan for use contracts having animals as their subject

As briefly mentioned in the previous subchapter (V.3.1.), the construction **of a loan for use** contract makes the process of taking the animal back from its possessor much easier than it would be in the case of concluding any other kind of contract. However, the possibility to terminate the contract under Polish law is more favorable for the lender (i.e. also for the foundations, which often use this kind of contract to transfer possession over an animal) than under German law. Both legal solutions are presented below one after the other.

According to Article 716 KC, an earlier termination of a loan for use contract is possible in cases where the party using an animal treats the animal improperly, or passes it to a third person without being authorized to do that by the other

1083 See: Subchapter IV.3.2. of this book "Results of the improper performance of contracts in reference to loan for use contracts having animals as their subject".

1084 See, with reference to German law, but applicable to Polish law as well: P. Rosbach, *Pferderecht*, pp. 127–130.

1085 See: SN, ruling from 7.4.2004, IV CK 231/03.

party, or forced to do that by circumstances. The right of the owner causing the early termination of a contract should be qualified as a sanction for the improper performance of the contract by the borrower. It is typical that the parties define how the animal can be used, and how it should be taken care of, but if they do not include such provisions in their agreement, then according to Article 712 KC, the animal should be used in a manner corresponding to its characteristics and purpose.[1086] It is underlined in the Polish literature that such behavior on the side of the party using an animal is understood as breach of a duty to care,[1087] which gains even more importance in reference in case of contracts having animals as their subject. Although the regulation of a lease contract under Polish law allows also for the earlier termination of a contract in case where the party using an animal treats the animal improperly or acts negligently when taking for it, the regulation of Article 667 § 2 KC referring to a lease contract does not allow such quick actions as Article 712 KC allows for in reference to loan for use contracts.[1088] Thus, in the case of a lease contract, the mistreatment of an animal has to occur at least twice, or the negligence in reference to the duty of care has to be strong enough that it threatens the health or life of an animal. Nevertheless, the standards applied to evaluate compliance with the duty to care should always be higher in reference to contracts involving animals, no matter whether it is a lease contract or a loan for use contract.

The possibility to terminate the contract with immediate effect is regulated differently in German law, where the German Civil Code does not contain a provision corresponding with Article 716 KC. Nevertheless, the possibility to terminate the contract earlier than provided previously in the parties' agreement can be deduced from the content of § 603 BGB. Although, according to Schreiber[1089] – unlike under Polish law – the person allowing for the usage of an animal is obliged to instruct the borrower not to mistreat an animal before terminating the contract (since the provisions concerning lease are applicable also to loan for use contracts in this matter – according to German literature[1090]), thus this legal measure has different consequences in German law, making it less favorable for the party allowing for the usage of an animal (e.g. foundations, which would prefer to have the possibility of taking the animal back as soon as

1086 See, with reference to Polish law: A. Kaźmierczyk, *Umowa*, p. 186.

1087 However, note that in this case the breach of duty is understood as the improper performance of the contract. W. Popiołek [in:] K. Pietrzykowski (ed.), *Kodeks cywilny*, Vol. II, p. 630; J. Gołaczyński [in:] E. Gniewek, P. Machnikowski (eds.), *Kodeks cywilny. Komentarz*, p. 1422; J. Górecki [in:] K. Osajda (ed.), *Kodeks cywilny. Komentarz. Tom IIIB*, pp. 683–685.

1088 See, with reference to Polish law: A. Kaźmierczyk, *Umowa…*, p. 187.

1089 A. Schreiber [in:] K. Tonner, A. Willingmann, M. Tabb (eds.), *Vertragsrecht*, p. 1146.

1090 *Idem*, compare also: A. Schreiber [in:] K. Tonner, A. Willingmann, M. Tabb (eds.), *Vertragsrecht*, p. 1148.

possible in the event of its mistreatment by the borrower). Nevertheless, the party leaving the animal for usage is also entitled to damages according to German law (as well as under Polish law, this right is based on the general provisions referring to contractual relationships).[1091]

Thus, the Polish legal system (unlike the German legal system) makes the loan for use contract more attractive for foundations allowing for the use of the animals trained by them. Namely, under Polish law, in the case of any other contract, the foundation would only be left with the possibility to counteract the mistreatment of the animal with the use of public law measures. Namely, Article 7 of Polish Animal Protection Act sets out the possibility to take the animal away from its owner on the grounds of a decision of the executive administration of the city/county (*Wójt/Burmistrz/Prezydent Miasta*), which can be issued as a result of the motion of a police officer, veterinarian doctor or a member of a non-profit organization whose statutory interest is based on the protection of animals.[1092]

In particular, the possibility of the earlier termination of a loan for use contract proves that it is a very useful legal construction in reference to legal relationships involving animals – at least under Polish law. The construction of a loan for use contract in the Polish legal system strengthens the position of a foundation as a party allowing the use of an animal, and gives the confidence that, even in case of any financial problems on the side of the foundation, it is the party that can collect the dog back easily. This allows the organization to at least check the health condition of a dog before passing it to another impaired person.

A very important difference between a loan for use contract and a lease contract can also be observed in the fact that in the case of a lease contract, the person acquiring the rented animal automatically steps into the legal position of the lessor.[1093] This regulation cannot be used for loan for use agreements *per analogiam.*[1094] Therefore, the organization allowing for the use of an animal can be sure that the animal should be returned to their hands regardless of the legal status of an animal, which can change over time due to the actions of the user and third parties, which the organization has no influence over. The same applies in the German legal system, where claims against the owner of an animal (in case

1091 With reference to German law, see: A. Schreiber [in:] K. Tonner, A. Willingmann, M. Tabb (eds.), *Vertragsrecht*, p. 1147. Under Polish law, the right to damages could be based on the general provisions of Article 471 KC, compare: J. Gołaczyński [in:] E. Gniewek, P. Machnikowski (eds.), *Kodeks cywilny. Komentarz*, pp. 1378.

1092 See: the legal measures allowing for temporary or permanently take away of an animal from its owner regulated in Article 7.1 of the Polish Animal Protection Act from 21.8.1997.

1093 See: Article 678 KC.

1094 See, with reference to Polish law: A. Kaźmierczyk, *Umowa…*, p. 39.

the person or entity giving the animal for use is not the owner) can be based on § 604 BGB.[1095]

However, it is worth recalling that loan for use contracts are not only used by foundations whose statutory aim is to train dogs for helping visually impaired people. It is also a courtesy relationship that occurs very often when taking care of animals being possessed (not necessary owned, since ownership of an animal on the side of a party leaving an animal for usage is not a necessary condition for concluding a loan for use contract[1096]) by friends, family members or other horse riders in the stable. However, in the event of an accident, deterioration in the animal's health or death, there is usually no more place for courtesy. At these moments, the legal provisions of the civil codes concerning liability for the deterioration or death of animal are especially important, since the loan for use contract is rarely concluded in writing.

In reference to a loan for use contract, the party leaving the animal to be used is also liable for any defects in the animal, though to a very limited extent. Thus, the institution of warranty is very limited with reference to courtesy-based relationships, as can be observed from the wording of Article 711 KC[1097] and § 600 BGB.[1098] The party allowing for the use of an animal in its possession is solely liable for defects (legal as well as factual) in that it may be obliged to pay damages incurred as a result of not informing the user of an animal about its defects – assuming that he was aware about these defects. This situation may occur, for example, when leaving a puppy at a friend's place for a weekend, and not making the person taking care for the dog aware that it should not be left alone in the apartment because it is very likely to cause damage to furniture/ shoes/etc. The same situation occurs in the case of leaving one's horse under a friend's supervision allowing him/her to use it and ride it, while not telling him/ her about certain dangerous habits of the horse, e. g. connected with reactions to certain objects (such as a violent reaction to using a crop) or actions (like mounting the horse). The same applies to other animals, like dogs (e. g. fear of the leash, dangerous reaction to a raised hand, etc.). This liability is not based on

1095 See, with reference to German law: A. Schreiber [in:] K. Tonner, A. Willingmann, M. Tabb (eds.), *Vertragsrecht*, p. 1148.

1096 See, with reference to Polish law: W. Popiołek [in:] K. Pietrzykowski (ed.), *Kodeks cywilny. Komentarz. Article 450–1088. Vol II*, Warszawa 2015, pp. 624; J. Górecki [in:] K. Osajda (ed.), *Kodeks cywilny. Komentarz. Tom IIIB*, , pp.681–683; J. Gołaczyński [in:] E. Gniewek, P. Machnikowski (ed.), *Kodeks cywilny. Komentarz*, p. 1376.

1097 Popiołek [in:] K. Pietrzykowski (ed.), *Kodeks cywilny*, Vol. II, pp. 626–627; J. Gołaczyński [in:] E. Gniewek, P. Machnikowski (eds.), *Kodeks cywilny. Komentarz*, p. 1419; J. Górecki [in:] K. Osajda (ed.), *Kodeks cywilny. Komentarz. Tom IIIB*, pp. 681–683.

1098 W. Weidenkaff [in:] O. Palandt, *Beck'sche Kurz-Kommentare: Palandt Bürgerliches Gesetzbuch mit Nebengesetzen*, München 2015, p. 911.

a warranty regime, but on the general rules of contractual liability[1099] and therefore on the principle of guilt (not on the principle of risk, as is the case with reference to the warranty liability, according to most representatives of the Polish doctrine).[1100] Certainly worth stressing here is that this liability is strictly dependent on the awareness of the party leaving an animal about the defect (and the unawareness of the other party, i. e. the party leaving an animal for use is not liable if the defect was easily visible).[1101]

Another issue that is gaining increased significance with reference to animals as subjects of loan for use contracts are the consequences of its possible health damage or death (which differentiates animals as living creatures from things). This problem arises in reference to Article 714 KC and § 605 BGB. According to Article 714 KC, the borrower is liable for the damage to or loss of the subject of a loan for use contract – thus, for the accidental death or damage of an animal. However, this liability arises only if he uses the animal in a manner contrary to the contract, or contrary to the nature or purpose of the animal, and secondly if, without authorization under the contract, or being forced by circumstances, he entrusts somebody else with the animal, and the animal would not have been lost or damaged if he had used it in an appropriate manner or had kept it himself.[1102] § 605 BGB defines the same situations (damage or loss of the subject of a loan for use contract – thus, an accidental death or damage of an animal) as grounds justifying the termination of the contract by the lender, however adds also a third situation to these reasons, namely the death of the borrower.[1103] This kind of liability is described in the literature as *casus mixtus* and can be described as a damage caused by a situation that would not have happened if the borrower had performed his duties properly (except of the situation of his death under BGB).[1104] It is usually difficult for the person leaving the animal for someone else's use to base a claim on Article 714 KC, since he is the one who bears the burden of proof in this case. The same applies in German law – thus it is the party

1099 See, with reference to Polish law: J. Górecki [in:] K. Osajda (ed.), *Kodeks cywilny. Komentarz. Tom IIIA*, pp. 681–683.

1100 See, with reference to Polish law: M. Podrecka, *Rękojmia za wady prawne rzeczy sprzedanej*, pp. 24; A. Brzozowski [in:] K. Pietrzykowski (ed.), *Kodeks cywilny. Komentarz. Article 450–1088. Vol II*, Warszawa 2013, p. 244.

1101 See, with reference to Polish law: J. Górecki [in:] K. Osajda (ed.), *Kodeks cywilny. Komentarz. Tom IIIA*, Warszawa, 2013, pp. 1450–1451.

1102 See: Article 714 KC.

1103 Compare: Remarks on the template of a contract of participation in horse-sharing (*Reitbeteiligungsvertrag*), A. Partikel, *Formularbuch für Sportverträge*, München 2015, pp. 237–238.

1104 See, with reference to Polish law: W. Popiołek [in:] K. Pietrzykowski (ed.), *Kodeks cywilny. Komentarz. Article 450–1088. Vol II*, Warszawa 2015, p. 629.

leaving the animal for usage, who has to prove that he is entitled to terminate the contract.[1105]

On the other hand, Article 718 KC and §§ 603 and 604 BGB refer to a situation where the loan for use contract expires due to objective circumstances and the borrower is obliged to return the animal in a non-deteriorated state, with the reservation that he is not liable for any deterioration being a natural consequence of the proper usage of the animal. Such deteriorations should be understood as medically predicted consequences of previous injuries that make the animal's movements increasingly difficult over time, as well as any health conditions connected with aging. However, the biggest risk connected with the usage of animals is the fact that they are not immortal and the time of their death can never be predicted and may come suddenly (whereas a deterioration in a movable good leading to it becoming no longer useful is a process that can be observed for a while, and the process of deterioration can usually be withheld if the right reaction occurs in good time). Thus, if an animal dies within the time period of a loan for use contract, the answer to the question, whether its death could have been avoided or not is always connected with serious legal consequences. In such a situation, each case has to be examined separately and must be followed by an autopsy and an official opinion of a veterinary doctor (whereas in the case of doubts leading to a legal dispute, each party may insist on having an opinion from a different, independent veterinary doctor). Thus, the possibility that the death could have been avoided when treating the animal with due care can never be excluded. The fact that the party leaving the animal for use cannot refuse to take the animal back – even in a deteriorated condition and even if this condition is a result of the borrower's negligence[1106] – raises more legal consequences in the case of animals than in the case of movables. Whereas a deteriorated thing may be simply left unused for a while, keeping an animal generates additional costs all the time – even if it cannot be used by its possessor. These costs not only involve feeding an animal (and – in the case of horses – also paying for its stall, which is often very expensive), but for any costs of medical treatment. Although the situation seems to be simpler in case of pets like dogs or cats, the medication of larger animals like horses, is often connected with its expensive transportation to a veterinary clinic specializing in a certain field of medicine. If the horse has been used in sports, the person who left it for usage is very likely to claim damages for a loss of profits as well. Therefore, it is very

1105 See, with reference to German law: A. Schreiber [in:] K. Tonner, A. Willingmann, M. Tabb (eds.), *Vertragsrecht*, p. 1148.

1106 See, with reference to Polish law: W. Popiołek [in:] K. Pietrzykowski (ed.), *Kodeks cywilny. Komentarz. Article 450–1088. Vol II*, Warszawa 2015, p. 631, and with reference to German law: A. Schreiber [in:] K. Tonner, A. Willingmann, M. Tabb (eds.), *Vertragsrecht*, pp. 1147–1148.

important to establish whether the death of an animal is accidental (in which case the responsibility of the borrower is based on *casus mixtus*, thus he still has the burden of proof) or occurred as a result of the borrower's negligence, i. e. lack of proper care for the animal, or its mistreatment.

VI. Final remarks

1. Conclusions in reference to the legal status of animals

The position of animals in the national legal system of Poland (with comparison to national legal system of Germany) and in the system of EU legal acts, as well as the proposal as to how the situation of animals might be changed, has been briefly presented in the first chapter of this book, followed with ethical foundations of this reasoning proposed by S. Stucki.[1107] After presenting the various groups of contracts involving animals in Chapters III–V, and combining the conclusions coming to mind after reading them with the philosophically-ethical background presented in Chapter II of this book, there is time for conclusions. In order to answer the question as to how the Polish legislator should actually change the legal position of animals in law,[1108] so that the conclusion of a contract, its performance and the results of the improper or non-performance of a contract could also be achieved with the respect that animals deserve, it necessary to give my opinion on all the ideas presented by S. Stucki in the second chapter[1109] of this book.

As already mentioned in Subchapter II.2.2. of this book, by defining a separate legal definition of an animal and by establishing a set of rules applicable to these objects of law (different than legal persons and different than things), it would be enough to change the way the animals are treated in the civil law. Therefore, in my opinion, it is not necessary to grant them the status of legal persons – as S. Stucki proposes[1110] – in order to (at least partially) achieve the idea of making humans their guardians – as G. Fraser proposes.[1111] Thus, there is no need to have a revolution in order to achieve a better legal position for

1107 S. Stucki, *Grundrechte für Tiere,* pp. 173–332.
1108 See: Subchapter II.2.2. of this book ("Animals as subjects or objects of law?").
1109 *Idem.*
1110 See: S. Stucki, *Grundrechte für Tiere*; Subchapter II.2.2. of this book.
1111 See: G. Fraser, *Legal personhood for animals in New Zealand*; Subchapter II.2.2. of this book.

animals, whereas this is also a challenge for the Polish jurisdiction and doctrine to show that animals are not inanimate objects of law, but rather a very specific kind of obligation, which results in several duties of the parties to that obligation.

The views represented by S. Stucki and G. Fraser – shown in the second chapter of this Dissertation[1112] – are very controversial. I believe that the time is yet to come for such laws to become part of our legal system and our legal culture,[1113] though it is definitely too early for that. An example presentation of national legal solutions improving the legal status of animals is presented in the subchapter below referring to *de lege ferenda* proposals in the Polish civil law. However, the EU could at least start to prepare their citizens for a change in how we perceive animals, e.g. by addressing more singular animal-related issues in its legal acts, or by making campaigns of a different kind to promote the idea of granting more rights to animals. Thus, although the EU is not able to harmonize the law by changing the position of animals to the extent of private law, it should be more consistent and include the statement that "animals are sentient beings" in all its legal acts.[1114] There should also be clear borders, of which the EU should not tolerate infringements (in reference to the administrative law), namely no longer tolerating the maltreatment of dogs[1115] or bulls[1116] or ritual slaughter,[1117] in modern Europe, regardless of national customs (e.g. prejudices that the castration of animals is against their nature; killing bulls for pleasure during *corrida*). Unfortunately, this remains for future considerations since – due to the

1112 See: G. Fraser, *Legal personhood for animals in New Zealand*; S. Stucki, *Grundrechte für Tiere* and Subchapter II.2.2. of this book.

1113 See: Subchapter II.3.4. of this book.

1114 In particular, I mean the inclusion of a statement that animals are sentient beings into Regulation (EU) 576/2013 on the non-commercial movement of pet animals, Regulation (EU) 1016/2012 on zootechnical and genealogical conditions for the breeding, trade in and entry into the Union of purebred breeding animals, hybrid breeding pigs and the germinal products thereof ('Animal Breeding Regulation') and all newly introduced EU legal acts. This formula has also not been included in Regulation (EU) No. 1143/2014 on the prevention and management of the introduction and spread of invasive alien species (IAS Regulation), COM/2013/0620 final – 2013/0307 (COD), though this is no longer in force.

1115 Compare the example presented in Subchapter II.3.4.

1116 Compare press articles referring to the problem of the *corrida*, e.g.: http://www.bbc.com/news/world-europe-38063778; https://www.theguardian.com/world/2010/jun/06/bull fighting-outlawed-catalonia (last visited: 6.9.2017). Compare the example presented in Subchapter II.3.4.

1117 Compare: E. Tuora-Schwierskott, *Rytualny ubój zwierząt w świetle wolności sumienia i wyznania oraz zasady proporcjonalności w ustawodawstwie i orzecznictwie Niemiec, Szwajcarii i USA*, Państwo i Prawo 2016, Issue 4, pp. 64–73; A. Młynarska-Sobaczewska, *Rytualne ofiary a moralność publiczna. Analiza argumentacji Trybunału Konstytucyjnego (K 52/13) i Sądu Najwyższego USA (508 U.S.520.1993),* Państwo i Prawo 2017, Issue 4, pp. 34–47.

lack of comprehensive legal measures – European Union is unable to rise above these customs.

2. Remarks *de lege ferenda* concerning animals in the Polish legal system (to the extent of private law)

As proven in Chapters III–V of this book, the fact that an animal constitutes the object of a contractual obligation significantly impacts the standards of concluding and performing that contract, as well as the results of non-performance and the improper performance of contracts by enlarging the scope of the parties' contractual duties. It is obvious that granting a separate legal status to animals would comprehensively change the way that the contract law provisions are interpreted and applied with reference to animals. However, at the same time this legal solution is impossible to impose in Poland (probably, as well as in most other EU Member States) due to prejudices of the Polish nation (and – probably – also in reference to other nations within the EU) connected with granting a different legal status to animals. As already mentioned, it is also impossible for such changes to come from the level of EU legislation, due to differences in legal culture within EU and the lack of competence of the EU legislator in these matters. Hence, the change in attitude to animals in Polish contract law must occur in the Polish contract law itself. This may come about by the introduction of singular legal provisions concerning animals to the Polish Civil Code, or by addressing this issue comprehensively in the doctrine and jurisprudence.

As it can be observed by reading this book, since the provisions of most of the contracts described in Chapter IV (excluding the commission contract, which is closely connected with sale of animals and the agency contract)[1118] are not included in the Polish or the German Civil Codes (or the German Commercial Code, since this is the place where the commission and agency contracts are regulated under German law),[1119] their applicability to animals is quite easy. Thus, there are no "black letter rules of law" that would fit better or worse to the applicability of these contracts to animals. Therefore, most of the rules come from usage and practice. As long as the Polish lawmaker leaves the qualification of teaching/training contracts, safe-keeping contracts and all "other" service contracts as undefined contracts, there is no need to change anything to make the law more adjustable to the needs of animals. Under German law, although these contracts are qualified as regular service contracts, thus they are not

1118 Compare: Subchapters III.1.2.1 and III.1.2.2 containing introductory remarks to commission and agency contracts.

1119 See: *Idem.*

undefined, there are also no specific provisions referring to their certain types and there is no need to change this. Nevertheless, the experience of the German jurisprudence and doctrine is incomparably larger than their equivalent in Poland. Thus, the Polish courts may derive knowledge and inspiration in this matter from the methodology of the interpretation and application of law perpetuated by the German courts in the fields of applicability of civil law provisions covering contracts for the transfer of ownership over goods, service contracts and contracts involving the use of somebody's things to animals. Acknowledgment of German rulings by Polish courts may serve not only the popularization of national breeding, farming and horse sports, but also the wellbeing of animals in general. However, it is important to note again that this should occur very carefully. Hence, the identity of a legal rule is not a guarantee of the same understanding of it in disparate legal systems.[1120]

This book shows that there is a wide range of contracts that involve animals. In addition, Chapter IV in particular shows not only that it is possible to conclude contracts specifically serving the wellbeing of animals , but also that many animal owners are willing to conclude such contracts. However, after acknowledging the description of the legal status of these contracts and practice, one question come to mind. Does this mean that the less specific the legal institutions chosen by the lawmaker are, the better it is for the animals? In other words: is it eligible to make a statement that providing less legal provisions with reference to a certain type of contract serves the wellbeing of animals?

The answer to the questions above is also clear. Since the lawmaker does not adjust provisions referring to any contracts to the case where an animal is the object of its contractual performance, and does not grant an animal any legal status that would be better than that of a pair of shoes – it is better for animals when the practice and usage work as they should. This is more the case with the German doctrine[1121] and jurisprudence,[1122] which are more experienced with reference to service contracts involving animals, and must be viewed more positively in comparison to Poland, which lacks judiciary rulings[1123] and suffi-

1120 E. Rott-Pietrzyk, F. Zoll [in:] M. Jagielska, E. Macierzyńska-Franaszczyk, E. Rott-Pietrzyk, F. Zoll, G. Żmij (eds.), *Limits of Harmonization and Convergence…*, p. 44; H. Honsell, *Die rhetorischen Wurzeln der juristischen Auslegung*, ZfPW 2016, p. 125.

1121 E.g.: M. Sommer, *Der Pferdekauf*; P. Rosbach, *Pferderecht;* J. Adolphsen, *Tierkauf* [in:] B. Dauner-Lieb, W. Langen, *BGB Schuldrecht. Nomos Kommentar.*

1122 Especially, the rulings: BGH, ruling from 19.1.2001 – V ZR 437/99; Apellation court in Menden, ruling from 26.2.2007, 4 C 11/07; BGH, ruling from 22.6.2005 – VIII ZR 281/04 (LG Oldenburg) presented in previous subchapters of this book.

1123 There are only one-off Polish rulings referring to the matters being subject of this book, see e.g. already mentioned rulings (both referring to sale of animals): SN, ruling from 11.8.1978 – III CRN 151/78 (which is already 40 years old, but still cited in the doctrine, due to the lack of modern rulings in these matters); SN, ruling from 25.9.2014 – II CSK 664/13.

cient literature (analyzing the problem deeply) covering these issues. Thus, as shown in Chapter IV, the German Civil Code does not include much more than the Polish Civil Code does in reference to service contracts involving animals, but the jurisprudence and doctrine does. This solution seems to serve the good of the animals, which can be treated with the respect they deserve, as there are no legal provisions that could lead to the soulless treatment of animals. The Germans have a long judicial practice in cases involving animals, and therefore German rulings should serve as a role model to the Polish courts and doctrinal research (as far as legal reasoning and methodology of law interpretation and application).

Taking into account the fact that, since the reform of the Polish Civil Code of 2014, there has been no single reference aimed at improving the treatment of animals in Polish contract law,[1124] and the fact that the German Civil Code has adjusted its civil law (i.e. also contract law) provisions to acknowledge the existence of animals on the market several times, it should be considered which of these legal solutions is in fact better for adjusting the legal provisions covering goods to animals.

These considerations should begin with **§ 903 BGB**, which states that the owner of an animal must, when exercising his powers, take into account the special provisions for the protection of animals. It is disputable whether the contents of § 903 BGB actually serve the well-being of animals or underline the owner's rights, which are similar to the owner's rights with reference to different objects of obligations. However, since – due to the content of Article 13 TFEU – all EU Member States include provisions stating that animals are sentient beings (in the meaning that EU and Member States must pay full attention to the welfare requirements of animals) in its legal systems, the **content** of § 903 BGB (especially when considering it in combination with § 90a BGB) itself should not trigger discussion, but its **place** in the German legal system as a whole. Although a similar regulation is provided by the combination of the provisions of Article 535 KC and Article 1 of the Polish Animal Protection Act, I am of the opinion that the inclusion of a provision confirming that the ownership rights with reference to animals are different to those with reference to things into national civil codes is a good solution. Thus, it is also used in other legal systems, not only the German one,[1125] and underlines the differences in the way that the contracting parties and courts should treat animals as the object of obligations. The in-

1124 The Polish Civil Code includes only one-off provisions of a more general nature, referring briefly to animals, whereas these provisions are not meant to serve the well-being of animals, see: Article 182 (but with reference to bees, which are not covered by the scope of this book), 424, 431, 432, 449^1, 846.

1125 See e.g.: § 494 of the Czech Civil Code § 641a of the Swiss Civil Code [ZGB]; § 285a of the Austrian Civil Code [*Allgemeines Bürgerliches Gesetzbuch.*

troduction of a similar provision into the Polish Civil Code would confirm that ownership rights with reference to animals are different than those in reference to things. In this case, the scope of modifications that are connected with the respective applicability of the provisions of law covering things to animals would be clearer and could simplify using the law in action. Additionally, the inclusion of this provision in a different legal act, probably referring to animal protection, seems to minimize the importance of the differences between animals – being a specific object of the obligations – and other goods.

Additionally, putting all the provisions aimed at enhancing the well-being of animals to a separate legal act creates an impression that this is a side issue and an object of administrative provisions, whereas I believe it is important to underline that the borders between public and private law are melting together[1126] and it is important to stress that animals may also be protected (although indirectly) by the provisions of private law to a wider extent.

Moving further to the results of the non-performance/improper performance of contracts in general, German law includes a very humane civil law provision referring to damages incurred as a result of the improper performance of a contract, i. e. in the case of buying/using/etc. an injured animal, whose curative treatment expenses had then to be covered. Thus, according to **(2) of § 251 BGB,** expenses incurred as a result of the curative treatment of an injured animal are not disproportionate merely because they significantly exceed the value of the animal. The lack of a similar legal provision in the Polish Civil Code makes the disproportion between the legal status of animals in the Polish and German law very transparent, therefore it is highly advisable for the Polish lawmaker to introduce it to the Polish Civil Code as well.

1126 In other words – as it was mentioned in the book – the public law provisions applicable to animals may impact the content of a contractual obligation. Firstly, this may occur by impacting these relationships by the mechanism included in Article 56 KC. Secondly, these public law provisions may consitute, according to one of the criteria under Article 353^1 KC, limiting the freedom of contract in such cases. In the case of infringing one of the legal criteria, the result included in Article 58 § 2 or § 3 arises. Thirdly, these legal provisions may also finally determine the standards of the due performance of the obligation according to Article 354 KC. With reference to the melting difference between private and public law, see: J. Nowacki,*Prawo publiczne – prawo prywatne*, Katowice 1992; W. Popiołek, *Znaczenie przepisów "prawa publicznego" różnych systemów prawnych dla stosunków umownych handlu zagranicznego*, Problemy Prawne Handlu Zagranicznego 1988, Issue 12, pp. 56–78; J. Łętowski, *W sprawie granicy międzyprawem publicznym a prywatnym* [in:] B. Kordasiewicz, E. Łętowska (eds.), *Prace z prawa cywilnego. Wydane dla uczczenia prany naukowej Profesora Józefa Piątowskiego*, pp. 353–362; R. Szczepaniak, *W zamkniętym kręgu podziału na prawo publiczne i prywatne, czyli o możliwości dochodzenia odsetek od zasądzonych kosztów procesu*, Studia Prawa Prywatnego 2015, Issue 3, pp. 49–59.

Another specific German civil law provision covered by the scope of this book refers to lease contracts and – due to the respective applicability of lease provisions to tenancy contracts[1127] – also to tenancy contracts. Thus, according to (1) of **§ 601 BGB**, the tenant must bear the customary costs of maintaining the thing lent; in the case of a gratuitous loan of an animal, such costs include the costs of feeding it. Although the fact that an animal has to be fed in order to be maintained in the same condition seems to be obvious and the lack of special regulations concerning leased animals in Polish law does not constitute any obstruction to applying provisions referring to things, it is clear that confirmation that animals deserve special treatment when offering its usage to a different person, deserves additional attention.

I believe that these few changes would be enough to signal the presence of animals as specific objects of obligations in the Polish Civil Code. Thus, as already shown using the example of service contracts, the lack of legal provisions referring to animals under the Polish and German legal systems does not mean their worse treatment, but actually the opposite – the possibility to create different new contracts aimed at the well-being of animals. Nevertheless, the choice of the German legislator to address the problem of animals as specific objects of obligations in the German Civil Code should be considered positively. Thus, a specific description on the use of every single provision covering goods to animals would not lead to a better understanding of its legal status, but differences in the ownership of an animal and a regular good should be underlined in the Civil Code of each country. Additionally, the German legal system deals well with brief legislation covering the problem of animals as specific objects of the obligations due to its rich jurisprudence in these matters. I believe that the jurisprudence and doctrine – based on the observation of practical usage – should address this problem in a more comprehensive way also in the Polish legal system, whereas only singular (but important) provisions should be added to the Polish Civil Code, using the German Civil Code as a pattern. Proposals of such changes are described below.

Concerning sale contracts, the idea that the owner of an animal must, when exercising his powers, take into account the special provisions for the protection of animals of § 903 BGB could be deepened by introducing to the Polish Civil Code a provision worded as: "*The seller has the right and obligation to take an interest in the animal's health and general condition after transferring ownership to the buyer, whereas the buyer is obliged to enable the seller to see the sold animal in order to check on its living conditions, as long as the frequency of these checks does not exceed the moral standards of a given society. In the event that the animal turns out to be maltreated, its previous owner/ seller is entitled to*

1127 See: § 581 (2) BGB.

issue a claim to repurchase the animal." In this case, there would be no doubts that this provision serves the well-being of an animal, i.e. that humans owe a duty of care and respect to animals and, additionally, it would constitute a bridge[1128] between animal protection using public law provisions and private law provisions, which may also lead to the protection of animal rights.

Introducing such a provision would strengthen the position of the animal's owner as its guardian, and would improve the standards of treating animals. Such a provision would definitely impact the standards of performance and the improper/non-performance of contracts having animals as objects of their contractual obligations by placing additional duties on the seller. However, these would be duties towards the sold animal rather than towards the buyer.

I would also suggest including in the Polish Civil Code a provision that animals could only be **donated** on the condition that the new owner takes sufficient care for an animal. This would mean that the previous owner would still have a duty to take care of the fate of the animals donated, and has some basic control over whether the new owner fulfils the animal's substantial needs. Such a provision could contain the wording: "*The donor has the right and obligation to take an interest in the animal's health and general condition after transferring ownership to the donee, whereas the donee is obliged to enable the donor to see the donated animal in order to check on its living conditions, as long as the frequency of these checks do not exceed the moral standards of a given society.*" Additionally, the scope of persons against which ingratitude may result in demanding that the object of the donation agreement be handed back, should be adjusted to also cover the donation of animals. Thus, although the applicability of Article 898 KC to animals is admitted by M. Goettel[1129] (the only representative of the Polish doctrine on these matters at the moment), addressing this provision directly to animals would, in my opinion, significantly change its status in the Polish civil law.

Through the implementation of changes proposed in this subchapter to the Polish Civil Code, the way the animals are seen and treated –by the lawmaker, as well as in the law in action – would be drastically improved by comprehensively granting the **position of being an animal's guardian to humans.** Moreover, in

1128 With reference to the melting difference between private and public law, see: J. Nowacki, *Prawo publiczne – prawo prywatne*, Katowice 1992; W. Popiołek, *Znaczenie przepisów "prawa publicznego" różnych systemów prawnych dla stosunków umownych handlu zagranicznego*, Problemy Prawne Handlu Zagranicznego 1988, Issue 12, pp. 56–78; J. Łętowski, *W sprawie granicy międzyprawem publicznym a prywatnym* [in:] B. Kordasiewicz, E. Łętowska (eds.), *Prace z prawa cywilnego. Wydane dla uczczenia prany naukowej Profesora Józefa Piątowskiego*, pp. 353–362; R. Szczepaniak, *W zamkniętym kręgu podziału na prawo publiczne i prywatne, czyli o możliwości dochodzenia odsetek od zasądzonych kosztów procesu*, Studia Prawa Prywatnego 2015, Issue 3, pp. 49–59.

1129 M. Goettel, *Sytuacja zwierzęcia w prawie cywilnym*, Warszawa 2013, pp, 155–156.

this way, the welfare of animals could be achieved without changing the legal position of animals in civil law. As mentioned in the previous subchapter, it is not necessary to grant the status of legal persons to animals – as S. Stucki proposes[1130] – in order to achieve the idea of making humans their guardians – which is closer to the idea of G. Fraser.[1131] Thus, my assumption made at the beginning of this book, namely that a revolution is not needed in order to achieve a better legal position of animals, has been positively proven. Whereas I consider S. Stucki's ideas concerning the need to make changes to the legal status of animals[1132] as unnecessary, the basic idea of G. Fraser[1133] deserves attention. Similarly, E. Łętowska, a representative of the Polish doctrine, argues primarily that, in the discussion on the legal status of animals, one should look at possibilities of adapting the legal status of an animal as defined under the law to be more practical.[1134] This way of reasoning should be employed in Poland also. Additionally, this should be achieved by using minimalistic tools. Although I believe that some changes to the Polish Civil Code are advisable with reference to animals (especially, in reference to ownership), it is certainly a case of "less is more". Therefore, the Polish jurisprudence and doctrine have the door wide open to create changes in raising the standards of treating animals that should be granted by the parties of obligations, and there are no obstacles to prevent the huge experience of the German jurisprudence and doctrine from being used to Poland's advantage, at least at some point. If the doctrine and jurisprudence would sufficiently address the problems described above, there would be no need to change the Polish Civil Code itself.

Summing up, I believe that the inclusion of a legal provision pointing out the differences between animals and goods into the Polish Civil Code – as it is § 903 BGB – (instead of locating it in a separate legal act) would serve the wellbeing of animals and would underline that they are a specific object of obligations. However, all other changes proposed above should be taken into account by the legislator solely as a last resort. **Thus, the problems addressed in this book could be comprehensively solved by the courts and doctrine** – which should be encouraged to publish opinions in that matter.

1130 See: S. Stucki, *Grundrechte für Tiere*; Subchapter II.2.2. of this book.
1131 See: G. Fraser, *Legal personhood for animals in New Zealand*; Subchapter II.2.2. of this book.
1132 See: S. Stucki, *Grundrechte für Tiere*; Subchapter II.2.2. of this book.
1133 See: G. Fraser, *Legal personhood for animals in New Zealand*; S. Stucki, *Grundrechte für Tiere* and Subchapter II.2.2. of this book.
1134 E. Łętowska, *Dwa aspekty praw zwierząt, dereifikacja i personifikacja* [in:] A. Szpunar (ed.), *Studia z Prawa Prywatnego. Księga pamiątkowa ku czci prof. dr B. Lewaszkiewicz-Petrykowskiej*, pp. 71–92.

It seems that the "door" that would open up the path for the Polish judicature to take the direction of interpreting and adjusting the private law provisions in reference to obligations to animals can be found in provisions including general clauses, like Article 56 KC, Article 65, Article 353[1] KC (in connection with Article 58 § 2 KC) and Article 354 KC. The general equity clauses included there could be helpful not only in defining the position of the parties to contracts referring to animals. This "door" may also – directly – lead to improvements in the legal situation of animals created by these various constructions of contract law. Therefore, general clauses could also have an additional function consisting in improving the wellbeing of animals in private law. Showing the direction of interpretation of private law provisions of various legal systems when applying them to obligations with animals as their objects may constitute precious inspiration for the Polish doctrine and a direction leading to animal welfare being placed at the highest level (in every particular case when it is necessary to do so). It is also possible that the experience of the German jurisprudence in these matters may allow the Polish judicature to follow the same path, or find a better path of its own.

References

Adekoya R., *How the EU transformed Poland,* The Guardian, https://www.theguardian.com/commentisfree/2014/may/01/eu-poland-10-years-economic.

Aderhold L., Grunewald B., Kingberg D., Paefgen W. (ed.), *Festschrift für Harm Peter Westermann zum 70. Geburtstag,* Köln 2008.

Adolphsen J., *Die Schuldrechtsreform und der Wegfall des Viehgewährleistungsrechts,* Agrarrecht 2001, No 7.

Adolphsen J. [in:] Dauner-Lieb B., Langen W., *BGB Schuldrecht. Nomos Kommentar,* Baden-Baden 2016.

Angelos J., *Why on earth is Greece in the EU? Reverence for the ancient Greeks led to the modern Greek crisis,* Politico 22 June 2015, http://www.politico.eu/article/why-is-greece-in-the-eu-grexit/.

Antoniuk J. [in:] Kaczmarek-Templin B., Stec P., Szostek D. (ed.), *Ustawa o prawach konsumenta. Kodeks cywilny (wyciąg). Komentarz,* Warszawa 2014.

Appleby M. C., Cussen V., Garces L., Lambert L. A., Turner J., *Long Distance Transport and Welfare of Farm Animals,* Wollingford/Cambridge 2008.

Appleby M. C., *The European Union Ban on Conventional Cages for Laying Hens: History and Prospects,* Journal of Applied Animal Welfare Science 2003, Vol. 6, Issue 2.

Badcock J., *Will Spain ever ban bullfighting?,* BBC News 3 December 2016.

Bagłaj E., *Polskiej potęgi hodowli koni arabskich by nie było, gdyby nie kilku ludzi, którzy kochali te zwierzęta,* Gazeta.pl 22 November 2016, http://weekend.gazeta.pl/weekend/1,152121,21011476,polskiej-potegi-konia-arabskiego-by-nie-bylo-gdyby-nie-wiedza.html.

Banaszak-Kulka A., *Kilka uwag o psach służbowych* [in:] Banaszak B. (ed.), *Przegląd Prawa i Administracji,* Vol. LXII, Wrocław 2004.

Banaszczyk Z. [in:] Pietrzykowski K. (ed.), *Kodeks cywilny. Komentarz,* Warszawa 2015.

Bar C. von, Clive E., Schulte-Nölke H. et al., *Principles, Definitions and Model Rules of European Private Law – Draft Common Frame of Reference (DCFR), Interim Outline Edition,* Munich 2009.

Barańczyk I. [in:] Karczewska D., Namysłowska M., Skoczny T., *Ustawa o prawach konsumenta,* Warszawa 2015.

Barański M., *Konstrukcja prawna umów o pośrednictwo,* Rejent 2010, Issue 9.

Basedow J., Hopt K. J., Zimmermann R. (eds.), *Max Planck Encyclopedia of European Private Law,* Oxford 2012.

BBC news, *The million stray dogs 'victims of the Greek debt crisis* (video), BBC news 3 October 2015, http://www.bbc.com/news/av/world-europe-34432580/a-million-stray-dogs-victims-of-greek-debt-crisis.

Becker M., *Grossbritannien, die EU und der Fall Skripal – Gelbe Karte, mehr geht doch nicht*, Spiegel Online 15 March 2018, http://www.spiegel.de/politik/ausland/fall-sergej-skripal-grossbritannien-sucht-nach-verbuendeten-a-1198269.html.

Beirne P., *From Animal Abuse to Interhuman Violence? A Critical Review of the Progression Thesis*, Society & Animals 2004, vol. 12, No 1.

Bentham J., *An Introduction To The Principles Of Morals And Legislation*, Oxford 1907 (1823).

Bentham J., *Wprowadzenie do zasad moralności i prawodawstwa* (Bogdan Nawroczyński trans.), Warszawa 1958.

Berger C. [in:] Stürner R. (ed.), *Jauernig, Kommentar zum BGB*, München 2015.

Berkowska E., Gwiazdowicz M., Sobolewski M., *Transport zwierząt – prawo, praktyka, perspektywy*, Kancelaria Sejmu – Biuro Studiów i Ekspertyz, April 2002, http://biurose.sejm.gov.pl/teksty_pdf/i-894.pdf.

Białocerkiewicz J., *Status prawny zwierząt. Prawa zwierząt czy prawna ochrona zwierząt*, Toruń 2005.

Bil T., Broniek A., Cincio A., Kiełbasa M. (consulted with Dannemann G., Fischer S. F., Zoll F.), *Kodeks cywilny – Civil code*, Warszawa 2011.

Bladowski B., *Umowa o dzieło i umowa zlecenia*, Warszawa 1987.

Błońska B., Gogłoza W., Klaus W., Woźniakowska-Fajst D. (eds.), *Sprawiedliwość dla zwierząt*, Warszawa 2017.

Bonell M., *The UNIDROIT Principles in Practice. Case law and Bibliography on the Principles of Commercial Contracts*, New York 2006.

Borggräfe J., *Der Sporttrainervertrag*, Frankfurt am Main 2006.

Braun W., *Geschäftsverträge*, Stuttgart 2007.

Breczko A., Andruszkiewicz M., *Przejawy reifikacji moralnej i prawnej zwierząt w XXI wieku* [in:] Pływaczewski E. W., Bryka J. (eds.), *Meandry prawa – teoria i praktyka. Księga jubileuszowa proz. Zw. Dra hab. Mieczysława Goettela*, Szczytno 2017, pp. 63–81.

Brennan B., *The starving dogs that give Spain a bad name*, Telegraph 22 March 2011, http://www.telegraph.co.uk/expat/expatlife/8382998/The-starving-dogs-that-give-Spain-a-bad-name.html.

Broom D., *Sentience and Animal Welfare*, Wallingford 2014.

Broß S., *Grundwerte und Grundrechte in Europa. Systematische und konstruktive Überlegungen* [in:] Robertson-von Trotha C. (ed.), *Kultur und Gerechtigkeit*, Baden-Baden 2007.

Brox H., Walker W., *Allgemeines Schuldrecht*, München 2015.

Brückner S., Kochhan C., *Die klassische Ausbildung des Pferdes – Basis für die langfristige Zufriedenheit des Käufers*, Piaffe 1/2011.

Brzozowski A., Jastrzębski J., Kaliński M., Kocot W. J., Skowrońska-Bocian A., *Zobowiązania. Część szczegółowa*, Warszawa 2017.

Brzozowski A. [in:] Pietrzykowski K. (ed.), *Kodeks cywilny. Komentarz*, Warszawa 2015.

Brzozowski A., *Odpowiedzialność przyjmującego zamówienie za wady dzieła*, Warszawa 1986.

Büdenbender U. [in:] Dauner-Lieb B., Langen W., *Anwaltkommentar BGB*, Bonn 2005.
Busch C., Schulte-Nölke H., *EU compendium: a practical tool for judges*, München 2011.
Busche J. [in:] Oetker H., *Handelsgesetzbuch. Kommentar*, München 2011.
Cahill D., Connery N., Kennedy T., Power V., *European Law*, Oxford 2011 (1987).
Carpenter S., *The devolution of conservation: why CITES must embrace community-based resource management*, 2 Arizona Journal of Environmental Law & Policy 1, 3–5 (2011).
Centrala Konsumentów Branderburgia (ed.), *Zakupy w Polsce – jak chronieni są konsumenci? Wykłady z sympozjum "Transgraniczna ochrona konsumentów w świetle europejskiej polityki ochrony konsumentów – perspektywa polsko-niemiecka"*, Akwigran 2007.
Clarck P., *I'm renting a dog*, Bloomberg, 1 March 2017, https://www.bloomberg.com/news/features/2017-03-01/i-m-renting-a-dog.
Cwajna A., *Możliwości wykorzystania prawa do wizerunku zwierząt w świetle prawa polskiego*, 25 February 2016, https://equista.pl/editorial/1120/prawo-mozliwosci-wy korzystania-wizerunku-zwierzat-w-swietle-prawa-polskiego.
Cwajna A., *Equista – Prawo: Wybrane umowy cywilnoprawne cz. IV umowa o trening konia lub jeźdźca*,15 March 2017, https://equista.pl/editorial/2120/prawo-wybrane-umowy-cywilnoprawne-cz.-iv-umowa-o-trening-konia-lub-jezdzca.
Czachórski W. (ed.), *Zobowiązania – Zarys wykładu*, Warszawa, 2012.
Czachórski W., *Zobowiązania. Zarys wykładu*, Warszawa 2002.
Czapliński W., Wyrozumska A., *Prawo międzynarodowe publiczne. Zagadnienia systemowe*, Warszawa 2004.
Czekała B., *Wypożyczalnia kur niosek, czyli australijski sposób na biznes*, 19 January 2016, https://www.topagrar.pl/articles/aktualnosci/wypozyczalnia-kur-niosek-czyli-austral ijski-sposob-na-biznes/.
Cześnik M., *Partycypacja wyborcza Polaków*, Instytut Spraw Publicznych, Warszawa, 2009, http://www.isp.org.pl/files/20145849250174351001263374709.pdf.
Deutsche Reiterliche Vereinigung e.V. Fédération Equestre Nationale (FN), *A Guide through the German Equestrian World – equestrian sports and breeding in Germany*, http://www.euroequestrian.eu/files/2/11/Horse_Sports_and_Breeding_Juli_2014.pdf.
Deutsche Reiterliche Vereinigung, *Zahlen und Fakten (2016)*, https://www.pferd-aktuell.de/fn-service/zahlen-fakten/zahlen-fakten.
Die Bundesvereinigung der Berufsreiter, *Welchem Reitlehrer kann ich trauen?*, St. Georg 2012, No 11.
Dobrodziej E., *Prawa i obowiązki stron w umowach zlecenia i o dzieło*, Bydgoszcz 1993.
Dobrodziej E., *Zatrudnienie na podstawie umów cywilno-prawnych. Aktualne przepisy. Wyjaśnienia, komentarze*, Bydgoszcz 2000.
Domagalski M., *Unia i jej władze nie mają wyraźnego i przetestowanego sposobu na przełożenie zaleceń na sankcje wobec Polski*, Rzeczpospolita 27 October 2016, http://www.rp.pl/Spor-o-Trybunal-Konstytucyjny/310279981-Zalecenia-Komisji-Europej skiej-wobec-TK-raczej-bez-sankcji.html.
Drapała P., *Glosa do uchwały SN z dnia 20 stycznia 2010 r., III CZP 125/09*, PiP 2012, Issue 2.
Drapała P., *Prowadzenie cudzych spraw bez zlecenia. Konstrukcja prawna*, Warszawa 2010.
Drapała P., *Świadczenie w miejsce wykonania (datio in solutum)*, Państwo i Prawo 2003, No 12.

Drozd E., *Recenzja pracy autorstwa A. Kleina, Elementy stosunku zobowiązaniowego*, PiP 1964, Issue 7.
Dybowski T., Pyrzyńska [in:] Łętowska E. (ed.), *System Prawa Prywatnego, vol. V, Prawo zobowiązań – część ogólna*, Warszawa 2013.
Ebert I., Schleuch A. [in:] Schulze R., Dörner H., Ebert I., Hoeren T., Kemper R., Saenger I., Schreiber K., Schulte-Nölke H., Staudinger A. (eds.), *Bürgerliches Gesetzbuch. Handkommentar*, Baden-Baden 2016.
Ehrlich E., Fundamental *Principles of the Sociology of Law*, New Brunswick/London 2009 (originally published on 1936 by Harvard University Press).
Eichelberger J., *Von neuen und gebrauchten Tieren – Zur Anwendbarkeit des § 475 Abs. 2 BGB auf den Tierkauf*, ZGS 2007, No 98.
Eichelberger J., Zentner M., *Tiere im Kaufrecht*, JuS 2009.
Elliott V., *Wypożyczalnia psów*, The Times/Onet.pl 13 May 2008, http://wiadomosci.onet.pl/kiosk/wypozyczalnia-psow/13mhm.
Emmerich V. [in:] Krüger W. (ed.), *Münchener Kommentar zum BGB, Vol. IV*, München 2016.
Emmerich V., Veit B. [in:] J. von Staudinger (ed.), *J. von Staudingers Kommentar zum Bürgerlichen Gesetzbuch: Staudinger BGB – Buch 2: Recht der Schuldverhältnisse*, Berlin 2005.
Englund L., Pringle J., *New diseases and increased risk of diseases in companion animals and horses due to transport*, Acta veterinaria Scandinavica, sup. 100.
Etel M., *Pojęcie przedsiębiorcy w prawie polskim i prawie Unii Europejskiej oraz w orzecznictwie sądowym*, Warszawa 2012.
European Union Directorate-General for Agriculture and Rural Development, *Agriculture In The European Union – Markets Statistical Information 2014*, http://ec.europa.eu/agriculture/markets-and-prices/market-statistics/index_en.htm.
Falkner G., Trein O., Hartlapp M., Leiber S. (eds.), *Complying with Europe. EU Harmonisation and Soft Law in the Member States*, Cambridge 2005.
Faust F. [in:] H. Bamberger, H. Roth, W. Hau, R. Poseck (eds.), *Beck'sche Online Kommentare, BeckOK, BGB*, 44. Ed., München 2017.
Fellmer E., Kiel P., *Rechtskunde für Pferdehalter und Reiter*, Stuttgart 1984.
Fischer L., *No animals were harmed…: Protecting chimpanzees from cruelty behind the curtain*, Hastings Commercial and Entrertainment Law Journal 27/2005.
Francione G., *Animal Rights and Animal welfare*, Rutgers L. Rev 48/1996.
Francione G., *Rain without Thunder – The ideology of the Animal Rights movement*, Philadelphia 1996.
Frąckowiak J. [in:] Rajski J. (ed.), *System Prawa Prywatnego, Vol. VII, Prawo zobowiązań – część szczegółowa*, Warszawa 2011.
Frankowski S. (ed.), *Introduction to Polish Law*, Warszawa 2005.
Fraser D., *Understanding Animal Welfare – the Science in its Cultural Context*, Ames 2008.
Fraser G., *Legal personhood for animals in New Zealand*, New Zealand 2016.
Fritzsche J. [in:] Bamberger H., Roth H., Hau W., Poseck R. (eds.), *Beck'sche Online Kommentare, BeckOK, BGB*, 44. Ed., München 2017.
Fuchs M. [in:] Bamberger H., Roth H. (ed.), *Beck'scher Online-Kommentar BGB*, München 2015.
Gadacz T., Milerski B., *Religia: Encyklopedia PWN*, Vol. 6, Warszawa 2002.

Gahn V. [in:] M. Schmid, A. Harz, *Fachanwaltskommentar. Mietrecht*, Köln, 2012.
Gawlik B., *Umowy mieszane – konstrukcja i ocena prawna*, Palestra 1974, Issue 5.
Gawlik Z. [in:] *Kodeks cywilny, Vol III, Zobowiązania. Część szczegółowa*, A. Kidyba (ed.), Warszawa 2014.
Geertz C., *The interpretation of cultures*, New York 2000.
Gehrlein M. [in:] Bamberger H., Roth H., Hau W., Poseck R. (eds.), *Beck'sche Online Kommentare, BeckOK, BGB*, 44. Ed., München 2017.
Gersdorf M., *Umowa o pracę. Umowa o dzieło. Umowa zlecenie*, Warszawa 1993.
Gniewek E., Machnikowski P. (eds.), *Kodeks cywilny. Komentarz*, Warszawa 2017.
Goettel M., *Sytuacja zwierzęcia w prawie cywilnym*, Warszawa 2013.
Gonzales J. A. R. L., *Direitos dos animais?*, https://lis-ulusiada.academia.edu/joségon zález.
Goodman P. S., *Spain's Long Economic Nightmare is finally over*, New York Times 28 July 2017, https://www.nytimes.com/2017/07/28/business/spain-europe-economy-recovery-unemployment.html?mcubz=1.
Górecki J., *Umowne prawo pierwokupu*, Kraków 2000.
Gregory N. G., *Physiology and Behaviour of Animal Suffering*, Oxford 2004.
Greven L., *Merkels Obergrenze*, Zeit online 21 July 2017, http://www.zeit.de/politik/deutschland/2017-07/fluechtlinge-obergrenze-angela-merkel-willkommenspolitik-ita lien-libyen.
Grochowski M., *Zbieg norm w zakresie rękojmi za wady rzeczy sprzedanej oraz błędu i podstępu (Zagadnienie prawne)*, Monitor Prawniczy 2012, No 19.
Grüneberg C. [in:] O. Palandt, *Beck'sche Kurz-Kommentare: Palandt Bürgerliches Gesetzbuch mit Nebengesetzen*, München 2015.
Grykowski B., *Fotografowanie zwierząt*, W todze i bez togi 8 December 2001, https://bartoszgrykowski.wordpress.com/2011/12/08/fotografowanie-zwierzat/.
Gudowski J. (ed.), *Kodeks cywilny. Komentarz. Zobowiązania*, Vol.IV, Warszawa 2017.
Gumowska A., Newsweek Polska 10.4.2016, http://www.newsweek.pl/polska/konie-ara bskie-smierc-klaczy-shirley-watts-w-janowie-podlaskim,artykuly,383683,1.html.
Gutmann T., *Recht als Kultur?*, Baden-Baden 2015.
Gutowski M., *Konwersja umowy stanowczej w przedwstępną wobec zmian kodeksu cywilnego*, PiP 2004, Issue 11.
Gutowski M., *Nieważność czynności prawnej*, Warszawa 2017.
Güttel I., *Ein Huhn fur drei Monate, bitte*, n-tv.de 24 April 2016, http://www.n-tv.de/panorama/Ein-Huhn-fuer-drei-Monate-bitte-article17531341.html.
Guzenda K., *Verbraucherrechte bei Lieferung einer vertragswidrigen Ware nach deutchem und polnischem Recht*, Frankfurt (Oder) 2007.
Gwiazdomorski J., *Umowa przedwstępna w kodeksie zobowiązań*, Czasopismo Prawnicze i Ekonomiczne 1936, Issue 30.
Habdas M., *Property and trust law in Poland*, The Netherlands 2015.
Habryn – Chojnacka E. [in:] Gutowski M. (ed.), *Kodeks cywilny, Vol I, Komentarz do Article 1–449[11]*, Warszawa 2016.
Haładyj K. [in:] K. Osajda (ed.), *Kodeks cywilny. Komentarz. Tom IIIA. Zobowiązania. Część ogólna*, Warszawa 2017.

Hantz K., Żukowska K., Grieger A., *Wymagania stawiane środkom transportu przy przewozie żywych zwierząt,* Autobusy: technika, eksploatacja, systemy transportowe 2016, Issue 8/17.

Harke J. [in:] Schulze R., Dörner H., Ebert I., Hoeren T., Kemper R., Saenger I., Schreiber K., Schulte-Nölke H., Staudinger A. (eds.), *Bürgerliches Gesetzbuch. Handkommentar,* Baden-Baden 2016.

Häublein M. [in:] Westermann H. (ed.), *Münchener Kommentar zum BGB, Vol. III,* München 2016.

Hegedus C., D., Pennbaker D. A., *Unlocking the case, (the film)* available athttps:// www.unlockingthecagethefilm.com.

Henklewski R., Florczyk A., Kinda W., *Punktowa skala w radiograficznej ocenie zdjęć rentgenowskich u koni z bolesnością grzbietu,* Życie weterynaryjne 2013, No 88 (10).

Herbert A., *If corporations can have legal personality, why not animals?,* Law Society of New South Wales, http://www.lawsociety.com.au/cs/groups/public/documents/inter netyounglawyers/023594.pdf.

Hoebel E., *The law of Primitive Man,* Cambridge, 1954.

Hoecke M. V. (ed.), *Epistemology and Methodology of Comparative Law,* Portland 2004.

Hofer S., *Der Schadenersatzanspruch des Käufers bei Sachmängeln – Grundsätze, Wertungen und Konstruktionen,* Archiv für die civilistische Praxis (ACP) 2001, Issue 2/201.

Hohloch G., *Culpa in contrahendo in private international law,* Problemy Prawne Handlu Zagranicznego, Issue 19/20.

Höpfner C. [in:] B. Gsell, W. Krüger, S. Lorenz, J. Mayer (ed.), *Beck-online Grosskommentar BGB,* München 2015.

Huber U., *statt der Leistung,* Archiv für die civilistische Praxis (ACP) 2010, Issue 3–4/210.

Hunt A., Wheeler B., *Brexit: All you need to know about the UK leaving the EU,* BBC News 3 March 2018, http://www.bbc.com/news/uk-politics-32810887.

Husa J., *Legal Culture vs. Legal Tradition – Different Epistemologies?,* Maastricht European Private Law Institute Working Paper 2012, Issue 18/2012, http://works.bepress.com/ jaakko_husa/23/.

Husa J., *Methodology of Comparative Law Today: From Paradoxes to Flexibility?,* Revue Internationale de Droit Comparé 2006, Vol. 58, No 4.

Hutton J., Dickson B. (eds.), *Endangered Species, Threatened Convention: The Past, Present and Future of CITES,* 2000.

Iacona J., *Behind closed curtains: the Exploitation of animals in the film industry,* Journal of animal & natural resource law XII/2016.

IBF International Consulting, VetEffecT, Wageningen University & Research Centre, Istituto Zooprofilattico Sperimentale dell'Abruzzo e del Molise "G. Caporale", *Study on the welfare of dogs and cats involved in commercial practices* (Specific Contract SANCO 2013/12364 – project financed by the European Commission), https://ec.europa.eu/ food/sites/food/files/animals/docs/aw_eu-strategy_study_dogs-cats-commercial-practices_en.pdf.

Inman P., Wearden G., *Greece plans return to bond market as Athens sees end in sight to austerity,* The Guardian 24 July 2017, https://www.theguardian.com/business/2017/jul/ 24/greece-return-bond-market-austerity-eurozone.

Jacyszyn J., *Przedsiębiorca w regulacjach prawnych, cz. I,* EP 2015, No 4.

Jagielska M., Macierzyńska-Franaszczyk E., Rott-Pietrzyk E., Zoll F., Żmij G. (eds.), *Limits of Harmonisation and Convergence. Dissimilarities in Similarities of Polish and German Contract Law*, Warszawa 2018.

Jezioro J. [in:] Gniewek E., Machnikowski P. (ed.), *Kodeks cywilny. Komentarz*, Warszawa 2017.

Jędrzejak M., *Uchodźcy będą mieli wpływ na polską gospodarkę*, Forbes 15 September 2015, https://www.forbes.pl/wiadomosci/jak-kryzys-z-uchodzcami-wplynie-na-zlote go/zmttp38.

Jędrzejewska A., *Koncepcja oświadczenia woli w prawie cywilnym*, Warszawa 1992.

Ju J. C., *When is an animal a legal person?*, Pacific Standard Magazine 28 April 2015, https://psmag.com/environment/is-a-chimpanzee-a-person.

Kaleta T., *Człowiek a zwierzę*, Wiedza i Życie 1996, issue 2, 2 http://archiwum. wiz.pl/1996/ 96023100.asp.

M. Kaliński M. [in:] Olejniczak A., *System Prawa Prywatnego. Prawo cywilne - część ogólna*, Warszawa 2014.

Kant E., *The Metaphysics of Morals*, Cambridge 1996.

Katner W. [in:] Karczewska D., Namysłowska M., Skoczny T., *Ustawa o prawach konsumenta*, Warszawa 2015.

Katner W. [in:] Stec M., *System Prawa Handlowego. Prawo Umów handlowych, Vol. V*, Warszawa 2017.

Katner, W. [in:] Rajski J. (ed.), *System Prawa Prywatnego, Vol. VII, Prawo zobowiązań - część szczegółowa*, Warszawa 2011.

Katner W. [in:] Katner W. (ed.), *System Prawa Prywatnego, Vol. IX, Prawo zobowiązań - umowy nienazwane*, Warszawa 2015.

Katner W., *Dylematy spójności Kodeksu spółek handlowych z Kodeksem cywilnym oraz Kodeksem rodzinnym i opiekuńczym - konferencja naukowa dla uczczenia 40lecia pracy naukowej Profesora Andrzeja Szajkowskiego w INP PAN (Warszawa, 23 września 2014 r.)*, Spółki handlowe jako przedsiębiorcy według Kodeksu cywilnego i Kodeksu spółek handlowych (dodatek MoP 7/2015).

Katner W., *Prawo działalności gospodarczej. Komentarz*, Warszawa 2003.

Kędzierska-Cieślak A., *Komis (zagadnienia cywilnoprawne)*, Warszawa 1973.

Kemptner D., *Der Einfluss des europäischen Rechts auf das polnische Zivilgesetzbuch*, Baden-Baden 2007.

Kern C., *Pachtrecht. Das gesamte pachtrecht mit Nebengebieten*, Berlin, 2012.

Kępiński M. [in:] Gutowski M. (ed.), *Kodeks cywilny, Vol I, Komentarz do Article 1–449[11]*, Warszawa 2016.

Kieninger E., *Wettbewerb der Privatrechtsordnungen in Europaischen Binnenmarkt*, Tübingen 2002.

Klein A., *Elementy zobowiązaniowego stosunku prawnego*, Wrocław 2005.

Klein A., *Ustawowe prawo odstąpienia*, Wrocław 1964.

Knapińska J., Madej K., *Niepełnosprawny z psem*, "Służba Pracownicza" 2010/11.

Kober A. [in:] Gsell B., Krüger W., Lorenz S., Mayer J. (ed.), *Beck-online Grosskommentar BGB*, München 2015.

Köbben A., *The logic of cross-cultural analysis: why exceptions?* [in:] Rokkan S. (ed.), *Comparative Research across Cultures and Nations*, Paris-The Hague 1968.

Koch A., Napierała J., *Umowy w obrocie gospodarczym*, Kraków 2006, Warszawa 2015.

Kocot J. W., *Odpowiedzialność przedkontraktowa,* Warszawa 2013.
Kocowski T. [in:] Borkowski A., Chełmoński A., Guziński M., Kiczka K., Kocowski T., Szydło M., Kieres L. (eds.), *Administracyjne prawo gospodarcze,* Wrocław 2009.
Koller I. [in:] Canaris C., Habersack M., Schäfer C., *Staub Handelsgesetzbuch Großkommentar,* Göttingen 2013.
Konopacki S., *Polska pięć lat w Unii Europejskiej,* Łódź 2009.
Konopka M., *10 - referendów akcesyjnych w 2003 roku,* UniaEuropejska.org - niezależny portal informacyjny o Unii Europejskiej, http://uniaeuropejska.org/10-referendw-akcesyjnych-w-2003-roku/.
Kozieł G. [in:] *Kodeks cywilny, Vol III, Zobowiązania. Część szczegółowa,* A. Kidyba (ed.), Warszawa 2014.
Kraemer L., *EU Environmental Law,* London, 2012.
Krajewski M. [in:] Łętowska E. (ed.), *System Prawa Prywatnego, Vol. V, Prawo zobowiązań - część ogólna,* Warszawa 2013.
Krajewski M., *Pierwotna niemożliwość świadczenia - między dwoma rozwiązaniami,* [in:] Olejniczak A., Haberko J., Pyrzyńska A., Sokołowska D., *Współczesne problemy prawa prywatnego,* Warszawa 2015.
Krawczyk J., *Haftung fuer Garantieerklaerungen im deutschen und polnischen Zivilrecht,* Konstanz 2015.
Kruczalak K., Rott-Pietrzyk E. [in:] Stec M., *System Prawa Handlowego. Prawo Umów handlowych, Vol. V,* Warszawa 2017.
Kufel J., *Umowa Agencyjna,* Poznań 1977.
Kunkiel-Kryńska A., *Metody harmonizacji prawa konsumenckiego w Unii Europejskiej i ich wpływ na procesy implementacyjne w państwach członkowskich,* Warszawa 2013.
Kwapiszewska-Antas M., *Człowiek wobec zwierząt na przestrzeni dziejów,* Słupskie Studia filozoficzne 2007, Issue 6, http://www.ssf.apsl.edu.pl/baza/wydawn/ssf06/kwapiszewska.pdf.
Kwaśnicki R.L., Lewandowski R., *Culpa in contrahendo w prawie polskim oraz niemieckim,* Prawo Spółek 2002, Issue 5.
Lasota K., *Verbraucherschutz im Internet nach polnischem Recht unter Berücksichtigung der europischen Rechtsangleichung,* München 2003.
Lazari-Radek K. & Singer P., *The Point Of View Of The Universe: Sidgwick And Contemporary Ethics,* Oxford 2014.
Lewandowska E., *Glosa do uchwały SN z dnia 20 stycznia 2010 r., III CZP 125/09,* Studia Prawnoustrojowe 2012, Issue 17.
Liberda E., *Odpowiedzialność kowali za wykonanie usługi,* Prawo i Konie 1 September 2014, http://prawoikonie.com/odpowiedzialnosc-kowali-za-wykonane-uslugi/.
Liljenstolpe C., *Horses in Europe,* Swedish University of Agricultural Sciences 2009, http://www.wbfsh.org/files/EU%20Equus%202009.pdf.
Locke J., *Some Thoughts Concerning Education,* London 1963.
Longchamps de Berier R., *Zobowiązania,* Lwów 1939.
Looschelders D., *Schuldrecht. Besonderer Teil,* Munchen 2012.
Lorenz S. [in:] Westermann H. (ed.), *Münchener Kommentar zum BGB, Vol. III,* München 2016.
Lubelska-Sazanów M., *Odpowiedzialność z tytułu rękojmi za wady fizyczne przy sprzedaży zwierząt,* Transformacje Prawa Prywatnego 2015, No 4.

Lubelska-Sazanów M., *The implementation of consumer directives into Polish law from the perspective of Directive 2011/83/EU of the European Parliament and of the Council of 25 October 2011 on consumer rights*, Právní ROZPRAVY, Vol. VI, Hradec Králové 2016.
Lubelska-Sazanów M., *The Wild Differences in Law when Trading in Wild Animals: a US and EU Perspective*, American Journal of Trade and Policy 2018, [S.l.], Vol. 4, No 3.
Lubelska-Sazanów M., *Zwierzę jako przedmiot świadczenia w umowach o użyywanie rzeczy* [in:] Pazdan M., Jagielska M., Rott-Pietrzyk E., Szpunar M. (eds.), *Rozprawy z prawa prywatnego: księga jubileuszowa dedykowana Profesorowi Wojciechowi Popiołkowi*, Warszawa 2017.
Ludwiczak W., *Umowa zlecenia*, Poznań 1955.
Lyster S., *International Wildlife Law: An Analysis of International Treaties concerned with the Conservation of Wildlife*, Cambridge 1993 (1985).
Łętowska E., *Dwa aspekty praw zwierząt, dereifikacja i personifikacja* [in:] Szpunar A. (ed.), *Studia z Prawa Prywatnego. Księga pamiątkowa ku czci prof. dr B. Lewaszkiewicz-Petrykowskiej*, Warszawa 1997.
Łętowska E. [in:] Łętowska E. (ed.), *System Prawa Prywatnego, vol. V, Prawo zobowiązań – część ogólna*, Warszawa 2013.
Łętowska E., Osajda K. [in:] Łętowska E. (ed.), *System Prawa Prywatnego, vol. V, Prawo zobowiązań – część ogólna*, Warszawa 2013.
Łętowska E., *Prawo umów konsumenckich*, Warszawa 2002.
Łętowski J., *W sprawie granicy międzyprawem publicznym a prywatnym* [in:] Kordasiewicz B., Łętowska E. (eds.), *Prace z prawa cywilnego. Wydane dla uczczenia prany naukowej Profesora Józefa Piątowskiego*, Wrocław/Warszawa/Kraków/Łódź 1985.
Łukaszewicz N., *Prawa zwierząt w kontekście społeczeństwa obywatelskiego i przeobrażeń cywilizacyjnych – praca magisterska na kierunku Stosunki międzynarodowe, Specjalność nauki polityczne na Wydziale Studiów Międzynarodowych i Politologicznych Uniwersytetu Łódzkiego*, Łódź 2010.
Machnicka A., *Przedkontraktowe porozumienia – umowa o negocjacje i list intencyjny. Studium prawnoporównawcze*, Warszawa 2007.
Machnikowski P. [in:] Gniewek E., Machnikowski P. (ed.), *Kodeks cywilny. Komentarz*, Warszawa 2017.
Machnikowski P., *Odpowiedzialność przedkontraktowa – jej podstawy, przesłanki i funkcje* [in:] Pazdan M., Popiołek W., Rott-Pietrzyk E., Szpunar M. (eds.), *Europeizacja prawa prywatnego*, Vol. I, Warszawa 2008.
Machnikowski P., *Swoboda umów według Article 353(1) KC. Konstrukcja prawna*, Warszawa 2005.
Machowska A., *Koncepcja zobowiązań rezultatu i starannego działania i jej doniosłość dla określenia odpowiedzialności kontraktowej*, KPP 2002, No 3.
Maestri M. de, Dominelli S. (eds.), *Party autonomy in European private (and) international law*, Rome 2014.
Magnus, U., *UN-Kaufrecht – Aktuelles zum CISG aufgespießt*, ZeUP 2017, Issue 1.
Malanczuk P., *Akehurst's Modern Introduction to International Law*, Routledge 1997.
Małysz F., *Kontrakty menedżerskie*, Służba Pracownicza 2012, Issue 8.
Mankowski P., *Rechtskultur*, Tübingen, 2016.
Mansel H. [in:] Stürner R. (ed.), *Jauernig, Kommentar zum BGB*, München 2015.

Maria G. A., *Public perception of farm animal welfare in Spain*, Livestock Science 2006, Vol. 3, Issue 103.

Markesinis S., Unberath H., Johnston A. C., *The German Law of Contract – A comparative Treatise*, Oxford 2006.

Martin R., *When CITES Works and When it Does Not* [in:] J. Hutton, B. Dickson (eds.), *Endangered Species, Threatened Convention: The Past, Present and Future of CITES*, 2000.

Marx N. F. Fallstricke [in:] Pferderechtsprozessen seit Abschaffung des Viehgewährleistungsrechts, NJW 2010, No 39.

Matusik G. [in:] Osajda K. (ed.), *Kodeks cywilny. Komentarz. Tom II. Własność I inne prawa rzeczowe, Ustawa o księgach wieczystych I hipotece (Article 2–22, 65–111[1]), Ustawa o zastawie rejestrowym i rejestrze zastawów*,, Warszawa 2017.

Mertens B., *Culpa in contrahendo beim zustande gekommenen Kaufvertrag nach der Schuldrechtsreform*, Archiv für die civilistische Praxis (ACP) 2003, Issue 6/203, pp. 818–854.

Merz-Perez L., Heide K., Silverman I., *Childhood cruelty to animals and subsequent violence against humans*, International Journal of Offender Therapy and Comparative Criminology 2001, vol. 45, No 5.

Michalak A., *Nowa Zelandia: Rzeka Whanganui została uznana za osobę prawną*, Rzeczpospolita 16 March 2017, http://www.rp.pl/Spoleczenstwo/170319159-Nowa-Zelandia-Rzeka-Whanganui-zostala-uznana-za-osobe-prawna.html.

Michałowska K., *Argumenty z prawa obcego w uzasadnieniu uchwał i orzeczeń Sądu Najwyższego*, [in:] Olejniczak A., Haberko J., Pyrzyńska A., Sokołowska D. (eds.), *Współczesne problemy prawa zobowiązań*, Warszawa 2015.

Micklitz H.-W., Purnhagen K. [in:] Säcker J. (ed.), *Münchener Kommentar zum BGB, Vol. I*, München 2015.

Mill J., *Rationale of judicial evidence, specially applied to English practice from the manuscripts of Jeremy Bentham* 475, IV (Book 8, Chapter 29), London 1827.

Morris D., *Nasza umowa ze zwierzętami*, Warszawa 1995.

Mrozowska M., *Umowy o zarz*ądzanie, Państwo i Prawo 1996, Issue 5.

Mudrock G., *Social structure*, New York 1949.

Müller-Glöge R. [in:] Henssler M. (ed.), *Münchener Kommentar zum BGB, Vol. IV*, München 2012.

Mycko-Katner I., *Umowa agencyjna*, Warszawa 2012.

Napierała J. [in:] Rajski J. (ed.), *System Prawa Prywatnego, Vol. VII, Prawo zobowiązań – część szczegółowa*, Warszawa 2011.

Norris R. T., *Transport of animals by sea*, Revue Scientifique et technique Office Intenational des Episooties 2005, Issue2/24.

Nowacki J., *Prawo publiczne – prawo prywatne*, Katowice 1992.

Nowacki J., *Odpowiednie stosowanie przepisów prawa*, PiP 1964, Issue 3.

Oexmann B., *Sachmangel Pferdekauf – von der Kasuistik zur Typologie*, Sozietät Dr. Oexmann 29 Jaunary 2007, http://www.oexmann.de/pferderecht/2/publikationen/jahr/2007/monat/01.

Ogiegło L. [in:] Pietrzykowski K. (ed.), *Kodeks cywilny. Komentarz*, Warszawa 2015.

Ogiegło L., *Usługi jako przedmiot stosunków obligacyjnych*, Katowice 1989.

Ogiegło L. [in:] Rajski J. (ed.), *System Prawa Prywatnego, Vol. VII, Prawo zobowiązań – część szczegółowa*, Warszawa 2011.

Ohanowicz A., Górski J., *Zarys prawa zobowiązań*, Warszawa 1970.

Oldfield S. F., *The Evolving Role of CITES in Regulating the International Timber Trade*, 22 Review Of European Comparative & International Environmental Law, 29/2013.

Olejniczak A. [in:] Olejniczak A. (ed.), *System Prawa Prywatnego, vol. VI, Prawo zobowiązań – część ogólna*, Warszawa 2014.

Olejniczak W. [in:] Rajski J. (ed.), *System Prawa Prywatnego. Volume VII. Prawo zobowiązań-część szczegółowa*, Warszawa 2011.

Olszewski J., Paszek A., *Umowy o dzieło, agencyjne, zlecenia. Objaśnienia i wzory*, Warszawa 2000.

Orlicki M. [in:] Gutowski M. (ed.), *Kodeks cywilny, Vol I, Komentarz do Article 1–449[11]*, Warszawa 2016.

Ortega E., Peñalosa J., *The Spanish economic crisis: key factors and growth challenges in the Euro area*, Documentos Ocasionales No 1201, Banco de España, https://www.bde.es/f/webbde/SES/Secciones/Publicaciones/PublicacionesSeriadas/DocumentosOcasionales/12/Fich/do1201e.pdf.

Osajda K. (ed.), *Kodeks cywilny. Komentarz. Tom II. Własność I inne prawa rzeczowe, Ustawa o księgach wieczystych I hipotece (Article 2–22, 65–111[1]), Ustawa o zastawie rejestrowym I rejestrze zastawów,*, Warszawa 2017.

Osajda K. (ed.), *Kodeks cywilny. Komentarz. Tom IIIA. Zobowiązania. Część ogólna*, Warszawa 2017.

Osajda K. (ed.), *Kodeks cywilny. Komentarz. Tom IIIB*, Warszawa 2017.

Pajor T., *Odpowiedzialność dłużnika za niewykonanie zobowiązania*, Warszawa 1982.

Panowicz-Lipska J. (ed.), *System Prawa Prywatnego*, Vol. 8, *Prawo zobowiązań – część szczegółowa*, Warszawa 2011.

PAP, *Kiedy wspólny system azylowy w Unii?*, Forbes 12 July 2011, https://www.forbes.pl/wiadomosci/o-rowne-traktowanie-azylantow-w-unii-europejskiej/327yh2n.

PAP, *Komisja Europejska stawia ultimatum Polsce, Czechom i Węgrom. Albo przyjęcie uchodźców albo Trybunał*, Newsweek Polska 6 September 2017, http://www.newsweek.pl/swiat/polityka/ke-stawia-ultimatum-polsce-przyjecie-uchodzcow-albo-trybunal,artykuly,415606,1.html.

Partikel A., *Formularbuch für Sportverträge*, München, 2015.

Pavlou L., *Greek Animal Rights Groups Disapprove of New Animal Law*, Greek Reporter 13 July 2011, http://greece.greekreporter.com/2011/07/13/disapproval-over-new-law-regarding-animals/.

Pazdan M. [in:] Pazdan M., (ed.), *System Prawa Prywatnego, vol. XX B, Prawo prywatne międzynarodowe*, Warszawa 2015.

Pecyna M., *Ustawa o sprzedaży konsumenckiej*, Warszawa 2004.

Pełczyńska-Nałęcz K., *Polska polityka wschodnia a Europejska Polityka Sąsiedzka*, Międzynarodowy Przegląd Polityczny 3–4 (8–9)/2004.

Peters A., *Global Animal Law: What it is and why we need it*, Transnational Environmental Law 2016, Issue 1, Vol. 5.

Peters F., *Der Anspruch auf Abnahme bei Kauf und Werkvertrag* [in:] Forstmoser P., Giger H., Heini A., Schluep W. (ed.), *Festschrift für Max Keller zum 65. Geburtstag*, Zürich 1989.

Pietrzykowski K. [in:] Pietrzykowski K. (ed.), *Kodeks cywilny. Komentarz*, Warszawa 2015. (ed.), *Kodeks cywilny. Komentarz*, Warszawa 2015.

T. Pietrzykowski, *Naturalizm i granice nauk prawnych. Esej z metodologii prawoznawstwa*, Warszawa 2017.

Pietrzykowski T., *Recenzja książki M. Rudego, A. Rudego, P. Mazura, Ubój rytualny w prawie administracyjnym, Warszawa 2013*, Prokuratura i Prawo 2014, Issue 3.

Pietrzykowski T., *Spór o prawa zwierząt*, Katowice 2007.

Pinillos R., Appleby M., Manteca X., Scott-Park F., Smith C., Velarde A., *One Welfare – a platform for improving human and animal welfare*, Veterinary Record 179 (16)/2016.

Pinior P. (ed.), *Evolution of private law – new approaches*, Katowice 2016.

Pisula W., *Psychologia zachowań eksploracyjnych zwierząt*, Gdańsk 2003.

Podrecka M., *Rękojmia za wady prawne rzeczy sprzedanej*, Warszawa 2011.

Poispil L., *Kapauku Papuans and their law*, New Haven 1958.

Pokrzywniak J., *Obowiązek lojalności jako element stosunku obligacyjnego*, MoP 2003, No 19.

Popiołek W., *Znaczenie przepisów "prawa publicznego" różnych systemów prawnych dla stosunków umownych handlu zagranicznego*, Problemy Prawne Handlu Zagranicznego 199, Issue 12.

Popiołek W. [in:] Pietrzykowski K. (ed.), *Kodeks cywilny. Komentarz*, Warszawa 2015.

Popper K., *Logik der Forschung* [trans. *The logic of scientific discovery*], Tübingen 1934.

Pound R., *Law in Books and Law in Action*, American Law Review 1910, Vol. 44, Issue I.

Preston N., *Understanding Ethics*, Sydney 2014.

Promińska U. [in:] Katner W. (ed.), *System Prawa Prywatnego, Vol. IX, Prawo zobowiązań – umowy nienawzwane*, Warszawa 2015.

Radcliffe-Brown A., *A note on Functionalist Anthropology*, Man 46/1946.

Radecki W., *Ustawy: o ochronie zwierząt, o doświadczeniach na zwierzętach – z komentarzem*, Warszawa 2007.

Radwański Z. (ed.), *System Prawa Prywatnego, Prawo cywilne – część ogólna, Vol. II*, Warszawa 2008.

Radwański Z., Panowicz-Lipska J., *Zobowiązania – część szczegółowa*, Warszawa 2015.

Radwański Z., *Podmioty prawa cywilnego w świetle zmian kodeksu cywilnego przeprowadzonych ustawą z dnia 14 lutego 2003 r.*, Przegląd Sądowy 2003, No 7–8.

Radwański Z., *Recenzja pracy autorstwa A. Kleina, Elementy stosunku zobowiązaniowego*, RPEiS 1965, Issue 1.

Radwański Z., *Uwagi o umowach mieszanych*, ZNUJ 1985, Issue 41.

Radwański Z., *Teoria umów*, Warszawa 1977.

Radwański Z., *Wykładnia oświadczeń woli składanych indywidualnym adresatom*, Wrocław/Warszawa/Kraków, 1992.

Radwański Z., *Zielona Księga. Optymalna wizja Kodeksu cywilnego Rzeczypospolitej Polskiej*, Ruch Prawniczy, Ekonomiczny i Socjologiczny 1/2007.

Rajski J. [in:] Rajski J. (ed.), *System Prawa Prywatnego. Volume VII. Prawo zobowiązań- część szczegółowa*, Warszawa 2011.

Rajski J. (ed.), *System Prawa Prywatnego, Vol. VII, Prawo zobowiązań – część szczegółowa*, Warszawa 2011.

Rankin J., *Greece in Europe: a short history*, The Guardian 3 July 2015, https://www.theguardian.com/world/2015/jul/03/greece-in-europe-a-short-history.

Reagan T., *The Case for Animal Rights,* Berkeley/Los Angeles 2004 (first published in 1983).

Reimann M., Zimmermann R. (eds.), *The Oxford handbook of comparative law,* Oxford 2008.

Rejman G., *Ochrona Prawa Zwierząt,* Studia Iuridica 2006, Issue XLVI.

Richardson P., *Why bullfighting is making Spain see red,* The Guardian 6 June 2010, https://www.theguardian.com/world/2010/jun/06/bullfighting-outlawed-catalonia.

Romanowski M., Kocot W., Kappes A. [in:] Katner W. (ed.), *System Prawa Prywatnego, Vol. IX, Prawo zobowiązań – umowy nienawzwane,* Warszawa 2015.

Rosbach P., *Pferderecht,* München 2011.

Rott-Pietrzyk E., *Commercial Agency Contracts and Freedom of Contract* [in:] Drygala T., Heiderhoff B., Staake M., Zmij G. (ed.), *Private Autonomy in Germany and in Poland and in Private European Sales Law,* Munich 2012.

Rott-Pietrzyk E., *Agent handlowy – regulacje polskie i europejskie,* Warszawa 2006.

Rott-Pietrzyk E., *Commercial Agency Contracts and Freedom of Contract* [in:] Drygala T., Heiderhoff B., Staake M., Zmij G. (ed.), *Private Autonomy in Germany and in Poland and in Private European Sales Law,* Munich 2012.

Rott-Pietrzyk E., *Glosa do wyroku Sądu Najwyższego z dnia 28 października 1999 r.*, II CKN 530/98, OSP 2000, No, 7/8.

Rott-Pietrzyk, E. [in:] Pazdan M., (ed.), *System Prawa Prywatnego, Vol. XX B, Prawo prywatne międzynarodowe,* Warszawa 2015.

Rott-Pietrzyk, E. [in:] Rajski J. (ed.), *System Prawa Prywatnego, Vol. VII, Prawo zobowiązań – część szczegółowa,* Warszawa 2011.

Rott-Pietrzyk E. [in:] Stec M., *System Prawa Handlowego. Prawo umów handlowych, Vol. V,* Warszawa 2017.

Rott-Pietrzyk E., *Klauzule generalne a wykonanie zobowiązania (z uwzględnieniem koncepcji systemu klauzul generalnych w projekcie KC)* [in:] Gniewek E., Górska K., Machnikowski P. (ed.), *Zaciąganie i wykonywanie zobowiązań,* Warszawa 2010.

Rott-Pietrzyk E., *Komentarz do Dyrektywy Rady nr 86/653 z 18 grudnia 1986 roku w sprawie harmonizacji praw państw członkowskich dotyczących niezależnych agentów handlowych,* Probemy Prawne Handlu Zagranicznego 2000, Issue 19/20.

Rott-Pietrzyk E., *Ochrona przedsiębiorcy jako strony słabszej na przykładzie agenta handlowego* [in:] Boratyńska M., *Księga Jubileuszowa ofiarowana Profesorowi Adamowi Zielińskiemu,* Warszawa 2016.

Rott-Pietrzyk E., *Umowa agencyjna w prawie polskim a standardy europejskie,* Kwartalnik Prawa Pryw. 1998, No 1.

Rott-Pietrzyk E., *Wygaśnięcie umowy agencyjnej,* Rejent 1999, No 9 (101).

Rott-Pietrzyk E., *Wykładnia oświadczenia woli (studium prawnoporównawcze),* Studia Prawa Prywatnego 2007, No 3–4.

Rott-Pietrzyk E., Grochowski M., *Prowizja agenta w czasie trwania umowy (imperatywny czy dyspozytywny charakter regulacji i wynikające z tego konsekwencje),* TPP 2018, Issue 4.

Roy E. A., *New Zealand river granted same legal rights as human being,* The Guardian 16 March 2017, https://www.theguardian.com/world/2017/mar/16/new-zealand-river-granted-same-legal-rights-as-human-being.

Rudy M., Rudy A., Mazur P., *Ubój rytualny w prawie administracyjnym,* Warszawa 2013.

Saenger I. [in:] Schulze R., Dörner H., Ebert I., Hoeren T., Kemper R., Saenger I., Schreiber K., Schulte-Nölke H., Staudinger A. (eds.), *Bürgerliches Gesetzbuch. Handkommentar,* Baden-Baden 2016.

Sandgren C., *On Empirical Legal Science,* Scandinavian studies in law 2000, Issue 40.

Sandøe P., Christiansen S., *The Ethics of Animal Use,* Copenhagen 2008.

Safjan M. [in:] Pietrzykowski K. (ed.), *Kodeks cywilny. Komentarz,* Warszawa 2015.

Schaper J., Kandelhard R., *Leistungsstörungen und Gewährleistungsrecht,* NJW 1997, Nr 13, p. 836.

Schmidt K., *Handelsrecht,* Köln 2014.

Schneider M., *Die Reitbeteiligung – Was man als Pferdebesitzer und Reiter zu Vertrag, Haftung und Versicherung wissen sollte!,* http://www.mps-pferderecht.de/die-reitbeteiligung-was-man-als-pferdebesitzer-und-reiter-zu-vertrag-haftung-und-versicherung-wissen-sollte.html.

Schnorbus Y., *Die richtlinienkonforme Rechtsfortbildung im nationalen Privatrecht,* Archiv für die civilistische Praxis (ACP) 2001, Issue 6/201.

Schreiber K. [in:] Schulze R., Dörner H., Ebert I., Hoeren T., Kemper R., Saenger I., Schreiber K., Schulte-Nölke H., Staudinger A. (eds.), *Bürgerliches Gesetzbuch. Handkommentar,* Baden-Baden 2016.

Schuhmacher D. [in:] M. Düsing, J. Martinez, *Beck'scher Kurzkommentare,* München 2016.

Schulte-Nölke H., Zoll F., Jansen N., Schulze R. (eds.), *Der Entwurf für ein optionales europäisches Kaufrecht,* München, 2012.

Schulze R. (ed.), *Common European Sales Law – Commentary,* Baden-Baden 2012.

Shyaam G., *The legal status of animals: The world rethinks its position,* Alternative Law Journal 2015, http://www.altlj.org/feature-articles/980-the-legal-status-of-animals-the-world-rethinks-its-position.

Siedlecka E., *Ziobro zlikwidował Komisję Kodyfikacyjną Prawa Cywilnego. Działała ponad 20 lat,* wyborcza.pl 17 December 2015, http://wyborcza.pl/1,75398,19359773,ziobro-zlikwidowal-komisje-kodyfikacyjna-prawa-cywilnego.html.

Siems M., *Comparative Law,* Cambridge 2014.

Sienkiewicz H., *Ogniem i mieczem, Warszawa 1884.*

Sienkiewicz H., *Pan Wołodyjowski,* Warszawa 1888.

Sienkiewicz H., *Potop,* Warszawa 1886.

Singer P., *Animal Liberation,* New York 1975.

Singer P., *Wyzwolenie Zwierząt* [Animal Liberation] (Anna Alichniewicz, Anna Szczęsna trans.), Warszawa 2004.

Siuda W., *Istota i zakres umowy o dzieło,* Poznań 1964.

Skowrońska-Bocian E., Warciński M. [in:] Pietrzykowski K. (ed.), *Kodeks cywilny. Komentarz,* Warszawa 2015.

Slomski M., *Die geschichtliche Entwicklung des polnischen Verbraucherkaufrechtes und die Umsetzung der Verbrauchsgüterkaufrichtlinie in Polen,* Hamburg 2011.

Smith A., *Purge at Poland's renowned stud farms pits against rich and famous,* The Guardian 8 April 2016, https://www.theguardian.com/world/2016/apr/08/purge-at-polands-renowned-stud-farms-pits-politicians-against-rich-and-famous.

Smith H., *Interview with Alexis Tsipras: "The worst is clearly behind us"*, The Guardian 24 July 2017, https://www.theguardian.com/world/2017/jul/24/alexis-tsipras-the-worst-is-clearly-behind-us.

Snitko-Pleszko M., *Kodeks cywilny po nowelizacji. Cz. II. Konsument, przedsiębiorca, przedsiębiorstwo, gospodarstwo rolne, oferta, aukcja i przetarg,* MOP 2003, No 10.

Sommer M., *Der Pferdekauf*, Münster/Westfalen 2000.

Sowery K., *Sentient beings and tradable products: the curious constitutional status of animals under Union law,* Common Market Law Review 2018, Issue 55.

Sprau H. [in:] Palandt O., *Beck'sche Kurz-Kommentare: Palandt Bürgerliches Gesetzbuch mit Nebengesetzen,* München 2015.

Stelmachowski A., *Wstęp do teorii prawa cywilnego,* Warszawa 1984.

Sten-Ziemons A., *Deutschland einig Pferdeland,* DW 20 July 2013, http://www.dw.com/de/deutschland-einig-pferdeland/a-16911941.

Strawiński P., *Życie po Brexicie,* Forbes 24 June 2016, https://www.forbes.pl/wiadomosci/brexit-jakie-beda-skutki-wyjscia-wielkiej-brytanii-z-ue/qgrxtrb.

Strus Z., *Przegląd orzecznictwa,* Palestra 2010, Issue 3.

Stucki S., *Grundrechte für Tiere: eine Kritik des geltenden Tierschutzrechts und rechtstheoretische Grundlegung von Tierrechten im Rahmen einer Neupositionierung des Tieres als Rechtssubjekt,* Baden- Baden 2016.

Sunstein C., Nussbaum M. (eds.), *Animal Rights: Current Debates and New Directions,* New York 2004.

Szczerbak E., *Polskie konie to już swiatowa, prestiżowa marka,* Polskie Radio 22 December 2015, https://www.polskieradio.pl/42/3725/Artykul/1560642,Polskie-konie-to-juz-swiatowa-prestizowa-marka.

Szpunar A., *Odstąpienie od umowy o przeniesienie własności nieruchomości,* Rejent 1995, Issue 6.

Sztejnert O., *Świadczenie wyrównawcze dla agenta albo jaki wpływ na polskie orzecznictwo może mieć nowelizacja niemieckiego HGB,* MoP 2010, No 14.

Szydło W. [in:] Gniewek E., Machnikowski P. (eds.), *Kodeks cywilny. Komentarz,* Warszawa 2017.

Tannenbaum J., *Veterinary ethics: Animal welfare, client relations, competition and collegiality,* St Louis 1995.

Tatarkiewicz W., *Historia filozofii,* Vol. 2, Warszawa 1988.

Tawse J., *Consumer attitudes towards farm animals and their welfare: a pig production case study,* Bioscience Horizons: The International Journal of Student Research 2010, Vol.3, Issue 2.

Taylor A., *Animals and Ethics: An Overview of the Philosophical Debate,* Toronto 2003.

Teichman A. [in:] Stürner R. (ed.), *Jauernig, Kommentar zum BGB,* München 2015.

Tonner K., Willingmann A., Tabb M. (eds.), *Vertragsrecht,* Köln 2010.

Topolewski K., *Umowa agencyjna według Kodeksu cywilnego. Wybrane problem de lege ferenda* [in:] Olejniczak A., Haberko J., Pyrzyńska A., Sokołowska D., *Współczesne problemy prawa prywatnego,* Warszawa 2015.

Tracz G., *Sposoby jednostronnej rezygnacji z zobowiązań umownych,* Warszawa/ Kraków 2007.

Trzaskowki, R. Granice swobody kształtowania treści i celu umów obligacyjnych, Kraków 2005.

Trzaskowski R. [in:] Bielska-Sobkowicz T., Ciepła H., Drapała P., Gudowski J., Trzaskowski R., Wiśniewski T., Żuławska C. (eds.), *Kodeks cywilny. Komentarz, Vol. IV, Zobowiązania: część szczegółowa,* Warszawa 2017.

Tulibacka M. [in:] Osajda K. (ed.), *Kodeks cywilny. Komentarz. Tom IIIB,* Warszawa 2017.

Tuora-Schwierskott E., *Rytualny ubój zwierząt w świetle wolności sumienia i wyznania oraz zasady proporcjonalności w ustawodawstwie i orzecznictwie Niemiec, Szwajcarii i USA*, Państwo i Prawo 2016, Issue 4.

Tylor E., *Primitive Culture: Researches into the Development of Mythology, Philosophy, Religion, Art, and Custom*, New York 1974 [1871].

Ulen T. S., *A Nobel Prize in Legal Science: Theory, Empirical Work, and the Scientific Method in the Study of Law,* Illinois Law Review 2002, Issue 4.

Van Hoecke M. (ed.), *Methodology of Legal Research. What Kind od Method for What Kind of Discipline?,* Oxford/Portland 2011.

Veissiera I., Butterworth A., Bock B., Roe E., *European approaches to ensure good animal welfare,* Applied Animal Behaviour Science 2008, Issue 4/113.

Verrinder J., McGrath V., Phillips C., *Science, Animal Ethics and the Law* [in:] D. Cao, S. White (eds.), *Animal Law and Welfare – International Perspectives,* Switzerland 2016.

Verrinder M., McGrath N., Philips C., *Science, Animal Ethics and Law* [in:] D. Cao, S. White (eds.), *Animal Law and Welfare – International Perspectives.*

Voy O., *Rechte und Pflichten einer Reitbeteiligung*, Reiter und Pferde 3/2007.

Waal F. de, *Are We Smart Enough to Know How Smart Animals Are?,* New York 2016.

Wagner C. [in:] Bamberger H., Roth H., Hau W., Poseck R. (eds.), *Beck'sche Online Kommentare, BeckOK, BGB*, 44. Ed., München 2017.

Walter Ł., *Umowa pensjonatowa – potrzebna czy nie?,* Konie i Rumaki 7/2012, http://www.konieirumaki.pl/pl/umowa-pensjonatowa.

Weidenkaff W. [in:] Palandt O., *Beck'sche Kurz-Kommentare: Palandt Bürgerliches Gesetzbuch mit Nebengesetzen*, München 2015.

Wertenbruch J., *Die Besonderheiten des Tierkaufs bei der Sachmängelgewährleistung,* NJW 2012, No 29.

Westermann H. [in:] Westermann H. (ed.), *Münchener Kommentar zum BGB, Vol. III,* München 2016.

Westermann H., *Zu den Gewährleistungsansprüche des Käufers*, ZGS 2005.

Westphalen E. G. von, *Der BGH auf der Suche nach dem Normpferd*, ZGS 2007.

White S., *Into the Void: International Law and the Protection of Animal Welfare,* Global Policy Journal 2013, Issue 4/4.

Widdows K., *What is an agreement in International Law?,* BYIL 50 1979.

Widło J., *Rękojmia za wady fizyczne w świetle nowelizacji Kodeksu cywilnego,* Monitor Prawniczy 4/2015, pp. 177–186.

Wilhelmsson T., *Towards a (Post)modern European Contract Law* [in:] Juridica International 6/2001.

Wise S. M., *Rattling the cage. Towards Legal Rights for Animals,* Cambridge, Mass.: Perseus Books, 2000. Włodyka S. (ed.), *System Prawa Handlowego, Vol. I,* Warszawa 2009.

Włodyka S. (ed.), *Prawo Umów Handlowych, Vol. V,* Warszawa 2017.

Wojciechowski J., *Ochrona zwierząt w UE – w dobrym kierunku zbyt małymi krokami* [in:] Gardocka T., Gruszczyńska A., *Status zwierzęcia. Zagadnienia filozoficzne i prawne*, Toruń 2012.

Wójcik S., *Odgraniczenie umowy o dzieło od umowy o pracę i od umowy zlecenia*, ZNUJ 1963, No 10.

Wójcik S., *Pojęcie umowy o dzieło*, S.C. 1963, t. IV.

Wojtas M., *Studien zum ausländisches und internationalen Privatrecht: Haftung für culpa in contrahendo*, Tübingen, 2017.

Wright J., Hensley C., *From Animal Cruelty to Serial Murder: Applying the Graduation Hypothesis*, International Journal of Offender Therapy and Comparative Criminology 2003, vol. 43, No 1.

Zagrobelny K. [in:] Gniewek E., Machnikowski P. (ed.), *Kodeks cywilny. Komentarz*, Warszawa 2017.

Zaradkiewicz K. [in:] Pietrzykowski K. (ed.), *Kodeks cywilny. Komentarz*, Warszawa 2015.

Ziembiński Z., *Metodologiczne zagadanienia prawoznawstwa*, Warszawa 1974.

Ziemiak M., *Requiem dla komisji kodyfikacyjnej*, Instytut Obywatelski 25 January 2016, http://www.instytutobywatelski.pl/24577/komentarze/requiem-dla-komisji-kodyfika cyjnej.

Zimmerman M., Dyson S., Murray R.: *Comparison of radiographic and scintigraphic findings of the spinous processes in the equine thoracolumbar region*, Vet. Radiol, Ultrasound 2001, No 52.

Zimmermann R. (ed.), *Zukunftsperspektiven der Rechtsvergleichung*, Tübingen 2006.

Zoll F. [in:] Popiołek W. (ed.), *System prawa handlowego. Międzynarodowe prawo handlowe, Vol. IX*,, Warszawa 2013.

Zoll F., *Rękojmia. Odpowiedzialność sprzedawcy w świetle znowelizowanych przepisów kodeksu cywilnego*, Warszawa 2018.

Online resources*

American Humane Association Guidelines, https://www.americanhumane.org/publication/guidelines-for-producersfilmmakers/.
Artyzm Art Gallery, *Konie w malarastwie polskim*, http://artyzm.com/theme.php?id=8t.
Athens guide, *Stray dogs*, https://www.athensguide.com/straydogs/.
Australian Cattle Dog Breeding Club in Germany: http://www.acdcd.de/images/pdf/Mietzuchtantrag.pdf.
"Z Peronówki" website: https://www.zperonowki.com/site/pl/node/582.
CITES Secretariat, https://cites.org/eng/disc/what.php.
European Union website: https://europa.eu/european-union/about-eu/institutions-bodies_pl.
European Commission on animal welfare: https://ec.europa.eu/food/animals/welfare/other_aspects_en, https://ec.europa.eu/food/animals/welfare/legislative_aspects_en; http://ec.europa.eu/food/animals/welfare/index_en.htm; https://ec.europa.eu/food/animals/welfare/main_achievements_en/.
European Commission, *An Introduction to CITES and its Implementation in the European Union* (2010), http://ec.europa.eu/environment/cites/pdf/trade_regulations/short_ref_guide.pdf, http://ec.europa.eu/environment/cites/legislation_en.htm.
European Commission, *EU Animal Welfare strategy: 2012–2015*, https://ec.europa.eu/food/sites/food/files/animals/docs/aw_brochure_strategy_en.pdf.
European Commission, *The European Union explained – Environment*, https://publications.europa.eu/pl/publication-detail/-/publication/3456359b-4cb4-4a6e-9586-6b9846931463/language-en.
European Commission, *The European Union explained – Internal Market*, https://publications.europa.eu/pl/publication-detail/-/publication/f85c0e8f-4cdf-4859-be26-f9c17e7fbb6f/language-en.
European Court of Human Rights website: http://www.echr.coe.int/Documents/UE_FAQ_ENG.pdf.
European Parliament, *Animal Welfare in the European Union*, a study for the PETI-Committee, http://www.europarl.europa.eu/RegData/etudes/STUD/2017/583114/IPOL_STU(2017)583114_EN.pdf.

* Views of the representatives of the doctrine and press articles available online are included in the Bibliography above.

European Parliament, *Sources and Scope of European Union Law,* http://www.europarl.europa.eu/ftu/pdf/en/FTU_1.2.1.pdf.

European Society of Dog and Animal Welfare – ESDAW: http://www.esdaw-eu.eu/the-eu-and-animal-welfare.html.

European Society of Dog and Animal Welfare (NGO), http://www.esdaw.eu/greece-massacre.html.

Eurostat, http://ec.europa.eu/eurostat/web/labour-market/earnings/database.

German Dalmatian Breeding Club website, http://www.cdf-dalmatinerverein.de/dokumente/Zuchtordnung_Stand_2014.pdf.

German foundation for visually impaired people *Stiftung Ostschweizerische Blindenführhundeschule,* https://o-b-s.ch/programm/einfuehrungslehrgang/.

German foundation for visually impaired people *Stiftung Schweizerische Schule für Blindenführhunde,* http://www.blindenhundeschule.ch/fuehrhunde/ein-fuehrhund-fuer-sie.html.

Gesetze im Internet, https://www.gesetze-im-internet.de/englisch_bgb/englisch_bgb.html#p2908.

Greek Animal Welfare Fund – GAWF: https://www.gawf.org.uk/what-we-do-1.

Greek charity Animal Protection Aegina Agistri (APAA), *Greece massacre,* http://www.aeginagreece.com/aegina/pages/articles/animals/animal_issues_greece.html.

Green book presenting changes proposed to the Polish Civil Code from 2007, edited by Z. Radwański, http://www.bip.ms.gov.pl/Data/Files/_public/bip/kkpc/zielona_ksiega.pdf.

Hannoveraner Horses Society, http://www.hannoveraner.com/hannoveraner-verband/, http://www.hannoveraner.com/hannoveraner-verband/auktionen/auktionsarchiv/auktionen-2016/verdener-/auktion-januar/auktionsbroschuere/.

Holsteiner Horses Society, http://holsteiner-verband.de/.

Horse pension "Country club", http://www.countryclub.nowyfolwark.pl/Media/Files/umowa-pensjonatowa-country-club.pdf.

Hundevermittlung Herzensache e.V., http://www.hundevermittlung-herzenssache.com/.cm4all/uproc.php/0/FORMULARE/Adoptions-Vertrag.pdf?cdp=a.

Janów Arabian stables, http://www.janow.arabians.pl/pl/historia/polskie-araby.php, http://www.prideofpoland.com/en/.

Ministry of Treasury Republic of Poland, https://www.msp.gov.pl/en/polish-economy/economic-news/5462,Polands-economic-progress-after-10-years-in-the-European-Union.html.

Moszna stables, http://moszna.pl/sprzedaz-koni/dzierzawa-koni-sportowych/.

Newfoundland breed website: http://www.neufieve.de/Frames/Eve/Welpen.htm.

Newspaper "Gallop", http://gallop.pl/zasady-dzierzawy-konia-umowa/.

Oldenburger Horses Society, http://oldenburger-pferde.net/.

Paros Animal Welfare Society – PAWS: http://paws.gr.

Pferd aktuell, *http://www.pferd-aktuell.de/ausbildung/berufsausbildung/berufsausbildung.*

Polish Ministry of Justice, https://bip.ms.gov.pl/pl/dzialalnosc/komisje-kodyfikacyjne/komisja-kodyfikacyjna-prawa-cywilnego/.

Pride of Poland auction (no longer organised), http://www.prideofpoland.pl/.

PZJ, *Doszkalanie kadr instruktorsko-trenerskich – Warunki oraz tryb przyznawania i pozbawiania licencji szkoleniowca oraz certyfikatu instruktora szkolenia podstawowego PZJ*, http://pzj.pl/sites/default/files/przepisy/doszkalanie_kadr_regulamin_2015_02_12.pdf.

PZJ, *Zawód jeździec, http://www.pzj.pl/node/zawód-jeździec.*

RöLF, http://www.bundestieraerztekammer.de/downloads/btk/leitlinien/RoentgenLeitfaden_2007.pdf.

Stucki S., *The Personhood Beyond the Human: On The "Animal Person" as Legal Persons* (video), Institute for Ethics and Emerging Technologies 31 December 2013, https://ieet.org/index.php/IEET2/more/personhood201401.

The human society website, available at: http://www.humanesociety.org/assets/pdfs/wildlife/exotics/state-laws-dangerous-wild-animals.pdf.

The human society, http://www.humanesociety.org/assets/pdfs/wildlife/exotics/state-laws-dangerous-wild-animals.pdf.

The Polish Law Collection, Translegis, www.legalis.pl.

United Nations, http://www.un.org/disabilities/default.asp?id=235.

Vis Maior Foundation, http://fundacjavismaior.pl/dzialania/psy-przewodniki/zostan-wlascicielem/.

Wzajemnie Pomocni Foundation, http://www.wzajemniepomocni.pl/images/umowa.pdf.

Zwierzęca Przystań Foundation, http://zwierzecaprzystan.pl/wp-content/uploads/2017/01/UMOWA-ADOPCYJNA-PSA.pdf.

Legal acts and public documents

Austrian Civil Code [*Allgemeines Bürgerliches Gesetzbuch*] of 1 May 1812, J.L. 946/1816, as amended.

Commission Implementing Regulation (EU) 2015/262 of 17 February 2015 laying down rules pursuant to Council Directives 90/427/EEC and 2009/156/EC as regards the methods for the identification of equidae (Equine Passport Regulation), OJ 59, 3 March 2015, pp. 1–53.

Commission Implementing Regulation (EU) No 577/2013 of 28 June 2013 on the model identification documents for the non-commercial movement of dogs, cats and ferrets, the establishment of lists of territories and third countries and the format, layout and language requirements of the declarations attesting compliance with certain conditions provided for in Regulation (EU) No 576/2013 of the European Parliament and of the Council Text with EEA relevance, OJ 178, 28 June 2013, pp. 109–148.

Commission Regulation (EC) No 865/2006 of 4 May 2006 laying down detailed rules concerning the implementation of Council Regulation (EC) No 338/97 on the protection of species of wild fauna and flora by regulating trade therein, OJ 166, 19 June 2006, pp. 1–69.

Commission staff working document – Annex to the Communication from the Commission to the European Parliament and the Council on a Community Action Plan on the Protection and Welfare of Animals 2006–2010 and Commission working document on a Community Action Plan on the Protection and Welfare of Animals 2006–2010 – Strategic basis for the proposed actions – Impact assessment {COM(2006) 13 final} {COM(2006) 14 final}, SEC/2006/0065.

Communication from the Commission to the European Parliament, the Council and the European Economic and Social Committee on the European Union Strategy for the Protection and Welfare of Animals 2012–2015, p. 5, available at: https://ec.europa.eu/food/sites/food/files/animals/docs/aw_eu_strategy_19012012_en.pdf.

Consolidated version of the Treaty on the Functioning of the European Union, OJ C 326, 26 October 2012, pp. 47–390.

Convention on International Trade in Endangered Species of Wild Fauna and Flora of 3 March 1973 [*Konwencja o międzynarodowym handlu dzikimi zwierzętami i roślinami gatunków zagrożonych wyginięciem sporządzona w Waszyngtonie dnia 3 marca 1973 r.*], Polish J.L. 1991 No 27, item. 112.

Council Directive 1999/22/EC of 29 March 1999 relating to the keeping of wild animals in zoos, OJ 94, 9 April 1999, pp. 24–26.

Council Directive 78/659 of 18 July 1978 on the quality of fresh waters needing protection or improvement in order to support fish life, OJ L222/1.

Council Directive 79/409/EEC of 2 April 1979 on the conservation of wild birds, OJ L103 of 25 April 1979, pp. 1–18.

Council Directive 90/425/EEC of 26 June 1990 concerning veterinary and zootechnical checks applicable in intra- Community trade in certain live animals and products with a view to the completion of the internal market. OJ 224, 18 August 1990, pp. 29–41.

Council Directive 92/43/EEC of 21 May 1992 on the conservation of natural habitats and of wild fauna and flora, OJ L206 of 22 July 1992, pp. 7–50.

Council Directive 92/65/EEC of 13 July 1992 laying down animal health requirements governing trade in and imports into the Community of animals, semen, ova and embryos not subject to animal health requirements laid down in specific Community rules referred to in Annex A (I) to Directive 90/425/EEC, OJ 268, 14 September 1992, pp. 54–72.

Council Directive 93/13/EEC of 5 April 1993 on unfair terms in consumer contracts, OJ 95, 21 April 1993, pp. 29–34.

Council Directive 98/58/EC of 20 July 1998 concerning the protection of animals kept for farming purposes, OJ 221, 8 August 1998, pp. 23–27.

Council Directive of 18 December 1986 on the coordination of the laws of the Member States relating to self-employed commercial agents (86/653/EEC), OJ 382, 31 December 1986, pp. 17–21.

Council Regulation (EC) No 1/2005 of 22 December 2004 on the protection of animals during transport and related operations and amending Directives 64/432/EEC and 93/119/EC and Regulation (EC) No 1255/97.

Council Regulation (EC) No 338/97 of 9 December 1996 on the protection of species of wild fauna and flora by regulating trade therein, OJ 61, 3 March 1997, pp. 1–69.

Czech Civil code [*Zákon č.*] of 3.2.2012, J.L. 89/2012, *občanský zákoník*, as amended.

Decision No 1386/2013/EU of the European Parliament and of the Council of 20 November 2013 on a General Union Environment Action Programme to 2020 'Living well, within the limits of our planet', OJ L from 28.12.2013, item 354, pp. 171–200.

Directive 1999/44/EC of the European Parliament and of the Council of 25 May 1999 on certain aspects of the sale of consumer things and associated guarantees, OJ 171, 7 July 1999, pp. 12–16.

Directive 2002/65/EC of the European Parliament and of the Council of 23 September 2002 concerning the distance marketing of consumer financial services and amending Council Directive 90/619/EEC and Directives 97/7/EC and 98/27/EC, OJ 271 of 9 October 2002, pp. 16–24.

Directive 2006/126/EC of the European Parliament and of the Council of 20 December 2006 on driving licences (Recast), OJ 403, 30 December 2006, pp. 18–60.

Directive 2011/83/EU of the European Parliament and of the Council of 25 October 2011 on consumer rights, amending Council Directive 93/13/EEC and Directive 1999/44/EC of the European Parliament and of the Council and repealing Council Directive 85/577/EEC and Directive 97/7/EC of the European Parliament and of the Council, OJ 304 of 22 November 2011, pp. 64–88.

Directive 2011/83/EU of the European Parliament and of the Council of 25 October 2011 on consumer rights, OJ 304, 22 November 2011, pp. 64–88.

Directive 79/923 of 12 December 2006 on the quality required of shellfish waters, OJ 281/47.

European Convention for the Protection of Animals during International Transport (Revised), 6 November 2003, ETS No 193.

European Convention for the Protection of Animals for Slaughter, 10 May 1979, ETS No 102.

European Convention for the Protection of Pet Animals, 13 November 1987, ETS No 125.

European Convention for the Protection of Vertebrate Animals used for Experimental and Other Scientific Purposes, 18 March 1986, ETS No 123.

European Convention on the Protection of Animals kept for Farming purposes, 10 March 1976, ETS No 087.

European treaty Series No 5, Convention for the Protection of Human Rights and Fundamental Freedoms, as amended.

Executive order concerning driving licences of 13 December 2010 [*Verordnung über die Zulassung von Personen zum Straßenverkehr/ Fahrerlaubnis-Verordnung – FeV*], OJ of 13 December 2010, Part I, item 1980, as amended.

German Animal Protection Act from 24 July 1972 in the version of 18 April 2006 (J.L. I p. 1206, item 1313), amendment of 28 July 2014, OJ. L p. 1308.

German Civil Code in the version promulgated on 2 January 2002, O J L of 8 January 2002, part I, No 2, item 2787, as amended.

German Commercial Code from 10 May 1987, OJ of 18.7.2017, Part I, item 2446, as amended.

German Emperor's Order concerning major defects and warranty terms for the trade of livestock from 27 March 1899 (J.L. Part III, item 402–3), which lost its legal binding force on 1 January 2002.

German Executive Act for the Protection of Farm Animals and Other Products Derived from Animals in the Household (*Verordnung zum Schutz landwirtschaftlicher Nutztiere und anderer zur Erzeugung tierischer Produkte gehaltener Tiere bei ihrer Haltung*) of 25 October 2001 in the version of 22 August 2006 (J.L. I p. 2043), last amendment of 5 February 2014 (J.L. p. 94).

German Executive Act referring to dogs (*Tierschutz-Hundeverordnung*) from 2 May 2001 (J.L. I p. 838), last amendment of 12 December 2013 (J.L. I p. 4145).

German Passenger Transport Act [*Personenbeförderungsgesetz*] of 8 August 1990 (BGBl. I S. 1690), as amended.

Minister of Food Industry and Agricultural Products' Purchase Ordinance of 7 October 1966 on the seller's responsibility for defects in certain types of animals (J.L. No 43, item 257).

Opinion of Advocate General Poiares Maduro on case C-465/04 from 25.10.2005.

Order on Standard Transport Terms for Tram and Trolley Bus Transport and Regular Public Transport Services with Motor Vehicles [Verordnung über die Allgemeinen Beförderungsbedingungen für den Straßenbahn – und Obusverkehr sowie den Linienverkehr mit Kraftfahrzeugen] of 27 February 1970 (BGBl. I S. 230), as amended.

Polish Act about Occupational and Social Rehabilitation and Hiring Impaired Persons of 27 August 1997 [*Ustawa* z *27.8.1997 r.* o *rehabilitacji zawodowej* i *społecznej* oraz *zatrudnianiu osób niepełnosprawnych*], J.L. 1997, No 123, item 776.
Polish Act on Consumer Rights from 30 May 2014, J.L. of 2014, item 827.
Polish Act on Freedom of Business Activity [*Ustawa o swobodzie Działalności Gospodarczej*] of 2 July 2004, J.L. of 2004 No 173 item 1807.
Polish Act on Drivers [*Ustawa o kierujących pojazdami*] of 5 January 2011, J.L. of 2011, No 30, item 151.
Polish Animal Protection Act from 21 August 1997 (J.L. 1997, No 111, item 724).
Polish Civil Code in the version promulgated on 23 April 1964, latest version: J.L. No 16, item 93, as amended.
Polish Economic Activity Act of 2 July 2004 (J.L. 2004 No 173 item 1807).
Polish Executive Act of the Ministry for Work and Social Politics of 1 April 2010 on issuing certificates confirming the status of a guide dog [*Rozporządzenie Ministra Pracy i Polityki Społecznej z 1.4.2010 r. w sprawie wydawania certyfikatów potwierdzających status psa asystującego*], J.L. 64, item 399.
Polish Minister's Act on the Seller's Responsibility for Defects in Certain Types of Animals from 7 October 1966 (J.L. No 43, item 257, as amended), which lost its legal binding force on 1 January 2015.
Polish Protection of Competition and Consumers Act [*Ustawa o ochronie konkurencji i konsumentów*] of 16 February 2007, J.L. of 2007, No 50 item 331.
Protocol of Amendment to the European Convention for the Protection of Animals kept for Farming Purposes, 6 February 1992, ETS No 145.
Protocol of amendment to the European Convention for the Protection of Vertebrate Animals used for Experimental and other Scientific Purposes, 22 June 1998, ETS No 170.
Regulation (EU) No 576/2013 of the European Parliament and the Council of 12 June 2013 on the non-commercial movement of pet animals and repealing Regulation (EC) No 998/2003, OJ 178, 28 June 2013, pp. 1–26.
Regulation (EU) No 1143/2014 of the European Parliament and of the Council of 22 October 2014 on the prevention and management of the introduction and spread of invasive alien species, OJ 317, 4 November 2014, pp. 35–55.
Regulation (EU) No 1143/2014 on the prevention and management of the introduction and spread of invasive alien species (IAS Regulation), COM/2013/0620 final - 2013/0307 (COD), no longer in force.
Report from the Commission Directorate General for Economic and Financial Affairs on *Economic Crisis in Europe: Causes, Consequences and Responses*, available at: http://ec.europa.eu/economy_finance/publications/pages/publication15887_en.pdf.
Report from the Commission on the application of the Commercial Agents Directive (COM (1996) 364 final, 23 July 1996).
Report from the Commission to the European Parliament and the Council on the implementation of Council Directive 98/58/EC concerning the protection of animals kept for farming purposes (COM(2016) 558 final), available at: http://eur-lex.europa.eu/legal-content/EN/TXT/?uri=CELEX:52016DC0558.

Report from the Commission to the European Parliament and the Council on the implementation of Council Directive 98/58/EC concerning the protection of animals kept for farming purposes (COM(2016) 558 final).

Report to the Commission on the Implementation of Directive 79/409/EEC on the Conservation of Wild Birds, Part I Composite Report on Overall Progress Achieved, Update for 1999–2001.

Rome I Regulation (Regulation (EC) No 593/2008 of the European Parliament and of the Council of 17 June 2008 on the law applicable to contractual obligations, OJ 177, 4 July 2008, pp. 6–16.

Treaty of Lisbon amending the Treaty on European Union and the Treaty establishing the European Community, OJ C 306, 17 December 2007, pp. 1–271.

Treaty on the Functioning of the European Union, OJ C 326, 26 October 2012, pp. 47–390.

United Nations Convention on Contracts for the International Sale of Goods, Vienna, 11 April 1980, S.Treaty Document Number 98-9 (1984), UN Document Number A/CONF 97/19, 1489 UNTS 3.

Court rulings

Polish court rulings

NSA Warszawa, ruling from 3 November 2011 – II OSK 1628/11, *Lex No 1151962.*
SA Gdańsk, ruling from 12 February 2013 – V ACa 1043/12, *Lex No 1313249.*
SA Gdańsk, ruling from 19 March 2015 – III AUa 2736/13, *LEX No 1415908.*
SA Gdańsk, ruling from 20 May 2016 – III AUa 2125/15, *LEX No 2091016.*
SA Katowice, ruling from 6. 2. 2018 – I ACa 907/17.
SA Kraków, ruling from 16 April 2013 – I ACa 235/13, *Legalis No 761361.*
SA Kraków, ruling from 17 June 2014 – I ACa 528/14, *Legalis No 1093155.*
SA Łódź, ruling from 19 June 2013 – III AUa 1511/12, *LEX No 1350370.*
SN, ruling from 11 March 2003 – V CKN 1829/00.
SN ruling from 22 March 2001 – V CKN 1599/00, *Legalis No 51929.*
SN, ruling from 7 April 1998 – II CKN 688/97, *Legalis No 348488.*
SN, ruling from 7 April 2004, IV CK 231/03, *Legalis No 71081.*
SN, ruling from 5 January 1999 – III CKN 783/98, *Legalis No 362262.*
SN, ruling from 10 January 2002 – II CKN 564/99, *OSP 2002 No 11, item 144.*
SN, ruling from 11 August 1978 – III CRN 151/78, *OSNC 1979/6/125.*
SN, ruling from 16 September 2011 – IV CSK 626/10, *Legalis No 411298.*
SN, ruling from 17 February 2005 – I CK 568/04, *LEX No 479349.*
SN, ruling from 18. 6. 2010 – V CSK 433/09, *Legalis* No *392593.*
SN, ruling from 19 September 2013 – I CSK 651/12, *Legalis* No 165585.
SN, ruling from 20 May 2010 – V CSK 387/09, *Legalis* No 381569.
SN, ruling from 24 November 1998 – I CKN 667/97, *Legalis* No 336426.
SN, ruling from 20 January 2010 – III CZP 125/09, OSNC 2010, No 7–8, pos. 108.
SN, ruling from 21 March 1977 – III CZP 11/77, *OSNCP 1977, No 8, item 132.*
SN, ruling from 25 September 2014 – II CSK 664/13, *OSNC – Supplementary collection 2015 No D, item 67, p. 161.*
SN, ruling from 26 February 2015 – III CZP 108/14, *OSNC 2016/1/2.*
SN, ruling from 28 October 1999 – II CKN 530/98, *OSNC 2000/5/88, OSP 2000/7–8/118.*
SN, ruling from 3 October 2014, V CSK 630/13, *OSNC 2015 No.7–8, item 96, p. 132, OSP 2016 No 12, item 113, p. 1630.*
SO Bydgoszcz, ruling from 23 October 2013 – VIII Ga 13/13, *LEX No 1719549.*

German court rulings

AG Essen, ruling from 31 August 2007 – 20 C 229/06, NZM 2008, 264.
AG Herne, ruling from 6 October 2003 – 5 C 85/02, *dejure.org*.
AG Krefeld, ruling from 1 September 2006 – 7 C 255/06, *BeckRS 2008, 21737.*
BGH, ruling from 9 June 1992 – VI ZR 49/91, NJW 1992, 2474.
BGH ruling from 21 April 2005 – Az. III ZR 293/04, NJW 2005, 2008.
BGH ruling from 29 March 2006, NJW 2006, 2250.
BGH, decision from 13 January 2015 – VI ZR 204/14, BeckRS 2015, 02514.
BGH, ruling from 11 July 2007 – VIII ZR 110/06, NJW 2007, 2619.
BGH, ruling from 13 April 2011 – VIII ZR 220/10, NJW 2011, 2278.
BGH, ruling from 14 February 2017 – VI ZR 434/15, NJW-RR 2017, 725.
BGH, ruling from 18 October 2017 – VIII ZR 32/16, NJW 2018, 150.
BGH, ruling from 18 December 1954 – II ZR 296/53, NJW 1955, 340.
BGH, ruling from 18 December 2002 – VIII ZR 123/02, NJW-RR 2003, 558.
BGH, ruling from 19 January 2001 – V ZR 437/99, NJW 2001, 1127.
BGH, ruling from 22 June 2005 – VIII ZR 1/05, NJW 2005, 3211.
BGH, ruling from 22 June 2005 – VIII ZR 281/04, NJW 2005, 2852.
BGH, ruling from 23 September 1981 – IV a ZR 185/80, NJW 1982, 43.
BGH, ruling from 24 February 2010 – VIII ZR 71/09, NJW 2010, 8.
BGH, ruling from 29 November 2006 – VIII ZR 92/06, NJW 2007, 1346.
BGH, ruling from 29 March 2006 – VIII ZR 173/05, NJW 2006, 2250.
BGH, ruling from 3 July 1985 – VIII ZR 152/84, NJW-RR 1986, 52.
BGH, ruling from 30 April 2013 – VI ZR 13/12, NJW 2013, 2661.
BGH, ruling from 7 December 2005 – VIII ZR 126/05, NJW 2006, 988.
BGH, ruling from 9 January 2008 – Az. VIII ZR 210/06, NJW 2008, 1371.
Finanzgericht Münster, ruling from 11 December 2014 – 5 K 3068/13 F, BB 2015, 1008.
LG Arnsberg, ruling from 13 October 2009 – 2 O 18/08, openJur 2011, 68900.
LG Darmstadt, ruling from 22 April 1998 – 21 S 263/97, VersR 2000, 732.
OLG Düsseldorf, ruling from 19.01.2017 – I-5 U 63/16, BeckRS 2017, 124397.
LG Fulda, ruling from 18 September 1992 – Az. 1 S 108/92, NJW-RR 1993, 886.
LG Göttingen, ruling from 17 October 2005 – 9 S 10/05, JurionRS 2005, 33564.
LG Krefeld, ruling from 13 April 2007 – 1 S 79/06, BeckRS 2008, 21784.
LG Lüneburg, ruling from 16 March 2004 – 4 O 322/03, BeckRS 2009, 77011.
LG Münster, ruling from 10 December 2004 – 10 O 716/03, BeckRS 2007, 06139.
LG Münster, ruling from 20 July 2007 – 10 O 240/06, NJOZ 2008, 434.
LG Verden, ruling from 16 February 2005 – 2 S 394/03, BeckRS 2009, 04445.
OLG Celle, ruling from 31 May 2006 – 7 U 252/05, BeckRS 2006, 14480.
OLG Düsseldorf, ruling from 16 April 2002 – 21 U 140/01, BeckRS 2005, 07217.
OLG Düsseldorf, ruling from 2 April 2004 – 14 U 213/03, NJOZ 2004, 1935.
OLG Düsseldorf, ruling from 9 November 2004 – 21 U 140/01, BeckRS 2005, 04146.
OLG Frankfurt a. M., ruling from 1 February 2011 – 16 U 119/10, BeckRS 2011, 05375.
OLG Frankfurt a. M., ruling from 17 July 2006 – 18 U 96/05, NJOZ 2007, 2046.
OLG Hamm ruling from 25 November 2015 – 12 U 62/14, BeckRS 2016, 05560.
OLG Hamm, ruling from 1 July 2005 – 11 U 43/04, BeckRS 2008, 15527.

OLG Hamm, ruling from 15 October 2004 – 19 U 75/04, BeckRS 2005, 13912.
OLG Hamm, ruling from 22 April 2015 – 14 U 19/14, NJW-RR 2015, 1114.
OLG Hamm, ruling from 27 August 2008 – 11 U 143/05, BeckRS 2010, 01835.
OLG Hamm, ruling from 5 June 2012 – Az. I-19 U 132/11, openJur 2012, 129605.
OLG Jena, ruling from 8 June 2016 – 7 U 573/15, BeckRS 2016, 102290.
OLG Koblenz, ruling from 12 September 2005 – 12 U 1047/04, BeckRS 2005, 13160.
OLG Koblenz, ruling from 18 January 2017 – 5 U 1021/16, NJW-RR 2017, 728.
OLG Koblenz, ruling from 23 April 2009 – 5 U 1124/08, NJW-RR 2009, 985.
OLG Koblenz, ruling from 7 January 2016 – 1 U 422/15, NJW-RR 2016, 474.
OLG Köln, ruling from 24 June 1994 – 20 U 11/94, NJW-RR 1995, 113.
OLG Menden, ruling from 26 February 2007 – 4 C 11/07, BeckRS 2007, 03278.
OLG Nürnberg, ruling from 29 March 2017 – 4 U 1162/13, NJW-RR 2017, 1173.
OLG Oldenburg, ruling from 17 June 2004 – 14 U 41/04, BeckRS 2009, 77009.
OLG Schleswig, ruling from 13 December 2005 – 3 U 42/05, BeckRS 2006, 04395.
OLG Stuttgart, ruling from 27 October 2004 – 3 U 198/03; BeckRS 2004, 11808.
OLG Stuttgart, ruling from 8 February 2006 – 3 U 28/05, BeckRS 2007, 10049.

Rulings of the European Court of Justice

Ruling of the European Court of Justice of 23. 3. 2006, *Honyvem Informazioni Commerciali v. Marielle de Zotti*, C-465/04, ECLI:EU:C:2006:199.
Ruling of the European Court of Justice of 23 April 2015, C-96/14, *Van Hove/CNP Assurances SA*, ECLI:EU:C:2015:262, NJW 2015, 1811.
Ruling of the European Court of Justice of 26 March 2009, C-348/07, *Turgay Semen/Deutsche Tamoil GmbH*, ECLI:EU:C:2009:195.
Ruling of the European Court of Justice of 28 July 2016, C-191/15, *Verein für Konsumenteninformation v Amazon EU Sarl*, ECLI:EU:C:2016:612.

European Parliament petitions

Petition 0094/2015 by Pia Berrend (Luxembourgish) on the terminology used for stray domestic animals in the proposal for a Regulation of the European Parliament and of the Council on Animal Health (COM/2013/0260), CM-PE 576,775 FdR 1085259.

Petition to the European Parliament 0103/2013 by Joron Dominique (French), on banning the use of animals in circuses in the EU, CM-PE529.943.

Petition to the European Parliament 0214/2013 by Ronald Schirmer and Annekatrin Pötschulat (German) on fur farming in Germany, CM-PE532.636.

Petition to the European Parliament 0224/2016 by P.A. (Italian) on cruelty to dogs in China, CM-PE 593,938 FdR 1109094.

Petition to the European Parliament 0251/2014 by Pia Berrend (Luxembourgish) on the mistreatment of stray dogs in Romania, CM-PE 557,378 FdR 1063572.

Petition to the European Parliament 0337/2013 by Lorenzo Croce (Italian) on the online sale of pets, CM-PE532.641.

Petition to the European Parliament 0471/2013 by Gian Marco Prampolini (Italian), bearing 27 signatures, on animal testing and vivisection for cosmetic research purposes, CM-PE 532,521 FdR 1032454.

Petition 0820/2015 by Annick Pillard (French) on prohibition of glue traps to catch rodents in the EU, CM-PE 587,741 FdR 1103203.

Petition to the European Parliament 0561/2014 by Sven Niederstrasser (German) on the abolition of the compulsory use of ear tags on free-range calves, CM-PE 557,396. FdR 1063594.

Petition to the European Parliament 0691/2013 by Julia Knorr Alonso (Spanish), on animal welfare in Spain and the European Union, CM-PE 532.588.

Petition to the European Parliament 0721/2014 by Joanna Swabe (British), on behalf of Human Society International, and two signatories, on the routine docking of pigs' tails, CM-PE 496.627.

Petition to the European Parliament 0723/2014 by M-J F. (Portuguese / Canadian) on Food safety and Free trade agreements, CM-PE 567.528 FdR 1071949.

Petition to the European Parliament 1024/2013 by Aurore Bardeau (French) seeking provisions to regulate animal euthanasia, CM-PE 537,427. FdR 1034194.

Petition to the European Parliament 1071/2014 by Linda Mäki-Sulkava (Finnish) on breeding of unhealthy traits in animals (dogs), CM-PE 576,720/REV FdR 1096600.

Petition to the European Parliament 1141/2014 by Fredrick Federley (Swedish), on the cutting of pigs' tails, CM-PE 496,627/REV.IV. FdR 1135280.

Petition to the European Parliament 1158/2013 by T.Ch. (Belgian), on Animal rights, CM-PE 535,954 FdR 1029899.

Petition to the European Parliament 1248/2013 by Pedro Pozas Terrados (Spanish) representing Projecto Gran Simio, CM-PE 536,100. FdR 103083.

Petition to the European Parliament 1307/2014 by A. K. (German) bearing 582 signatures, on a ban on the use of ear tags for the identification of cattle, CM-PE 565,121. FdR 1070347.

Petition to the European Parliament 1320/2015 by Susanne Prahm (German) supported by 8 co-signatories, on the ill-treatment of cats and dogs in China, CM-PE 587,562 FdR 1102178.

Petition to the European Parliament 1336/2015 by Patrick Katzer (German) on a ban on scientific experiments on primates, CM-PE 587,555 FdR 1102171.

Petition to the European Parliament 1379/2015 by Gisela Urban and Gabriele Menzel (German) on behalf of several animal welfare organisations, supported by 4,680 co-signatories, on the protection of humans and animals against toxins and pesticides, CM-PE 587.768.

Petition to the European Parliament 1417/2015 by M.V. (Italian) on animal cruelty in China, CM-PE 587,562 FdR 1102178.

Petition to the European Parliament 1546/2014 by R. P. S. (Spanish) against the immobilisation of horses with pliers, CM-PE 576,732/REV FdR 1103133.

Petition to the European Parliament 1553/2013 by Diana Patricia Giraldo Tejada (Spanish) on the protection of animal rights in Spain, CM-PE 576,732/REV FdR 1103133.

Petition to the European Parliament 1560/2014 by Corinna Haussmann (German) on the use of helium in place of CO2 for stunning animals for slaughter, CM-PE 567,571. FdR 1071995. 74.

Petition to the European Parliament 1619/2013 by C.J. (German), on a ban on hunting all songbirds and penalties for countries failing to comply – CM-PE 541,576 FdR 1039634.

Petition to the European Parliament 2218/2013 by C.J. (German) on banning the import of leather, leather goods and fur from China, CM-PE 564,828 FdR 106759.

Petition to the European Parliament 2301/2014 by Moona Hellsten (Finnish), on the cruel treatment of animals in a zoo (Zoo du Mont) in Toulon, France, CM-PE 571,580 FdR 1077802.

Petition to the European Parliament 2377/2013 by G.J. (German) on the use of ear tags for the identification of livestock, – CM-PE 546,947 FdR 1048514.

Petition to the European Parliament 2391/2013 by C.J. (Dutch), on a ban on birdcages containing zinc, CM-PE 578,575 FdR 1088088.